Continuous Architecture

Sustainable Architecture in an Agile and Cloud-Centric World

Continuous Architecture

Sustainable Architecture in an Agile and Cloud-Centric World

Murat Erder

Pierre Pureur

AMSTERDAM • BOSTON • HEIDELBERG • LONDON
NEW YORK • OXFORD • PARIS • SAN DIEGO
SAN FRANCISCO • SINGAPORE • SYDNEY • TOKYO

Morgan Kaufmann is an imprint of Elsevier

Acquiring Editor: Todd Green
Editorial Project Manager: Lindsay Lawrence
Project Manager: Punithavathy Govindaradjane
Designer: Matthew Limbert

Morgan Kaufmann is an imprint of Elsevier
225 Wyman Street, Waltham, MA 02451, USA

ISBN: 978-0-12-803284-8

British Library Cataloguing-in-Publication Data
A catalogue record for this book is available from the British Library.

Library of Congress Cataloging-in-Publication Data
A catalog record for this book is available from the Library of Congress.

For information on all Morgan Kaufmann publications
visit our website at www.mkp.com

To my sons, Hakan and Ozan, and my love, Pinar,

who all provided invaluable support

M.E.

To Kathy,

wife, friend, partner, confidant, and gentle critic

P.P.

Contents

Foreword by Kurt Bittner

Customers expect more today than ever before. In an instant-on, ever-connected world, they have more choices than ever before. Their memories are short, as is their patience; their brand loyalty is fleeting. Your connection with them must be constantly renewed through new products and new experiences. What you cannot give them, they will find elsewhere. Responding to their needs by creating great experiences has become the new competitive differentiator.

Old "waterfall" ways of developing software have been largely replaced by Agile approaches at the leading edge of new application development, in which modularity, delivery speed, and flexibility are essential. It still lingers where older, monolithic application architectures prevent changing in small increments. Even there, as applications are replaced, refactored, or retired, waterfall approaches are losing their grip.

Agile is changing as well, infused by DevOps and Continuous Delivery practices that remove barriers that prevent teams from moving faster. Infrastructure as Code and cloud-based environments, Continuous Integration, automated deployment, and API-based automated testing are reshaping the ways organizations deliver software.

Software architecture has, to date, lagged behind, but not for long. Software architecture's concerns—namely, modularity, maintainability, scalability, security, adaptability, and a host of other -ilities—are at the heart of what makes software successful. Achieving these goals does not happen by accident, but the old ways of architecting does not work either. Continuous Delivery has introduced continuous change, and with it, the need for a continuous approach to software architecture.

A former colleague, Philippe Kruchten, himself a leader in advancing the software architecture profession, used to tell a joke that asked, "How do you get a good software architecture?" and responded "Hire a good software architect!" There is some truth in that, yet it is also misleading. Software architecture is not the unique domain of software architects; every developer needs to concern themselves with architectural considerations. Unintended consequences are everywhere, and developers must be able to understand the architectural implications of the continual decisions they make.

Moment to moment, applications change and adapt. The word "architecture" itself is a metaphor—and perhaps one that is wearing out. We are not building buildings, bridges, or Greek temples. Software today bears more resemblance to living organisms that are born, grow, change over time, and eventually die. When we are successful at "architecting," they adapt fairly fluidly; when the architecture is less successful, they become cumbersome, hard to change and support, and eventually succumb to small flaws accumulated over time.

Yet architecture is still an apt enough metaphor for now. Successful buildings must anticipate how they will be used, how they will deal with stresses put on them, and how they will remain adaptable and relevant over time. We must recognize that just as software is rapidly evolving, our notion of software architecture must evolve apace as well. That is where this book comes at just the right time.

I have known Murat and Pierre for a very long time and have worked with them on a variety of initiatives over the years. They bring together an understanding of Agile software development but also an appreciation of what intentional software architecture practices can bring. In our rush to deliver applications continuously, we need these applications to be adaptable and modular. We need to be able to replace everything in the application over time without killing the host.

Continuous Architecture principles do just that. They bring together a long-term view of the inevitable evolution of the application over time coupled with modern continuous software delivery techniques. This book will help you to bring those views together as well, making software architecture not just something practiced by software architects and not just at the beginning of the application life cycle but continuously throughout the entire life of the application.

This book is organized around six principles:

1. **Architect products, not projects.** Take the long view. Recognize that software lives a long time. Decades, if you are lucky. Build it with that in mind.
2. **Focus on quality attributes, not on functional requirements.** Worry about performance, scalability, and security. Nonfunctional requirements shape application architecture far more than functional requirements.
3. **Delay design decisions until they are absolutely necessary.** Do not overbuild. Do not anticipate problems that have not occurred and may never occur.
4. **Architect for change—leverage "the power of small."** Expect change. Embrace change. Welcome it. Make the architecture resilient enough to accommodate change.
5. **Architect for build, test, and deploy.** Use modularity to make it easy to build, test, and deploy the application incrementally and continuously.
6. **Model the organization after the design of the system.** Recognize that the organizational structure often strongly influences the application architecture. The organizational structure creates architectural biases that need to be recognized and sometimes overcome.

Focusing on principles avoids the inevitable problem with processes: No one process works for everyone, but these principles truly do work for everyone. These six principles permeate the book, and that is a good thing—it gives you, the reader, the chance to see these principles in practice.

I think this book is an important addition to the dialog about software architecture's role in continuous delivery and represents an important evolutionary step toward a new kind of software architecture—one that can be defined and evolved incrementally and continuously across a series of rapid releases.

Kurt Bittner
Principal Analyst at Forrester Research, Boulder, CO
June 24, 2015

Foreword by Peter Eeles

Approaches to the development and delivery of information technology solutions have evolved significantly over the past decade or so. Traditional "waterfall" development approaches, although still relevant today for a certain class of system, have been complemented with iterative development; Agile development; and most recently, scaled (or disciplined) Agile development that brings Agile to the enterprise. A more recent evolution is often referred to as "DevOps," which, at its heart, moves us beyond development and into the world of *delivery*. This is not simply about connecting development and operations; it is fundamentally about enabling a "software supply chain" that focuses on helping our delivery projects get from an idea to production as quickly as possible, enabling rapid feedback and evolution of our solutions. The aspiration is one of *Continuous Delivery.*

A Continuous Delivery approach is particularly important for organizations looking to capitalize on technology trends, such as "mobile," in which much is often unknown (have you ever tried to define all of the requirements for a mobile app up front?) and in which convergence on the requirements and solution can only be achieved through a series of incremental releases of the solution to end users and feedback obtained at the end of each iteration. A more recent evolution, still, is "cloud," which can further accelerate the delivery of solutions by removing common impediments to many projects, such as the rapid provisioning of infrastructure to support the development, testing, and execution of the solutions being created.

The prominence of new and exciting approaches, such as Agile, DevOps, and cloud, often downplays a characteristic that is fundamental to the success of all of them—architecture. For example, even hardcore Agile evangelists will tell you that they do at least some design up front (and, as Grady Booch succinctly put it, "Architecture *is* design, but not all design is architecture"); otherwise, how could the work of a team be coordinated without chaos ensuing? Similarly, in a DevOps world, how can the work of development and operations be coordinated unless there is some (architectural) consensus on the deployment units that allow development artifacts (e.g., software components) to be aligned with operations constructs (e.g., the placement of software components on hardware nodes)?

Enter *Continuous Architecture*, the subject of this book and a highly timely and highly relevant addition to our collective knowledge. This book considers a number of themes that are often treated as subjects in their own right (e.g., Agile, DevOps, and cloud) and carefully blends them with our rich heritage of architecture-centric thinking, resulting in a unifying and practical work that will benefit many readers.

Rooted on six principles that the authors have identified (and that provide a common theme throughout), this book will possibly provide answers to questions that you have not even thought of yet. The book is especially relevant to those of us who often spend our time working within large enterprises, applying Agile, DevOps, and other approaches on our path to successful project delivery.

Peter Eeles
Chief Architect for IT at IBM Rational

Acknowledgments

This book was a long time in the making. It started as a project back in 2004, when we both worked for a large US consulting firm. We felt at the time that we had a lot to share in the field of Software Architecture and Software Engineering and that it would be important to pass that knowledge and experience on to others. We wrote and published four articles and put the project on hold due to other priorities. We finally restarted this project a year ago, and would like to thank the following people for encouraging us and helping us bring this project past the finish line.

Kurt Bittner for guiding us from the beginning and acting as a reviewer. Peter Eeles for invaluable feedback while reviewing the book. Eoin Woods and Phillipe Krutchen who provided insight and ideas. Jan Bosch, Dean Leffingwell and James Watters for their endorsements. Sarah Marangoni for her guidance on the publishing world. Lindsay Lawrence and Todd Green from Elsevier who supported and collaborated with us during the entire process. Manuel Barbero who first proposed that we should put our thoughts in a book back in 2004. Patrick Griffin from Travelers who helped us with some of the graphics in this book.

Chapter 1

Introduction to Continuous Architecture

"We are called to be architects of the future, not its victims.
—R. Buckminster Fuller

Both of us call ourselves architects because we believe there is no better explanation of what we do every day at work. Through our careers covering software and hardware vendors, management consultancy firms, and large financial institutions, we have predominantly done work that can be labeled as software, solution, and enterprise architecture.

However, when we say we are architects, we always have a need to qualify it; we believe an explanation is required to separate ourselves from the stereotype of an IT architect that adds no value. Most readers are probably familiar with the common expression of: "I am an architect, but I deliver/write code/engage with clients" (fill in with your choice of an activity that is perceived as valuable).

How has this notion of the ivory tower architect become so predominant? We are confident that we are not alone in this mindset. We also believe that architects who exhibit the infamous qualities of abstract mad scientists, technology tinkerers, or presentation junkies are a minority of practitioners. A majority of architects work effectively as part of software delivery teams, most of the time probably not even calling themselves architects. In essence, all software has an architecture, and most software products have a small set of senior developers who create a consistent architecture regardless of whether it is documented or not.

Through our careers, we have also noticed the increasing speed of delivery expected from IT practitioners within enterprises. At the same time, the ease of use and 24/7 expectations of end users are driven by the overwhelming expansion of technology in our daily lives—we have progressed from PCs to tablets to smartphones to wearable technology. Today software delivery teams are expected to operate on an Internet time and scale. This has significantly increased the demand for and resulted in the widening adoption of Agile and Continuous Delivery practices.

As a result, the pendulum has swung away from traditional software architecture practices and in particular Enterprise Architecture. We do not believe that the pendulum will swing back to these traditional practices. However, there is still a need for an architectural approach that can encompass Continuous Delivery, providing it with a broader architectural perspective. This is the main topic addressed in this book. Before we define Continuous Architecture, let us first provide a definition of software architecture and then consider the historical perspective.

WHAT DO WE MEAN BY ARCHITECTURE?

When we talk about architecture, we are concerned with software architecture. How do we define *software architecture*? Let us look at a few common definitions.

According to the Wikipedia entry maintained by IFIP WG 2.10[1] on software architecture:

> *Software architecture refers to the high level structures of a software system, the discipline of creating such structures, and the documentation of these structures. It is the set of structures needed to reason about the software system. Each structure comprises software elements, relations among them, and properties of both elements and relations. The architecture of a software system is a metaphor, analogous to the architecture of a building.*

The International Standards Organization and Institute of Electrical and Electronics Engineers (IEEE) use the following definition*:

> *Architecture: the fundamental concepts or properties of a system in its environment embodied in its elements, their relationships, and in the principles of its design and evolution.*

Specifically, we are dealing in this book with the IT concerns of software development within a commercial enterprise.

The four most common reasons for developing a software architecture are to:

1. **Define the guiding principles and standards.** Architecture is a vision of the future, and supporting tools to help you get there.
2. **Develop architecture models.** In this case, architecture is concerned with abstracting at an appropriate level to make business and technical decisions.

*This is known as ISO42010 or ISO/IEC/IEEE 42010.

3. **Build common services.** The services could be systems or organizations. Architecture can be defined as focusing on defining interfaces.
4. **Create a roadmap to an IT future state.** Architecture deals with transition planning activities that lead to the successful implementation of an IT blueprint.

In accordance with these goals, building a large software system in an effective and efficient manner requires a blueprint—commonly referred to as a "software architecture." Such an architecture includes descriptive models (defined in both business and technology terms) to aid decision makers in understanding how the entity operates today and how it wants to operate in the future and prescriptive models to help the project team successfully transition to its desired IT state.

HISTORICAL PERSPECTIVE

Let's look at a brief history of the evolution of the computer and software industry. Our objective here is not to provide a comprehensive history but highlight a few key developments to put Continuous Architecture in a historical perspective.

While looking at the history of computer technology, it is interesting to look at two aspects, the major technology "epochs" versus concepts

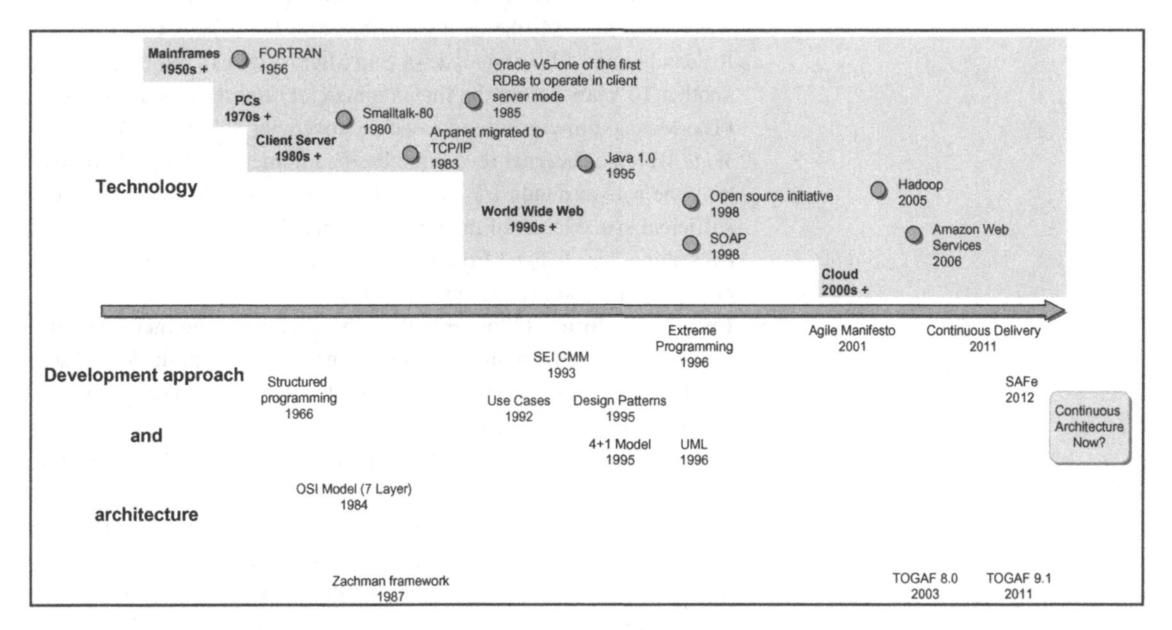

■ **FIGURE 1.1** Technology and architecture timeline.

evolving in software development and software architecture. We can articulate the major epochs in the computer industry as:

1. **The age of the mainframe (1950s +):** This started basically in the 1950s with the main computing paradigm being mainframe computers. These were expensive and powerful machines that enabled large corporations to start automating certain aspects of their businesses as well as supporting scientific development.
2. **Getting personal (1970s +):** This is when *PCs* (Personal Computers) as we know them today were introduced. It was a huge leap forward in the sense that computing power could be put in one machine that could sit on a desk. This enabled individuals to interact with computers in a much more "personal" manner. However, most individual users of such technology were still in large companies and research institutions.
3. **Distributing the load (1980s +):** As computers evolved in capacity and started becoming networked, the concept of *client server* architecture started evolving. This resulted in a view that not all software needed to run on a single computer but that the computing burden could be shared. At that time, client server architecture and how best to distribute responsibilities were major architectural topics. As the client server paradigm evolved, so did the concept of networked computers.
4. **Era of connectivity (1990s +):** The "network is the computer" term was coined in 1984 (the term is attributed to John Gage, Chief Researcher and fifth employee of Sun Microsystems), but it took another 10 years before the first commercial browser was introduced (The Mosaic browser was released in November 1993). The *World Wide Web* and Internet revolution has had tremendous impact on not only the software industry but also the entire world. We do not have sufficient space to detail its impact, but needless to say that everything has changed from the way we shop to the way we communicate and even to how our gadgets interact.
5. **Back to the future (2000s +):** With the ubiquitous Internet came the opportunity to unleash us from dependency on physical devices. The ability to store and retrieve information from the *cloud* creates even further opportunities, as well as challenges.

   For example, we do not always physically own the books we buy on our e-readers.[2] The company that sells us the books is the owner of the content and has the right to remove it, which would not be an option for old physical books. We will leave the ethical discussion of the Internet and cloud computing to other authors and go back to our architecture storyline.

   The cloud era has also enabled enterprises to only acquire the required software and compute capacity. We call this era "back to the

> future" because we are back to the model of leasing capacity, which was exactly the model in the mainframe days. The only difference is that we are implementing the model in a highly interconnected, standardized, and real-time world.

The computer and software world will continue to evolve, with the next phase currently coming from mobile devices and wearable computers. What has not changed during this approximately half a century journey is the fact that developers still write code. What is also interesting is that productivity among developers is still quite varied, and creativity is still associated with the developer role. Basically, we still are in a software as a craft stage and have not been able to fulfill the industrial revolution and automation that have been promised at each stage in the journey.

What has changed, though, is the speed at which we are expected to execute, as well as the scale in which we need to operate. Quarterly release cycles are no longer relevant, and commercial solutions have to cater to increasing demands from end users in terms of performance, usability, and scalability.

Figure 1.1 highlights some interesting data points in the five epochs we have listed in the brief history of the commercial computer and software industry.

Let us now look at how the approach to software development and architecture has evolved during this journey. As stated before, some things have not changed. Structured programming has been with us for most of the journey and highlights key elements any current architect and developer would recognize: creating logical structure based on modularity.

The 1980s saw some key architectural patterns starting to evolve. The Open System Interconnection (OSI) Model in the network domain was an excellent example of creating a layered architecture. Enterprise Architecture concepts can be considered to have been jump-started with the introduction of the Zachman framework, which created a technology taxonomy that is still valid today.

The early to mid-1990s saw an explosion of ideas, from use cases to UML and Extreme Programming (XP). This was when object-oriented programming was the rage, which resulted in a series of efforts to create methodologies and techniques for this new world. It was also at the beginning of the Internet explosion, although we were not quite there.

The impact of the Internet era and the demand for quicker delivery of software resulted in the *Agile Manifesto* being published. An interesting footnote is that this was published right after the dot-com bubble burst. Over time, we have seen a gradual acceptance of the Agile approach and its evolution to Continuous Delivery and DevOps concepts.

In parallel, the Enterprise Architecture concept has gone through several waves of popularity and disillusionment. The fact that The Open Group Architecture Forum (TOGAF) standard is still active is an attestation that there still is demand for addressing enterprise-wide architectural concerns.

However, we believe that the concept of software architecture and in particular Enterprise Architecture is becoming less relevant for developers in large enterprises. Even if Enterprise Architecture groups exist, their impact on the day-to-day development is limited.

The activities of the Enterprise Architecture groups fail what we call the "junior developer" litmus test. This litmus test acknowledges that a lot of architectural decisions are made by developers in action—where the rubber hits the road. The litmus test validates if a junior developer on a team makes his or her decisions based on guidance from architects.

We believe that the gap between the Agile delivery and architecture practices within a commercial enterprise is wider than before. This is where Continuous Architecture comes in; it is a set of principles and tools targeted at addressing this gap.

Another way of looking at Continuous Architecture is by using an analogy based on real-life architecture. If our objective is to build a cathedral, an Agile developer will start shoveling, but an enterprise architect will look at a 5-year plan. The goal of Continuous Architecture is to bridge this gap (Figure 1.2).

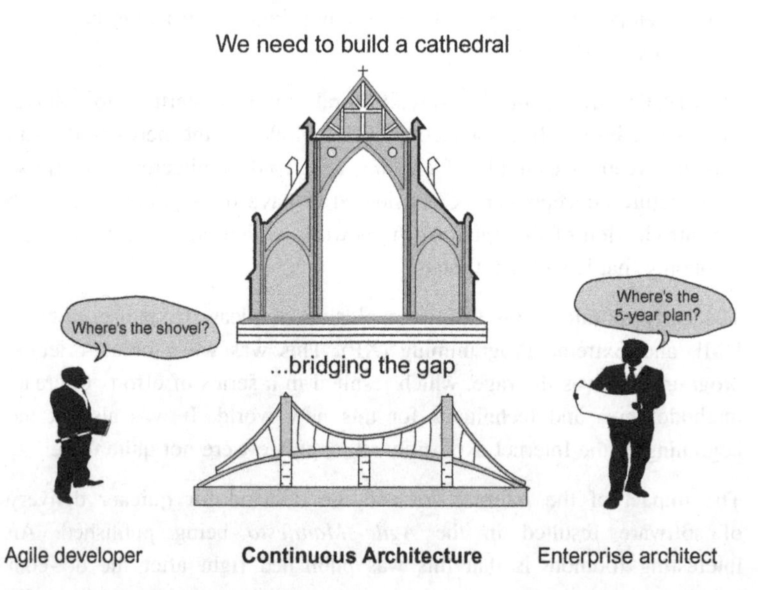

■ **FIGURE 1.2** The Continuous Architecture context.

CURRENT CHALLENGES WITH SOFTWARE ARCHITECTURE

Now that we have a historical perspective, let us look at the state of software and Enterprise Architecture today. We can identify three main challenges with the current state of software architecture within most commercial organizations:

1. Focus on technology details rather than business context
2. Perception of architects as not delivering solutions or adding value
3. Inability of architecture practices to address the increase in speed of IT delivery

Software architectures are driven by business goals, yet gaining a deep understanding of the business and its needs is not done very often in architecture projects. Architecture teams tend to spend considerable amounts of time documenting the current state of existing systems and then creating elaborate "architecture blueprints" that try to fix the perceived shortcomings. Unfortunately, these blueprints are usually derived from current IT trends or fads; for example, most architectures designed these days include some amount of service definitions, cloud computing, and big data, regardless of their applicability to the problem at hand. The root cause of this problem may be that most IT architects are more comfortable solving technology problems than they are at solving business problems.

A second issue with architecture lies with the concept of "Enterprise Architecture" and Enterprise Architecture organizations. Broadly speaking, architects fall into two categories: solution architects and enterprise architects. Enterprise architects may be further categorized according to the discipline they are specialized in, such as application, information, security, or infrastructure. Whereas enterprise architects are normally located in a central group, solution architecture organizations may be either centralized or distributed.

Solution architects focus on providing project-level architectures, but enterprise architects attempt to create strategies, architecture plans, architecture standards, and architecture frameworks for the whole enterprise. In turn, solution architects are expected to abide by those strategies, plans, standards, and frameworks when working on a project. Because enterprise architects are not close to the day-to-day business processes, the artifacts they produce may not be considered very useful by the project teams and may even be seen as hindrances.

In addition, the implication of the solution versus enterprise architect terminology is that enterprise architects are not perceived as focused on providing solutions and therefore are perceived as being potentially part of the problem. Often, enterprise architects are portrayed as academic, theoretical, and out of touch with the day-to-day realities of delivering and maintaining IT systems. Of course, the same is sometimes said about some solution architects, too, or even about anyone who plays an "architect" role on a project.

A third issue with architecture is the accelerating speed of IT delivery. As the pace of the business cycles increases, the IT function is expected by their business partners to deliver systems more rapidly. A new class of systems has emerged: the "systems of engagement," which provide capabilities that support the interactions between the outside world (prospects, customers, and other companies) and the enterprise. Because of advances in software engineering as well as the availability of new enabling technologies, the approach used for architecting modern systems that require agility is different from the approach used to architect older systems. This has created the need for a "two-speed architecture" approach, leveraging tools and techniques to architect "systems of engagement" that are fundamentally different from the tools and techniques used to architect the older "systems of record."

The planning processes associated with Enterprise Architecture are best suited to the older systems of record, which do not need to change as often as the newer systems of engagement. "Old school" enterprise architects insist on using the same set of strategies, frameworks, and standards for every system, including the newer systems of engagement, and this attitude creates a further disconnect among the business, the software developers, and the architects.

Given these three issues, we have to accept that traditional architecture has failed. It is not surprising that Enterprise Architecture groups are being disbanded and that even the most practical of the solution architects are just tolerated in a world where agility and speed of delivery are paramount.

Architecture in an (increasingly) Agile World

The first Agile methodology, XP, was created by Kent Beck in March 1996 when he was working at Chrysler.[3] The first book on Agile (*Extreme Programming Explained*) was published in October 1999,[4] which was followed by several publications on various Agile methodologies inspired by XP.

Since then, adoption of these methodologies has been nothing short of explosive, and Agile methodologies have been maturing so quickly that

Agile is rapidly becoming "old news." Even the most conservative companies have started looking into Agile. Techniques such as pair programming, test-driven development, and Continuous Integration have become mainstream. How have software architecture practitioners responded to the Agile tidal wave? Poorly, in our opinion.

- **The beginnings: architecture and extreme programming:** In the beginning, Agile (i.e., XP) and architecture ignored each other. In the minds of XP practitioners, architects were part of the "red tape" that they believed was counterproductive and were trying to eliminate. If a role or an activity was not seen as directly correlated with the development of executable code, the XP response was to eliminate it, and architecture was considered part of this category.

  In the XP approach, the architecture "emerges" from code building and refactoring activities, hence the term "emergent architecture," derived from the concept of "emergence" ("In philosophy, systems theory, science, and art, emergence is a process whereby larger entities, patterns, and regularities arise through interactions among smaller or simpler entities that themselves do not exhibit such properties"[5]). There is no longer any need for architects to create explicit architectural designs because "the best architectures, requirements and design emerge from self-organizing teams."[6]

  Unfortunately, this approach does not scale well as new requirements are identified; as refactoring activities become more and more complex, lengthy, and costly; and as systems grow in size. The systems tend to struggle to meet their quality attribute requirements, and meeting these requirements often requires even more refactoring.

  In addition, without some kind of documented architecture, it is difficult to accurately predict infrastructure needs for development, testing, and production activities. Infrastructure items such as servers, storage, and networks may have long lead times, and not being able to forecast the demand for those items results in lengthy project delays.

  So how did most software architects react to the first Agile wave? Mostly by ignoring it. They expected Agile to fade away and firmly believed that the pendulum would swing back to serious "modern" Iterative methodologies such as the Rational Unified Process (RUP) that were deferent to architects by explicitly including architecture activities. (Please see the Glossary for a definition of RUP.)
- **Where we are: architecture and the Scaled Agile Framework (SAFe):** As we all know, traditional software architects didn't get their wish—Agile did not fade away. Architects realized that Agile was here to stay and that they could help Agile teams, and simultaneously Agile teams realized that they needed some help from those pesky architects if they

wanted their systems to scale, be reliable, be secure, and still meet their performance goals. (Please see the Glossary for a definition of SAFe.)

As a result, architects have started thinking about adapting their methodologies to become more "Agile friendly." For example, the third edition (published in 2013) of *Software Architecture in Practice* by Len Bass, Paul Clements, and Rick Kazman includes a chapter called "Architecture in Agile Projects" (Part Three, "Architecture in the Life Cycle," Chapter 15[7]).

At the same time, some of the Agile approaches and methodologies have started including formal architecture steps. One of the best examples of this evolution is the Scaled Agile Framework (SAFe), created by Dean Leffingwell. SAFe specifically includes architecture steps grouped into an "Architecture Runway" (see Glossary for a definition of Architecture Runway) and leverages the concept of "Intentional Architecture," described by Dean Leffingwell as "an enterprise practice designed to produce and evolve robust system architectures in an Agile fashion."[8]

- **Where we are going: Continuous Delivery:** The next step in this evolution is the realization by software developers that developing software in an Agile fashion is not enough. They also need to deliver that software quickly to test and production environments so that it can be used by real-life users. This realization is driving the adoption of Continuous Delivery by software development teams, and again, software architects are slow in responding to this trend and adapting their architecture methodologies and tools to support this approach. We clearly need a new way of looking at architecture in a Continuous Delivery world.

Architecture in a Continuous Delivery and Cloud-Centric World

Let us look more specifically at Continuous Delivery. According to Wikipedia:

> *Continuous Delivery (CD) is a software engineering approach in which teams keep producing valuable software in short cycles and ensure that the software can be reliably released at any time. It is used in software development to automate and improve the process of software delivery. Techniques such as automated testing and continuous integration (CI) allow software to be developed to a high standard and easily packaged and deployed to test environments, resulting in the ability to rapidly, reliably and repeatedly push out enhancements and bug fixes to customers at low risk and with minimal manual overhead.*[9,10]

As the pace of business innovation is accelerating and becoming more and more software driven (as the venture capitalist Marc Andreessen noted when he observed that "software is eating the world"), there is increasing pressure on corporate IT to deliver software more rapidly, and Continuous Delivery offers a potential solution to this challenge.

The main objective of Continuous Delivery is to respond quickly to business needs by frequently delivering high-quality software in rapid cycles. Unlike traditional software delivery approaches that emphasize the importance of delivering various documents such as requirements, architecture, and design specifications, the overall goal of Continuous Delivery is to produce production-quality software rapidly in an incremental manner. Instead of validating various artifacts produced as part of the Software Development Life Cycle (SDLC), quality is enforced by systematically testing the software components using automated tests. The software components produced as a result of each rapid delivery cycle (sometimes called "Sprints" in Agile terminology) may or may not be deployed to production immediately, but they are of production quality.

In addition, the current adoption of cloud-centric models is also enabling Continuous Delivery. These models include the following:

- **Infrastructure as a Service (IaaS):** The ability to rapidly provision computing resources such as servers, storage, and networks, which can be located either within the enterprise ("Private Cloud"), outside the enterprise ("Public Cloud"), or both ("Hybrid Cloud")
- **Platform as a Service (PaaS):** The ability to rapidly provision application computing services such as middleware (e.g., application servers, message queuing services, load balancers) and database services. Similar to IaaS, those services can be delivered internally (Private Cloud), externally (Public Cloud), or both (Hybrid Cloud).
- **Software as a Service (SaaS):** The ability to rapidly provision business applications such as email and real-time collaboration. Similar to IaaS, those services can be delivered internally (Private Cloud), externally (Public Cloud), or both (Hybrid Cloud).

Among these three models, the PaaS model is the most beneficial to a Continuous Delivery approach because it enables application developers to provision the application computing services they require to run their applications, using self-service tools. Using this approach, the cloud is morphing from an environment for running applications to a new model where it becomes the application architecture itself.

All of this sounds great—can you imagine going from sitting down with your business partners on Monday morning to delivering a new, fully tested capability before the end of the week? For example, Amazon deploys code every 14 seconds on average. Amazon was able to roll out its new "Prime Now" product in exactly 111 days, starting from the day the initial press release was written to the day Prime Now became available to customers!

So what is stopping the average enterprise from fully adopting Continuous Delivery? We have no shortage of modern software development methodologies. Agile software development approaches enable the development teams to create and enhance applications at a rapid pace, and these methodologies are becoming mainstream, at least for teams working on the modern systems of engagement referred to earlier in this chapter. Cloud service models enable the developers to provision application environments and deploy applications to testing and production environments using self-service tools. So what is preventing the adoption of Continuous Delivery?

Despite recent advances in making software development more Agile, delivering projects to production still feels like tackling a major challenge every time. The handoffs among development groups, testing groups, and operations groups are rarely smooth. Typically, these handoffs are associated with a number of challenges such as manual processes; lack of communication among developers, testers, and operations; and inadequate processes and tools that slow down the entire software delivery process. We strongly believe that there is a need for an architectural approach that can encompass Continuous Delivery, providing it with a broader architectural perspective. We believe that "Continuous Architecture" provides this perspective.

CONTINUOUS ARCHITECTURE DEFINITION

What is Continuous Architecture? We believe that it is an architecture style that follows six simple principles:

1. **Architect products, not just solutions for projects.** Architecting products is more efficient than just designing point solutions to projects and focuses the team on its customers.
2. **Focus on Quality Attributes, not on functional requirements.** Quality attribute requirements drive the architecture.
3. **Delay design decisions until they are absolutely necessary.** Design architectures based on facts, not on guesses. There is no point in designing and implementing capabilities that may never be used; it is a waste of time and resources.
4. **Architect for change—leverage "the power of small."** Big, monolithic, tightly coupled components are hard to change. Instead, leverage small, loosely coupled services.

5. **Architect for build, test, and deploy.** Most architecture methodologies exclusively focus on software building activities, but we believe that architects should be concerned about testing and deployment activities in order to support Continuous Delivery.
6. **Model the organization after the design of the system.** The way teams are organized drives the architecture and design of the systems they are working on.

These principles are described in detail in Chapter 2 of this book, and they are complemented by a number of well-known tools such as Value Chains, Utility Trees, Decision Logs, and QFD matrices, to name a few. These tools are described in detail in this book and, together with the principles, assist architects in defining the key components of software architecture, such as:

- The context of the system
- The key functional requirements that will impact the architecture
- The Quality Attributes that drive the architecture
- The architecture and design decisions
- The architecture blueprints (Figure 1.3)

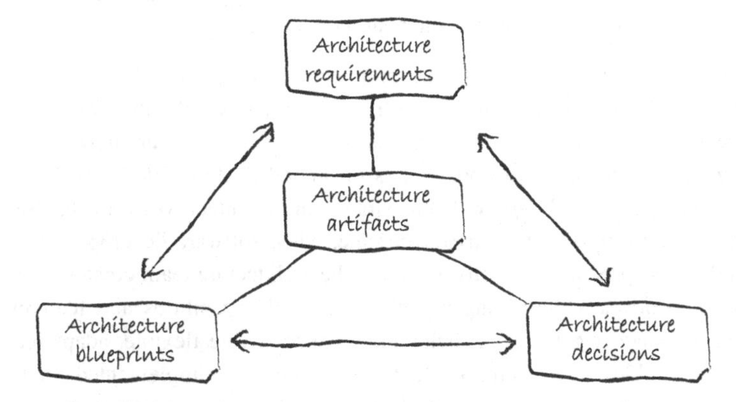

■ **FIGURE 1.3** Key components of software architecture.

Interestingly, the components of software architecture do not exist in isolation and are interrelated (see Figure 1.1). We argue that creating an architecture is making a series of compromises among the requirements, the decisions, the blueprints, and even the ultimate architecture artifact—the executable code itself.

For example, a decision made as a result of a performance requirement is very likely to affect most other quality attribute requirements, such as usability or configurability, and drive other decisions that will impact the architecture blueprints and eventually the capabilities being delivered by the executable code. Paraphrasing Otto von Bismarck, we could say that "architecture is the art of the possible!"[11]

So why is Continuous Architecture different from other architecture methodologies? To begin with, we do not think of it as a methodology. This book describes a series of principles, tools, techniques, and ideas that can be thought of as an architect's toolbox to effectively deal with Continuous Delivery projects. There is no preset order or process to follow for using these principles, tools, techniques, and ideas, and using any of them is not mandatory. We have found them effective on the projects we have worked on, but they are dynamic and adaptable in nature. Our hope is that readers will be inspired by this book to adapt the contents of our "Continuous Architecture toolbox" and extend it with new ideas on how to provide architecture support to projects that want to deliver robust and effective software capabilities rapidly.

We strongly believe that leveraging the contents of our Continuous Architecture toolbox will help architects address and eliminate the bottlenecks that we described in the previous section. The goal of the Continuous Architecture context is to speed up the software development and delivery process by systematically applying an architecture perspective and discipline continuously throughout the process.

Unlike most traditional software architecture approaches that focus on the software design and construction aspects of the Software Development Life Cycle, Continuous Architecture brings an architecture perspective to the overall process, as illustrated by *Principle 5: Architect for build, test, and deploy*. It encourages the architect to avoid the Big Architecture up Front (BArF) syndrome, when software developers wait and do not produce any software while the architecture team creates complicated artifacts describing complex technical capabilities and features that may never get used. It helps the architect create flexible, adaptable, and nimble architectures that are quickly implemented into executable code that can be rapidly tested and deployed to production so that the users of the system can provide feedback, which is the ultimate validation of an architecture.

In addition, the Continuous Architecture approach focuses on delivering software rather than documentation. Unlike traditional architecture methodologies, artifacts are viewed as a means, not as an end.

The Benefits of Continuous Architecture

The cost–quality–time triangle is a well-known project management aid that basically states the key constraints of any project (Figure 1.4).

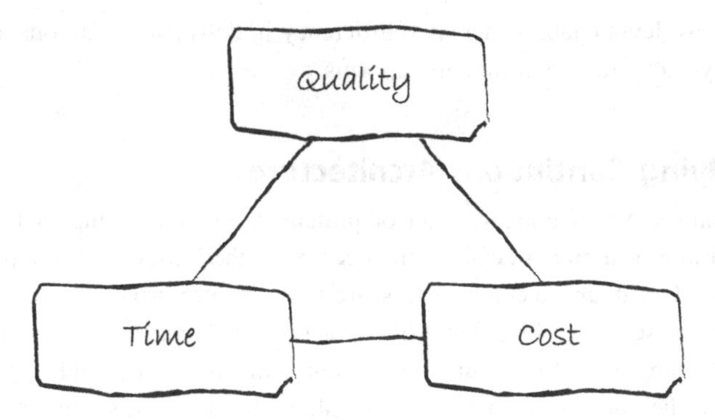

■ **FIGURE 1.4** Cost–quality–time triangle.

The basic premise is that it is not possible to optimize all three corners of the triangle; you are asked to pick any of the two corners and sacrifice the third.

We do not claim that Continuous Architecture solves this problem, but the triangle does present a good context to think about benefits of Continuous Architecture. If we identify good architecture as representing quality in a software solution, then with Continuous Architecture, we have a mechanism that helps us balance time and cost. Another way of saying this is that Continuous Architecture helps us balance time and cost constraints while not sacrificing quality.

The time dimension is a key aspect of Continuous Architecture. We believe that architectural practices should be aligned with Agile practices and not contradict them. In other words, we are continuously developing and improving the architecture rather than doing it once and creating the BARF. As we will see in detail further in this book, Continuous Architecture puts special emphasis on Quality Attributes (*Principle 2: Focus on Quality Attributes, not on functional requirements*). We believe that cost is one of the Quality Attributes that is often overlooked but is critical in making the correct architectural decisions. In summary, Continuous Architecture does not solve the cost–quality–time triangle, but it gives us tools to balance it while maintaining quality.

An element that the cost–quality–time triangle does not address is sustainability. Most large enterprises have a complex technology and application landscape as a result of years of business change and IT initiatives. Agile and Continuous Development practices focus on delivering solutions and ignore addressing this complexity. Continuous Architecture tackles this complexity and strives to create a sustainable model for individual software applications as well as the overall enterprise.

Applying Continuous Architecture at the individual application level enables a sustainable delivery model and a coherent technology platform resilient against future change. Applying Continuous Architecture at the enterprise level enables increased efficiency in delivering solutions and a healthy ecosystem of common platforms.

Applying Continuous Architecture

Continuous Architecture is a set of principles and supporting tools. We do not aim to define a detailed architecture methodology or development process. Our main objective is to share a set of core principles and tools we have seen work in real-life practice. So applying Continuous Architecture is really about understanding the principles and applying them to the context of your environment. While doing this, you can also decide about the tools you would want to implement.

We are responding to the current challenge of creating a solid architectural foundation in the world of Agile and Continuous Delivery. However, this does not mean that applying Continuous Delivery is a prerequisite for adopting the Continuous Architecture approach. We realize that some companies may not be ready to adapt Agile methodologies. Moreover, even if a company is fully committed to Agile methodologies, there may be situations, such as working with a third-party software package, when other approaches such as Iterative or Incremental approaches may be more appropriate (Figure 1.5).

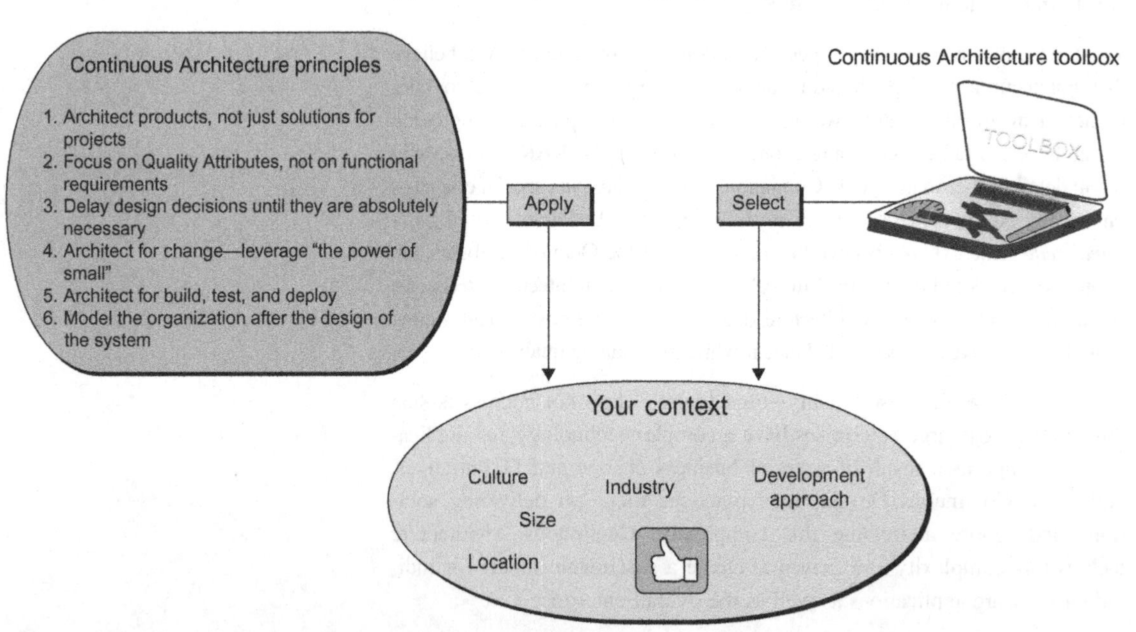

■ FIGURE 1.5 Applying Continuous Architecture.

Does this mean that Continuous Architecture would not work in this situation? Absolutely not. This is one of the key benefits of the "toolbox" approach. Its contents can be easily adapted to work with Iterative or Incremental instead of Agile approaches.

Continuous Architecture also operates in two dimensions, time and scale (Figure 1.6). The time dimension addresses how we enable architectural practices in a world of increasingly rapid delivery cycles. Although the scale dimension looks at the level we are operating at, we believe that the Continuous Architectural principles apply consistently at all scales, but the level of focus and the tools used might vary.

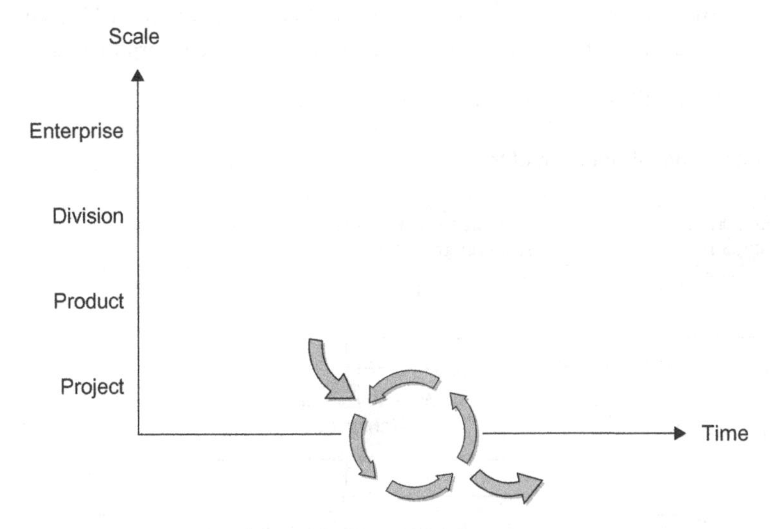

■ **FIGURE 1.6** Continuous Architecture dimensions.

STRUCTURE OF THE BOOK

The book consists of four logical blocks. We start off by setting the context and introducing key terms. This is done in the current chapter, which sets the context, and in Chapter 2, which details the six key principles of Continuous Architecture.

Then we introduce the tools we recommend to use while applying Continuous Architecture. To do this, we follow the four key elements of any software development project: requirements, design, delivery, and testing (or validation). While explaining the tools, we also highlight how the principles can be applied in each of these activities. We do present the activities from requirements to validation in a sequential manner, but this does not mean that we recommend a traditional Waterfall method.

We are just following the logical way of thinking about these activities. Regardless of how Agile you are or how many parallel tasks you conduct to develop software, you still need to understand requirements, design and develop your system, and validate that it operates as expected.

We then elaborate on the Continuous Architecture principles with a detailed case study.

In the last three chapters of the book, we expand on the topic of applying Continuous Architecture within the Enterprise. We start off by discussing the role of the architect in the current context of Agile and Continuous Delivery. We finally focus on applying Continuous Architecture at an Enterprise scale. We then discuss the topic of Enterprise Services, which we believe are important to create efficient architectures at the Enterprise scale.

Figure 1.7 illustrates the structure of the book.

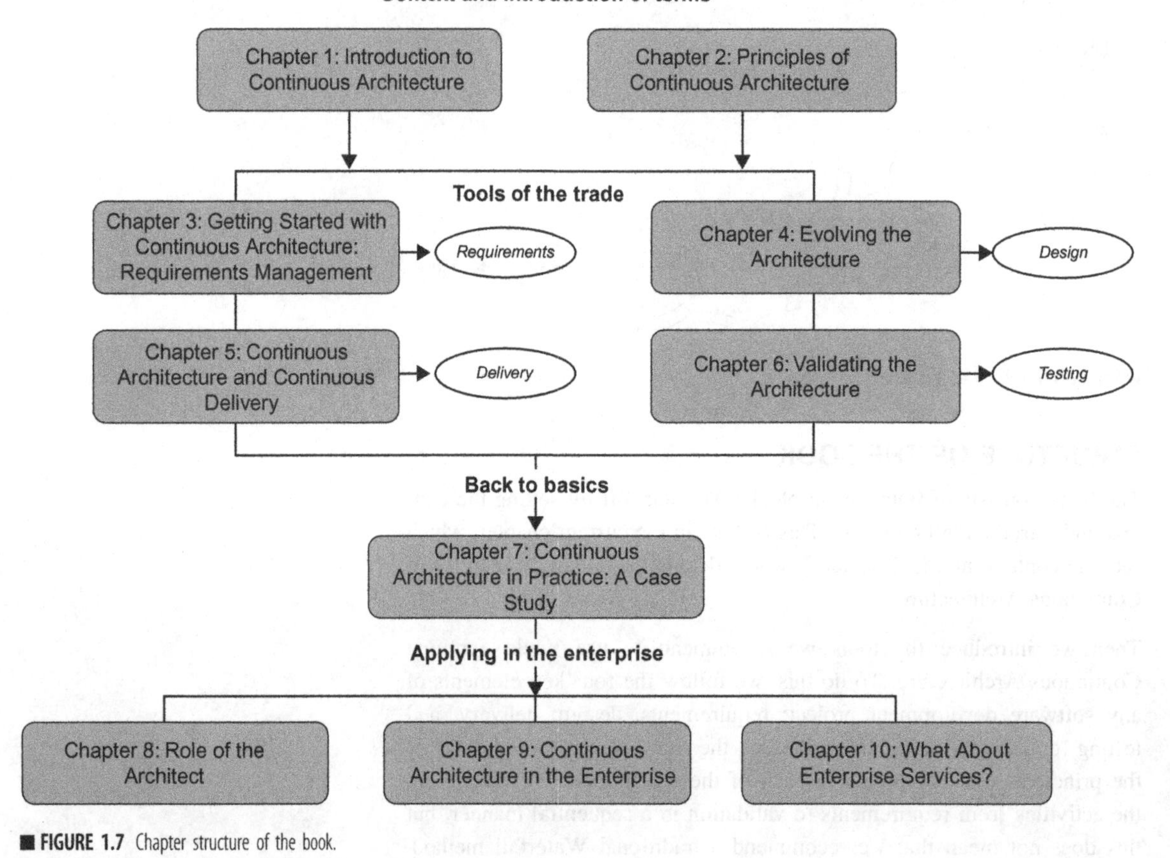

■ **FIGURE 1.7** Chapter structure of the book.

ENDNOTES

1. International Federation for Information Processing (IFIP) Working Group 2.10, <http://www.softwarearchitectureportal.org/>.
2. King M. Amazon wipes customer's Kindle and deletes account with no explanation. The Guardian, October 22, 2012. <http://www.theguardian.com/money/2012/oct/22/amazon-wipes-customers-kindle-deletes-account/>.
3. Extreme programming. Wikipedia, <https://en.wikipedia.org/wiki/Extreme_programming/>.
4. Computerworld, December 2001. Computerworld-appdev-92.
5. Emergence. Wikipedia, <https://en.wikipedia.org/wiki/Emergence/>.
6. Agile Manifesto. Principles behind the Agile Manifesto, <http://www.agilemanifesto.org/principles.html/>.
7. Bass L, Clements P, Kazman R. Software architecture in practice. 3rd ed. Addison-Wesley Professional; 2012.
8. Leffingwell D. Agile architecture: what is intentional architecture? <http://scalingsoftwareagilityblog.com/agile-architecture-what-is-intentional-architecture/>.
9. Continuous delivery. Wikipedia, <https://en.wikipedia.org/wiki/Continuous_delivery/>.
10. Chen L. Continuous delivery: huge benefits, but challenges too. IEEE Softw 2015;32(2):50.
11. von Bismarck O. Die Politik ist die Lehre vom Möglichen (Politics are the art of the possible). In Fürst Bismarck: neue Tischgespräche und Interviews, vol. 1, p. 248.

Chapter 2

Principles of Continuous Architecture

Il semble que la perfection soit atteinte non quand il n'y a plus rien à ajouter, mais quand il n'y a plus rien à retrancher.

(It seems that perfection would be attained not when there is no longer anything to add, but when there is no longer anything to take away.)

—Antoine de St. Exupery, *Terre des Hommes*, 1939

The concept of Continuous Architecture arose as a response to the need for an architectural approach that is able to support very rapid delivery cycles as well as more traditional delivery models. Because of advances in software engineering as well as the availability of new enabling technologies, the approach used for architecting modern systems that require agility (our "systems of engagement") is different from the approach we used to architect older systems (e.g., our "systems of record" and "systems of operation"). As a result, we can deliver modern applications (including systems of engagement, systems of record, and systems of operation) rapidly, sustainably, and with high quality using a Continuous Delivery (see Glossary) approach, which is enabled by using a Continuous Architecture approach.

But what is Continuous Architecture? We believe that it can be defined as an architecture style that follows six simple principles:

1. Architect products, not just solutions for projects.
2. Focus on Quality Attributes, not on functional requirements.
3. Delay design decisions until they are absolutely necessary.
4. Architect for change—leverage "the power of small."
5. Architect for build, test, and deploy.
6. Model the organization after the design of the system.

These principles are depicted in Figure 2.1 and are discussed in detail in the following sections.

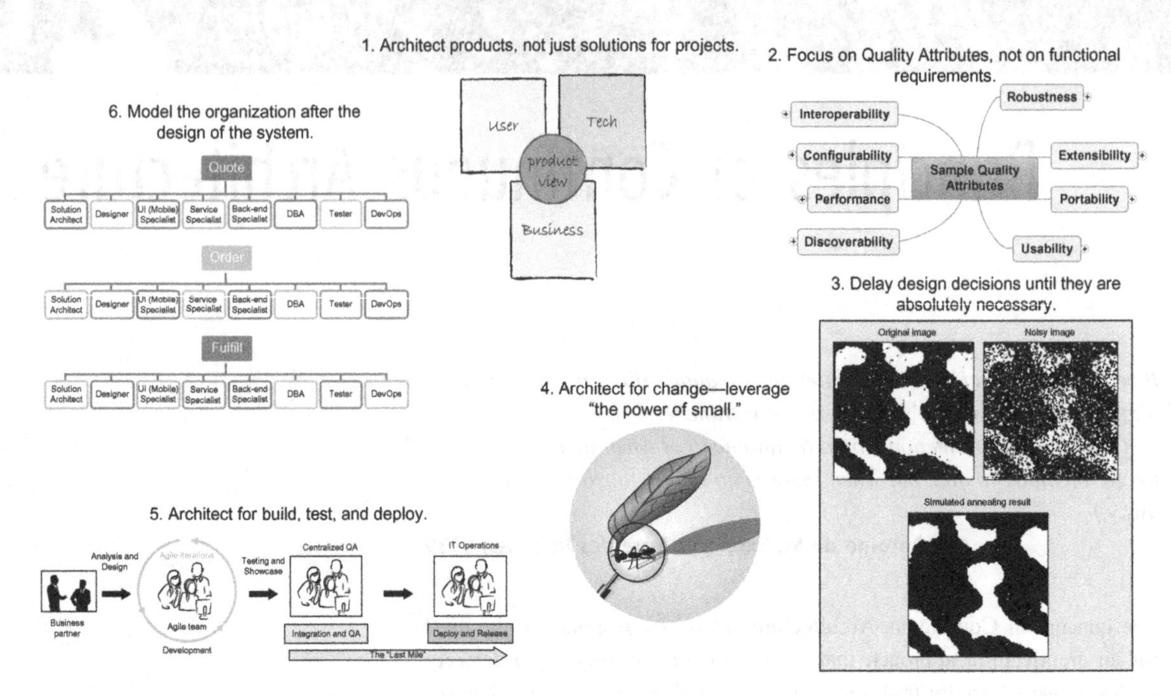

■ **FIGURE 2.1** Continuous Architecture principles.

> **WHEN SHOULD CONTINUOUS DELIVERY BE USED?**
>
> With respect to release cycles and deployment mechanisms, modern architectures need to function at multiple speeds. An IT organization is going to have a "portfolio" of applications, some of which can support high rates of change (because of their loosely coupled architectures) and some of which cannot be released very fast because they are tightly coupled and therefore tend to be brittle.
>
> A "Continuous Architecture approach" takes this into account and is able to deal with differing release rates. Systems of engagement (especially mobile

PRINCIPLE 1: ARCHITECT PRODUCTS, NOT JUST SOLUTIONS FOR PROJECTS

Architects generally tend to fall into two broad categories: those who concentrate on projects ("Solution Architecture," which focuses on the architecture of a single application and is relatively short term in its focus) and those who work on company-wide strategies ("Enterprise Architecture," which focuses on cross-application issues over the lifetime of those applications). While a project-only focus may lead to making short-term architecture decisions, an enterprise-only focus may be perceived as theoretical and impractical. After all, who can accurately predict which technologies Systems of Engagement will need to use in even just a few short years? Will customers be using tablets, smartphones, intelligent watches, glasses, or even some new device still waiting to be invented?

How can we solve this challenge? Projects are temporary in nature and are meant to deliver a well-defined result. In reality, projects rarely exist in isolation; they are often part of a larger endeavor (sometimes called a "program") that exists in order to enhance a product or service. Looking at the architecture required by a project in isolation can be misleading and hides the need for a longer term product-level architecture, which is more strategic in nature than the project-level architecture.

What Is a Software Product?

The concepts of a software product and its associated software product management are critical to the Continuous Architecture approach. Principle 1 states to "Architect products, not just solutions for projects," but what do we mean by "product"?

Most IT shops do not think of themselves as a company in the business of building, selling, and maintaining software products for their customers; instead, they think in terms of delivering applications to their business partners. However, software has become critical to the ability of the partners to serve customers; it has become the strategic enabler. "As software takes a central role in modern business models, application delivery has become the key enabler of disruption."[1] This is forcing IT shops to think differently about the way they deliver software.

In fact, there is little difference at a conceptual level between the processes followed by vendors of commercial software and IT groups of companies that are not in the software business.

One of the key differences is that processes used by successful software companies tend to be more efficient than those used by companies that think of their software as merely supporting their businesses. In today's world, every company needs to think of its applications like a commercial software company; for every application, there has to be a clear understanding of market needs and user requirements. These are reflected in a product definition and a product roadmap. In other words, every company needs software product management.

But what is product management? A good definition we have found is:

> *Product Management is the activity of "product" ownership from Product Conception to Product Withdrawal. It is without any doubt an essential business discipline whereby the Product Manager is analogous to the conductor of an orchestra—without the conductor, uncontrolled pandemonium sets in with each instrument fighting to be heard in continuous cycle of disarray.*[2]

A product management focus is essential for Continuous Architecture because it forces the organization to focus on creating products with repeatable processes, with well-understood customer needs and sustainable business cases. It creates within the IT organization a sense of ownership that leads to better business results.

and cloud applications) lend themselves to a Continuous Delivery approach. Systems of record and systems of operation are usually not a good fit for Continuous Delivery because traditional tightly coupled architectures often require substantial rewrites to keep pace with evolving business needs, and enhancements are often postponed until the need becomes critical.

As we will see further in this chapter as part of our discussion of *Principle 4: Architect for change—leverage "the power of small,"* loosely coupled architectures enable rapid changes. However, uncoupling monolithic architectures is often a significant challenge.

Using a Continuous Delivery approach, IT teams can rapidly and safely implement new requirements from the business by creating a regular, controlled, and highly automated delivery pipeline. Using this approach, an IT organization is able to move from a traditional model in which business partners specify requirements to one in which they switch to "testable hypothesis." This in turn creates a new, high-speed IT function that sits alongside the legacy IT function. Using this approach, the high-speed IT function focuses on the systems of engagement for a few business areas. Continuous Architecture principles and tools can be applied in both high-speed and legacy IT environments.

The concept of software product management further refines this:

> *Software product management is the process of managing software that is built and implemented as a product, taking into account life-cycle considerations and generally with a wide audience. It is the discipline and business process which governs a product from its inception to the market or customer delivery and service in order to generate biggest possible value to the business. This is in contrast to software that is delivered in an ad hoc manner, typically to a limited clientele, e.g. service.*[3,4]

To illustrate this, consider an IT group in a large U.S. financial services corporation that has received a request from its business partners to build and implement a new web-based online system to allow prospective customers to compare one of their offerings to the competitions' offerings; we will call this the "WebShop" system. The team decides to leverage the Continuous Architecture approach to support the delivery of this new system.

The team starts its Continuous Architecture journey by applying *Principle 1: Architect products, not just solutions for projects.* The team looks at existing products and searches for similarities with the "WebShop" system that it is building—in contrast with the approach used by many software development teams when building a new system: "Let's build from scratch!"

As they do this, the team discovers that the "WebShop" system is similar to an existing web-based system that allows customers to get quotes and purchase products. Working with the product manager for this system, the team jointly reviews the roadmap and finds that the plan was to implement a competitive price comparison capability, so it made sense to consolidate the two projects.

With the similarities identified, the team decides to consolidate the functional and Quality Attribute Requirements (QARs) between projects and designs an architecture to support both projects. This is made possible by adopting a product management focus and discipline.

Leveraging "Architect Products, Not Just Solutions for Projects" in Practice

Because creating and maintaining an architecture is an expensive task, it makes sense to leverage it across multiple projects. In that context, a product-level architecture can be reused many times, avoiding rework and promoting planned software reuse as opposed to random reuse paradigms that seldom work. (For an in-depth discussion of this topic please see Fowler et al.[5]) Using this approach, individual projects are instantiated from common product architectures.

More and more IT organizations have started using a new, product-oriented approach to software development. Using this approach, product-centric development teams partner with both their customers and business stakeholders and own the business results that their software delivers. As IT organizations evolve from a project-centric focus to a product-centric focus, software architecture must lead the way by focusing on products. Continuous Architecture's focus on products and product lines blurs the distinction between solution architects and enterprise architects. Continuous Architecture enables architectures to evolve into strategic assets that can be leveraged continuously and rapidly to deliver business value.

PRINCIPLE 2: FOCUS ON QUALITY ATTRIBUTES, NOT ON FUNCTIONAL REQUIREMENTS

The requirements of any IT system can be classified into the following two categories:

1. **Functional requirements:** Functional requirements describe the business capabilities that the system must provide, as well as its behavior at run-time. Common approaches for documenting functional requirements include Use Cases (if an Iterative methodology is being used) and User Stories (if an Agile methodology is being used).
2. **Nonfunctional requirements:** These requirements describe the "Quality Attributes" that the system must meet in delivering functional requirements. They are usually classified into "Quality Attribute Requirements" (defined as "qualifications of the functional requirements or of the overall product") and "constraints," which are "design decisions with zero degrees of freedom." Figure 2.2 depicts a set of sample Quality Attributes that we may identify as part of our requirements.

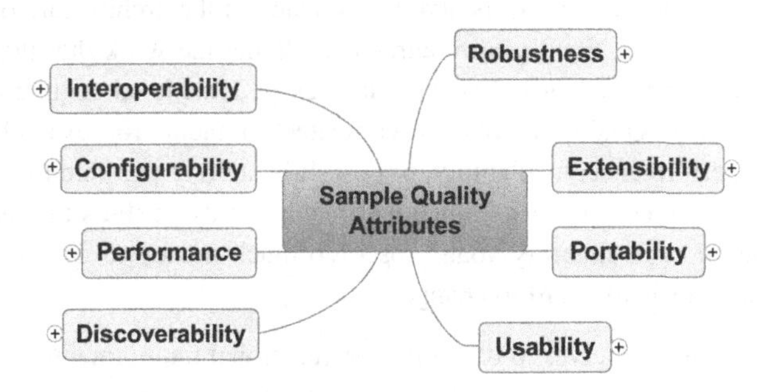

■ **FIGURE 2.2** Sample Quality Attributes.

DON'T THINK FUNCTIONAL REQUIREMENTS; THINK FASTER TIME TO FEEDBACK

The traditional requirements paradigm centers on interviewing subject matter experts (SMEs) who provide requirements that the system must satisfy. These SMEs are sometimes actual users of the system, but more frequently they are representatives from the business who are merely familiar with the users of the system. When SMEs guess what the needs of real users are and the best ways to satisfy those needs, the results often fall short.

The problem is the SME paradigm itself. No one person can represent the needs of all users, no matter how hard they try. The problem goes deeper: The conscious mind often cannot express what is really needed, and only knows what it doesn't like when it sees it. As a result, the surest path to success is to put something out there that minimally satisfies some need, sometimes called a minimum viable product, and then improve upon that in rapid cycles.[7]

CLARIFYING REQUIREMENTS IS IMPORTANT

Philippe Kruchten tells the following story about the importance of clarifying requirements. Back in 1992, Philippe was leading the architecture team for the Canadian Air Traffic Control System, and the team had a requirement of "125 ms time to process a new position message from the Radar Processing System, from its arrival

Intuitively, we gravitate toward functional requirements. For example, Philippe Kruchten, in his seminal article,[6] recommends focusing on a "small subset of important scenarios—instances of use cases—to show that the elements of the four views work together seamlessly.... These scenarios are an abstraction of the most important requirements," which are generally assumed to be functional requirements.

Whereas these requirements tend to be well documented and carefully reviewed by the business stakeholders, quality attribute requirements tend to be more succinct (usually provided as a simple list that may fit on a single page) and perhaps not as carefully scrutinized. Real-life examples of poorly documented quality attributes requirements include:

- "The system must operate 24/7."
- "The system must be extremely user friendly."
- "The system must be very fast" (our personal favorite).

However, quality attribute requirements often have a more significant impact on the architecture of a product. Specifically, the architecture of a system determines how well the nonfunctional requirements will be implemented by our system. The architect makes architectural and design decisions in order to implement Quality Attributes, and those decisions often are compromises, since a decision made to better implement a given Quality Attribute may negatively impact the implementation of other Quality Attributes.

Therefore, accurately understanding quality attribute requirements is one of the most critical prerequisites to adequately designing a system. Using an Architecture Tradeoff Analysis Method (ATAM) utility tree and architecture scenarios (refer to the Glossary for definitions of Architecture Tradeoff Analysis Method utility tree and architecture scenario) is a very effective approach to capture and document quality attribute requirements. (See Chapter 3 for more details on leveraging user stories for this purpose.)

As for functional requirements and their impact on the architecture of our systems, of course, functional requirements define the work that the system must do but do not define *how* it does it. Functional requirements generally have Quality Attributes associated to them, for example, in terms of performance, availability, or cost. It is entirely possible to design a system that meets all of its functional requirements yet fails to meet its performance or availability goals, costs too much money to develop and to maintain, or is too hard to change.

When we limit ourselves to designing for functional requirements without taking into account quality attribute requirements, we end up with a large number of candidate architectures. Designing for quality attribute requirements enables us to limit the candidate architectures to a few choices, and usually one candidate will satisfy all of our requirements.

PRINCIPLE 3: DELAY DESIGN DECISIONS UNTIL THEY ARE ABSOLUTELY NECESSARY

The second principle of Continuous Architecture provides us with guidance to make architectural and design decisions to satisfy quality attribute requirements and not to focus exclusively on functional requirements. Functional requirements often change frequently, especially if we are architecting one of those "systems of engagement" delivered over a mobile device whose User Interface (UI) is likely to change frequently in response to changing customer needs, competitive response, and ever-evolving mobile technology. What Principle 3 advocates is to make design decisions only when facts are known, instead of overcompensating for unknown requirements (in particular quality attribute requirements). According to the Continuous Architecture approach, architectural decisions are a core unit of work for an architect and should be explicitly managed.

Even quality attribute requirements are subject to change or at least to underestimation. When a mobile or web application's popularity goes "viral," even the most carefully crafted applications can collapse under the unexpected load. In addition, performance and availability targets may be vaguely described as Service-Level Agreements (SLAs) or Objectives (SLOs) are not always clear. A common practice is to err on the side of conservatism when describing objectives that may result in unrealistic requirements.

"Modifiability" is especially hard to quantify or to describe; how do you measure the capability of a system to respond to changes that are not yet known? Responding to poorly defined "modifiability" or "configurability" requirements may lead the architect to unnecessarily introduce complex components. For example, it may seem appropriate for an architect to include a rules engine into her design to implement a set of business rules. This approach would enable future-proofing the solution to any change or addition to the business rules. However, the same architect may discover a few years later that this kind of flexibility was not really necessary.

One of the problems with rules engines is that they tend to take control of the architecture over time because the rules engine often becomes tightly coupled with nearly every aspect of the architecture. This additional complexity is also often unwarranted; it is often simpler and less costly to implement business rules in a traditional programming language if they do not change often. Low rates of rules change and low

entry in the Area Control Center till all displays are up-to-date."

After trying very hard to meet the 125 ms for several months, I was hiking one day, looking at a secondary radar slowly rotating (I think it was the one on the top of Mount Parke on Mayne island, just across from Vancouver Airport). I thought, "Mmm, there is already a 12–20 second lag in the position of the plane, why would they bother with 125 ms?" (Note: Primary radar uses an echo of an object. Secondary radar sends a message, "Who are you?" and the aircraft responds automatically with its ID and its altitude; see http://en.wikipedia.org/wiki/Secondary_surveillance_radar [Figure 2.3]. It looks like this: https://www.youtube.com/watch?v = Z0mpzIBWVG4. I knew all this because I am a pilot.)

Then I thought, "In 125 ms, how far across the screen can an aircraft go, assuming a supersonic jet . . . and full magnification?" Some back-of-the-envelope computation gave me about 1/2 pixel! When I had located the author of the requirement, he told me: "Mmm, I allocated 15 seconds to the radar itself (rotation), 1 second for the radar processing system, 4 seconds for transmission, through various microwave equipment. That left 1 second in the ACC. Breaking this down between all equipment in there, router, front end, and so on, it left 125 ms for your processing, guys, updating and displaying the position. . . ." These may not have been his exact words because this happened a long time ago, but this was the general line. Before Agile methodologies made it a "standard," it was useful for the architects to have direct access to the customer, often on site and in this case being able to speak the same language (French).

Philippe's story clearly stresses that it is important for an architect to question everything and not to assume that requirements as stated are absolute.

■ FIGURE 2.3 Airport radar. *Used under license from Shutterstock.com.*

complexity usually do not justify the added complexity and expense associated with a rules engine. When following this approach (i.e., writing rules in the code itself), it is useful to identify the rules (perhaps with some sort of comment) so they can be easily located later.

Figure 2.4 depicts two examples of commonly used three-tier architectures: one without a rules engine (rules are embedded in each tier, either as configuration or as part of the application code) and one with a rules engine. In the second example, the rules engine is tightly coupled with each tier. We may face a long and expensive project if we ever need to replace or eliminate it.

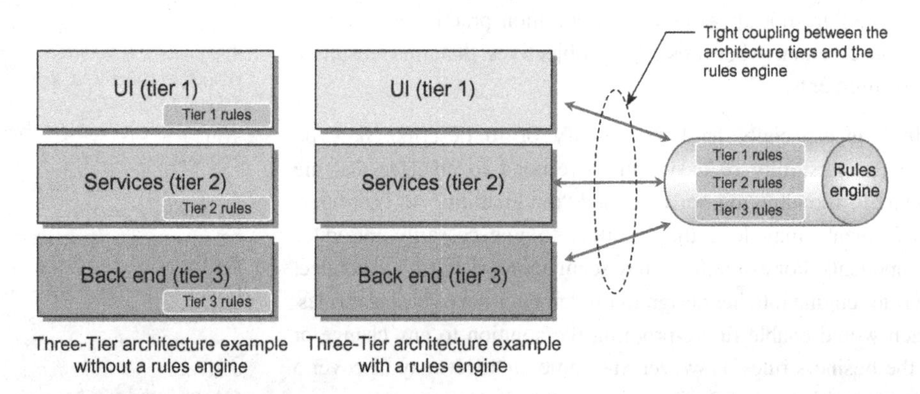

■ FIGURE 2.4 Two commonly used three-tier architectures.

We recommend making design decisions based on known facts, not guesses. Chapter 4 describes how to leverage a Six-Sigma technique (Quality Function Deployment [QFD]) to make sound architecture and design decisions. One key recommendation of Continuous Architecture is to encourage architects to document the rationale behind architecture and design decisions and to base decisions on facts, not fiction.

As we move away from Waterfall application development life cycles involving large requirement documents and evolve toward the rapid delivery of a viable product, we need to create Minimum Viable Architectures (MVAs) to support the rapid delivery of those products. This concept is discussed in more detail in Chapter 7.

To that effect, limiting the budget spent on architecting is a good thing; it forces the team to think in terms of a Minimum Viable Architecture that starts small and is only expanded when absolutely necessary. Too often, a team will solve problems that do not exist and yet fail to anticipate a crippling challenge that kills the application. Getting to an executable architecture quickly and then evolving it are essential for modern applications.

DELAYING DESIGN DECISIONS AND SIMULATED ANNEALING

An interesting parallel can be made between the principle of delaying design decisions and a technique called simulated annealing, which is a probabilistic technique used for solving optimization problems.

Image processing is one area where this technique is used. Basically, if you want to clean up a noisy image, instead of applying a deterministic model, you iterate over the image thousands of times. At each iteration, you make a decision for a particular pixel based on the value of its neighbors. The interesting part is that in the early iterations, you allow a high value of uncertainty in that decision, that is, you make a probabilistic guess. As iterations evolve, you restrict the uncertainty of the probabilistic jump. So the image cools down, just like steel cooling down when you anneal it, hence the "simulated annealing" term.

How does this relate to architectural decisions? Simply put, if you cool down the image too quickly, it cracks—just like steel cracking if you cool it down too quickly. The same concept applies for architectural decisions: If you make too many decisions early on in the process, your architecture will fracture.

Figure 2.5 provides an example of simulated annealing applied to image processing.

PRINCIPLE 4: ARCHITECT FOR CHANGE—LEVERAGE "THE POWER OF SMALL"

The third principle of Continuous Architecture implies that the architecture and the design of the system will change as requirements—especially nonfunctional requirements—emerge. Change is unavoidable; the challenge is to achieve architectural consistency while evolving it at the same time. But how does an architect create a design that is based on the few nonfunctional requirements known at the beginning of a project and yet is resilient to change?

This is where the fourth principle of Continuous Architecture comes to our rescue. The answer lies in basing the architecture on smaller, loosely coupled components and to replace (not change) those components as new requirements emerge. Using loosely coupled components is not a new idea; it has been around since at least the 1980s. In fact, David Parnas' work on information hiding and modular programming back in the early 1970s introduced this concept, and the Simula language implemented similar ideas in the 1960s.

But what is loose coupling? According to Wikipedia, "In computing and systems design, a loosely coupled system is one in which each of its components has, or makes use of, little or no knowledge of the definitions of other separate components," and this concept was introduced by Karl Weick in 1976. Coupling refers to the degree of direct knowledge that one component has of another. The objective of using loose coupling is to reduce the risk that a change made within one

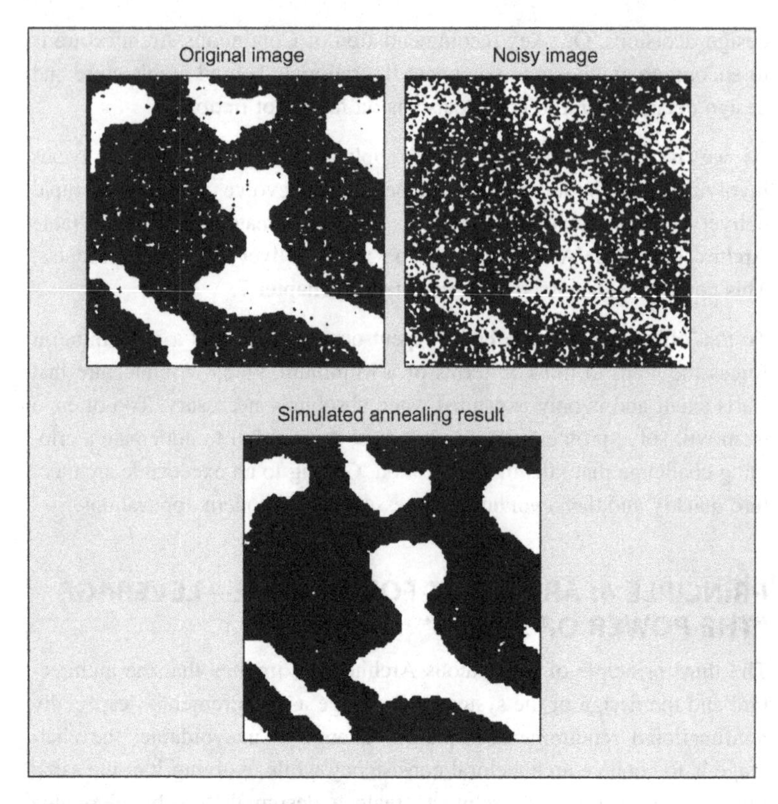

■ **FIGURE 2.5** Simulated annealing example.

component will result in an unintended behavior in another component. Limiting interconnections between components can help isolate problems and simplify testing, maintenance, and troubleshooting.

A loosely coupled system has been broken down into a set of highly independent components that can be independently replaced. Loose coupling can create challenges when a high degree of interaction between or among components is required. For example, in some mobile applications, a high degree of element interaction is necessary for synchronization of data in real time between the front end and the back end. To meet demanding response time requirements and to keep the design simple, the architect may need to implement some direct calls between front-end and back-end components, therefore increasing the coupling between those components.

Therefore, similar to any other design approach, loose coupling needs to be used carefully, with a full understanding of the requirements. Another benefit of loose coupling and replaceability is that they enable the delay of design decisions, and even the reversal of some decisions, by substituting different implementations of services. To do this, the services must be partitioned to appropriately separate concerns.

In a nutshell, architecting for change requires enabling interoperability while avoiding coupling. Keeping the robustness principle in mind is a good Continuous Architecture practice!

But what about using small components? According to Wikipedia, "The Unix philosophy emphasizes building short, simple, clear, modular, and extendable code that can be easily maintained and repurposed by developers other than its creators. The Unix philosophy favors composability as opposed to monolithic design – from Wikipedia 'The Unix Philosophy'." "Microservices" are a good example of applying this design philosophy beyond the Unix Operating System. Using this approach, many services are designed as small, simple units of code with as few responsibilities as possible (a single responsibility would be optimal), but when leveraged together, they can become extremely powerful. The "microservice" approach can be thought of as a refinement of Service-Oriented Architectures (SOAs).

Amazon provides a good illustration of this approach because it is strongly committed to microservices. Using this design philosophy, the system needs to be architected so that each of its capabilities is consumable independently and on demand. The concept behind this design approach is that applications should be built from components that do a few things well, are easily understandable, and are easily replaceable if requirements change. These components should be easy to understand and small enough to be thrown away and replaced if necessary.

In practice, building a system entirely from microservices today could be a stretch because integration and deployment challenges can become overwhelming as the number of microservices grows exponentially. However, significant progress is being made in managing and deploying microservices, and it is very likely that building a large system entirely with microservices will become a viable proposition in the near future. In the meantime, microservices can be leveraged for designing the parts of the system that are most likely to change—and therefore making the entire application more resilient to change. Microservices are a critical tool in the Continuous Architecture toolbox because they enable loose coupling of services as well as replaceability and therefore quick and reliable delivery of new functionality.

THE ROBUSTNESS PRINCIPLE, ALSO KNOWN AS POSTEL'S LAW

This principle is "Be conservative in what you do, be liberal in what you accept from others," often reworded as "Be conservative in what you send, be liberal in what you accept."[8] In other words, code that sends commands or data to other machines (or to other programs on the same machine) should conform completely to the specifications, but code that receives input should accept nonconformant input as long as the meaning is clear.

CONTINUOUS ARCHITECTURE VERSUS "EMERGENT ARCHITECTURE"

Please note that we are not talking about the "emergent architecture" process of some Agile projects here. Those projects apply *Agile Manifesto* principle 11 ("The best architectures, requirements and designs emerge from self-organizing teams"), and this results in architectures that usually require significant amounts of refactoring as new requirements emerge.

This approach may be appropriate for smaller projects, but for larger systems, some amount of architecture planning and governance are required up front to ensure that quality attributes requirements are met and that appropriate infrastructure is available in time to support development, testing, and implementation activities.

PRINCIPLE 5: ARCHITECT FOR BUILD, TEST, AND DEPLOY

So far the first four principles of Continuous Architecture are not specific to projects using the Continuous Delivery approach. This approach changes with the *Principle 5: Architect for build, test, and deploy.* Adopting a Continuous Delivery model implies that all phases of the Software Development Life Cycle (SDLC) need to be optimized for Continuous Delivery. Adopting an Agile methodology such as Scrum is a good first step toward Continuous Delivery but it is not enough by itself.

Let's use a simple example to illustrate this point. Let's return to the IT group in a large U.S. financial services corporation that we introduced in this chapter, as part of our discussion of *Principle 1: Architect products, not just solutions for projects.*

The company has an excellent track record of delivering projects on time and within budget, and their focus is on stability and security rather than time to market. Major software releases follow a quarterly schedule, and minor releases are delivered on a monthly basis. Historically, the company has been using a "Waterfall" approach for its Software Development Life Cycle, with some recent attempts at moving toward a more Iterative approach (really a "fast Waterfall") and even some Agile pilots for small projects. The infrastructure is optimized for this delivery schedule; it uses fixed, predefined "silos" (common to all applications) for its centralized Quality Assurance (QA) testing group to test the new versions of its application software before it is deployed in production as part of its release schedule.

The IT organization decides to use some of the Agile techniques as well as a Continuous Integration approach to building software and delivers the "WebShop" on time, with few defects. (See the Glossary for a definition of Continuous Integration.) The company's only concern is that despite adopting Agile techniques and Continuous Integration practices—including some automated tests as part of each build—the vast majority of defects are found during Quality Assurance testing. In addition, deployment of application software to the various testing environments and to the production environment is still a long and error-prone process.

After the system has been delivered, the company's business partners want to quickly make several changes to the User Interfaces and change some business rules. They also want to have multiple versions of the application in production to test various hypotheses and understand which User Interface configuration works better with their target audience (this approach is known as "champion/challenger" testing or A/B testing).

The IT group discovers that its skills and processes are not well adapted to this new situation. Adopting Agile techniques enables them to optimize the "design/build" phase of the Software Development Life Cycle, but the cross-system integration, testing, and deployment processes (described as the "last mile" in Figure 2.6) remain a bottleneck and prevent the group from achieving its rapid delivery goal.

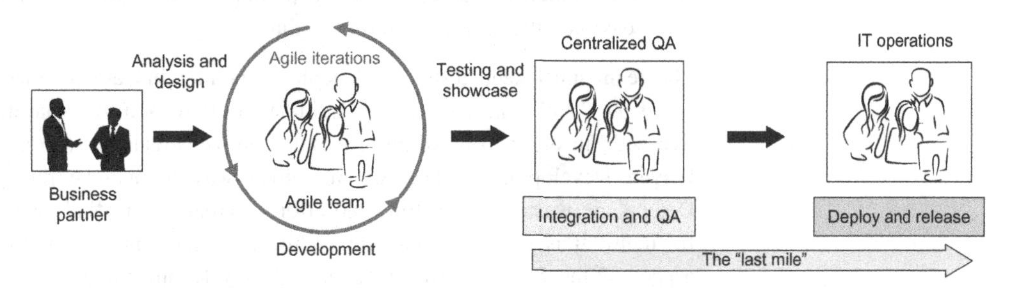

■ **FIGURE 2.6** Traditional deployment process.

Attempts at speeding up existing integration, testing, and deployment processes by taking shortcuts result in errors and production issues. In effect, the team is attempting to force a process designed to release software on a monthly cycle to release on a weekly (or even faster) cadence, and the process is no longer functioning smoothly.

What could they have done differently? The architecture needs to be optimized for the whole Software Development Life Cycle process, not just the "design/build" phase of the process. In Continuous Architecture, the architect needs to take into account the integration, testing, and deployment requirements, and user stories are an excellent way to document those requirements. Each iteration includes a design/build, integration/testing, and deployment component (Figure 2.7).

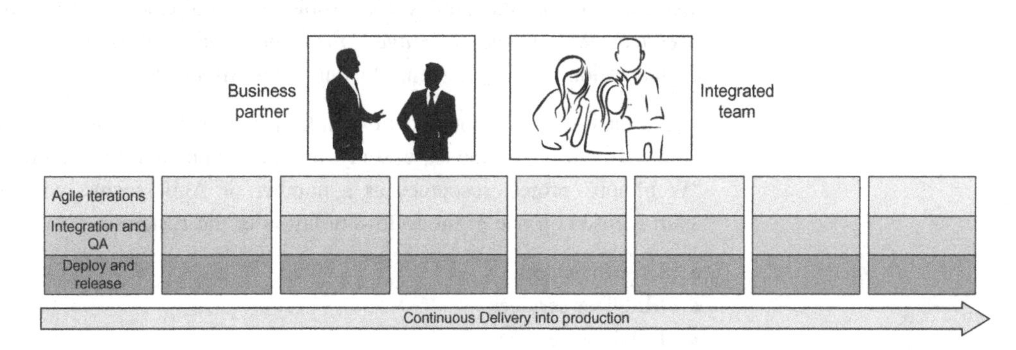

■ **FIGURE 2.7** Continuous Delivery process.

In practice, this is achieved by designing small, Application Programming Interface (API)-testable services and components as well as leveraging Service Virtualization in order to enable testing of applications and systems when not all the services are available. It also means keeping coupling of components to an absolute minimum (remember *Principle 4: Architect for change—leverage "the power of small"* and the robustness principle). Finally, it means avoiding putting business logic in hard to test areas such the messaging infrastructure.

The team must keep testing and deployment in mind at all times and avoid the "We'll fix it in testing" attitude so often used to create defective code in order to make an artificial deadline. Practices such as Test Driven Development (TDD) are are great way to achieve this goal. Defects are waste; it takes time and effort to create them, find them, and fix them! It is very important for architects to take into account every aspect of the Software Development Life Cycle, including testing and deployment, when creating and evolving modern architectures in order to enable Continuous Delivery.

PRINCIPLE 6: MODEL THE ORGANIZATION AFTER THE DESIGN OF THE SYSTEM

The first five principles deal with process and technology, but what about the third dimension of every IT project we are involved in—people? How does Continuous Architecture impact the organization of software delivery teams, or conversely, how can we better organize teams to support Continuous Delivery?

First let's discuss some scoping considerations here. For Continuous Architecture to be effective, we need to include all constituents in the delivery team, not only those responsible for the build activities (designers and developers) but also the groups responsible for testing and deployment, as well as the groups responsible for requirements (*Principle 4: Architect for change—leverage "the power of small"*) and support. Collaboration is a key element of Continuous Architecture.

Going back to our hypothetical example from our discussion of Principle 1, the IT group in the case study initially attempted to organize the "WebShop" project resources as a number of Agile teams, with each team focused on one of the following layers of the system:

- User Interfaces
- Mid-Tier services
- Database services
- Back-end interface services

They quickly discovered that this approach was counterproductive. Organizing teams in layers did not promote collaboration. Instead, it created communication issues.

In addition, the adoption of Agile techniques varied by teams: the User Interface team decided to be as "Agile" as possible, but the team responsible for the services interfacing with back-end systems elected to follow their traditional "Waterfall" approach. Using several Software Development Life Cycle approaches simultaneously created more misunderstandings and communication issues.

Because back-end interface services were not ready for testing until the end of the Waterfall development cycle, the User Interface and midtier services developers had to "stub out" their calls to those services during iteration testing, which prevented them from testing with realistic test cases and resulted in the majority of the defects being discovered in the Quality Assurance phase. This in turn resulted in significant unplanned rework to fix those defects. In addition, working sessions between the teams were few and far between. That lack of communication contributed to additional misunderstandings resulting in more defects.

What happened here to our hapless IT team is that they were the victims of what is known in the IT community as "Conway's law." Back in 1968 (according to Wikipedia), computer programmer Melvin Conway introduced a concept that has since became known as "Conway's law" at the National Symposium on Modular Programming: "Organizations which design systems . . . are constrained to produce designs which are copies of the communication structures of these organizations."

This was further elaborated by James O. Coplien and Neil B. Harrison as follows: "If the parts of an organization (e.g. teams, departments, or subdivisions) do not closely reflect the essential parts of the product, or if the relationships between organizations do not reflect the relationships between product parts, then the project will be in trouble. . . . Therefore: Make sure the organization is compatible with the product architecture."[9] Putting Conway's law to work for you—rather than against you—means organizing your teams after the design of the system you are working on in order to promote interoperability.

Returning to our hypothetical example from our discussion of Principle 1, it would have been much better to organize the teams vertically (i.e., by capability being delivered) rather than by architecture layer.

For example, if "fulfill an order" is one of the capabilities being delivered by the application, we would create a "fulfill an order" team with the following roles. Please note that this is a role structure and not an organization chart.

Some of the roles (Architect, Designer, DBA) are likely to be filled by the same individual across all teams:

- Solution architect
- Designer
- User Interface specialist
- Service specialist
- Back-end specialist
- Database Administrator (DBA)
- Tester
- Operations specialist

Organizing teams by capability or product feature promotes effective communications among team members. Teams that use that approach discover that the vast majority of issues are identified early in the software development process. Issues are solved before they turn into unpleasant surprises at the end of the project or before they turn into defects in production.

One last word of caution about *Principle 6: Model the organization after the design of the system.* Most organizations are hamstrung by their heritage and have a hard time changing, so expect to overcome resistance to change when applying this principle. Go slow, implement change in small increments, and demonstrate benefits as you go to convince your colleagues and turn them into allies.

SUMMARY

In this chapter, we defined "Continuous Architecture" as an architecture approach that follows the following six principles:

1. Architect products, not just solutions for projects.
2. Focus on Quality Attributes, not on functional requirements.
3. Delay design decisions until they are absolutely necessary.
4. Architect for change—leverage "the power of small."
5. Architect for build, test, and deploy.
6. Model the organization after the design of the system.

As a result, Continuous Architecture enables the following capabilities:

- They are resilient to change.
- They are testable.
- They can respond to feedback. In fact, they are driven by feedback.

The next chapters in this book discuss in detail the techniques and tools used in the Continuous Architecture approach and illustrate those tools and techniques with a case study.

ENDNOTES

1. Lo Giudice D, Bittner K. Define a software delivery strategy for business innovation. Forrester Report, July 25, 2014.
2. Best Practice Product Management. <Productmanager.co.uk>.
3. Software Product Management. <https://en.wikipedia.org/wiki/Software_product_management>.
4. Ebert C. Software product management. Crosstalk 2009;22(1):15–199.
5. Fowler M, Beck K, Brant J, Opdyke W. Refactoring: improving the design of existing code. July 8, 1999.
6. Kruchten P. The 4 + 1 view model of architecture. IEEE, November 1995.
7. Bittner K. Software requirement practices are ripe for disruption. Forrester Research, April 2014.
8. The robustness principle. <https://en.wikipedia.org/wiki/Robustness_pr>.
9. Coplien J, Harrison N. Patterns of Agile Software Development. Addison-Wesley; 2004.

Chapter 3

Getting Started with Continuous Architecture: Requirements Management

"Would you tell me, please, which way I ought to go from here?"
"That depends a good deal on where you want to get to," said the Cat.
"I don't much care where—" said Alice.
"Then it doesn't matter which way you go," said the Cat.

—Lewis Carroll, *Alice in Wonderland*

Unlike Alice, we know where we want to get to on the Continuous Architecture journey: We would like to implement an architecture approach to effectively support Continuous Delivery—and it does matter which way we go!

In this chapter, we will take the first steps toward that journey, starting with requirements management. We will cover in detail the practices and techniques that are required at this stage. We will also cover the toolset available to architects to implement those practices and techniques.

Why is it important for the architect to use an effective and efficient way of managing requirements? Consider the following example. A large financial institution decides to implement a brand-new enterprise customer system. Senior leadership knows that each of the company's business units manages its customers independently. They believe that an enterprise customer system would enable them to create significant business opportunities by enabling cross-selling of existing customers by multiple business units and leveraging resources across the enterprise in their marketing and selling processes.

This company has a seasoned architecture team, and some of its architects have experience with implementing customer systems in similar companies. They select the best contractor they can find and organize a number of offsite workshops and working groups to ensure that they have buy-in from the various business units across the enterprise and to gather requirements. These requirements are documented in voluminous Microsoft Word documents and describe numerous functional requirements from the various business units. Unfortunately, some of these requirements conflict with each other and are not prioritized. In addition, the documents do not include any Quality Attribute Requirements (QARs) beyond some vague statements such as "The system must be fast and must be able to scale."

Using the large requirement documents, the architecture team and their contractor create an even larger Request for Proposals (RFP), send the RFP to a few vendors, and select a software package after a lengthy process based on their perception (reinforced by the vendor) that this software package is "easily customizable." The team signs a contract with the vendor and proceeds to customize the software to their requirements. This task turns out to be difficult because some of the requirements are ambiguous, and they lack access to business executives who could prioritize conflicting requirements. In addition, the vendor has to make significant unexpected changes to the architecture to accommodate some of the requirements. The changes negatively impact the performance and scalability of the software package but neither the vendor nor the project team feel that those are serious issues since there are no quality attribute requirements that set performance or scalability targets for the system.

A year later as time and money run out, they attempt to implement the new enterprise customer system. Unfortunately, the system falls short of expectations. The performance of the new system is inadequate, and the new system cannot even handle their existing customer base. In addition, many business units feel that most of their requirements have not been implemented and have been pushed to a future phase of the project. Several attempts at remediating those issues fail, and the new system is eventually decommissioned.

What went wrong? How can we develop architectures that enable the business instead of constraining it? The challenges faced on that project were not just about requirements management, but we believe that managing requirements well is a key success factor in any IT project, and poor requirement management was one of the main reasons why this project failed.

This chapter outlines an approach to modeling the business as well as identifying and managing requirements by leveraging the concepts of product management, value chains, user stories, and architecture scenarios within the context of creating and evolving in a Continuous Architecture manner whether at a product level or at the enterprise level.

We begin by contrasting functional requirements and Quality Attributes. We then outline the objectives of value chains and user stories. Next, we describe value chains and user stories in more detail and provide relevant examples for each, as well as guidelines for using these techniques as part of a Continuous

Architecture approach. Finally, we discuss how architecture scenarios can be leveraged to identify and manage quality attribute requirements.

FUNCTIONAL REQUIREMENTS VERSUS QUALITY ATTRIBUTES

As mentioned in Chapter 2, requirements for a software system fall into the following two categories:

1. **Functional requirements:** These requirements describe the business capabilities that the system must provide, as well as its behavior at run-time.
2. **Non-functional requirements:** These requirements describe the "Quality Attributes" that the system must meet in delivering functional requirements.

As we saw in Chapter 2, functional requirements are usually well documented and carefully reviewed by the business stakeholders, but Quality Attributes are documented in a much more succinct manner. They may be provided as a simple list that may fit on a single page and perhaps not as carefully scrutinized.

However, our view is that Quality Attributes drive the architecture design. As stated by Bass et al., "Whether a system will be able to exhibit its desired (or required) Quality Attributes is substantially determined by its architecture."[1] The architect's role is to make architectural and design decisions in order to implement Quality Attributes, and those decisions often are compromises because a decision made to better implement a given Quality Attribute may negatively impact the implementation of other Quality Attributes. Accurately understanding quality attribute requirements is one of the most critical prerequisites to adequately designing a system.

Let's illustrate this with an example by returning to the IT group introduced in Chapter 2. The group has identified the following top three Quality Attributes for the "WebShop" system, in priority order:

1. Cost effectiveness of the total life cycle of the system, not just development costs
2. Performance
3. Usability

Listing cost effectiveness as the top Quality Attribute is not unreasonable for a financial institution; most financial companies are concerned about the cost of their IT function, especially if they happen to operate in the retail sector (e.g., retail banks, personal insurance carriers). However, very few teams *explicitly* design for cost effectiveness and risk ignoring a key Quality Attribute; they often either create an application system that

WHAT IS THE MEAN STACK?

MEAN (which is an acronym that refers to the first letters of its four components; please refer to Davis[2] for more information on the MEAN stack) is an open-source solution stack for building dynamic web and mobile web sites. MEAN includes the following products (Figure 3.1):

1. MongoDB, a document, NoSQL database
2. Express, a web applications framework for NodeJS
3. Angular, a JavaScript UI web development framework
4. Node.js, a software platform for scalable server-side and networking applications

Some of the benefits of using the MEAN stack are as follows: speed of development and fast prototyping, ability to make changes quickly and easily, automated testing, native support for web technologies, easy migration to production, ease of scale (both vertically and horizontally), and support by most cloud PaaS providers.

■ **FIGURE 3.1** The MEAN stack.

is expensive to run and to maintain, or they risk having to change the architecture after the system has been built in order to make it affordable.

Because our team leverages *Principle 2: Focus on Quality Attributes, not on functional requirements*, it keeps cost effectiveness in mind when making architecture, design, and product selection decisions. Some of the decisions the team makes as a result are:

- The team leverages open source products instead of proprietary products. In this case, the team decides to leverage the MEAN stack to build the "WebShop" system. This decision not only decreases the infrastructure cost for the project, but it also allows the team to use the same data structure (JSON [JavaScript Object Notation]) in all components of the system, therefore avoiding expensive and time-consuming transformations. In addition, it gives them the flexibility to deploy code without changes to their private cloud, as well as to major cloud Platform as a Service (PaaS) providers. It also gives them the option of providing a mobile User Interface (UI) as well as a web User Interface at the cost of a relatively small effort.
- The team leverages JavaScript as its development language for both User Interface and server side. Because JavaScript is a scripting language, it minimizes developers' downtime and enables quick and easy changes to the code base.
- The team leverages a cloud infrastructure for development and most of its testing, therefore further decreasing infrastructure costs

What about functional requirements? Functional requirements define the work that the system must do but do not define *how* it does it. Functional requirements generally have Quality Attributes associated to them, for example, in terms of performance, availability, or cost. Designing for quality attribute requirements enables us to limit the candidate architectures to a few choices and select the architecture that best satisfies all our requirements.

Finally, remember the trend away from "Big Requirement Documents" (BRDs) and toward faster time to feedback. Many functional "requirements" documented in Big Requirement Documents are not really required and sometimes not even nice to have. Implementing Continuous Delivery means optimizing every component of the Software Development Life Cycle, including requirements gathering.

Focusing requirements on defining products in terms of addressing specific problems to be solved and the explicit outcomes is a great way to achieve this. As stated by Kurt Bittner:

> *An outcome is either satisfied or it is not; outcomes are the appropriate units of scope for a release, not requirements. A requirement that does not contribute to satisfying an in-scope outcome is superfluous. When requirements become disconnected from outcomes, scoping discussions become complex and contentious, subject to mere whim and opinion. The result is usually wasted time, effort, and money.*[3]

LEVERAGING VALUE CHAINS TO UNDERSTAND THE FUNCTIONAL SCOPE OF A PRODUCT

Now that we have provided an overview of functional and quality attribute requirements, let us first look at techniques for eliciting functional requirements. Traditionally, the goal of technology is to enable a business to function in an efficient and flexible manner. However, this role is changing. In today's world, technology also enables new business models and interactive conversations with customers. All technical decisions need to be grounded on business models and objectives.

As a result, it is only natural that the first logical step in the Continuous Architecture approach is to understand the functional scope of the product or project we are building. We use value chains to better understand and describe this functional scope. The objectives of developing a value chain are to:

- Understand the "why" and "what" of the business. Why are we in business? What are the core activities that provide value to our clients and us?

- Understand the "how" of the business. How do we actually execute within the core activities of our business?
- Understand the "whom" of the business. Who are the internal and external users of our technology?

The Big Picture: The Value Chain

The role of the "value chain" is to depict activities ("chevrons") of the enterprise that are involved in generating value, as well as the supporting areas. Figure 3.2 depicts a sample value chain for a financial trading institution.

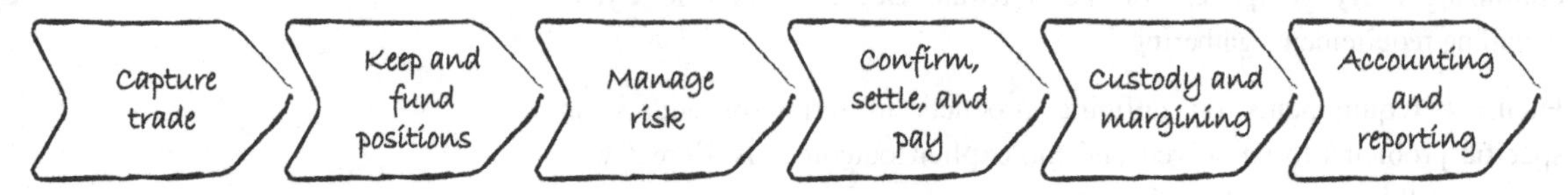

■ **FIGURE 3.2** Sample trading value chain.

The value chain should easily answer the question "Why are we in business?" The trading example clearly shows that the goal of the organization is to capture trades, process, and maintain them. The chevrons of Figure 3.2 are defined as follows:

- **Capture trade:** The activities involved in generating trades for the organization. These can be trades created by its own broker or dealers, automated systems, or feeds from other partner institutions (e.g., investment managers).
- **Keep and fund positions:** The activities of tracking the portfolio of trades, their market values, and their status as well as how they are funded
- **Manage risk:** The activities of looking at the overall exposure the organization has based upon the portfolios it is managing
- **Confirm, settle, and pay:** The activities involved with confirming the execution of trades, ensuring that the necessary procedures are followed for the traded instruments to actually change ownership and all involved parties' payments are processed
- **Custody and margining:** The activities involved in managing the ownership of instruments that the organization has acquired
- **Accounting and reporting:** The activities ensuring that the organization's assets and liabilities are reported in a consistent manner within regulatory and firm requirements

A value chain provides an overview of the business by depicting major processes that collectively generate value for the organization and its clients.

A value chain is a long-lasting view of the business. As long as the core business does not change, the same value chain can be used by the organization for years. One of the first authors to introduce the value chain concept was Michael Porter in 1985.[4]

The value chain is a simple high-level picture of the business that is depicted in a single view for easy comprehension. The software architecture objectives of developing a value chain are:

- It provides a single overview that shows the major elements of the business.
- It provides an anchor point that can be used as a launchpad for more detailed views from business, financial, and technical perspectives.
- It summarizes existing information regarding the "emergent" architectural condition of the organization.
- It defines a common notation and vocabulary for more detailed business and technical architecture work.

The former example focuses on the core activities of the organization and ignores the supporting activities such as research and human resources. These supplemental activities can be shown as horizontal bars cutting across all chevrons. Figure 3.3 is a sample value chain for a lending organization.

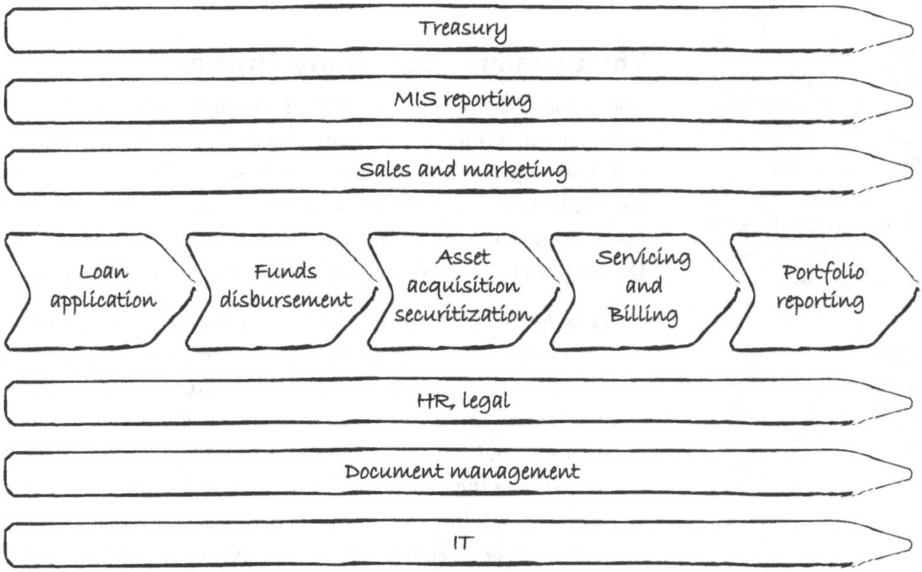

FIGURE 3.3 Sample lending value chain.

WHAT ABOUT BUSINESS CAPABILITIES?

The concept of "business capabilities" has recently become popular, especially with business architects. What are business capabilities?

A business capability is what a company needs to do to execute its business strategy (e.g., enable ePayments, tailor solutions at point of sale, demonstrate product concepts with customers, combine elastic and non-elastic materials side by side, etc.). Another way to think about capabilities is that they are a collection or container of people, process and technology that is addressable for a specific purpose.[5]

Business capabilities can be used effectively to succinctly describe and document the chevrons in a value chain. However, there is a risk in using business capabilities: The team may be tempted to decompose them into successive levels of detail (levels 0, 1, 2, 3, and so on) and create a voluminous and detailed "business capability model" (very much the same way as teams were creating voluminous "process decomposition models" a few years ago), which does not offer any value to support the Continuous Architecture approach.

In the Continuous Architecture approach, business capabilities can be used to describe value chain chevrons at a high level, and user stories can be used to "animate" the value chain.

Normally, we put shared services elements under the central chevrons and management and client-focused elements above the central chevrons. Even though modeling the supporting services is beneficial from a completeness perspective, exclude these unless they are of particular interest to the architecture effort. This is in line with our pragmatic approach of focusing on what really matters and not "boiling the ocean."

The core chevrons for the above example are:

- **Loan application:** The activities involved with applying for a loan
- **Funds disbursement:** The actual disbursement of the loan amounts
- **Asset acquisition or securitization:** Acquisition of loans from other organizations and securitizing the organization's assets (in this case loans) in the marketplace
- **Servicing and billing:** The activities involved with supporting the loans, billing, sending of statements, responding to client inquiries, and so on
- **Portfolio reporting:** Reporting on the financial balance of the entire asset base of the organization

The value chain gives us the "what," but to understand the business, we also need to understand the "how," as well as the "who." This is where the dynamics come into the picture.

The Dynamics: User Story Themes

The value chain is great at setting the high-level context, but to drive architectural definitions, we want to animate the value chain. User stories (see Glossary for a definition of user stories)[6] are one well-recognized technique that can help us animate the value chain. The concept of "user stories" is popular with Agile development teams and Continuous Delivery teams. User stories are defined by Wikipedia as follows:

> *In software development and product management, a user story is one or more sentences in the everyday or business language of the end user or user of a system that captures what a user does or needs to do as part of his or her job function. User stories are used with agile software development methodologies as the basis for defining the functions a business system must provide, and to facilitate requirements management. It captures the 'who', 'what' and 'why' of a requirement in a simple, concise way, often limited in detail by what can be hand-written on a small paper notecard.*[7]

User stories are a great way to explore a value chain; each chevron or set of business capabilities can be described in detail by a set of user stories as well as a set of test cases that define the outcomes of the stories. However, user stories can be at a too granular level for larger scale architectural decisions. We recommend to group user stories (and test cases) in one of three ways:

- They can be grouped into "user story themes." We will use this term here to keep the terminology as neutral as possible.
- Alternatively, they can be grouped into use cases. We like the convenience of using use cases to group user stories, but we do not advocate using a traditional use case analysis approach (see later discussion). Also, we are aware that using this terminology may feel slightly behind the times to some Agile methodology practitioners.
- Finally, they can be grouped into "features"[8] if an Agile terminology (e.g., Scaled Agile Framework [SAFe]; see Scaled Agile Framework[9] for more details on this methodology) is preferred.

Regardless of the approach being used for organizing user stories and test cases, it is important not to drill down into detailing them too early in the process. Keep in mind that in the Continuous Architecture approach, quality attribute requirements and their associated architecture scenarios drive the architecture design. Detailed user stories and test cases are not important at architecture design time. User stories and test cases should be documented in detail when the software is being written—and not before.

Let us use the loan servicing organization from our previous example to explain those concepts. We know from the value chain that the first two chevrons are loan application and funds disbursement. But what actually happens, and who is involved in these activities? We can get this information by looking at the user story themes and the associated user stories for each chevron (Figure 3.4). Note that we have used the traditional use case notation which we find very useful (see call out on leveraging use cases for more detail).

As can be seen from Figure 3.4, we now know more about how our business operates. We have determined three main events (apply for loan, disburse loan, and pay fees), which we will call user stories themes (or alternatively, either "use cases" or "features"), and eight roles (applicant, guarantor, lender, credit bureau, core processing, loan origination, servicing, and designated recipient), which we will call actors. The user story themes tell us the "how" and the actors the "who" of the business.

Going back to our loan servicing organization, we find that we have five external actors, the applicant, lender, guarantor, credit bureau, and

LEVERAGING USE CASES TO GROUP USER STORIES: WHAT IS DIFFERENT ABOUT OUR APPROACH?

In traditional use case modeling,[10] you differentiate between actors and use cases by looking at the boundary of the system you are modeling, whether it is a software system or a business. Anything that is outside of the system and needs to interact with the system is called an *actor*, and the activities they require the system to perform are called *use cases*. The next step in the analysis is to describe the use cases in detail ("detailing a use case"), optionally using various Unified Modeling Language (UML) tools. This may result in voluminous descriptions of requirements, which we do not recommend.

In our approach, we leverage the use case concepts of boundaries and actors, but we do not detail use cases. We just use them as a convenient grouping for user stories and test cases.

Use cases are not as prevalent as they used to be in the software industry. In essence, they have become so much part of the common language that we believe they no longer are understood in their original intent. We still find the original definition of use cases useful for analyzing architecture requirements.

Regardless of whether you call them user story themes or use cases, the main objective is to animate the value chain from the perspective of an end user.

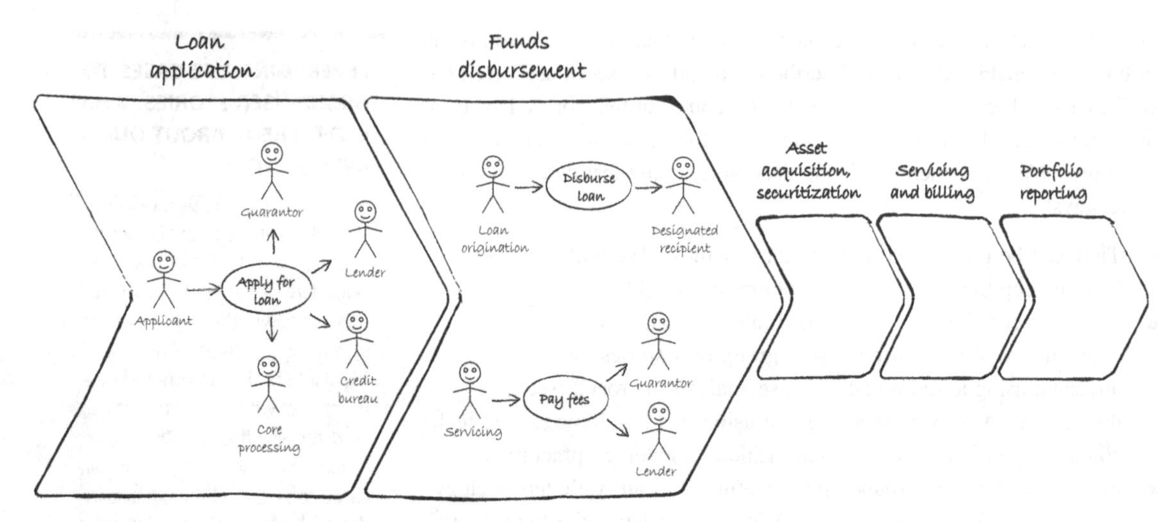

■ **FIGURE 3.4** Lending value chain and user story themes.

> **USER STORY THEME: APPLY FOR A LOAN**
>
> This theme represents the flow of events that take place when the applicant applies for a loan (including both certification and guarantee activities). This theme includes the following user stories:
>
> 1. Match the loan program entered by the applicant to a loan program offered by a guarantor–lender combination.
> 2. Obtain a loan guarantee from the guarantor, if applicable (electronic or manual). For certain loans, blanket or default guarantees apply that make it unnecessary to get explicit approval from the guarantor. However, the guarantor is informed of the loan.
> 3. Obtain the applicant's credit rating from the credit bureau.

designated recipient. From this, we can understand the core business revolves around connecting three of these actors, the applicant, lender, and guarantor. We can also infer that the organization in question is not a lender itself but acts as a broker among the lender, the applicant, and the guarantor of the loan.

The model tells us that we have three internal organizations (i.e., actors) active. In the funds disbursement chevron, the loan origination actor ensures the loans go to the designated recipient, which could be the bank of the applicant or an entity such as a university that directly receives the loan. At the same time the servicing actor pays fees to the guarantors and lenders. The core processing actor is where the loan applications are received and processed.

Analyzing User Story Themes

Assume that for our loan servicing organization, our goal is to define an architecture blueprint, primarily the components we need at a logical level to support our business. The first step is to write a brief outline of the user story theme, listing the user stories included in this theme.

This outline is very high level but is adequate for our purpose because our goal is to understand and describe the business and not create detailed business requirements at this time.

The next step is to create a high-level sequence diagram (sequence diagrams are an integral part of the Unified Modeling Language) outlining the major components that will be involved in the user story theme (Figure 3.5).

This sequence diagram highlights the need for one major system for originations and two supporting components, an imaging service and a formatting service. You can see that we have started making architectural decisions already in the process of drawing a sequence diagram. When we make decisions on such matters, it is not usually in the confines of one sequence diagram but across the breadth of the overall architecture. Other sequence diagrams we would have developed would have pointed out a need for common services such as the imaging and formatting services.

Another architectural decision could have been to split the loan origination system into separate systems based on the types of loans processed. This is not only determined by architectural preference but is also influenced by the current environment of the organization.

4. Perform risk analysis and assign rates.
5. Obtain underwriting (nonguaranteed loans).
6. Perform exception processing, such as credit rejection, application changes, and missing borrower information. All exception-processing activities have to be communicated to the applicant, lender, and guarantor when appropriate.
7. Obtain final approval and inform the appropriate parties or notify the borrower of the denied loan.

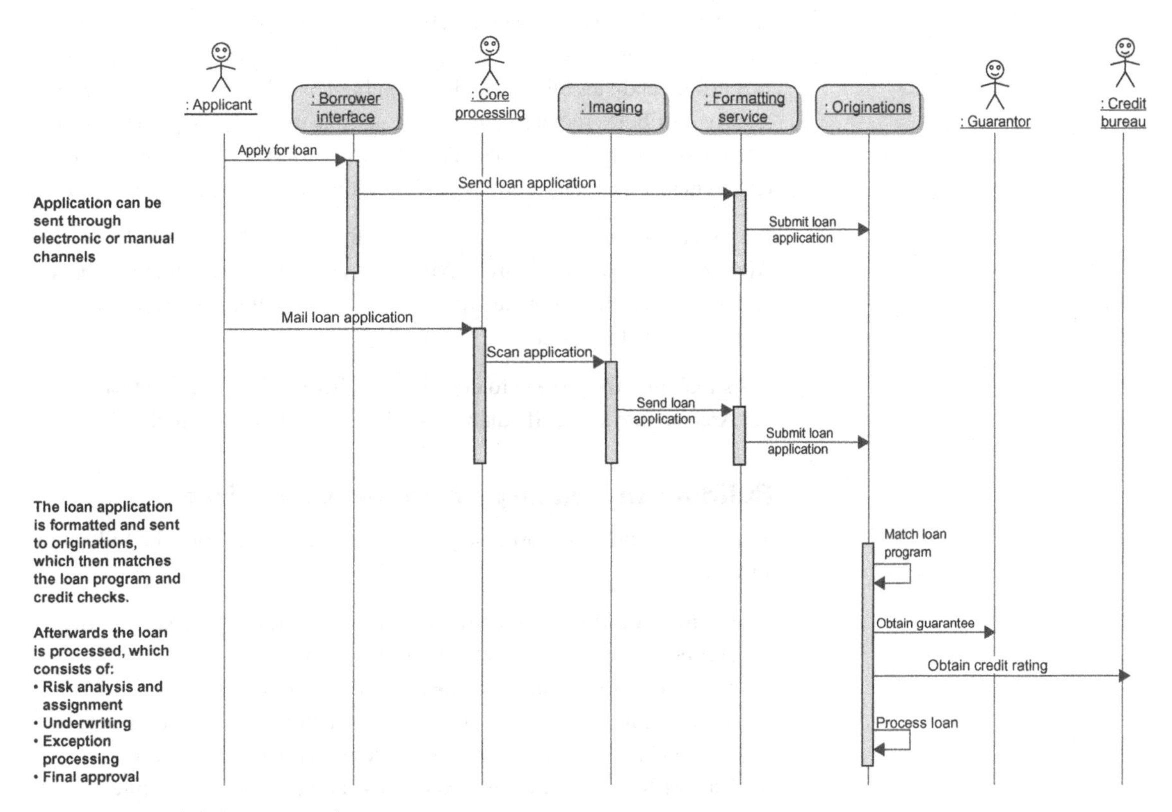

■ **FIGURE 3.5** "Apply for loan" sequence diagram.

USING ARCHITECTURE SCENARIOS FOR QUALITY ATTRIBUTE REQUIREMENTS

In the previous section, we presented an approach to leverage two tools (value chains and user story themes) to define the "functional" scope of our Continuous Architecture project, specifically what the architecture is intended to deliver. However, experienced architects know that a given set of business capabilities can often be delivered by several different architectures. Because each functional requirement (or each set of functional requirements) usually has associated Quality Attributes, the optimum architecture is the one that best satisfies the quality attribute requirements.

In the Continuous Architecture approach, the goal of the architect is to precisely elicit and describe the quality attribute requirements that she will use to design the architecture. But how do we describe Quality Attributes? Quality Attribute names do not provide specific enough information. For example, what do we mean by "configurability"? "Configurability" could refer to a requirement to adapt a system to different infrastructures, or it could refer to a totally different requirement to change the business rules of a system. Terms such as "availability," "security," and "usability" can be as ambiguous. Attempting to document quality attribute requirements using an unstructured approach is not satisfactory because the vocabulary used to describe the quality attribute requirements may vary a lot depending on the perspective of the author.

We recommend to leverage the Utility Tree technique from the Architecture Tradeoff Analysis Method (ATAM). Documenting architecture scenarios that "animate" quality attribute requirements is a key component of this technique.

Let's look into the process to document quality attribute requirements using the Architecture Tradeoff Analysis Method utility tree in more detail.

Building the Quality Attributes Utility Tree

The Architecture Tradeoff Analysis Method utility tree uses the following structure:

- **Highest level:** Quality Attribute requirement (performance, security, configurability, cost effectiveness, and so on)
    - **Next level:** Quality Attribute requirement refinements. For example, "latency" is one of the refinements of "performance," and "access control" is one of the refinements of "security"
- **Lowest level:** Architecture scenarios—at least one architecture scenario per Quality Attribute refinement

As we discussed earlier in this chapter, in the Continuous Architecture approach, we document the following three attributes for each architecture scenario:

- **Stimulus:** This portion of the architecture scenario describes what a user of the system would do to initiate the architecture scenario. For example, in the case study described earlier in this chapter, 20 concurrent users accessed the "WebShop" system simultaneously.
- **Response:** This portion of the architecture scenario describes how the system would be expected to respond to the stimulus. In the case study, the response is defined as "The system handles those requests and responds within an acceptable response delay."
- **Measurement:** The final portion of the architecture scenario quantifies the response to the stimulus, which is "within 3 seconds" in this case.

Optionally, the following three attributes are used in Architecture Tradeoff Analysis Method to further document the architecture scenario, although in practice, we seldom use them in the Continuous Architecture approach:

- **Source:** The entity that initiates the stimulus. In practice, this information is either self-evident or can be included in the stimulus portion of the architecture scenario. For most of the "WebShop" architecture scenarios, the stimulus would be the end user of the system.
- **Environment:** The context in which the stimulus occurs, including the system's state or any unusual conditions in effect. For most of the "WebShop" architecture scenarios, the environment would be specified as "under normal conditions" and can be omitted. However, if we wanted to document an availability scenario, we might specify the environment as "one of the servers is down."
- **Artifact:** The component of the system that responds to the stimulus. Because the architecture of the system has not been designed yet, this information is not usually known yet, although we will use this attribute when testing the architecture. For the "WebShop" systems, artifacts would include the User Interface components, the services layer, and the back-end systems.

Quality Attribute Details

Some Quality Attributes such as performance, security, and availability are common to most systems. Other Quality Attributes such as portability and cost effectiveness may be more specific to some systems (although we would be hard-pressed to come up with an architecture example in the financial services sector that is not driven by cost effectiveness!).

Capturing and Maintaining the Utility Tree Electronically

The Software Engineering Institute does not recommend any specific tool to capture and maintain utility trees. A simple way to do this is to use a **spreadsheet** that can be managed using one of the popular spreadsheet management software packages, such as Microsoft Excel. Unfortunately, this approach does not provide a graphical representation of the utility tree, and we have found that graphical representations are useful during design work sessions.

Another approach is to use a diagramming tool, for example, either Microsoft PowerPoint or Microsoft Visio. This approach provides a good visual representation, but maintenance is difficult: What if a Quality Attribute qualifier needs to be split into two qualifiers? Scenarios are easy to move between qualifiers if that happens.

So far, the best approach we have found is to use a mind mapping software package such as Mindjet MindManager. This software seems to combine the best of both worlds—good graphical representation with the ability to expand or hide Quality Attributes, qualifiers, and architecture scenarios, as well as ease of maintenance. In addition, this software package has good import–export utilities that can be used to exchange data with popular software packages such as Microsoft Office components.

We will present a very brief description of a few common quality attribute requirements in this section, and we strongly encourage the reader to refer to Bass et al.[1] for an in-depth discussion of these quality attribute requirements, including sample scenarios that can be easily customized to be used as part of the Continuous Architecture toolbox.

Performance

This can be defined as "the ability of a system to allocate its computational resources to requests for service in a manner that will satisfy timing requirements."[10] For this Quality Attribute, we are clearly concerned about timing and computational resources and need to define how to measure these two variables. At a risk of stating the obvious, it is critical to define clear, realistic, and measurable objectives from our business partners to evaluate the performance of a system.

Two sets of measurements are usually monitored for this quality attribute:

- The first set of measurements defines the performance of the system in terms of timings from the end user's viewpoint under various loads (full peak load, half peak load, and so on). The application load is a key component of this measurement because most applications have an acceptable response time under light or no load.
- The second set of measurements defines the computational resources used by the application for the load, and assesses if the planned physical configuration of the application is sufficient to support the expected usage load, plus a safety margin. This measurement can be complemented by "stress testing" the system, which means increasing the load until the performance of the system becomes unacceptable or the system stops working.

Availability

This can be defined as "the probability that a system will work as required when required during the period of a mission.... Availability includes non-operational periods associated with reliability, maintenance, and logistics.... This is measured in terms of nines. Five-9's means less than 5 minutes when the system is not operating correctly over the span of one year."[12]

As companies operate more and more globally and our applications become an integral part of the life of customers and employees, the "period of a mission" has evolved from 8 hours per day for 5 days per week (8/5) to 24 hours per day for 7 days per week (24/7). The expectation for a "system of engagement" delivered to a customer or a prospect on their mobile device is that the system will be available regardless of the time of the day (or night) and the day of the week.

As for performance, it is critical to define clear, realistic, and measurable objectives from our business partners to evaluate the availability of a system, keeping the "cost-effectiveness" Quality Attribute in mind (see later discussion). Going from four 9s to five 9s often represents a substantial investment in money, time, and infrastructure that may not make sense, especially if all other applications used by a company can barely achieve three or four 9s. Table 3.1 illustrates how downtime exponentially decreases as the "9s" increase:

Table 3.1 Impact of "9s" on downtime

Availability	Downtime per Year
One 9	40 days
Two 9s	4 days
Three 9s	9 hours
Four 9s	50 mns
Five 9s	5 mns
Six 9s	30 s

Going back to the "mobile shopping" system, is the cost of losing a few sales if the system is not available 15 minutes each week enough to offset the cost of the redundant infrastructure required to achieve a five 9s objective?

In addition to the "9s," the most common metrics used to measure system availability are Mean Time To Recovery (MTTR, the average length of time required to restore operation to a normal level that meets the system's service-level objectives) and Mean Active Maintenance Down Time (MAMDT, which measures the amount of time while the system is unavailable because of planned maintenance activity to the software or hardware components).

The architecture scenarios that may be associated with this quality attribute include:

- Detecting a fault (either in a software or hardware component)
- Recovering from a fault
- Preventing a fault

Cost effectiveness

Cost effectiveness is not commonly included in the list of quality attribute requirements for a system, yet it is almost always a factor. It is associated with cost-effectiveness analysis, which is defined as "a form of economic analysis that compares the relative costs and outcomes (effects) of two or more courses of action."[13,14]

In the field of building architecture, architects routinely propose several options to their customers based on cost. Taking cost into account is imperative for most of their projects. In the Continuous Architecture approach, cost effectiveness is an important consideration.

Let us state a very important point one more time: Limiting the budget spent on architecting is a good thing; it forces the team to think in terms of a **Minimum Viable Architecture** that **starts small** and is only **expanded when absolutely necessary**.

Getting to an executable architecture quickly and then evolving it is essential for modern applications. Unfortunately, some architect teams design their systems independently of any budgetary considerations (some do not even know the allocated budget) and as a result end up with a design that their company cannot afford.

Some interesting scenarios that can be associated with this Quality Attribute include:

- Decrease or increase of budget by a significant amount: Would less money significantly impact the final product? Would more money allow the team to deliver a better product faster?
- Decrease or increase of infrastructure cost: Could the system run on a smaller infrastructure? Could a hybrid cloud strategy be leveraged, and would it save money?
- Use open source instead of proprietary products: Would the quality of the product suffer?

Gaining a good understanding of quality attribute requirements is a critical step in the Continuous Architecture approach. These requirements are a key driver in the architecture design. Simply put, a good architecture design cannot be created without a deep understanding of the quality attribute requirements of the system.

Architecture scenarios and utility tree are two powerful tools to elicit and analyze quality attribute requirements, and they should be leveraged by the architect as much as possible. These tools enable the architect to get a deep understanding of aspects of the system such as cost effectiveness and time to market that may not be taken into account in the architecture otherwise.

GATHERING AND MANAGING REQUIREMENTS

Now that we have defined some key concepts and tools, we can focus on some techniques for gathering and managing requirements. There are three basic techniques for gathering requirements: stakeholder interviews, Joint Requirements Development (JRD) sessions, and conversations with the business partners or product owner (which assume that the business partners are co-located with the team). These three techniques can be used independently or can be combined into a requirements gathering process.[15,16]

Regardless of the technique being used, the goal of the requirements gathering process is to provide the right level of information for the stage the project is at. Unlike the traditional Waterfall process in which every requirement is fully documented at the start of the project, signed off on by various stakeholders, and artificially "frozen in time," we recommend an Agile, "just in time" process for gathering requirements. There is no need to drill down on a requirement until detailed information for that requirement is required by the project.

Similar to other artifacts generated as part of the Continuous Architecture approach, requirements evolve continuously. They should be reviewed as needed by the product or project stakeholders, but they remain a living thing, evolving based on feedback, until the product is delivered to and accepted by customers.

Stakeholder Interviews

Stakeholder interviews are usually associated with "Waterfall" styles of Software Development Life Cycles (SDLCs). They are a traditional process for eliciting requirements and focus on the perspectives and perceived needs of the stakeholder. They may provide a good understanding of the stakeholder's unique business processes and business rules, and the in-person nature of the interviews provides a more relaxed environment where concepts and ideas may be thoroughly investigated.

The danger with this approach is that it may yield a level of detail that's unnecessary at the stage the project is at, and give a "Waterfall" flavor to a Continuous Delivery project. However when properly used in conjunction with Joint Requirement Development sessions and/or Conversations with the stakeholders, they can be a very effective tool for eliciting requirements.

Joint Requirements Development Sessions

Joint Requirements Development sessions are generally associated with Iterative software development methodologies and are sometimes confused with Joint Application Design (JAD) sessions. Joint Requirements Development and Joint Application Design sessions are similar, but Joint Requirements Development sessions focus on requirements, and Joint Application Design sessions focus on design features to be implemented to reflect the requirements.

Joint Requirements Development sessions are very effective at eliciting and documenting cross-functional requirements that may not be adequately identified in stakeholder Interviews. Joint Requirements Development sessions need to follow a defined process and should be facilitated by a trained facilitator, wherein stakeholders participate in discussions to elicit requirements, analyze their details, and uncover cross-functional implications. Having a dedicated scribe to document the discussion is extremely helpful for these sessions.

As for stakeholder interviews, the danger with the Joint Requirements Developments is that they may yield too low a level of detail and give a "Waterfall" flavor to a Continuous Delivery project. It is therefore critical that the Joint Requirements Development facilitator actively manages the level of detail for the requirements and does not allow the discussion to dive at too low a level.

Conversations with Business Partners (or with the Product Owner)

Conversations with the business partners are associated with Agile Software Development Life Cycle methodologies. They assume that the business partners or the business owner of the project (or product being developed) are co-located with the design, development, and testing teams. Agile methodologies try to stay away from using the word "requirements" because Agile practitioners believe that the word carries an expectation that "requirements" must be implemented as specified. Instead, they prefer to leverage user stories.

Simply put, user stories represent a "promise for a conversation" between the development team and the product owner (or the business partner).[15]

This technique can be used with non-Agile Software Development Life Cycle methodologies. It works well in conjunction with the other two approaches (stakeholder interviews and Joint Requirements Developments) to elicit and document the right level of detail at the appropriate time.

Going back to the IT team first mentioned in Chapter 2, it elects to combine the three techniques as follows:

- The team does a quick round of interviews to document the functional requirements and Quality Attributes for the "WebShop" system at *a high level of detail.* The team documents the functional requirements by leveraging user story themes and user stories, as well as the acceptance criteria as part of the user stories. The team documents the quality attribute requirements for the new system by leveraging an Architecture Tradeoff Analysis Method utility tree. Typically, this activity should be done in a couple of days.
- The team runs a half-day Joint Requirements Development session to ensure that it did not miss any cross-functional requirements and updates the user story themes, the user stories, and the Architecture Tradeoff Analysis Method utility tree as required.
- The team leverages the "conversations" with its business partners as needed when details are required as part of design and construction activities.

As a result, the team very quickly creates a succinct document that summarizes the capabilities that the "WebShop" system needs to deliver, and they only elicit and document implementation details when required. The team focuses on defining a product in terms of "testable hypotheses" and outcomes and stays away from the "Big Requirement Document" syndrome!

Managing Functional Requirements

What do we mean by "requirements management"?

> *The purpose of requirements management is to ensure that an organization documents, verifies, and meets the needs and expectations of its customers and internal or external stakeholders. Requirements management begins with the analysis and elicitation of the objectives and constraints of the organization. Requirements management further includes supporting planning for requirements, integrating requirements and the organization for working with them (attributes for requirements), as well as relationships with other information delivering against requirements, and changes for these.*[17,18]

In the Continuous Architecture approach, we are primarily concerned with managing quality attribute requirements. However, properly managing functional requirements is equally important. As already discussed, requirements can be gathered using interviews, Joint requirements development sessions, conversations with the business stakeholders or product manager, or a combination of those approaches. We are suggesting documenting functional requirements using features and user stories, but the format used to document these requirements is not critical—bulleted lists of requirements or even free-form Microsoft Word documents work as well, providing that the level of detail is appropriate.

The key point to keep in mind when eliciting functional requirements is to keep them at the right level of detail and not prematurely drill down on a requirement just because that information is available from a business partner who is too willing and anxious to tell us not only what she needs but also how to implement that feature.

What do we mean by "**the right level of detail**"? At the start of the process, it is just a "promise for a conversation" level; then levels of detail are added as the project progresses and as conversations with the business partners take place. The objective is to capture enough detail to support the current phase of the process—and no more. For example, the following information is unnecessary from an architectural perspective:

- Detailed algorithms for calculation of charges and fees
- Validation rules for User Interface fields

Remember that there will be plenty of time to drill into details during conversations among the designers, the developers, and their business partners at implementation time. Also remember that there is no need to document details that may become irrelevant or obsolete at implementation time because the capability being documented may not end up being what actually gets implemented, depending on feedback obtained along the way.

Managing Quality Attribute Requirements

As mentioned earlier, we recommend using a technique called the "utility tree" from the Architecture Tradeoff Analysis Method to manage quality attribute requirements.

> *The output of the utility tree-generation step is a prioritization of specific quality attribute requirements, realized as scenarios. The utility tree serves to make concrete the quality attribute requirements, forcing the architect and customer representatives to define the relevant quality requirements precisely.*[10]

Applying this technique to the "WebShop" system, the quality attribute requirements are shown in the Architecture Tradeoff Analysis Method utility tree in Figure 3.6.

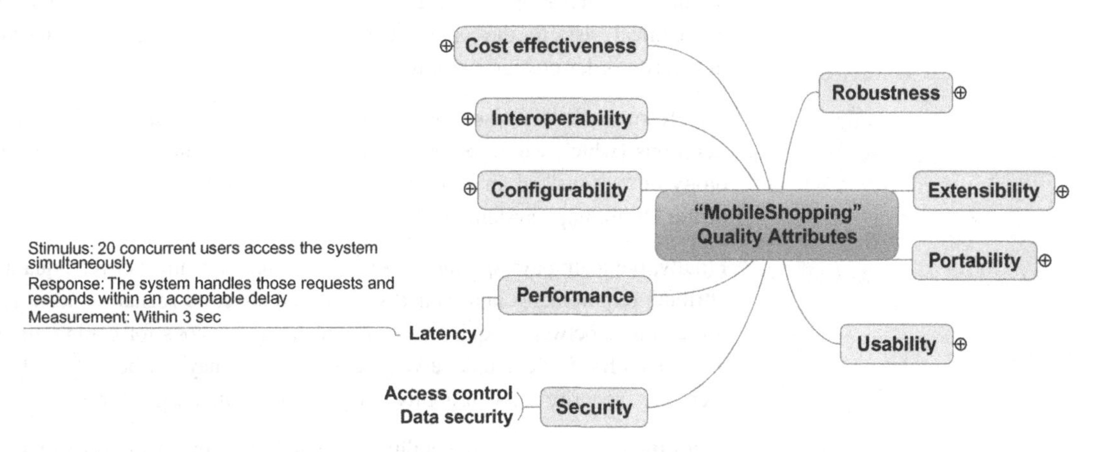

■ **FIGURE 3.6** "MobileShopping" utility tree.

Their goal in building a utility tree is to identify, prioritize, and refine their most important quality attribute requirements; the tree can be seen as a top-down tool for documenting and analyzing the key quality attribute requirements for the "WebShop" system. The team uses the following process to build the tree:

1. The team records its quality attribute requirements as the highest level nodes of the tree. In this example, these are performance, security, configurability, cost effectiveness, and so on.

2. The team further refines each quality attribute requirement with the next level of nodes. In this case, "latency" is one of the refinements of "performance," and "security" is further refined by "access control" and "data security."
3. The final step is to identify at least one architecture scenario (see Glossary for a definition of architecture scenario) for each quality attribute requirement refinement and record the architecture scenarios as the leaves of the utility tree, as well as their attributes. For example, the team documents the following attributes for the performance/latency architecture scenario:
   a. **Stimulus:** Twenty concurrent users to access the "WebShop" system simultaneously
   b. **Response:** The system handles those requests and responds within an acceptable response delay
   c. **Measurement**: Within 3 seconds

Each architecture scenario is then prioritized in the order of importance to the business partners or product manager. An interesting aspect of this approach is that each architecture scenario can also be viewed as a technical risk to the project, and the list of architecture scenarios in priority order creates a risk register.

The team uses this risk register to prioritize the various architecture iterations (which would be called "elaborations" in an Iterative methodology or "sprints" in an Agile world) required to design the architecture of the "WebShop" system.

Finally, the team pays special attention to the relationships between quality attribute requirements and their associated architecture scenarios, identifying conflicts between requirements and making decisions for compromises and trade-offs. For example, a very secure system may not be very usable; therefore "security" and "usability" may conflict with each other.

"Performance" and "configurability" are another common example of two quality attribute requirements conflicting with each other because the design techniques used for configurability (e.g., storing user-modifiable configuration parameters) in a database may interfere with the performance of a system. "Cost effectiveness" may interfere with several other quality attribute requirements such as configurability or portability that may increase the development and testing effort and therefore the cost of building and maintaining the system.

In fact, most architecture and design decisions are trade-offs between or among two or more quality attribute requirements. Chapter 4 explores this topic in more depth and discusses the importance of architectural decisions. It is therefore critical to record all architectural decisions in a

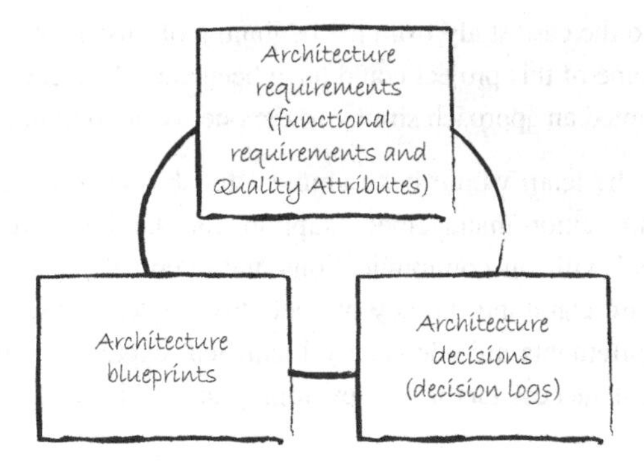

■ **FIGURE 3.7** Interrelationships among architecture artifacts.

"decision log" documenting clearly the decision, its context, and the rationale for making the decision.

Figure 3.7 depicts the interrelationships among architecture artifacts. Architecture requirements (both functional requirements and Quality Attributes) drive architecture decisions. Those decisions drive the creation and the evolution of the architecture blueprints. However, decisions also impact requirements, and blueprints impact decisions; each artifact ends up being a trade-off that needs to take into account the other artifacts.

There is nothing wrong in making compromises and trade-offs as part of creating and evolving the architecture; in fact, they are almost unavoidable. Issues are created when implicit or undocumented decisions are made and nobody remembers a few months later what was decided or why it was decided until a problem occurs, so please remember to document your architecture and design decisions in a decision log!

SUMMARY

In this chapter, we took the first steps on the Continuous Architecture journey, starting with requirements management. We covered in detail the practices and processes that can be followed at this stage. We also described the topics used by the architect to initiate this process, including the following:

- What is the difference between functional requirements and Quality Attributes, and why are Quality Attributes important when designing the Architecture?
- How do we gather and manage requirements?
- What are value chains and user stories, and why are they important to understand functional scope in the Continuous Architecture approach?
- Why are architecture scenarios important for identifying and managing quality attribute requirements? What specific tools are available to document these requirements?

Going back to the case study from the beginning of this chapter, we believe that the outcome of this project could have been very different if the project team had adopted an approach similar to the one we are outlining here.

Specifically, the team would have enjoyed full business stakeholder participation and senior management support for the initiative instead of having to deal with miscommunications and eventually distrust between the architecture team and the key project stakeholders. Ensuring that key business requirements are adequately identified, captured, and documented is a critical success factor for developing an architecture.

ENDNOTES

1. Bass L, Clements P, Kazman R. Software architecture in practice. 3rd ed. Addison Wesley; 2012.
2. Davis S. Mastering MEAN: Introducing the MEAN Stack, September 9, 2014. <http://www.ibm.com/developerworks/library/wa-mean1/index.html/>.
3. Bittner K. Software requirement practices are ripe for disruption. Forrester Research, April 2014.
4. Porter M. Competitive advantage: creating and sustaining superior performance. New York: Free Press; London: Collier Macmillan; 1985.
5. Capability management in business. Wikipedia, <https://en.wikipedia.org/wiki/Capability_management_in_business/>.
6. Scaled Agile Framework. Stories Abstract, July 15, 2014. <http://www.scaledagileframework.com/stories/>.
7. Wikipedia. User:FlorianBauer79/sandbox, <https://en.wikipedia.org/wiki/User:FlorianBauer79/sandbox/>.
8. Scaled Agile Framework. Feature Abstract, July 22, 2014. <http://www.scaledagileframework.com/feature/>.
9. Scaled Agile Framework. Scaled Agile Framework 3.0, <http://www.scaledagileframework.com/>.
10. Use case modeling was introduced by Ivar Jacobson in his seminal book. Jacobson I, et al. Object-oriented software engineering a use case driven approach, Addison-Wesley; 1992.
11. Clements P, Kazman R, Klein M. Evaluating software architectures—methods and case studies. Addison-Wesley; 2002.
12. Availability. <https://en.wikipedia.org/wiki/Availability>.
13. Cost Effectiveness Analysis. <https://en.wikipedia.org/wiki/Cost-effectiveness_analysis>.
14. Bleichrodt H, Quiggin J. Life-cycle preferences over consumption and health: when is cost-effectiveness analysis equivalent to cost-benefit analysis? J Health Econ 1999;18(6):681–708.
15. Leffingwell D, Widrig D. Managing software requirements: a use case approach. 2nd ed. Addison-Wesley; 2003.
16. Cohn M. User stories applied: for Agile software development. Addison-Wesley; 2004.
17. Requirements Management. <https://en.wikipedia.org/wiki/Requirements_management>.
18. Stellman A, Greene J. Applied software project management. O'Reilly Media; 2005.

Chapter 4

Evolving the Architecture

Complexity is a natural trajectory, it is the course of most everything, it just happens. Simplification is innovation by design.

—Story Musgrave

In Chapter 3, we started our Continuous Architecture journey by looking at the area of requirements management. We discussed how the Continuous Architecture principles can be applied and introduced a set of relevant tools for requirements management. In this chapter, we will take the next logical step in our journey and focus on the topic of design. The design of an architecture is not a one-time activity. Rather, it consists of a series of activities and decisions that take place over time that result in the architecture evolving as more facts are known. As a result, we call this chapter "Evolving the Architecture." In this chapter, we focus on a few key topics that we believe are critical for evolving the architecture from the perspective of Continuous Architecture.

The first topic we will focus on is architectural decisions. They are the elemental building blocks of creating an architecture. If architects do nothing else, they need to ensure that architectural decisions are made. We will look at the role of decisions, provide examples, and discuss how decisions can be utilized successfully.

For the second topic we will look into prioritization and determining which architectural features are relevant to the problem at hand. The overall purpose is to make sure that business drivers and requirements drive the architecture. For this, we will demonstrate how to use an established Six Sigma technique called Quality Function Deployment (QFD).

The final topic we will discuss is transition planning. Defining a target architecture is a significant effort on its own, but creating a transition plan on how to realize the target is even more challenging. To address this challenge, we will present a technique called plateaus and waves.

ARCHITECTURAL DECISIONS

Role of Decisions in Architecture

If you ask most people what the most visible out from architecture is, they will most likely point to a fancy diagram that highlights key components and their interactions. Usually, the more color and complexity it has, the better. The diagram should be too difficult to read on a normal page and require a special large-scale printer to produce. Architects want to look smart, and producing a complex diagram shows that the architect can solve extremely difficult problems! Although such diagrams give the authors and readers the false sense of being in control, they normally have limited impact on driving any architectural change.

Part of this is because of a lack of effective communication, which is a key challenge faced by architects. To be successful, architects need to spend the same amount of time socializing their architecture as they spend on developing it. We will cover the topic of collaboration and communication in more depth in Chapter 10.

Even if an architect is extremely successful in communicating, what is the key unit of work of an architect? Is it a fancy diagram, a logical model, a running prototype? Continuous Architecture states that the unit of work of an architect is an architectural decision. As a result, the most important output of any architectural activity is the set of decisions made along the product development journey. It comes as a surprise that so little effort is spent in most organizations on arriving at and documenting architectural decisions in a consistent and understandable manner.

Let us first provide an example of what we mean by architectural decisions and then discuss aspects around how to implement them.

Architectural Decision Example

Figure 4.1 is a slightly simplified version of an architectural decision. (Specific values for the requirements have been removed on purpose to make the example generic.)

Although you do not need to use this exact template for documenting the architectural decision, some key points are worth mentioning:

- It is important to clearly articulate all constraints related to a decision—architecture is in essence finding the optimal solution within the constraints given to us.

TOPIC

Access to data for use in simulations by desktop applications by business users spread across global regions.

Context

A new application is to become the access portal for end user access to market data. Key requirements are:

* Clients integrating market data with their desktop applications to run simulations
* Clients subscribing to a subject of interest to view only data relevant to them.

Constraints

No	Description
C-01	Access to data will be via the http protocol. Implications: A client pull-based consumption model is implied, rather than a push model.
C-02	Zero client footprint. Data must be delivered to users without the need to install additional client-side software. Implications: This constraint limits the options available.

Quality Attributes

NFR	Description
QA-01 Scalability & Capacity/ Geographical	**User base** Users are distributed across the US, Europe, and Asia Pacific, with the following projected numbers: *Region* | *Clients* *US* *Europe* *Asia*
QA-02 Scalability & Capacity	**Current Volumes** Region | Clients | Peak usage US Europe Asia **Projected Volumes** Region | Clients | Peak usage US Europe AP
QA-03 Data Sources	95% are static payloads 5% live objects changing once a second The sources provide message notification for changed data.
QA-04 Data Volume	Average object size = XKB Typically data size = XKB to YKB Maximum size = ZMB

Decision

Subject Area	Desktop Data Distribution
Decision Name	Managed service for distributing market data for desktop applications
Alternatives	1. **Current Web Hosting configuration:** The current hosting architecture is a shared managed service, where each instance has strict limits on the number of concurrent sessions, threads and memory that can be consumed by an application. This configuration ensures that a particular application is prevented from impacting the performance of other applications deployed on the infrastructure. Unless additional memory is available the NFR around the size of the data cache cannot be met. Additionally the volume of potential requests from clients cannot be supported with the current configuration.

■ **FIGURE 4.1** Architecture decision template.

	2. New event based http server: Implement new event based http server that does not leverage a thread per client model, has a standard module to support integration with caching layer via pass through access to the cache via configuration. ***Pros:*** • More efficient scalability than a thread per client based server • Less moving parts than a standard hosting service ***Cons:*** • Introduces a new technology to the organization. Will require additional engineering to setup, and the acquisition of appropriate skills. • No support for advanced functionality eg high availability – though no specific requirements for this have been articulated. **3. Application Server + Caching :** ***Pros:*** • Leverages standard components • Enables deployment of all components within application server container. • Minimizes inter process communication – both components can be hosted in the same container. • Could have a lower TCO due to leveraging existing engineered solutions. ***Cons***: • The use of complex caching is overkill, given the requirements and is not a good fit for the use case as specified in the caching standard and COE literature • The cost of deployment is high. • No native http interface; this means potentially more moving parts to access the cached data. **4. Web Messaging:** Web Messaging utilizing the messaging service over http via a push based mechanism. ***Pros:*** o Messaging service already exists within the organization ***Cons:*** o Only supports a push based model. Will require additional client side code to consume data. This does not meet constraint C-02.
Decision	Option 2: New event based http server
Rationale	• Option 1 is not viable due to the constraints of the environment already listed • Option 2 was performance tested and deemed suitable to meet the NFRs • Option 3 is not viable due to high deployment costs and complex architecture • Option 4 can be eliminated due to it not supporting constraint C-02
Decision Maker	
Ratified by	

■ **FIGURE 4.1** *(Continued)*

- As stated in *Principle 2: Focus on Quality Attributes, not on functional requirements*, it is important to explicitly document nonfunctional requirements, i.e., Quality Attributes.
- All options considered and rationales for coming to the decision have to be articulated.

Finally, there is one piece of critical information on the example architectural decision: Who has made this decision and when? Appropriate accountability and visibility of decisions are essential.

ACCOUNTABILITY FOR DECISIONS

In his excellent book *Visual Explanations*,[1] Edward Tufte provides an incisive analysis of the decision to launch the Space Shuttle *Challenger*. Over 10 pages of detailed analysis, Tufte demonstrates the multiple failings of communication that resulted in the shuttle being launched in a temperature too low; resulting in the fatal O-ring failure. The day before the launch the rocket engineers prepared a presentation outlining the temperature concerns. As Tufte describes: "The charts were unconvincing; the arguments against the launch failed; the Challenger blew-up." One of the most interesting points raised by Tufte was that the title chart and all other displays used did not provide the names of the people who had prepared the material.

Making and Governing Design Decisions

We recommend not only documenting architectural decisions but also defining the architectural decisions you need to make up front and identifying the dependencies between them. Figure 4.2 is an example of the architectural decisions required in defining an integration approach for a specific business area.

It is appropriate to remember at this point *Principle 3: Delay design decisions until they are absolutely necessary*. What we are saying here is not in conflict with this principle. It is important to clearly understand all the architectural decisions that you need to make, or as Donald Rumsfeld said, the known unknowns. Then as more data becomes available, you can start making and documenting the decisions.

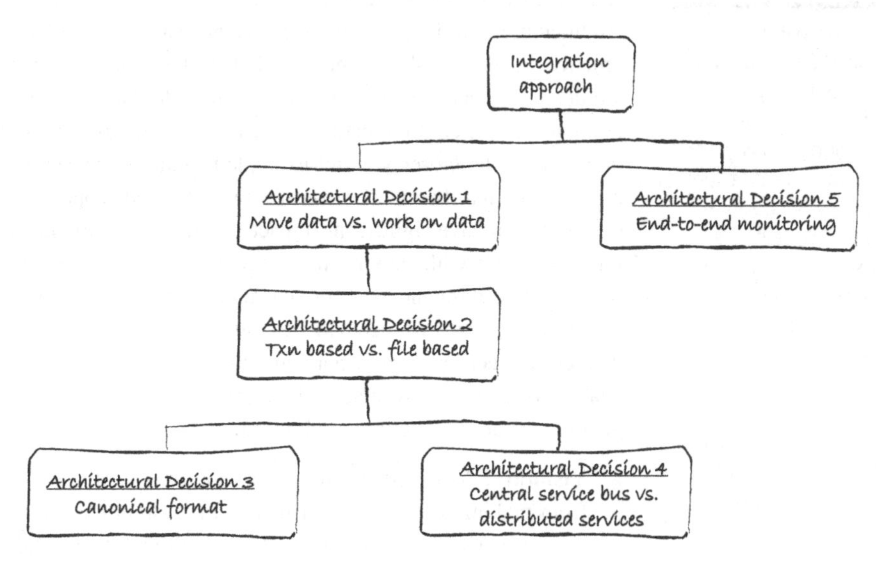

■ **FIGURE 4.2** Relating architectural decisions.

Now let us look at the different types of architectural decisions in an enterprise. Figure 4.3 demonstrates how architectural decisions are made in a typical enterprise.

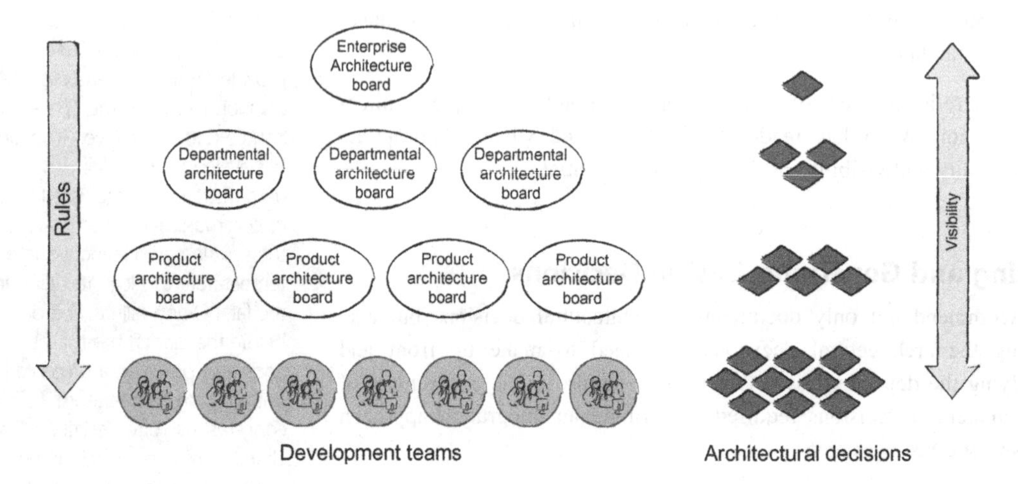

■ FIGURE 4.3 Levels of architecture decisions.

> The principle of delaying architectural decisions until they are required should not be seen as a lack of focus on proper architectural design. This is really driven by how you interpret "until they are absolutely necessary." If you believe that certain decisions are key for creating a solid foundation for your product, then you definitely should focus on them. What we are really trying to espouse is not to overcomplicate your architecture by assuming a target state that is not clearly defined or a set of requirements that may never come.

If we assume that an enterprise has set up effective governance bodies that ratify decisions, it is only natural that the higher up you go, fewer decisions are made and fewer reviews are conducted. (This can also be explained by the fact that high-level governance bodies lack the context and bandwidth to conduct detailed reviews.) As a result, the Enterprise Architecture board makes much fewer decisions than product-level governance boards. It should be noted that the scope and significance of architectural decisions also increase with scale. However, most decisions that can impact an architecture are driven on the ground by implementation teams. The closer you get to implementation, the more decisions are made. Although they tend to be of a more limited scope, over time, these decisions can have significant impact on the overall architecture. There is nothing wrong with making more decisions at this level. The last thing we would recommend is to create unnecessary burden and bureaucracy on project teams that need to be Agile and quickly make decisions to deliver on their project. There are two elements that we believe will enable us to take advantage of aligning Agile project teams to wider governance around architectural decisions:

- **Visibility:** As stated before, we do not want to stop project teams from making decisions aligned with their rhythm of delivery. However, we also do not want the overall architecture of a product or enterprise compromised by team/project-level decisions. Examples abound of project teams putting a stored procedure here and there to meet their immediate deliverables. The end result is a brittle architecture that is very expensive to refactor. Creating visibility of architectural decisions at all levels of the organization and sharing these among different teams will greatly reduce the probability of significant architectural compromises occurring. This is not technically difficult; all you need to do is agree on how to document an architectural decision (you can use a version of the template presented earlier in this chapter) and use existing communication and social media channels available in the organization. Although technically not difficult, creating a mechanism for sharing architectural decisions is still difficult to implement, mainly because it requires discipline, perseverance, and open communication.

- **Rules:** In reality, the probability of project teams compromising the architecture will greatly be reduced if they are given clear rules to adhere to. For example, if there are clear rules around where and how to implement stored procedures, then the simple example of creating a brittle architecture by writing stored procedures in random places of the architecture can be avoided. If you go back to the diagram around decisions, the main job of higher governance bodies is not to make decisions but to define rules.

We would also like to note that applying *Principle 4: Architect for change—leverage "the power of small"* and *Principle 6: Model the organization after the design of the system* greatly reduces the impact of unforeseen and unknown architectural decisions. Applying these principles clearly scopes the impact of an architectural decision and ensures that all parties that participate in the decision have sufficient context.

The concept of delaying design decisions has been discussed extensively in Agile forums, and the term "the last responsible moment"[2] is a good representation of *Principle 3: Delay design decisions until they are absolutely necessary.* We also recommend that readers refer to a blog written by Rebecca Wirfs-Brock[3] on this topic.

Are what we call rules different from architectural principles and standards? We used the term "rule" deliberately in the context of architectural decisions. You can say that a rule is a type of architectural decision. We believe that architectural decisions make an immediate impact on the architecture being developed. As a result, general guidance provided for development teams is not an architectural decision but a rule.

Instead of *rule*, we could have used the term *policy* or *principle.*

Principles do have a significant role in architectural decisions. According to dictionary.com, one definition of a principle is "an adopted rule or method for application inaction." According to this definition, we can say that a principle is a type of rule. The litmus test for an architectural principle is, "Can it be used while making an architectural decision?" For example, "All applications must be scalable" is not a principle; rather, it is a statement of general intent.

Agile and Architectural Decisions

Let us now look into architectural decisions within the context of Agile development. Currently, there is a large amount of discussion around how architectural decisions align with Agile development. If you follow a purist Agile approach, then you will be very wary of any high-level architectural direction from the ivory tower. The team will make necessary decisions and refactor them when the need arises. On the other side, there is a view that architectural decisions are key for Agile to scale and link in with the wider enterprise context.

The term *policy* can seem to be more applicable. Again, let us look at the dictionary.com definition of policy: "a definite course of action adopted for the sake of expediency, facility, etc." Policy does have the implication of driven by a governing body, such as a political government or department, and can be associated with a more bureaucratic mindset. The term *policy* also implies a level of general guidance, where there is a level of implementation detail left for further interpretation.

In contrast to the above two options, we prefer the term *rule* because it implies a clear set of constraints applied to architectural decisions. They can be general architectural principles, standards, or policies.

We believe that applying the recommendations outlined in this section will greatly help bridge the Agile versus enterprise architecture gap. By clearly defining all the architectural decisions you need to make, you are basically creating your architectural backlog. You can decide if you want to incorporate resolving any of the architectural decisions within your normal backlog, or you can keep the architectural decision backlog separate. The key point is not to lose track of these architectural decisions. If you apply the concept from Iterative development of focusing on architecturally significant scenarios first, then your initial set of sprints basically becomes focused on resolving key architectural decisions (Figure 4.4).

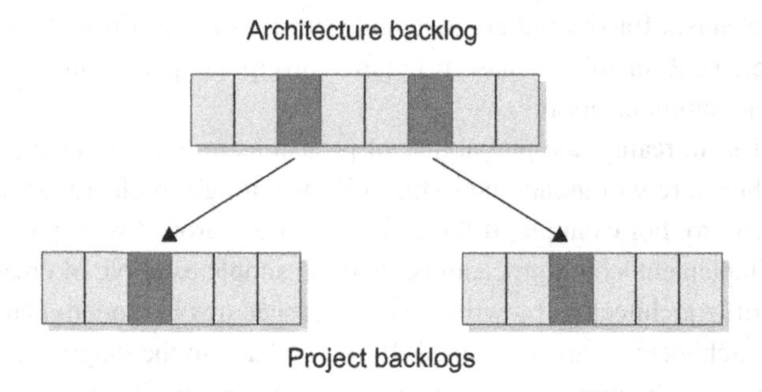

■ **FIGURE 4.4** Architecture and project backlogs.

If you then make your architectural backlog visible to other teams and relevant architecture groups, then you have created full transparency over how you are evolving your architecture. As long as you abide by the rules set by the enterprise, you should not need to do anything else to align with the enterprise view.

When you have an architectural backlog, you have to decide who prioritizes it. Just as with a project backlog, it is important to have the voice of the customer at the forefront. There are two approaches that can work for this. The first one is to have the project teams represent the voice of the customer in prioritizing the architectural backlog. The second one is to have direct representation from the business in prioritizing the backlog. We recommend including the business as much as possible in the evolution of the architecture. As a result, our recommendation would be the second approach. It goes without saying that the exact dynamics of the projects and culture of the organization will help drive the approach you take.

PRIORITIZING: USING QUALITY FUNCTION DEPLOYMENT

It is obvious that architectural decisions are not made in a vacuum; all the work has to be driven by the overall business context of the organization and the particular objectives of the problem domain, whether it is a product, application, or project. It is also important to note that quite a few architectural decisions are compromises between different quality drivers (e.g., performance vs. flexibility). The objective should be to evolve architectures that support requirements and explicitly deal with conflicting quality drivers. For this, we recommend leveraging a Six Sigma technique called QFD. QFD is a systematic method for tying product and service design decisions directly to customer wants and needs. This helps address a key architecture challenge around providing traceability between business drivers (e.g., faster time to market, improving quality or service, or controlling costs) and architectural decisions. It also enables traceability between Quality Attributes and architectural decisions.

Similar to many manufacturing organizations that cater to consumer markets, information technology (IT) organizations must respond to their users' changing demands while simultaneously supporting ongoing operations. As with many larger manufacturing organizations, the complexity of the delivery system (which in the case of IT means applications, data, and IT infrastructure) does not lend itself to rapid change without significant capital investment. To effectively manage these challenges, IT organizations need to adopt the same type of engineering-oriented mindset that has proven so effective in other types of businesses in which success is tightly coupled to effective design and the use of technology.

Quality Function Deployment helps in translating customer needs into technical requirements. QFD was developed in Japan in the late 1960s by Professors Shigeru Mizuno and Yoji Akao. It was part of a larger focus on quality management and initially deployed within the automobile industry in the 1970s. QFD has spread to multiple global industries, including the software engineering industry. The overall QFD process and methodology cover a wide area of aligning product design to customer requirements.[4,5] For our purposes, we will use the central concept of QFD, which is called the house of quality.

The QFD technique is based on a simple concept: It enables transformations from a prioritized set of drivers to a set of candidate enablers, ensuring that the requirements can be traced throughout the design.

As a simple example of QFD usage, assume that you are designing a new system for a nonprofit entity that organizes international sporting events. Your team has interviewed the key users who have expressed desired benefits for the new system. Those benefits, in order of priority, are:

- Better service for the athletes—for example, better response to participants' queries, requests for special accommodations, and requests for special transportation needs between the event venues and the airport
- Faster response to problems that could arise during an event
- Improved service for the officials
- Increased integrity for the sporting events through improved authentication of athletes' credentials

Assume also that your team has collected a list of functional requirements for the system, which include:

- Obtaining day passes on the spot for athletes so they can attend several events on a given day when they are not participating in any events themselves
- Checking accreditation of athletes, officials, and other participants
- Accommodating issues such as special requests for computer or telecommunications equipment as the athletes check in at their accommodations
- Auctioning tickets to the public in case some tickets remain unsold right before an event

The problem is that your users cannot agree on the priorities of their requirements, and the budget allocated to the project is not sufficient to implement all requirements. You need to select two of the four requirements for implementation. How do you achieve this goal?

For this, you can leverage QFD, linking the benefits to the requirements. (Note that functional requirements do not need to be the primary input into the QFD process. The purpose is to provide an example.) Figure 4.5 shows the results of this process.

In Figure 4.5 and all of this chapter's QFD examples, the numbers have the following meaning:

- The numbers in the 'weight' or 'importance' column represent the weights assigned to each benefit. In this example, the four identified benefits have been given weightings of 10 to 7 from most important to least.

Key:
Θ Strong relationship
○ Moderate relationship
▲ Weak relationship

		1 Accommodate issues	2 Auction tickets	3 Obtain day pass	4 Check accreditation	1 Weight	2 Rank	
Better service to games participants	1	Θ	○		○	10.0	1.0	1
Faster response to problems	2	Θ				9.0	2.0	2
Better service to officials	3	Θ	○	○		9.0	2.0	3
Better integrity for the games	4	○			○	7.0	4.0	4
Correlation to benefits	1	273	57	27	51			
Rank	2	1	2	4	3			
		1	2	3	4			

■ **FIGURE 4.5** Quality function deployment example.

- The symbols (Θ, ○, ▲) represent the correlation between the "what" (e.g., better service to officials) and the "how" (e.g., obtain day pass). The usual relationship weights are 9 for a strong relationship, 3 for a moderate relationship, and 1 for a weak relationship.
- The numbers in the 'correlation to' row represent the result of the QFD calculation—in this case, benefit weight times relationship value (strong, moderate, or weak) assigned during the QFD process.

The QFD technique shows "accommodate issues" as the most important requirement to satisfy followed by "auction tickets," "check accreditation," and "obtain day pass." Our decision is therefore to implement "accommodate issues" and "auction tickets" in the first release of the system.

From this simple example, you can see that the QFD technique lets us correlate how well the design criteria will meet the customer needs. This example is a simplified utilization of the house of quality. In its full scope, the house of quality is shown in Figure 4.6.

By leveraging the house of quality, the team can identify neglected needs and find design features that might not necessarily meet any needs. The elements of the house of quality that we used in our simplified example are highlighted in dark grey.

An additional QFD feature that we can use is the correlation matrix, otherwise known as the roof of the house. This addresses the fact that not all

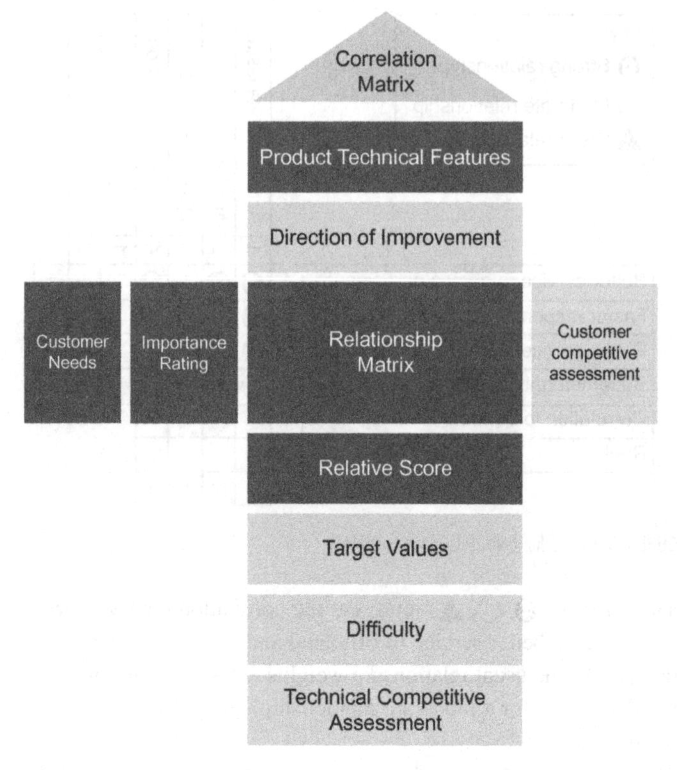

■ **FIGURE 4.6** The house of quality.

features can coexist when seeking to meet customer requirements: a positive correlation indicates that two design elements complement each other. A negative correlation denotes a possible interference between the implementation of these design elements.

The house of quality tool includes other optional components, such as the following:

- A competitive assessment of customer needs: The QFD team uses this to assess the team's customer needs against its perceived competition.
- A competitive assessment of technical features: This ranks the product's technical features against the competition.
- Difficulty: This is used to indicate the ease of implementation of the product's technical features.
- Target values: This is used to identify a target value for a "technical feature." For example, we can give a five 9s target for the availability feature.

- Direction of improvement: This identifies in which direction a feature would improve. For example, availability will improve with additional 9s.

Normally, we do not use these additional components in our architecture approach. The QFD technique is geared toward addressing all elements of product design, including elements such as competitive analysis and voice of the customer. However, from a Continuous Architecture viewpoint, we recommend using the core elements, which are highlighted in dark grey in Figure 4.6. In addition, using the correlation matrix is very good for analyzing conflicting design features. However, please note that the data used in the correlation matrix is not part of the numerical calculations performed.

In summary, think of QFD as a structured mechanism for documenting justifications for decisions and assumptions that architecture design participants must make.

Using Quality Function Deployment in Different Scenarios

The beauty of QFD is that at the highest level it is a great mechanism for correlating "whats" to "hows." You can decide how to interpret these terms and chain QFD matrixes. As a result, the "how" of one matrix becomes the "what" of a subsequent matrix.

Some of the more common usage scenarios we have encountered include the following:

1. **Prioritizing user requirements and Quality Attributes:** This use of QFD occurs when you identify functional and nonfunctional architecture requirements from multiple stakeholders. (We can define *architecture requirement* as a requirement that is critical to the development of the architecture.) Using QFD, the team correlates the requirements to the key business drivers. The team can also use QFD in this scenario to clarify the business program's priorities by correlating the programs to the business vision and strategies. Finally, the team might leverage QFD to prioritize the architecture principles by correlating them to the business vision and strategies.
2. **Translating requirements into an architecture design:** This type of QFD usage concerns prioritizing and selecting design choices. Prioritized requirements from the requirements prioritization scenario serve as inputs to this process. The team prioritizes and selects the architecture designs and features by relating them to the QFD input set. Similarly, the team can select technology products by correlating

them to the QFD input set. Further correlation to architecture principles can refine both selections of designs, features, and technology products.

3. **Planning releases:** The third QFD usage category involves sequencing rollout phases. Again, the prioritized requirements serve as inputs. The team prioritizes and selects the platform's components to be rolled out in sequence to ensure a smooth transition between the current and the future IT states by correlating them against the QFD input set.

The following diagram demonstrates how these different houses of quality can be integrated together. Note that there are multiples options on how you can set up QFD matrixes. Initially, it is easy to get carried away and try to correlate everything to everything. We recommend that you use the tool at key decision points where prioritization is required in a nonbiased way from multiple stakeholders (Figure 4.7).

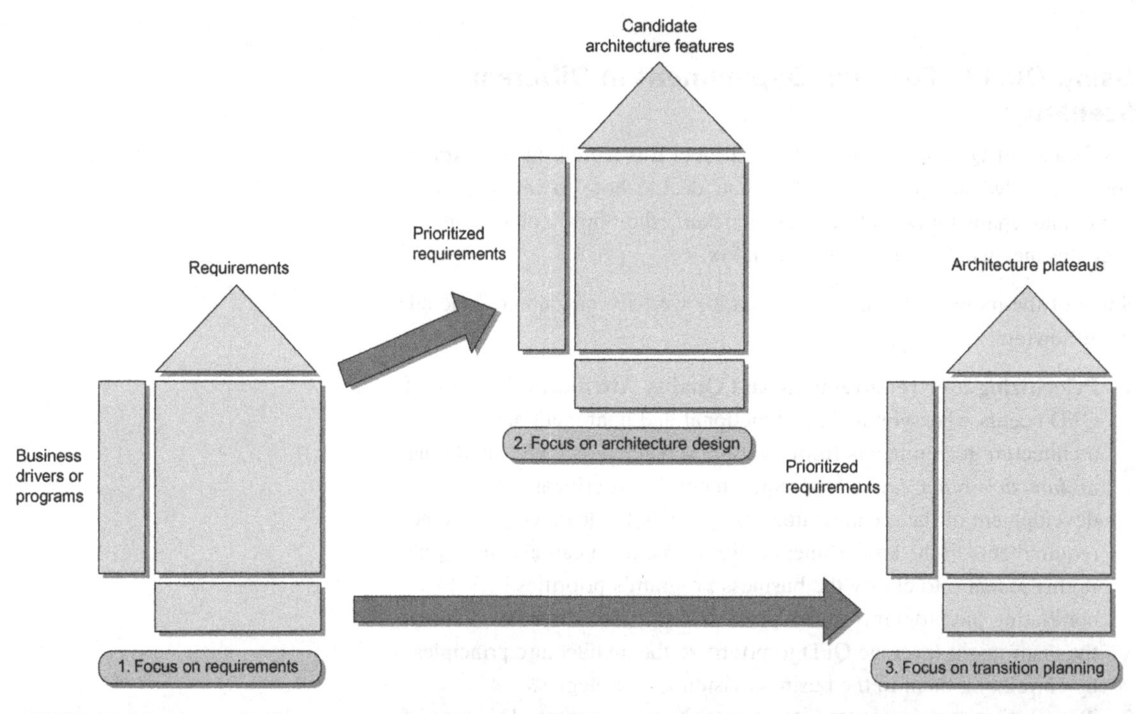

■ **FIGURE 4.7** Linking houses of quality.

Let us now provide two examples of how to use QFD. The first one is focused on prioritizing user requirements and Quality Attributes, and the second one illustrates translating requirements into an architecture design.

Business Drivers to Quality Attributes

Our first scenario uses QFD to link Quality Attributes to the business drivers. One of the input parameters to the QFD process is a set of priorities for the business drivers, and the QFD process lets the team prioritize the requirements against these. A simple example illustrates this scenario.

Assume you are in the requirements phase of a major project for a financial services institution. The architecture team has gathered a list of business drivers. As the following list indicates, the team has prioritized the business drivers and has given each driver a weight, with 50 being the maximum weight. The higher the weight, the more important the driver.

- Control costs (weight 5), such as the cost of delivering and operating new application systems.
- Decrease time to market (weight 18).
- Enable customers to have a single view of firm X (weight 41).
- Improve quality of service (weight 13).
- Improve the financial services institution's ability to answer questions from business users (weight 4).

Your team has also collected a list of potential nonfunctional Quality Attributes, as shown in Table 4.1.

Table 4.1 Quality attribute requirements collected by the team

Quality Attribute	Level	Architecture Topics Addressed
Performance	Run-time	Intercomponent communication; dividing functionality to exploit parallelism
Security	Run-time	Specialized components (secure kernels, firewalls, and authentication servers)
Availability	Run-time	Fault tolerance, redundant components, and controlling component interactions
Usability	Run-time	Linked to modifiability; important cost-control quality; error handling, error avoidance, and user satisfaction
Consistency	Run-time	Ability for the system to return consistent results when used by several clients
Modifiability	Build	Modularized, encapsulated components
Portability	Build	Portability layer
Reusability	Build	Loose coupling between components
Integratability	Build	Compatible interconnection mechanisms, consistent interfaces
Testability	Build	Modularized, encapsulating components

Prioritizing a list can sometimes get quite difficult. In workshops, you can always try giving participants a certain number of votes and tabulate the results. One great technique we have found useful is pair-wise comparison.[5] In this approach, you basically compare two items at a time and make a call if one of them is preferable to the other or if they carry the same weight. If you basically go through your entire list with this approach and let a basic Excel template do the calculations for you, the result quickly becomes a prioritized list, which is much more data driven. We have even found that the technique works outside of the context of a workshop. In one example, we gave the template to 10 different individuals and averaged their responses. Although probably not the most scientific approach, this exercise ended up with a prioritized list that all stakeholders agreed to.

The team can now organize a prioritization workshop with the key stakeholders. During this workshop, the team asks the stakeholders to review the list of business drivers, confirm their assigned priorities, and review the list of candidate Quality Attributes for completeness.

It is now time to use the QFD tool. Before the workshop, the team inputs the business drivers, their weights, and the candidate Quality Attributes into the tool, and a team member's laptop computer screen projects the QFD house of quality. This team member will act as the scribe for the exercise and will capture the exercise results in real time, providing instant feedback to the workshop attendees.

For each requirement in every column, the group asks, "Does this requirement contribute to the realization of this driver strongly, moderately, weakly, or not at all?"As the group agrees on a contribution level, the scribe records it by using the appropriate symbol as Figure 4.8 shows. It is critical that the group address each column, at least for the first few requirements, until the workshop attendees are comfortable with the process.

When all relationships are determined, the system automatically calculates the rankings for the requirements (as Figure 4.8 shows). This is an iterative process, and the workshop leader should explain this to the participants before the workshop attendees start determining the relationships. This iterative approach lets the participants reach agreement faster on the contribution levels. No decision is final, and you can revisit decisions later. The iterative approach also lets the team review and adjust the relationships after the first pass is completed. In practice, more than two iterations are seldom required, and teams make few adjustments during the second iteration.

In addition to determining the relation between the requirements and Quality Attributes, the team also focuses on the "roof of the house." In this exercise, the workshop participants are asked to determine if there is a positive, a negative, or no correlation between different Quality Attributes. Inputting of these values does not impact any calculated values but is used to analyze any architectural conflict between Quality Attributes.

When reviewing the results of the QFD exercise, the clustering of requirements is more important than their ranking, so the team should review the score of each requirement in relation to the others. For this example, we would have three clusters:

- First cluster: integrability, consistency, modifiability, and testability
- Second cluster: security, reusability, and portability
- Third cluster: availability and performance

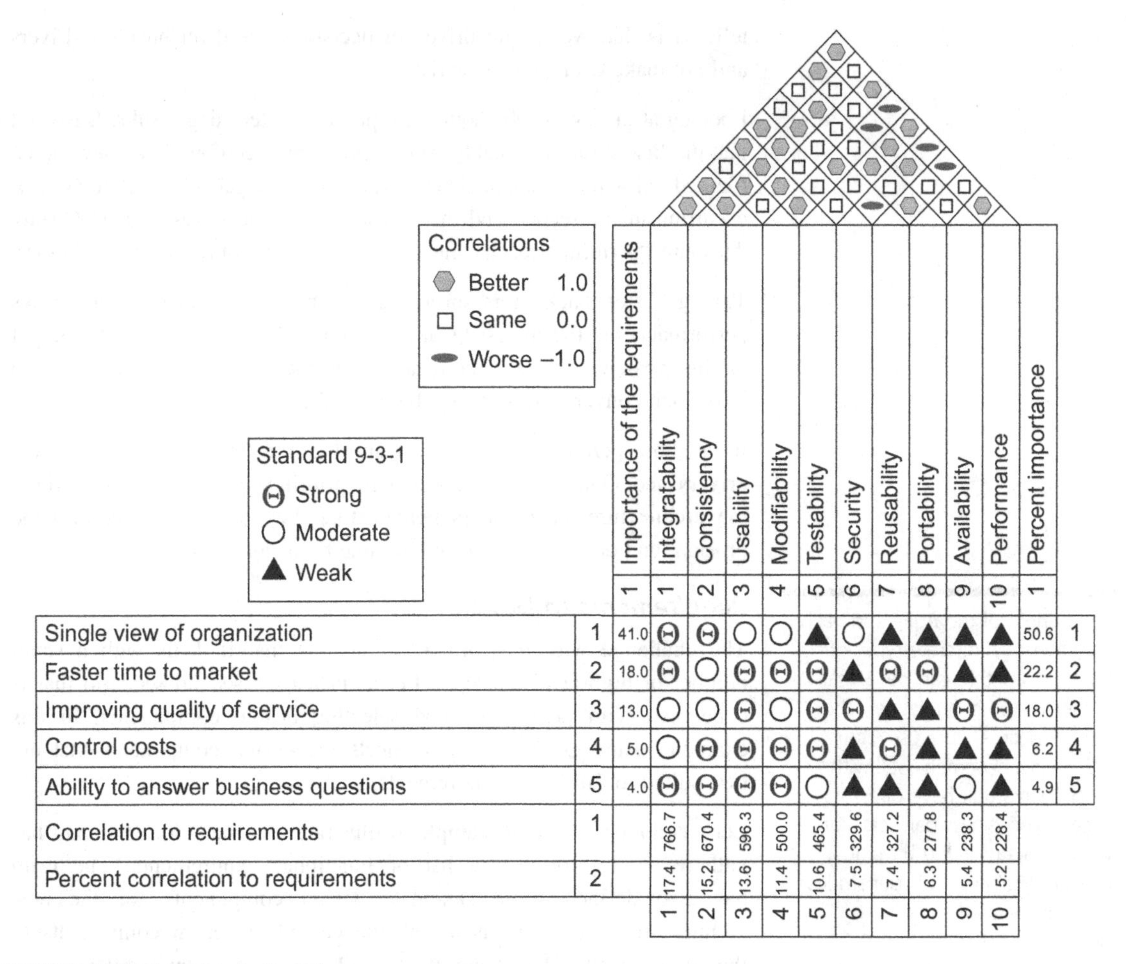

■ **FIGURE 4.8** Requirements to Quality Attributes.

This tells our design team that focusing on availability and performance is not as critical as focusing on building loosely coupled components that are modifiable and testable. This might sound counterintuitive, but that is what the business drivers have told us. If there is disagreement in the result, then the business drivers or the correlation factors can be revisited. This technique also helps us implement *Principle 3: Delay design decisions until they are absolutely necessary*. Why unnecessarily architect a solution for Quality Attributes that are not strongly driven by business requirements? It can still be argued that by not focusing on such key elements such as availability and performance, we are building ourselves problems for the future, or what can be called technical debt. These are all factors that architects have to consider. What Continuous Architecture tells us is that we should drive our decisions based on business drivers and not make decisions too early.

Looking at the roof of the house also produces interesting results. It is good that the first cluster of Quality Attributes support each other, so they can be focused on without contradicting each other. Negative correlations start occurring in the second and third clusters, with the lowest ranked Quality Attribute, "performance," having the highest number of negative correlations.

Taking a step back, it is surprising to find an organization that ranks performance as the lowest Quality Attribute, but that is what the output of this particular QFD demonstrates. The fact that the tool forces us to have such conversations is valuable in itself.

In a short period of time, the team has managed to elicit business drivers and Quality Attributes and to prioritize them. More important, the architecture stakeholders believe that they had key input into the process, and decisions are fully traceable by using QFD.

The benefit of the Agile approach is to focus on discrete types of functionality that can be implemented in a relatively short period of time—the user story. This works extremely well with small teams that have direct access to business partners. But what happens if you have an unmanageable set of user stories and a disparate business population? How do you categorize and prioritize these user stories? In addition, how can you summarize the value of what you are delivering to senior business and IT stakeholders? There is an inherit challenge in scaling user stories and providing a consistent narrative of linking them to business drivers.

This is an area where the QFD approach can also be very valuable. In his online article,[6] John Livingston discusses this topic in detail.

Requirements to Design

The challenge with the former example is that it deals with a small number of high-level concepts. Let us provide a second scenario that is concerned with prioritizing and selecting design components. In this example, using QFD, the team selects the design components that are best suited to fulfill the requirements.

Let's continue with our example to illustrate this scenario. The team has gathered and prioritized a list of functional requirements. The team has also defined some candidate design components for the new architecture. They must now link the candidate design components to the requirements. The team uses QFD in a workshop similar to the prioritization workshop with the key stakeholders that we discussed earlier. Figure 4.9 shows the results of the QFD workshop. For ease of readability, on Figure 4.9 we have removed the detailed QFD calculations. Only the ranking of the calculations are presented.

As a result of this workshop, the team has a clear idea of which architectural components are required to support the prioritized requirements. It might seem obvious that the foundations of creating a common messaging standard with a bus are required first. However, it is interesting that components such as the trade compression service and exception processing are low on the priority list.

In summary, we have discovered that the QFD approach yields the following advantages:

Standard 9-3-1

Symbol	Meaning	Value
Θ	Strong	1.0
○	Moderate	0.0
▲	Weak	–1

		1 Common messaging standards	2 Integration bus	3 XML/JSON Protocol to JSON Protocol	4 CAB data store with common API	5 Securities master with common API	6 Industry D/B I/F service	7 ADP interfaces service	8 Security depository I/F service	9 Customer interface service	10 Consolidated logical trade data store	11 Trade validation service	12 Trade compression service	13 Exception processing	2 Percent of importance	
Trade data prescreened or validated for exception processing prior to execution	1	Θ	○	Θ	Θ	Θ	○			○	Θ	Θ		○	4.2	1
Customer order/trade data electronically captured and fed into an STP environment	2	Θ	Θ	○	○	Θ	▲			○	Θ	Θ	○	○	4.2	2
Prescreened trade data routed through industry databases for enrichment	3	Θ	○	Θ	▲	○	Θ				Θ	Θ			4.2	3
Trade status information maintained and distributed through trade management system	4	Θ	Θ	○	▲	○	▲		○		Θ	Θ	Θ		4.2	4
Common repository of trade information	5	Θ	○	Θ	Θ	Θ	○				Θ	○	Θ	○	4.2	5
Real-time STP environment	6	Θ	Θ	○	Θ	Θ	Θ	Θ	Θ	Θ	Θ	Θ	Θ	Θ	4.2	6
Orders placed electronically into a centralized order management system on a real-time basis	7	Θ	Θ	Θ	Θ	○				○	○	○			4.2	7
Orders managed through a centralized order management system	8	Θ	Θ	○	○	○			○		○	○		○	4.2	8
Standardized order processes across products	9	Θ	○	Θ	○	○	▲		○		○	○	Θ	○	4.2	9
Electronic trade tickets	10	○	▲	○	Θ	○				○	▲	▲		○	4.2	10
Trade processing standardized across products wherever possible. Detailed procedures created by product when necessary	11	Θ	▲	Θ	○	Θ		○			Θ	○	○		4.2	11
All steps of execution automated	12	○	Θ	○	○	○	○	Θ	Θ	Θ	○	○	▲	Θ	4.2	12
Trades input into trade processing system without time lag from original execution	13	○	Θ	○	○	○	○	○		▲	▲	Θ			4.2	13
Electronic tickets routed to operations for input	14	○	○	○	○	○					▲	○	▲		1.4	14
Execution data including price, quantity, and counter-party captured electronically in real time	15	Θ	○	○	Θ	Θ	○			▲	○	Θ			4.2	15
All trades matched to internal sources in an automated manner for tracking and audit trail	16	Θ	Θ	Θ	○	Θ			○		Θ	▲			1.4	16
Electronic matching of salesperson and trader sides of trade	17	Θ	▲	Θ	○	○					○	▲			1.4	17
Automated feeds to settlement systems	18	○	Θ	▲	○	○	▲	Θ	Θ		Θ	▲			4.2	18
Automated crossing engines	19	Θ	Θ	Θ	Θ	Θ	○		Θ		Θ				4.2	19
Automated order routing based on liquidity and best execution	20	Θ	Θ	○	○	Θ	▲				○				1.4	20
Automated links to clearing agents and clearing houses	21	○	▲	○	▲	○	▲		Θ		○				4.2	21
Automated linkage of street-side transaction to customer-side confirmation	22	○	▲	○	Θ	○				Θ	○				4.2	22
Allocation and split instructions captured automatically and verified for processing	23	▲	Θ	○	Θ	○	▲			○	▲				1.4	23
Trade management system handles all trade states	24	Θ	▲	○	▲	Θ					Θ				4.2	24
Exception-based processing	25	Θ	Θ	Θ	Θ	Θ					○	Θ			4.2	25
Centralized confirmation factories used for settlement activities	26	Θ	Θ	Θ	Θ	Θ					▲				4.2	26
Electronic confirmations	27	○	▲	○	Θ	○				Θ	○				4.2	27
Electronic receipt of allocation instructions	28	○	▲	○	○	○				○	○				1.4	28

FIGURE 4.9 Requirements to components.

- You can identify and address key customer needs.
- You can prioritize business requirements and drive design and implementation planning activities.
- Business stakeholders can participate in the design process.
- Design decisions can be linked to business drivers.

This example clearly demonstrates the value of QFD, which is a strong tool for the architect to use to assist in areas where prioritization is critical.

MANAGING CHANGE: TRANSITIONAL ARCHITECTURES

So far we have discussed the topics of architectural decisions and prioritization. These topics can be implemented at any scale, from a single project to a large enterprise solution. Our last topic, which talks about managing change, is more relevant as you move up the scale from a single project and start taking a product suite, departmental, or enterprise view.

Most large-scale IT efforts, especially if they have a strong architecture focus, start with a long, expensive effort to define the current state followed by production of an abundant set of future-state blueprints. Such descriptive views of future architectures often include excessive detail. Given the uncertainty of reaching the future architectural state, the effort into creating this level of detail is usually wasted. Too often, this approach results in implementation efforts that significantly exceed their budget and planned timeframe and do not meet expectations. We believe that even the best architecture models and blueprints do not help much with the actual implementation of the large-scale change over time. It is really important to define the actions required to realize the desired architecture, shifting your view from the *descriptive* to the *prescriptive*.

Here is the Continuous Architecture version of the prescriptive approach: Why not briefly document the current state of the architecture, define the desired state at the conceptual level, and finally define transitional architectures on the way to reaching that goal? In other words, we introduce the idea of evolving the architecture. By following this approach, we can quickly learn which areas to focus on before moving forward with the architecture models and blueprints. This method also yields several important benefits, including a focus on delivering architecture features that matter most to the business: effective risk mitigation, expectation management, and requirements traceability, as well as lower costs.

A Model of Architecture Transitions

Let's start by introducing the concept of *architecture transitions*, the foundation of our approach. To develop an IT architecture, we leverage a model of transitions between IT states: the A-to-B-to-C model. On a time continuum, A is the architecture at the current point, C is the desired future architecture, and B architectures are transition points along the path from A to C. We believe that at A, the current architectural state of the IT environment, most enterprises are dissatisfied with the support their IT environment provides.

Our approach to evolving the architecture uses three simple steps shown in Figure 4.10.

1. Understand the "as-is" state, A.
2. Envision the desired future state, C.
3. Define and build the transitional architectures, B.

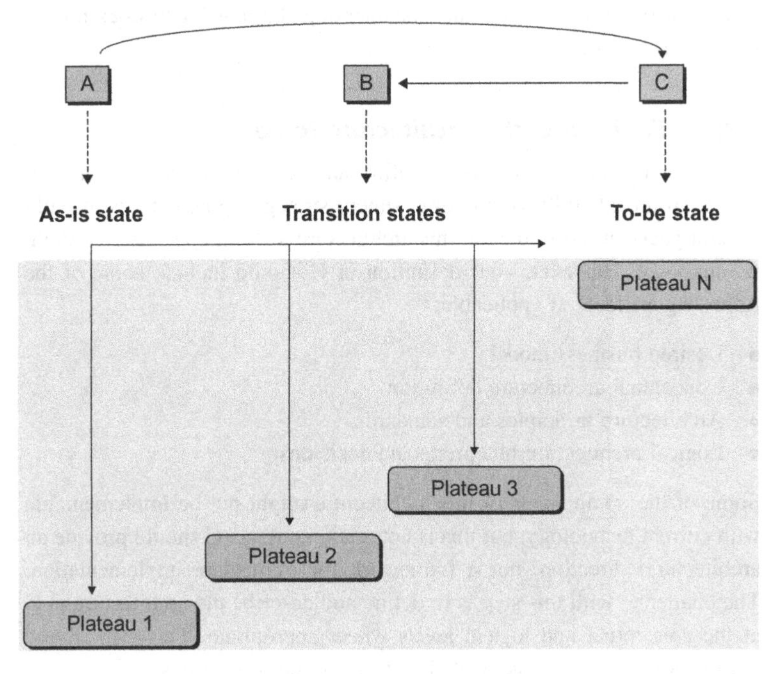

■ **FIGURE 4.10** Transitional architecture overview.

Let's review these steps in more detail.

Step 1: Understand A, the As-Is State

This step's objective is to gain an understanding of the current state, focusing on current business processes and technical architecture, and to document this understanding. An excellent way to document business processes is by animating value chains (discussed in Chapter 3). The prime reason for performing this exercise is to create an architecture baseline that you can leverage to build the first transitional architecture. Another important reason is to comprehend the issues associated with the current state so you can create the future vision.

The challenge with this step is using the appropriate level of detail. Not enough detailed information makes step 3 (Define and build the transitional architectures) difficult to accomplish because the architecture baseline is too vague for effective planning. On the other hand, too much detail makes it difficult to focus on important issues; it also creates planning problems because step 1 becomes a time- and resource-consuming exercise. In practice, we have found that the most effective approach is to constrain this step, both in time and resources, to ensure that the team in charge of understanding and documenting the as-is state does not go into excessive detail.

Step 2: Envision C, the Architecture to Be

The objective of this step is to define an ideal future state, with your IT environment fully supporting stated strategic goals. C is usually several years in the future, so this architecture's technology details might be unknown. However, your definition of C should include some of the following artifacts, if applicable:

- Desired business model
- Conceptual architecture definition
- Architecture principles and standards
- Logical architecture blueprints and decisions

Some of the components of this architecture might not be implementable with current technology, but this is not really an issue. C should provide an architectural direction, not a framework for immediate implementation. The challenge with this step is to define and describe the architecture at C at the conceptual and logical levels where appropriate. This step should not include physical implementation details or considerations.

Step 3: Define B′, B″, B‴..., the Transitional Architectures

The third and final step in our process is to define the transitional architectures—B′, B″, B‴, and so on. To define these architectures, we follow a gap analysis process between A and C (the architecture baseline and the to-be architecture). As a result, we create a series of transitional architectures at the logical level that are refinements of the to-be architecture.

The goal of implementing this series of architectures is to minimize the technology risk created by the amount of change between A and C. The transitional architectures draw heavily on the to-be architecture; this keeps the rework caused by the transition process to a minimum.

As part of this step, we also define and document the first one or two transitional architectures (B′ and B″) at the physical level, including some of the following artifacts as appropriate:

- Architectural decisions
- Technology product standards
- Logical and physical architecture blueprints
- Appropriate design and implementation patterns

But how do we define these transitional architectures, and what do they look like? To address these questions, we must first introduce the concepts of plateaus and waves.

Infrastructure Plateaus and Application Waves

Most IT implementation efforts involve two types of change:

- Delivering business functionality via application software components
- Implementing significant architectural change. This can be change in *infrastructure components* (e.g., integration middleware, hardware) or introduction of key architectural components (e.g., key applications, enterprise services).

The first realization that comes to the architect's mind in thinking about a transitional architecture is that business functionality can be delivered in smaller chunks than introducing new architectural components. Because key architectural changes can have significant repercussions on the application layer, you should introduce these changes less frequently than application changes. We express this fundamental difference by using the following terms for architecture planning purposes:

- *Plateaus* describe the successive states of significant architectural change.
- *Waves* describe the series of application architecture releases during a plateau. (In a Continuous Delivery world, waves become continuous.)

Plateaus provide the support framework that enables a series of waves to deliver business functionality. Although the term "plateau" sounds like a fancy new way of saying "phase," we chose this term with care. To implement a new architecture within a complex environment, you must move forward in measurable, discrete steps and introduce change at predefined intervals. The word "plateau" indicates a period of steady state, in which no major architectural changes occur. The objective here is to create a stable architectural platform, which the development organization can use for a predefined period of time to create value for the business users. The obvious question is, "How long should a plateau last?" If it is too long, the next change introduced will be too large and risky; if it is too short, you will be in constant change mode. Most of the projects we have worked on have used a plateau period of 6 months.

In defining plateaus, we use the following guidelines:

- Build each plateau with technology that exists at the initiation point.
- Each plateau should provide a business benefit, which ideally should be articulated with metrics.
- Define only the current plateau and the next one in detail.
- Clearly articulate the architectural decisions you expect to address in the current plateau.
- Each plateau should last approximately 6 months.

After a plateau is in place, the developers need not worry about major architectural changes that can potentially affect their productivity; basically, they can deliver business functionality by producing a series of waves upon a stable platform. There are no strict guidelines on how many waves developers should deliver for a given plateau, nor is there a strict definition of a wave. The main goal is to deliver business functionality in a manner mutually agreed with business users and IT. As a result, the mechanism by which an organization defines, communicates, and delivers waves depends on its existing culture. If you are developing in an Agile model, then your waves become aligned to your sprints.

What Does a Transitional Architecture Look Like?

How you define a transitional architecture depends on the scale that you are operating at. A detailed transitional architecture covering an entire enterprise can be quite complex. Regardless of its complexity, effectively communicating a transitional architecture is as important as getting the details correct. Primarily, the transitional architecture plateaus should reflect the discrete nature of the architecture as it progresses toward an end state; the waves should clearly identify the series of business functionality made available. If done effectively, the transitional architecture itself should be all you need to communicate your architecture.

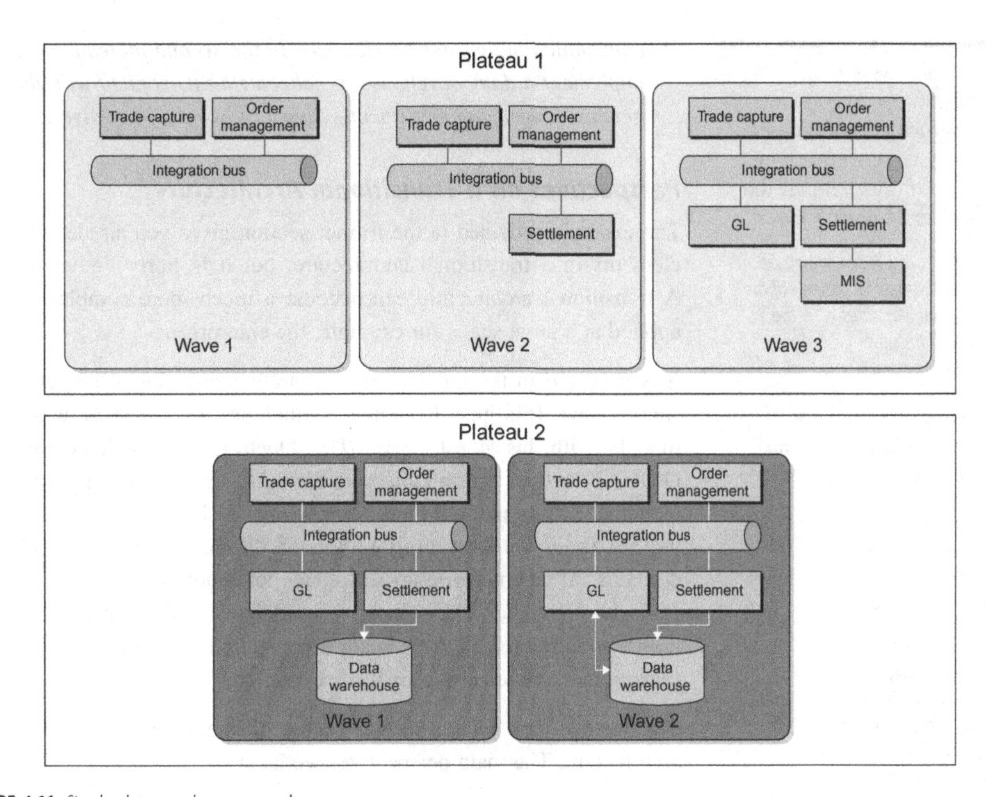

■ **FIGURE 4.11** Simple plateau and wave example.

Let's start by reviewing a simple example, depicted in Figure 4.11. This example shows a simplified version of a transitional architecture developed for an organization that wanted to integrate its front-to-back office capabilities, with a focus on creating an extensible reporting infrastructure. This example clearly articulates how to achieve the transition to a fully integrated architecture through two distinct plateaus and three waves within the first plateau. For a majority of stakeholders, this simple diagram sufficiently describes what we want our architecture to be and how we can get there.

If we added a caption to the picture, it would read something like this:

> *The future state is to have a common data warehouse with all the applications communicating via an integration bus. We reach this state by gradually increasing the number of applications in a series of waves that leverage the integration bus infrastructure that we provide in the first plateau. By wave 3, we have trade capture, order management, settlement, and general ledger*

In *Software and Systems Architecture*,[7] Rozanski and Woods provide a structured overview of key architectural concepts. They define two terms that are related to our concept of perspectives:

An architectural view is a representation of one or more structural aspects of an architecture that illustrates how the architecture addresses one or more concerned held by one or more of its stakeholders.[7]

An architectural viewpoint is a collection of patterns, templates, and conventions for constructing one type of view.[7]

Examples of viewpoints include development, operational, functional, and information.

An architectural perspective is a collection of architectural activities, tactics, and guidelines that are used to ensure that a system exhibits a particular set of related quality properties that require consideration across a number of the systems architectural views.[7]

Examples of perspectives include security, performance, and regulation.

It should be noted that what we called a perspective is closer to the concept of a viewpoint. However, what we refer to as Quality Attributes is the same concept as what they call a perspective. The book then goes on to define in detail how to use viewpoints and perspectives for defining an architecture. Similar to other methods for defining and modeling an architecture, the techniques described in *Software and Systems Architecture* can be used in conjunction with the Continuous Architecture approach.

communicating via the service bus. In the second plateau, we implement a data warehouse, synchronizing its content with the general ledger and settlement systems in two distinct waves.

Perspectives on a Transitional Architecture

The example provided in the former section gives you an idea of the key elements in a transitional architecture, but it is fairly limited in detail. A transitional architecture can become a much more complex endeavor applied at a large scale, for example, the enterprise.

It is accepted in the industry that an architecture cannot be defined in a single view. (Philippe Krutchen created one of the most widely used models with his 4 + 1 view. The Open Group Architecture Forum (TOGAF) defines four architecture views: business, data, application, and technical.) If we try to define a transitional architecture for a large scale, we are faced with the proliferation of different views and technology domains. At an enterprise level, we can potentially deal with every aspect of technology: networks, security, middleware, desktops, and applications. In addition, any large-scale organization will have to consider the transitional architecture in light of several concurrent projects.

We use the term *perspective* to define different views of a transitional architecture. The main perspectives we have are:

- *Plateau perspective* depicts the state of a particular plateau, including all the domains in scope.
- *Domain perspective* depicts how the plateau will look from the perspective of a particular technical domain such as network, applications, or security.
- *Project perspective* depicts how the plateau affects ongoing projects and vice versa.
- *Wave perspective* depicts how the waves of application functionality arrive within the context of a particular plateau.

Now let's look at a case study to see how these perspectives work.

Case Study

In our example, the company's main business is to service loans. The company originates loans itself and acquires loans from other financial institutions. From its traditional mainframe-based environment, it is migrating to a newer set of event-driven and component-based applications. At the same time, the company has started deploying Agile development in most of its software delivery projects.

Our team wants to develop an architecture for all major technology domains. The team has already provided a view of this company in terms of an animated value chain in Chapter 3. This helps set the business context. In addition, the team conducts a simplified current state analysis. Then the team develops a future-state conceptual model to guide the overall direction and logical alternatives for each domain. The domains they identify are application tools, data warehouse, middleware, platform, security, workflow, network, and system management. However, for this example, we have simplified the transitional architecture model by grouping those domains into two more general, high-level domains: data and technology infrastructure.

The transitional architecture consists of a set of plateaus for all domains within scope and a series of waves delivered on the plateaus. For this project, the team identifies four infrastructure plateaus and 10 application waves. To convey the information to the various audiences, they invoke different perspectives of the transitional architecture. Figure 4.12 outlines

Waves

Wave 1

1. Accounting and billing
   - Components accessible via information bus but not yet directory enabled
2. Client management
   - Release 3.0
   - Utilizes directory services
   - Legacy client management system retired

Wave 2

1. Imaging
   - Replacement system implemented
2. Credit rating engine
   - Available via information bus

Data

Corporate Data Warehouse

1. Financial modelling data mart fed from data warehouse
2. Weekly (instead of monthly) updates of financial reporting

Data Marts

1. Budgeting and servicing data marts implemented
2. Excel spreadsheets for finance discontinued
3. Metadata
   - Metadata repository for shared data implemented

Infrastructure

Information Bus

1. Mainframe components linked to information bus

Security

1. New authentication engine implemented

System Management

1. Fault and performance management implemented
2. Backup tools consolidated

Platform

1. Windows XP retirement complete

■ **FIGURE 4.12** Plateau perspective for the third plateau.

the plateau perspective for the third plateau. The plateau definition includes three streams: waves, data, and infrastructure.

By reviewing this example, we can quickly understand the implications of the plateau. We describe a plateau as an end state; we have to document the set of activities necessary for reaching the end state in a more detailed project plan. Let's examine the impacts of plateau 3 for each of the streams.

- The waves column lists all the updates to the applications that will be delivered in plateau 3. In the first wave, accounting and billing will become available, and a new client management release of the system will replace the legacy application. The second wave involves a replacement of the imaging application and a new credit rating engine available through the information bus.
- The data column describes the main changes to the data environment that will have occurred by the end of the plateau. In this example, the main changes are the implementation of new data marts and a first instance of a metadata repository.
- The infrastructure column describes the main changes to the infrastructure that will take effect by the end of the plateau. These fall into four major areas: information bus, network, system management, and platforms.

The teams responsible for the accounting and billing, client management, and credit rating engine follow an Agile approach, but the imaging system and data mart and data warehouse teams follow a more traditional system life cycle. So how do these different teams interact with the transitional architecture? As can be seen from Figure 4.12, the plateau definition enforces on the teams major milestones but does not dictate the details of how they will get to these milestones. So the impact on both Agile and Waterfall-oriented development teams is the same: they have to plan toward reaching the milestones.

The credit rating team has implemented an Agile approach and already has an existing backlog of client-driven features they need to implement. Based on the input from the plateau definition, they add an additional story to their backlog: integration with the information bus. Similarly, the accounting and billing and client management teams update their backlogs as well.

An interesting aspect to consider is if it makes sense to have a combined view of these backlogs at the plateau level. As illustrated in Figure 4.13, there is no reason that all the plateau stories cannot be combined and viewed collectively. This is similar to the program backlog concept

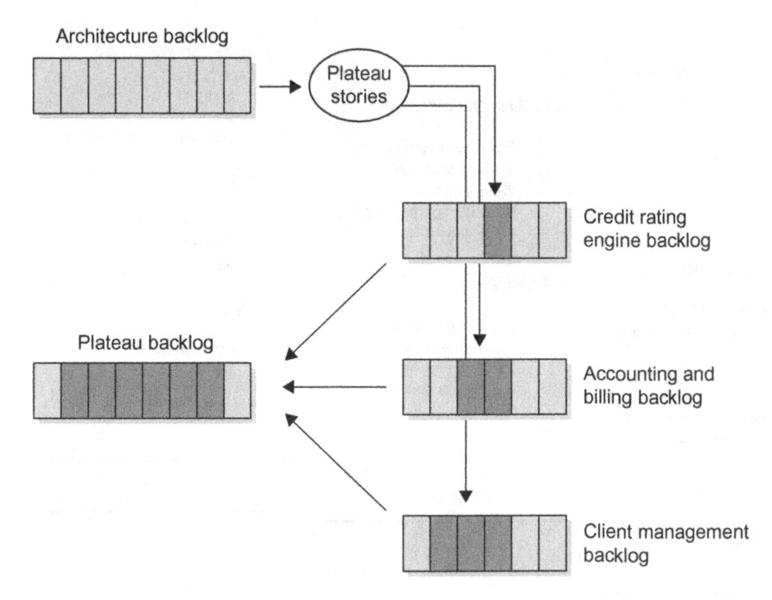

■ **FIGURE 4.13** Impact of plateau design on backlogs.

illustrated in the Scaled Agile Framework (SAFe) approach.[8] Such a view would minimally be beneficial for creating a transparent view across all the activities within the plateau.

If we take one more step and align this view with our concept of having an architecture backlog, we can see that actually, the plateau stories are driven by the decisions that get made as part of a wider architecture backlog. We could further expand and have architectural decision backlogs at the individual component (e.g., credit rating engine) level. Although it might seem theoretically appealing to have multiple backlogs linked to each other, we should remember to keep our world simple. In summary, the key idea is to enable both an Agile approach at the component level with an architectural journey at a larger scale. At the same time, we want to create traceability and visibility between these different levels.

The larger the scale, the more critical dependency management becomes. We recommend keeping a dependency matrix, not only for architectural decisions but also between components and delivery milestones.

The view of plateau 3 shown in Figure 4.12 would be of interest to senior business and IT management, architects, and project managers, who must align their projects with the plateaus. But what if we want to know the

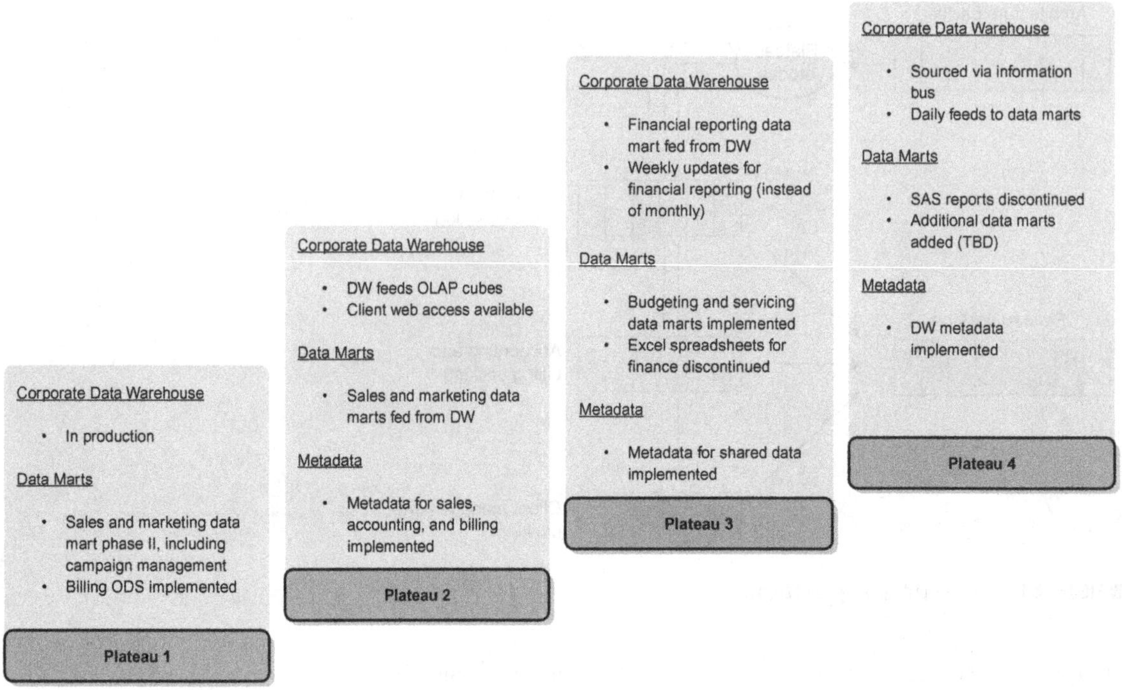

Corporate Data Warehouse
- In production

Data Marts
- Sales and marketing data mart phase II, including campaign management
- Billing ODS implemented

Plateau 1

Corporate Data Warehouse
- DW feeds OLAP cubes
- Client web access available

Data Marts
- Sales and marketing data marts fed from DW

Metadata
- Metadata for sales, accounting, and billing implemented

Plateau 2

Corporate Data Warehouse
- Financial reporting data mart fed from DW
- Weekly updates for financial reporting (instead of monthly)

Data Marts
- Budgeting and servicing data marts implemented
- Excel spreadsheets for finance discontinued

Metadata
- Metadata for shared data implemented

Plateau 3

Corporate Data Warehouse
- Sourced via information bus
- Daily feeds to data marts

Data Marts
- SAS reports discontinued
- Additional data marts added (TBD)

Metadata
- DW metadata implemented

Plateau 4

■ **FIGURE 4.14** Domain perspective.

impact on the data warehouse environment? In Figure 4.14, the data warehouse domain perspective answers this question, clearly identifying the major steps that the data warehouse domain must implement.

The project perspective, which has a structure similar to that of a domain perspective, defines the impact of the architecture plateaus on a particular project over time. Finally, the wave perspective outlines the series of functionality to be delivered over time. At a minimum, you should define the waves at the level documented in Figure 4.12, but we recommend detailing the functionality in terms of functionality delivered and implementation considerations. If adopting an Agile approach, the project and wave perspectives should be detailed in terms of sprints. For a fully Agile organization, the concept of waves can actually seem redundant and should not be introduced if it adds additional complexity.

What About Agile and Iterative Development?

The concept of Iterative development in the 1990s followed by Agile development in the 2000s has taken the software development world by storm. So, are we advocating an alternative approach to these best practices that are so predominant in the industry? In contrast, we believe that transitional architectures complement Agile and Iterative development and in fact address gaps that might result from using these approaches.

Iterative development is especially effective for mitigating the risks associated with integrating the various components of an application system. As a result, the Iterative development process gives priority to the implementation of the features associated with the largest architectural coverage. Most of the architecture complexities are included in the first iteration or iterations.

In contrast, Agile focuses on delivery against user stories in manageable increments or sprints. If you take this to the extreme, the architecture evolves and will be refactored as new requirements or challenges with the architecture arise.

Neither of these approaches directly addresses issues associated with the rollout of architectural change at scale. In contrast, a transitional architecture framework seeks to mitigate implementation difficulties in both the application and the infrastructure aspects. In this framework, we can use Agile or Iterative approaches to define application waves. The plateaus, however, provide successive stable environments that enable the iterations to deliver business functionality while minimizing technology risk. Thus, transitional architectures can be used to extend the Agile and Iterative development concepts to address infrastructure, large-scale architectural change, and functionality implementation issues.

Continuous Architecture moves in two dimensions, time and scale. The concepts and techniques introduced in this chapter are relevant in particular as you move up the dimension of scale. Applying concepts of Agile at a project level is relatively easy. Most IT groups successfully implement Agile principles. The challenge starts when you start operating at a larger scale. From our perspective, the minimum scale to develop an architecture would be at the product level. An approach that is gaining traction about applying Agile at a larger scale is called SAFe.[8] Two of SAFe's principles are directly aligned with our recommendations on architectural decisions:

Alignment focuses on coordination among different teams and programs, with particular focus on aligning the backlogs. Our concept of implementing an architectural decision backlog can be used to extend this principle.

Transparency is another principle that is similar to our recommendation on creating explicit visibility of architectural decisions.

SAFe also has the concept of architecture epics. These represent large technology initiatives, cutting across multiple products and teams. We see these as analogous to our plateaus, which focus on significant architectural change.

Refactoring

The topic of refactoring is one of the key tenets of Agile development. It is recognized that refactoring can happen at two levels, code and architecture. In both cases, functional behavior does not change. The focus is to improve the Quality Attributes, including better performance, scalability, and flexibility. The main difference between refactoring code and architecture is the scale at which you are operating. When refactoring at the code level, the work can be done by a single developer and focuses on the internals of a component. When refactoring at the architecture level, the work involves larger teams and focuses on dependencies between components as well as between components and the underlying infrastructure.

While refactoring code, the key question is the benefit gained versus the effort. If refactoring a complex set of code is deemed too time consuming, it might be a better option to rewrite the code. This becomes even easier if your architecture is aligned with *Principle 4: Architect for change—leverage "the power of small."*

At the architecture level, addressing refactoring questions is a little more complex. What is called refactoring versus rearchitecture? At what point do multiple attempts at refactoring start contradicting each other? You refactor for flexibility first and then refactor for performance, and may undo the changes you had done in the former attempt as part of this process.

In Continuous Architecture, our recommendation is to drive the architecture in a more consistent manner by applying the techniques described in this chapter:

- Keep an architectural backlog and know in advance the key architectural decisions you need to make.
- Prioritize these decisions based on quality factors that are driven by business priorities. Leverage QFD to manage this prioritization and the "top of the house" to watch out for conflict in different design options.
- Manage major change through transitional architecture and the concept of plateaus.

By leveraging these basic steps we believe that you should be much more in control of your architectural destiny while still maintaining an Agile approach.

Transitional Architectures in Practice

Creating a transitional architecture can seem like a daunting task. Although we do not advocate any strict process, we have identified several best practices that we leverage as parts of a repeatable process:

- **Create the framework.** Start by deciding on the number of plateaus and waves you want to identify. As a first approximation, use the 6-month rule for the plateaus. Identify waves. Interact with the business and prioritize the functionalities it requires. Make sure to communicate the effort associated with each discrete item of functionality so that the business can base the prioritization not just on what it wants but also on a cost–benefit view.
- **Identify waves.** Interact with the business and prioritize the functionalities it requires. Group the functionality into waves. This is a high-level exercise and should be able to be sorted out in a series of workshops and not immense requirements documents. This prioritized set of functionality is your first strawman for waves.

- **Map the plateaus.** After you have identified the waves, map them onto the plateaus. At this point, plateaus have no reference to infrastructure elements; they are a set of steady states on which you are distributing a series of functionalities. Next you will identify the steady-state infrastructure components required to support the waves. Align plateaus. For each domain, identify each discrete step (e.g., reference data available via the information bus) that the transitional architecture will identify. Distribute these discrete steps onto the plateaus with an eye on the waves that they need to support. This part of the analysis is a fine balancing act, making sure that each plateau is evenly balanced and provides true business benefit. Start with the end in mind but be pragmatic. At this point, you have either clearly documented your future state or have a clear idea of what the vision is. Start by identifying the critical steps you must take to get to the future (or desired) state. Be realistic in your assumptions and do not try to accomplish too much in each plateau.
- **Validate plateaus and waves.** Validate each wave and plateau using "what if" scenarios to ensure that the proposed transitional architecture framework is flexible enough to support business and technology changes over time. In addition, each wave and plateau should provide a business benefit, which you must clearly be able to articulate.
- **Contextualize.** Identify and incorporate technology constraints. Most of these will be results of current ongoing projects. Documenting the effect of these on the architecture will help put the changes you can influence in context.
- **Iterate.** Iterate over the plateaus. Look at each plateau individually and assess balance, feasibility (including budget constraints), and dependencies. Iterate over the domains and take a cross-plateau view to make sure that the domain is progressing coherently, with all constraints and dependencies understood. This step is critical because it ensures proper mitigation of technology and implementation risks.

Traditional brainstorming materials, such as flipcharts and post-it notes, facilitate this process. For example, using post-its to describe each piece of wave functionality and discrete infrastructure change lets you easily move these steps from one plateau to another. Color coding makes it easy to identify domains, and numbering is helpful for determining dependencies. We also encourage you to leverage QFD for prioritizing requirements and for grouping those requirements into waves and plateaus.

Most importantly, as the work develops, each plateau and wave will start gaining an identity based on the steps that it contains. (We find that giving each plateau a short recognizable name is also very helpful.) It is important to capture this identity and document the plateau's business value. This business value is critical for your successful communication of the transitional architecture. You can only achieve buy-in from all the stakeholders by articulating what each plateau is accomplishing, briefly and understandably.

For example, building on our earlier description of Figure 4.11, we might say something like this:

> *The future state is to have a data warehouse and supporting data model with all the applications communicating via an enterprise service bus. We reach this state by gradually increasing the number of applications that use the service bus:*

- *In plateau 1, wave 1, trade capture and order management will communicate in a common manner that will enable quicker and more accurate processing of trades.*
- *In plateau 1, wave 2, we will add settlement to the fold, giving the client-facing account managers access to valuable data.*
- *Plateau 1, wave 3 will be more internally focused, linking the general ledger to the integration bus and adding management information system capabilities to settlement.*
- *In plateau 2, we do not make any business changes but greatly enhance the maintenance and cost of the environment by implementing a common data warehouse (wave 1) and synchronizing this with the general ledger (wave 2).*

An important aspect of designing transitional architectures is to define them at the appropriate level of detail. Keep in mind that business drivers, priorities, technologies, and organizations change. Consequently, spending an enormous amount of time detailing every step of a transitional architecture is a wasted effort. We recommend documenting only the first plateau at an immediately actionable level of detail. Keep the other plateaus at the level of abstraction of the examples in this chapter. Finally, to mitigate risk and continuously improve the architecture design and implementation process, go through the following checklist at the end of each plateau:

- Is my plan and budget adequate to continue on to the next plateau? Should I adjust them?
- What are my go and no-go architecture decisions? Should I simplify the architecture and eliminate features that no longer provide a benefit or might not be implementable? Should I add any new features to the architecture?

- What are the lessons learned during the implementation of the current plateau? How do they apply to future plateaus?

We have observed that defining transitional architectures with this approach yields several advantages:

- It helps you identify and focus on delivering the architecture features that deliver the most value to business users.
- You identify implementation risks early in the process and ensure their adequate mitigation.
- You create a stable architectural environment for application developers while incrementally improving the underlying infrastructure.
- You can link architecture decisions to business requirements and demonstrate this linkage to the business users.
- You can communicate the architecture to a wide audience as a progression of actionable steps along the dimension of time.

APPLYING THE CONTINUOUS ARCHITECTURE PRINCIPLES

Now that we have discussed three key elements in evolving an architecture, let us circle back to our six Continuous Architecture principles and see how they relate to these topics.

Architectural Decisions

The most obvious principle in this area is *Principle 3: Delay design decisions until they are absolutely necessary.* What we are mainly advocating related to this principle is to create an architecture backlog and then focus only on the decisions you need to make. It is important to note that the only driver for making an architectural decision does not have to be exclusively related to the immediate delivery at hand. You can also make decisions that you think are required for the long-term stability of the product or enterprise. This is where *Principle 1: Architect products, not just solutions for projects* comes in. The scope of your architectural decision backlog should not be based on a project or application scope but should minimally deal with decisions required for a product. *Principle 5: Architect for build, test, and deploy* dictates that the scope of your architectural decisions are not limited to only the product but also include architectural decisions impacting the full development life cycle.

Principle 4: Architect for change—leverage "the power of small" and *Principle 2: Focus on Quality Attributes, not on functional requirements* are enabling principles. Basically, you should apply these while making your architectural decisions. They should provide the guidance you require to build out your architecture.

If you apply *Principle 6: Model the organization after the design of the system*, then by its nature, your architectural decisions become much more localized. In other words, the number of stakeholders required to come to a particular decision is minimized. This helps resolve organizational friction and enables speed of delivery. That does not mean that there will not be architectural decisions that span components; actually defining the components themselves is an architectural decision. So the concepts of providing visibility and rules are still very relevant.

Prioritizing: Quality Function Deployment

Let us start with *Principle 2: Focus on Quality Attributes, not on functional requirements*. It is clear from our description that QFD provides additional support to this principle; in essence, it enables us to focus on the Quality Attributes that are higher priority for achieving the business objectives. We can also link our Quality Attributes to functional requirements. In other words, QFD enables us to bring more nuance to this principle. We do not need to ignore functional requirements; we can easily integrate them to the Quality Attributes. However, architectural decisions should still focus on driving through Quality Attributes.

Similarly, QFD enables us to prioritize architectural features and decisions. As a result, it is another input into *Principle 3: Delay design decisions until they are absolutely necessary* by giving us guidance on which architectural features and decisions are more important than others.

Principle 1: Architect products, not just solutions for projects tells us to focus on products. One key element in applying product management is to develop your product based on customer demand and market competition. This is exactly what QFD was designed to address. If you are a product manager, you can use the full feature set of QFD in driving your product features based on the voice of the customer.

Principle 4: Architect for change—leverage "the power of small" makes sure that the requirements and architectural features you prioritized are atomic units of work that are loosely coupled. As demonstrated in our requirements to design example, having a component-based architecture enables effective prioritization. If we had built the roof of the house of quality in that example, we should see relatively little positive or negative correlation between our components. This can be used as a checkpoint to determine the coupling between your components.

Similar to what we discussed in regard to design decisions, *Principle 6: Model the organization after the design of the system* and *Principle 5: Architect for build, test, and deploy* help in effectively scoping the prioritization exercises you need to conduct.

Transitional Architectures

The first principle to look at is *Principle 1: Architect products, not just solutions for projects.* All products are expected to have a roadmap that describes the feature sets that will be added to the product over time. This is driven by customer demand, which as discussed can be input into the QFD process. The relationship between transitional architectures and product roadmaps are twofold. First, the techniques used for developing transitional architectures can be used for developing the roadmap. Secondarily, if the scopes of transitional architectures span multiple products, then the product roadmap has to be aligned with the plateaus. This can easily be accomplished by introducing an additional perspective focused on the products being analyzed.

Applying *Principle 2: Focus on Quality Qttributes, not on functional requirements* will help drive through how the plateaus and waves are defined. In particular, the impact of Quality Attributes on defining infrastructure plateaus should not be overlooked. Using QFD in the design of plateaus and waves will help drive the prioritization activities.

Principle 3: Delay design decisions until they are absolutely necessary can be applied from two aspects. First you should make sure that the architectural decisions that helped define the plateaus and waves are clearly articulated and communicated. In addition, you should align the architectural decision backlog with the transitional architectures. Basically, you should have an idea of what architectural decisions are required to reach the next plateau.

Principle 4: Architect for change—leverage "the power of small" will help drive the components that go into different plateaus and waves. The more you apply this principle, the easier you will find your transitional planning because you will be able to "reconfigure" or "refactor" your transitional architecture relatively easy.

Once again *Principle 6: Model the organization after the design of the system* and *Principle 5: Architect for build, test, and deploy* help in effectively scoping the transitional architecture you need to design.

SUMMARY

This chapter has focused on the tools that are relevant for evolving the architecture, in particular:

- We started with architectural decisions, which are a non-negotiable element of any architecture, explicitly or implicitly. We defined what we mean by an architectural decision and presented our views on how to approach architectural decisions. Our main recommendation in this space is to explicitly document and communicate architectural decisions: create your decision backlog.
- Then we focused on the topic of prioritization. A common challenge in product management in general and architecture in particular is the ability to link key features to the business drivers. We looked into using an existing Six Sigma technique called QFD.
- Finally, we looked at how we can approach transition planning. This becomes even more relevant when the scope of the architecture effort spans more than one product, for example, a particular department or the enterprise. We introduced the concepts of plateaus and waves that help structure a transition plan that enables large-scale architectural change while catering to multiple delivery cycles.

We believe that using such tools will greatly increase the effectiveness of your architecture regardless of what process or methodology you are using. In the next chapter, we will focus on the next logical step in our journey: Continuous Architecture and Continuous Delivery.

ENDNOTES

1. Tufte T. Visual explanations: images and quantities, evidence and narrative; 1997.
2. Poppendieck M, Poppendieck T. Lean software development: an Agile toolkit; 2003.
3. The Responsible Designer. Agile Architecture Myths #2 Architecture Decisions Should Be Made At the Last Responsible Moment, January 18, 2001. <http://wirfs-brock.com/blog/2011/01/18/agile-architecture-myths-2-architecture-decisions-should-be-made-at-the-last-responsible-moment/>.
4. Akao Y. Quality function deployment: integrating customer requirements into product design. Productivity Press, NY; 1990.
5. Mizuno S, Akao Y. QFD: the Customer-Driven Approach to Quality Planning & Deployment. Quality Resources; Asian Productivity Organization, Tokyo; 1994.

6. Livingston J. A spoonful of QFD helps the Agile go down, November 21, 2007. <http://www.qfdonline.com/archives/>.
7. Rozanski N, Woods E. Software systems architecture. 2nd ed. Addison-Wesley; 2012.
8. Scaled Agile Framework. Scaled Agile Framework 3.0, <http://www.scaledagileframework.com/>.

Chapter 5

Continuous Architecture and Continuous Delivery

Without continual growth and progress, such words as improvement, achievement and success have no meaning.

—Benjamin Franklin

The principal goal of Continuous Delivery is to adapt and respond quickly to business needs by delivering high-quality software in rapid cycles. Agile software development practices enable development teams to create and enhance applications at a rapid pace. However, the handoff between development groups, testing groups, and operations groups is rarely smooth. Typically, this handoff is associated with a number of challenges such as manual processes; lack of communication among developers, testers, and operations; and inadequate processes and tools that slow down the entire software delivery process.

A Continuous Architecture approach can address and eliminate these bottlenecks. The goal of Continuous Architecture in the Continuous Delivery context is to speed up the software development and delivery process by systematically applying an architecture perspective and discipline continuously throughout the process. This chapter focuses on describing how to bring an architecture perspective to the overall process (sometimes referred to as the "DevOps" process) as well as to the following five key components of that process:

- Continuous feedback and monitoring
- Continuous Integration (CI)
- Continuous release and deployment
- Continuous testing
- Hybrid cloud deployment

CONTINUOUS ARCHITECTURE AND THE DEVOPS PROCESS

What Is "DevOps"?

"DevOps (a portmanteau of "**dev**elopment" and "**op**erations") is an application delivery philosophy that stresses communication, collaboration, and integration between software developers and their information technology (IT) counterparts in operations. DevOps is a response to the interdependence of software development and IT operations. It aims to help an organization rapidly produce software products and services."[1,2,3] DevOps is also defined as "an approach based on lean and Agile principles in which business owners and the development, operations and Quality Assurance (QA) departments collaborate to deliver software in a continuous manner that enables the business to more quickly seize market opportunities and reduce the time to include customer feedback."[4]

Although simple in concept, DevOps is seldom effectively implemented in traditional organizations. To adopt a DevOps approach, organizations typically need to make the following changes:

- Involve business, development, Quality Assurance (QA), and operations throughout the entire software delivery process.
- Eliminate manual testing and deployment processes by implementing new highly automated processes.
- Avoid large, infrequent code releases (especially quarterly and less frequently) by frequently releasing application code in smaller releases.
- Make measurement and feedback loops an integral part of the entire application delivery cycle, including feedback from production.
- Build applications to take advantage of a hybrid cloud model. This means making it possible for components to be hosted when it makes the most sense depending on the phase of the Software Development Life Cycle (SDLC). For example, the system could be architected to leverage a public cloud infrastructure to perform large-scale performance tests.

Implementing effective DevOps requires changing the culture as well as the structure of the IT organization, not just processes and tools.

> *The essence of DevOps is to design a system in which people are held responsible for the consequences of their actions – and indeed, one in which the right thing to do is also the easiest thing to do.*[5]

Let's illustrate this point by returning to the Continuous Architecture journey of the IT group that we first introduced in Chapter 2 and further discussed in Chapter 3.

DevOps Without Continuous Architecture

As mentioned in Chapter 2, the IT group in our case study has elected to use some of the Agile techniques as well as a Continuous Integration approach for building and delivering the "WebShop" system. They are convinced that they are already fully leveraging a "DevOps" approach by creating a separate DevOps team, but unfortunately, their software deployment process has many issues.

Typically, it takes them a significant amount of time (sometimes a day or more) to move software from a development environment to a testing environment, and their application sometimes exhibits a different behavior depending on the environment it is running in. The developers are focused on implementing new features, and they assume that if an application successfully passes its unit and integration tests, it will pass the Quality Assurance tests and will run in production. In addition, they assume that the existing application components will keep on running when new components are implemented, which is unfortunately often not the case.

Operations, on the other hand, focuses on maintaining stability and minimizing change. They see increasing the speed of delivery as a threat to stability and try to minimize the frequency of software releases. They view monthly deployments as minimally acceptable but quarterly releases as ideal.

Deployment is done using homegrown scripts that need to be modified for each application release. Developers are not allowed to configure their application software on the virtual servers within the testing environments, so they provide configuration instructions via email to the "DevOps" team. Using that configuration information, DevOps then manually configures the application software in the testing environment. This approach is error prone and involves many "trial and error" iterations before the software is correctly configured and ready for testing.

The highly manual nature of this approach creates delays in the software delivery process and introduces new instabilities; capabilities that developers have successfully tested in their own environments fail in new ways when run in the testing environments. The situation often gets worse when application code is released to the production environment. Let's look into what happened here and caused this issue.

Their management had heard of the "DevOps" concept from vendor presentations and recognized its potential but unfortunately did not fully understand it before implementing it. They created a separate "DevOps group." This group was staffed with members of an existing release management function, which amounted to renaming their release management group to "DevOps."

In effect, they did not fully leverage *Principle 5: Architect for build, test, and deploy*. Specifically, they failed to understand that "DevOps" means development and operations, working together to remove barriers, handoffs, and valueless activities from the application delivery life cycle. All they did was to rename an existing function, keeping all the processes and workflow the same.

A Continuous Architecture Roadmap for Implementing DevOps

Given their testing and deployment challenges, the team decides to try a new approach for deploying and testing the "WebShop" system.

Figure 5.1 depicts their roadmap for implementing an optimal DevOps process.

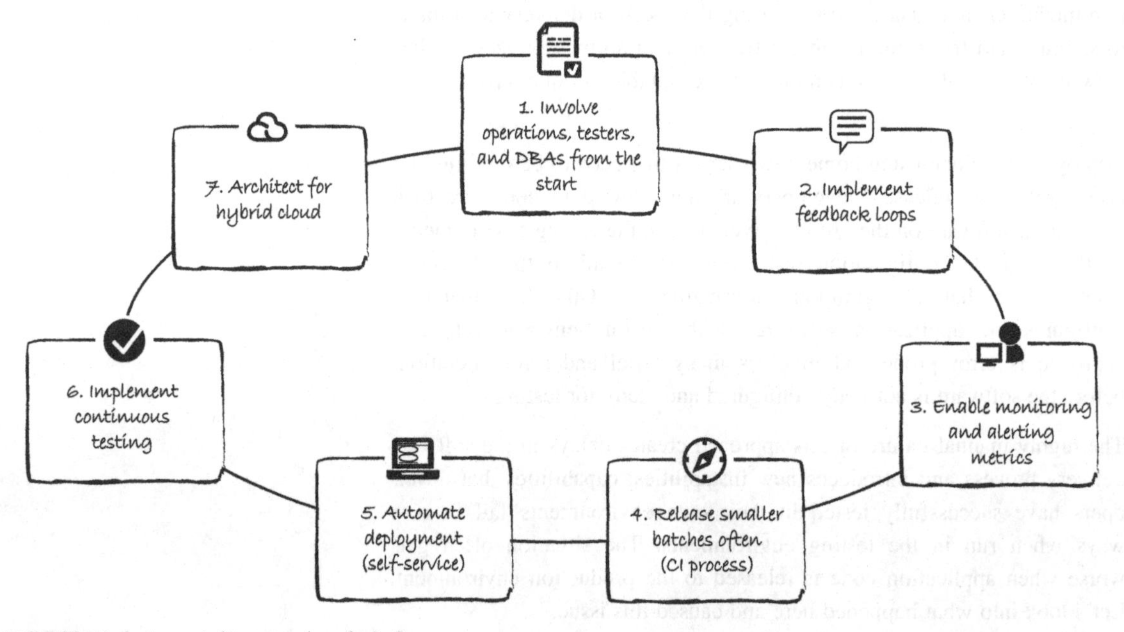

■ **FIGURE 5.1** Continuous Architecture roadmap for DevOps.

Their first priority is to fix their cultural and communication challenges, leaving technical challenges for later. They leverage *Principle 6: Model the organization after the design of the system*, and they include a tester, a database administrator (DBA), and an operations specialist as part of each capability team. For example, the "fulfill an order" capability team now includes the following roles:

- Solution architect
- Designer
- User Interface (UI) specialist
- Service specialist
- Back-end specialist
- **Database Administrator (DBA)**
- **Tester**
- **Operations specialist**

The roles in **bold** are the ones that were added as part of this effort.

The team immediately notices a significant improvement in the testing and deployment processes. Because every project stakeholder is now part of the project since its inception, communication issues are now few and far between. There are no more unpleasant surprises: Database Administrators, testers, and operations specialists are participating in the design and development of each technical capability provided by the new system and are able to voice concerns early in the life cycle. Potential testing and deployment problems are anticipated and solutions to those problems are quickly designed and implemented.

Learning from this success, IT management realizes that there is no need for a separate "DevOps" group and going forward will form cross-functional teams as needed, eliminating specialist teams. However, the team is unable to quantify the process improvements because they are not yet systematically collecting feedback or metrics.

The team's second step for implementing DevOps is to build on their first success and to implement a **continuous feedback loop** at each step of the software release and deployment process. The feedback loop is initially implemented with basic, simple tools. They start with a Microsoft SharePoint site for sharing information and some simple scripting techniques to gather data.

Because they have used basic tools and not overarchitected a solution, this simple approach leverages *Principle 3: Delay design decisions until they are absolutely necessary.* It provides very valuable information on their deployment and testing process. Although software deployments are still done using homegrown scripts, the customization of those scripts generates fewer errors. Overall, the software deployment process gets faster and more reliable, and the team learns something about automating deployments.

They also decide to extend this concept to collecting feedback from customers by implementing some basic instrumentation capabilities in their application software, such as reporting on which input fields are used and in which sequence and which capabilities are used. Also, by knowing which features are being used, they can tell which features are not being used. The feedback provides their business partners with information about which application capabilities are valuable to their customers. This enables the business partners to focus future development on the most valuable capabilities and reduces waste caused by developing and implementing features that are rarely or never used.

The team's third step for implementing an optimal DevOps process is to systematically monitor the software release and deployment process, generate alerts when errors are encountered, and start collecting metrics on those alerts. As a result, the whole team believes that they are part of the process, and the developers enjoy fixing these alerts as much as delivering stories.

Based on those metrics, they start having regular, fact-based discussions with their operations and testing groups, and they make further improvements to their software deployment and release process. As a result, they eliminate more issues and are able to decrease release cycle times even more. See the section "Continuous Architecture, Continuous Feedback, and Continuous Monitoring" for more details on how Continuous Architecture can help with implementing feedback loops and monitoring the software release and deployment process.

With the process improvements they have made so far, and especially based on the software deployment metrics they are now collecting, the team members suspect that there may be a correlation between the size of their software deployment batches and the number of errors encountered during the deployment process. Smaller, more frequent deployments seem to generate fewer issues, and the operations team (which is separate from the now defunct DevOps team) is getting more comfortable with the deployment process and the associated scripts.

As an experiment, they decide to break down a large release into a series of smaller releases to deploy those smaller "batches" more frequently. This results in further improvements to the process and additional decreases in both software deployment time and deployment errors. Breaking down the large deployment batches into smaller units leads them to implement an improved and more effective software development and deployment process. They also increasingly leverage *Principle 4: Architect for change—leverage "the power of small"* and use more microservices in their architecture. In addition, they make it a practice to design those microservices for failure and not just to handle "happy paths" to make testing easier.

The team's fifth step for implementing their DevOps process is to eliminate homegrown scripts and implement some automated deployment tools. These tools provide them with better monitoring and alerting as well as more accurate metrics. In addition, the tools allow them to implement a "self-service" model, which enables developers to deploy their new software (or software changes) to the testing environments without involving another group. In addition, they implement a "**delivery pipeline**," which is a single path to production for all changes to the "WebShop" system, including application code, database structure, infrastructure, and environment changes (the "Continuous Architecture and Continuous Release and Deployment" section in this chapter discusses the delivery pipeline in more detail).

The team's sixth step for implementing an optimal DevOps process is to implement a "continuous testing" approach and automate their testing processes. A critical component in this step is to leverage *Principle 5: Architect for build, test, and deploy.* This approach ensures that every service is independently tested. As mentioned in our earlier discussion of Continuous Architecture principles in Chapter 2, this can be achieved by leveraging a number of techniques, including small, Application Programming Interface (API)-testable services and components as well as service virtualization (the "Continuous Architecture and Continuous Testing" section in this chapter discusses those techniques in more details.)

The team's seventh and final step for implementing its DevOps process is to start architecting the software so it can be deployed on hybrid cloud infrastructures. This enables them to quickly provision new environments and to scale those environments in a very cost-effective manner by leveraging public cloud infrastructures. For example, the team is able to quickly build a performance environment to perform stress testing on the new "WebShop" system and to find out the maximum number of concurrent users who can simultaneously access the system with an acceptable response time. (The "Continuous Architecture and Hybrid Cloud Deployment" section discusses some techniques that can be used for architecting applications that can run on hybrid cloud infrastructures.) By following this seven step roadmap our "WebShop" team has significantly improved their ability to develop and release software in a continuous manner.

The next sections in this chapter provide more details on how the Continuous Architecture "Toolbox" can be leveraged to enable and optimize the following key building elements of the DevOps process:

- Continuous feedback and continuous monitoring
- Continuous Integration
- Continuous release and deployment
- Continuous testing
- Hybrid cloud deployment

CONTINUOUS ARCHITECTURE, CONTINUOUS FEEDBACK, AND CONTINUOUS MONITORING

What Do We Mean by "Continuous Feedback Loop"?

Feedback is essential to effective software delivery. Agile processes use some of the following tools to obtain feedback:

- Pair programming
- Unit tests
- Continuous Integration
- Daily scrums
- Sprints

As we saw earlier in this chapter, implementing a continuous feedback loop is a key building block of the DevOps process, but the DevOps tools used are different from the tools used by Agile methodologies. They include tools to implement a continuous feedback loop by collecting information from the software release and deployment process, creating a simple dashboard that summarizes the information, and organizing daily meetings with all stakeholders to review results and design changes.

What is a "feedback loop"? In simple terms, a process has a feedback loop when the results of running the process are used to improve how the process itself works in the future.

Leveraging the Continuous Architecture approach, the steps of implementing a DevOps continuous feedback loop are as follows:

1. **Collect feedback** either from deployment scripts or from an integrated tool that automates the delivery pipeline. The key here is not to start the process by implementing a complex dashboard that may take a significant amount of time and money to get up and running. As we saw earlier in this chapter, the team in the case study leveraged a Microsoft SharePoint site and some simple script instrumentation techniques to achieve this.

2. **Assess feedback.** Root cause analysis needs to be part of the event handling process. Form a multidisciplinary team that includes developers, operations, and testers. The goal of this team is to analyze the root causes of issues that may have occurred during the software release and deployment process; for example, why was a component deployed incorrectly, or why did it take twice the expected amount of time to deploy a component?
3. **Work incrementally.** Design small *incremental* changes to the process based on the root cause analysis. It is much better to make a series of small changes that can be easily undone than a large change that may have unexpected results. These changes need to be reviewed and agreed on by all the stakeholders.
4. **Schedule incrementally.** Changes need to be scheduled carefully so that each one builds on the results of the previous one. Making multiple changes at once is risky because their results may offset each other: One change may increase process stability, but another change may accidentally create stability issues under certain conditions. If both changes are made at the same time, it becomes difficult to determine which change should be retained and which one should be eliminated. Again, this step is a joint effort involving all the stakeholders.
5. **Implement changes** and go back to step 1 (collect feedback).

Figure 5.2 depicts this process.

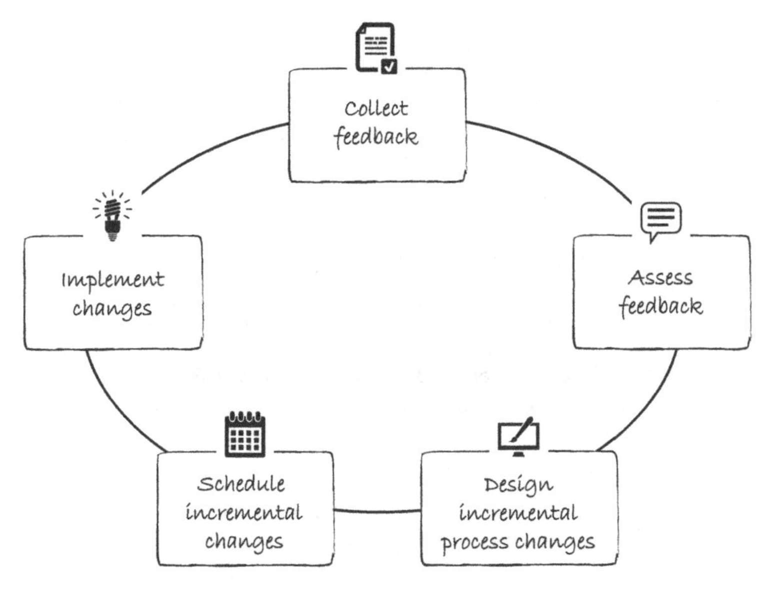

■ **FIGURE 5.2** The DevOps continuous feedback loop.

What Is Continuous Monitoring?

Continuous monitoring enables developers and testers to understand the performance and availability of their application during both the pre-production and the production phases. Continuous monitoring provides the team with early feedback that can be used for improving the usability of the application, as well as analyzing issues encountered while testing the application.

The key to continuous monitoring is to put effective instrumentation in the User Interface layer as well as in each of the services that the application uses. Instrumentation can have a negative impact on performance, and that impact can be felt when mobile User Interfaces are instrumented, so it is important to be able to turn monitoring on and off.

Similar to our approach to designing services for automated testing described in the "Continuous Architecture and Continuous Testing" section, services must be designed for continuous monitoring by including instrumentation as one of the core capabilities provided by a service rather than retrofitting instrumentation after the service has been developed.

Figure 5.3 provides an overview of how an application such as "WebShop" from our case study can be instrumented to provide effective monitoring. (Please note that this instrumentation approach is similar to the instrumentation approach used for enterprise services, as discussed in Chapter 10.)

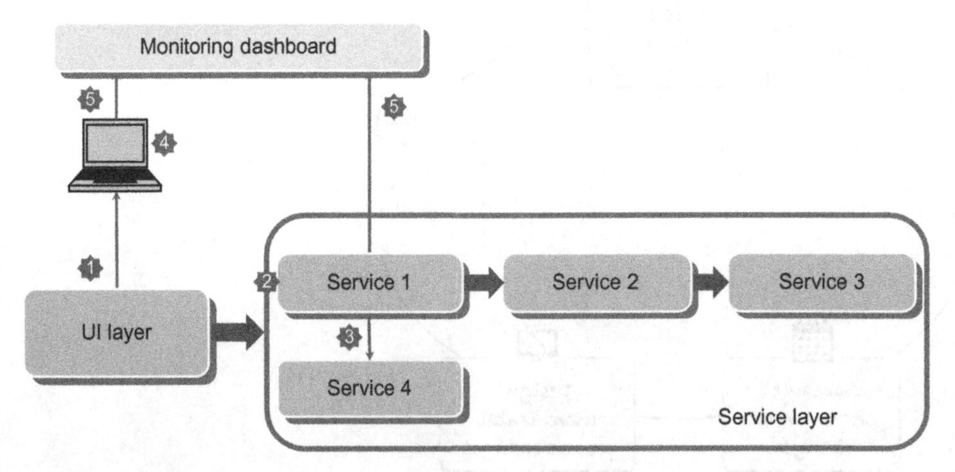

■ **FIGURE 5.3** Monitoring an application.

The instrumentation and monitoring of an application need to provide the following capabilities:

1. Instrumentation to report on both the usage and the health of the User Interface layer of the application: For example, which User Interface fields are being used by the end user, and in which sequence? Which paths are being followed, and which paths are seldom or never used? Is the User Interface layer functioning normally, and is the response time acceptable under load?
2. Instrumentation to report on the usage and health of each service used by the User Interface layer: How is the service being used, which paths are being followed, and are the service and all of its components working normally? (Please refer to Chapter 10 for a definition of *service health*.)
3. Instrumentation to report on the usage and health of other services called by the primary services, which are themselves directly called by the User Interface layer.
4. Instrumentation to report on the health of each client of the User Interface layer: Is the response time within the service-level agreements? Is the resource pool of the client at an acceptable level?
5. A monitoring dashboard that reports on the utilization and health of the application by leveraging instrumentation data: This could be a real-time dashboard or even a report produced at frequent intervals.

The same approach also applies to **customer feedback**. Application instrumentation enables business partners to analyze customer behavior and pinpoint customer pain points. This in turn can be used to discover unused functionality within applications and focus future development on creating valuable features that customers really want. For example, we may discover that the ability to navigate screens randomly instead of following a fixed workflow is seldom used by our customers, so why waste resources delivering that capability? Instrumentation features are also able to limit waste caused by developing and implementing features which are rarely or never used.

CONTINUOUS ARCHITECTURE AND THE CONTINUOUS INTEGRATION PROCESS

Understanding Continuous Integration is key to understanding Continuous Delivery and therefore to understanding how Continuous Architecture can support this process.

What Is Continuous Integration?

Continuous Integration is a software development practice in which developers integrate, build, and test their work frequently, typically supported by automation. Each integration cycle happens on a Continuous Integration Build Server, which performs the following seven steps, in order:

1. Detect changes in the source code repository tool. Subversion is an example of a source code repository tool.
2. Extract the source code changes from the source code repository tool and move them to the Continuous Integration Build Server.
3. Compile the source code changes.
4. Perform quality validation–related tasks such as running automated unit tests and performing automated architecture verification, design validation, and code quality analysis. These tasks are optional in the Continuous Integration process, but they are strongly recommended as enforcing quality as early in the process as possible is a key attribute of the Continuous Architecture approach.
5. Check the new compiled code back into the Source Code Repository tool.
6. Report build status to designated stakeholders.
7. Optionally package and deploy successfully integrated code to the testing environment.

The Continuous Integration process is depicted at a high level in Figure 5.4.

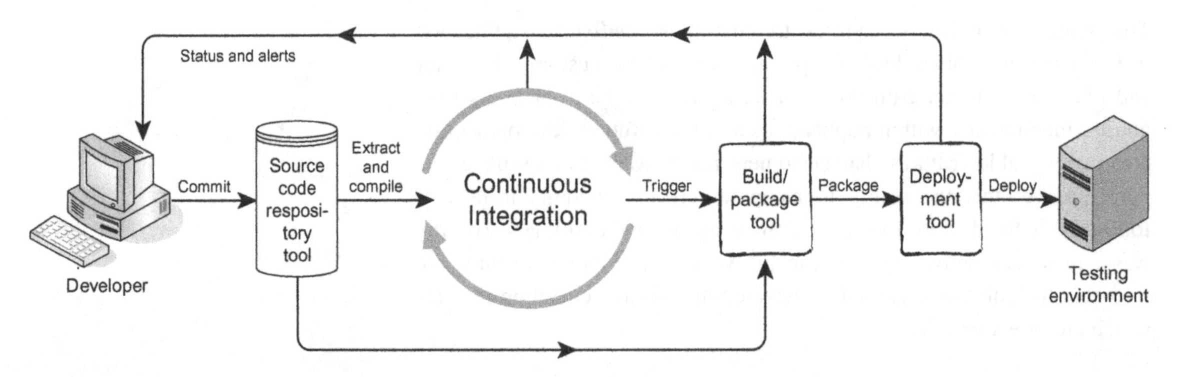

■ FIGURE 5.4 Sample overall Continuous Integration process.

Going back to the case study, the team decides to implement a Continuous Integration process as part of the fourth step in their DevOps roadmap (see the "Continuous Architecture and the DevOps Process" section). They leverage *Principle 3: Delay design decisions until they are absolutely necessary* when architecting their Continuous Integration process and select simple tools that are either already used by their organization or inexpensive open source tools. Their goal is to better understand what they need from the Continuous Integration process before they commit to expensive third-party vendor tools. They decide to use the following tools:

- Jenkins: an open source software tool used to provide Continuous Integration services such as monitoring changes in the versioning and revision control system, initiating build and packaging activities, and providing monitoring facilities such as a dashboard showing success and failures in the process
- Subversion (SVN): an open source software versioning and revision control system, distributed as free software under the Apache License
- A number of static code analysis and automated testing tools such as Microsoft's FxCop and NUnit, an open source unit testing framework
- An internal tool to perform builds and software packaging
- A vendor software deployment tool already in use in the organization

Figure 5.5 provides a depiction of the team's Continuous Integration process.

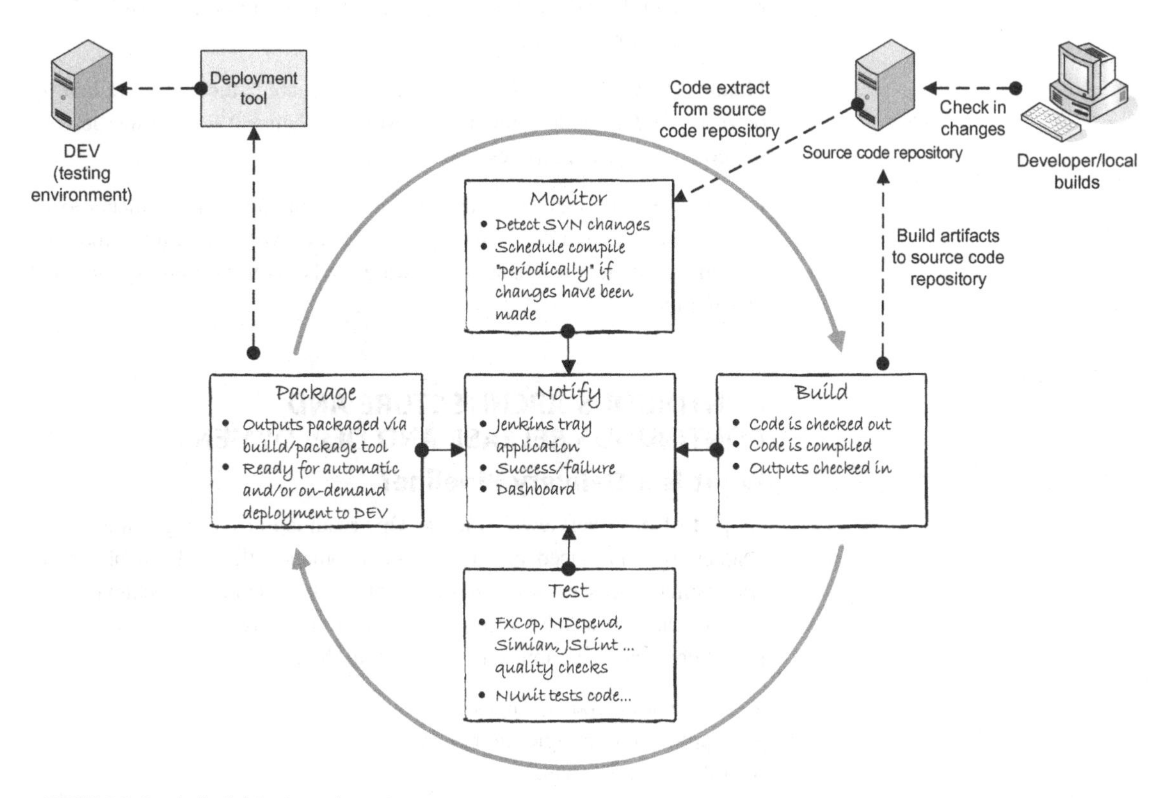

■ **FIGURE 5.5** Sample detailed Continuous Integration process.

What Are the Benefits of Continuous Integration?

The team in our case study discovers that leveraging Continuous Integration provides a number of benefits compared with a traditional approach when source code changes are compiled, integrated, and tested on a less frequent basis (typically once a week or less often).

They are now able to detect software integration problems early, which means that the problems are fixed continuously with no last-minute scramble to do so before a major version of the software is being prepared for release.

In addition, developers get immediate feedback on the quality, functionality, and even system-wide impact of the code they are writing. Providing immediate feedback is essential to the Continuous Architecture approach.

Also, immediate and automated unit testing of changes takes place as part of the Continuous Integration process. Immediate architecture, design, and code quality validation checks take place as part of the compilation, build, and deployment process. (Please refer to Chapter 6 for more details on these techniques.)

Finally, the Continuous Integration process enables the early availability of an up-to-date build (including latest code changes) for testing, demonstration, or release purposes.

In a nutshell, the team was able to make significant improvements to its software release and deployment process with a very small investment by combining some open source software tools with existing vendor and internal tools.

CONTINUOUS ARCHITECTURE AND CONTINUOUS RELEASE AND DEPLOYMENT

What Is a Delivery Pipeline?

As part of our overview of the DevOps roadmap at the beginning of this chapter, we introduced the concept of automating the build, deployment, and testing processes as much as possible. A key element in achieving this is to implement a delivery pipeline, which is a single path to production for all changes to an application, including the following items:

- Application code changes
- Application configuration changes
- Infrastructure changes
- Environment changes

- Database structure (schema) changes
- Business rules changes (if a Rules Engine is being used)
- Messaging or integration middleware changes

The goal of the delivery pipeline is to implement standardized processes for building, deploying, and testing applications. Ideally, an effective delivery pipeline should include the following components:

1. Version control tool
2. Continuous Integration process and tools
3. A self-service, automated deployment toolset
4. A self-service, automated testing toolset

From an infrastructure perspective, the deployment toolset provides the capability to automate the provisioning of environments. To achieve this goal, different infrastructure techniques are available, including server, storage, and network virtualization and cloud-based approaches (Infrastructure as a Service [IaaS] and Platform as a Service [PaaS]).

Figure 5.6 depicts the various components of a delivery pipeline.

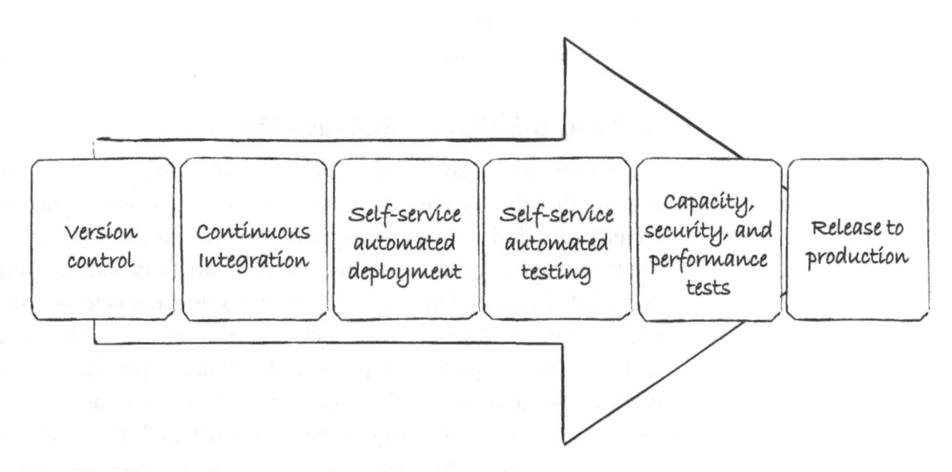

■ **FIGURE 5.6** A simplified delivery pipeline.

In addition, a delivery pipeline provides the following capabilities:

- Visibility to the team of the risk associated with application changes
- Self-service capabilities for deployment and testing: The developers are in control of all aspects of the deployment and testing processes.

- Status of applications currently in each environment (test, preproduction, production)
- Change traceability of all application changes, including application code changes, application configuration changes, infrastructure changes, environment changes, database structure (schema) changes, and business rules changes (if a rules engine is being used), integration and middleware changes.

When a delivery pipeline is used, each change to the application is systematically validated at every step of the deployment process to ensure that it can be released. These validations are effected using a series of automated tests. Candidate changes that successfully pass the tests are placed in a "release queue" for deployment to test, preproduction, and production environments.

A delivery pipeline is a key component of the Continuous Delivery process, and the architect needs to ensure that it is properly architected, designed, and implemented to meet the team's requirements by leveraging *Principle 5: Architect for build, test, and deploy.* As with any aspect of Continuous Architecture, quality attribute requirements are especially important, especially if a decision is made to use a vendor tool to implement this component.

Making a Software Release Decision

In the Continuous Architecture approach—just like in Agile development and in the Continuous Delivery process—we consider requirements, architecture, design, and other specification documents as living artifacts. The team continues to iterate through those artifacts until the software is delivered, and therefore they are never really "complete"—and they do not receive "approvals" or "sign-offs." They can—and they should—be reviewed by the project or product stakeholders periodically to ensure that the system being developed meets expectations. However, as the saying goes, "The map is not the territory." From a Continuous Architecture perspective, we believe that the architecture is best reflected in the system in production and not in any models or documents describing it. Reviewing an architecture document is not the same as reviewing the architecture. Because the team is delivering continuously, the actual output should be reviewed as soon as feasible instead of reviewing the artifacts that are a proxy for the real product.

The traditional "software release approval" process does not work well in the context of the Continuous Delivery process. There are a number of ways to improve the software release process to implement continuous delivery, and we will briefly describe the following three approaches from an architecture viewpoint:

- Team-wide consensus
- Testers as gatekeepers
- Continuous deployment

Team-Wide Consensus

Continuous Delivery requires a different approach to software release than classic software releases. One way to implement this revised approach is to make the release decision by consensus, such as when the release decision is made by a vote of the participants in the stories to be implemented. Or the combined team could also decide by vote when the application is ready to move to production—anything from simple majority to unanimous agreement. Giving the architect the right to veto the software release decision if she or he believes that technical risks have not been addressed properly, or that the architecture has not been implemented satisfactorily, can ensure architectural quality requirements are met. In practice, this works best for small teams.

Quality Assurance as Gatekeeper

One way to defer the software release decision is to make Quality Assurance responsible for it. This approach may seem to be the easiest option to implement in most organizations, but it may not be the most effective. First, it assumes that the IT organization still includes a Quality Assurance group separate from application development. As explained in the callout "The Quality Assurance Group in a Continuous Delivery World," many companies have eliminated their formal Quality Assurance organizations and have moved the testing function back to the developers. This approach positions the Quality Assurance organization as the "process police," which goes against the culture of collaboration that is at the foundation of the DevOps process. It may also not be what Quality Assurance wants to do. Finally, we believe that the architect should have the right to veto the software release decision if necessary, as explained in the section "Team-Wide Consensus."

Continuous Deployment

The goal of Continuous Deployment is to shrink the time to market of software development by asking, "What would it take to release to production with every commit?" This approach is being used by companies such as Facebook and Twitter. It implies that the combined development, testing, and operations team needs to have code that is near production ready every time a significant change is made to the application, which is easier said than done.

Some of the techniques used by those companies include deploying code to production "dark" (not executing) and then activating it over time with the use of configuration rules. These techniques may also include having two production environments, the "live" environment and the "model office" environment. New code is first deployed in the "model office" environment and submitted to a final round of testing. Assuming that this testing is successful, the two environments are switched—the "model" office becomes "live" and vice versa.

Needless to say, the Continuous Deployment approach requires a strong architecture oversight and team discipline to make sure that a release does not degrade the quality or value realized by customers or the benefits realized by customers. (Please refer to Chapter 6 for a discussion of some of the tools that can be used for this purpose.) This approach is also much more suitable for systems of engagement than for systems of record. In the case of systems of record, financial loss can result if something does not work right. If someone's personal financial information gets shared with the wrong person, the result could be catastrophic.

Which approach is best? The answer depends on organizational culture and IT context. The three approaches presented here are examples; the right one needs to be tailored to each individual situation. The key is to realize that the traditional software release approval process is not compatible with Continuous Delivery and to involve the whole team, including architects, developers, testers, and operations specialists, to design an appropriate process.

CONTINUOUS ARCHITECTURE AND CONTINUOUS TESTING

What Is Continuous Testing?

Continuous testing uses automated approaches to significantly improve the speed of testing by taking a so-called "shift-left" approach, which integrates the Quality Assurance and development phases. This approach may include a set of automated testing workflows, which can be combined with analytics and metrics to provide a clear, fact-based picture of the quality of the software being delivered. This approach is illustrated in Figure 5.7.

Leveraging a continuous testing approach provides project teams with feedback on the quality of the software that they are building. It also allows them to test earlier and with greater coverage by removing testing

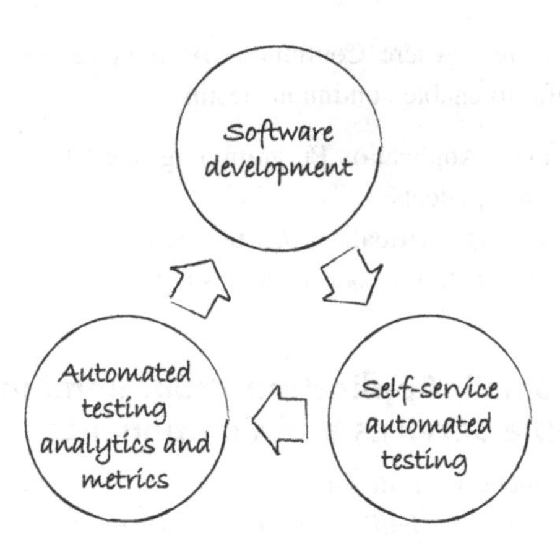

■ **FIGURE 5.7** Sample automated testing approach.

bottlenecks such as access to shared testing environments and having to wait for the User Interface to stabilize. For example, test environments hosted on the mainframe typically need to be scheduled in advance, and a simple test scripting issue may cause significant delays by causing a test to fail, to miss its testing window, and to be rescheduled at a later date when the test environment becomes available again.

Some of the benefits of continuous testing are as follows:

- Shift testing activities to the "left" of the Software Development Life Cycle and integrate them into software development activities.
- Integrate the testing, development, and operations teams in each step of the Software Development Life Cycle.
- Automate testing as much as possible to continuously test key capabilities being delivered.
- Provide business partners with early and continuous feedback on the capabilities being delivered.
- Remove test environment availability bottlenecks so that those environments are continuously available.
- Actively and continuously manage quality across the whole delivery pipeline.

How Can We Architect for Continuous Testing?

Continuous testing relies on automating deployment and testing processes as much as possible and ensuring that every component of the application can be tested as soon as it is developed—an approach referred to as "shifting left" testing. We discussed some techniques for automating deployment in the previous section in this chapter, and we will discuss some of the techniques for "shifting left" testing as well as automating testing in this section.

There are three areas where Continuous Architecture practices may be especially helpful to enable continuous testing:

- Designing small, Application Programming Interface (API)-testable services and components
- Leveraging a service virtualization approach
- Architecting test data for continuous testing

Designing Small, Application Programming Interface (API)-Testable Services and Components

As previously mentioned in Chapter 1 as part of the discussion of *Principle 5: Architect for build, test, and deploy*, services need to be fully tested independently of the other components of the applications. The goal here is to fully test each service as it is built, so that there are very few unpleasant surprises when the services are put together when the application is assembled as part of the integration testing process.

This is best achieved by doing the following:

1. Architecting, designing, and implementing small, Application Programming Interface (API)-testable services
2. Keeping coupling of components to an absolute minimum (remember *Principle 4: Architect for change—leverage "the power of small"* and the robustness principle; as explained in Chapter 2, the robustness principle, also known as Postel's law, is defined as "Be conservative in what you do, be liberal in what you accept from others")
3. Avoiding putting business logic in hard to test areas such as the messaging infrastructure

The key question for an architect following the Continuous Architecture approach when creating a new service should be: "Can this service be easily and fully tested as a stand-alone unit?"

Service Virtualization

Service virtualization is defined as follows:

> *In software engineering, service virtualization is a method to emulate the behavior of specific components in heterogeneous component-based applications such as API-driven applications, cloud-based applications and service-oriented architectures. It is used to provide software development and QA/testing teams access to dependent system components that are needed to exercise an application under test (AUT), but are unavailable or difficult-to-access for development and testing purposes. With the behavior of*

the dependent components "virtualized," testing and development can proceed without accessing the actual live components.[6,7,8]

Modern applications such as the "WebShop" system include numerous components and services. These components and services may be developed by different teams working on different timeframes, and waiting for every service to be fully ready in order to test would defeat the purpose of Continuous Delivery because it would push testing to the end of the project.

Leveraging service virtualization is a very effective approach to enable testing of applications when not all of the services are yet available or when one of the testing environments (e.g., a mainframe testing environment) is in high demand and needs to be scheduled in advance.

Service virtualization gives developers and testers a way to deal with this. Simulations of services can be quickly created and used to "shift left" integration testing back into the early development and test cycles. Overall, this approach significantly reduces risk and cuts release times.

How does service virtualization work? Let's return to the case study discussed in the first section of this chapter. The team wants to implement a continuous testing approach. Unfortunately, the "WebShop" application relies on a number of back-end services that are hosted on a mainframe. Testing time on the mainframe is in high demand and needs to be reserved in advance, which conflicts with the continuous testing approach.

To resolve this issue, the team decides to leverage a vendor's service virtualization tool to test the service tier of the "WebShop" system without accessing the mainframe-based back-end services. They use the service virtualization tool to create a virtual service by analyzing its service interface definition (inbound/outbound messages), as well as its runtime behavior. After the virtual service has been created, it can be deployed to the team's distributed test environments and used continuously to test the "WebShop" application. Figure 5.8 depicts at a high level how this process works.

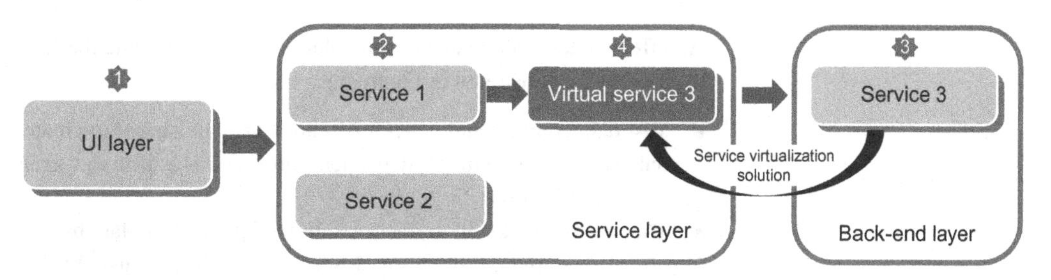

■ **FIGURE 5.8** Testing the "WebShop" application with a virtual service.

The testing process can be broken down into the following components:

1. The User Interface layer of "WebShop" invokes Service 1 in the Service Layer. This layer is implemented on a distributed infrastructure.
2. Service 1 calls Service 3 in the back-end layer. That layer is implemented on a mainframe-based infrastructure.
3. The team uses the service virtualization tool to create a distributed, virtualized version of Service 3.
4. Virtual Service 3 is implemented on the distributed infrastructure. The team is now able to run a wide range of tests (including performance tests) without having to involve the mainframe.

Architecting Test Data for Continuous Testing

Having a robust and fully automated test data management solution in place is a prerequisite for continuous testing, and the solution needs to be properly architected as part of the Continuous Architecture approach. Copying a production database to create test data without masking sensitive fields is not a good way to generate test data, and recreating test data from scratch for every series of tests is extremely inefficient, especially if this is done without the benefit of an automated tool.

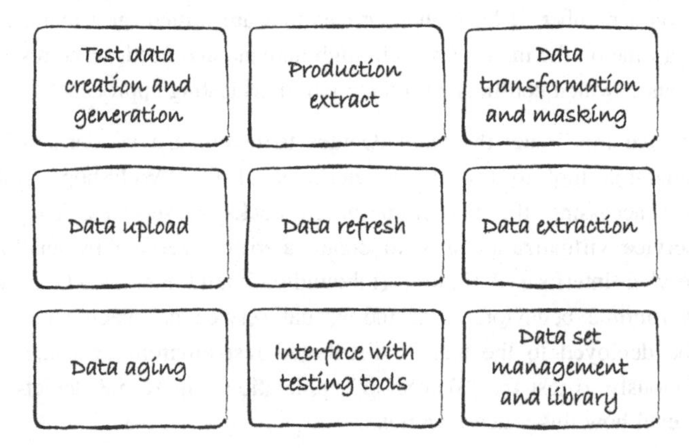

■ FIGURE 5.9 Representative test data management capabilities.

An effective test data management solution needs to provide the following capabilities, as illustrated in Figure 5.9:

- Test data creation and generation capability: the ability to create new, bulk sets of data with all dependent information as if it was generated by the application
- The ability to take an extract or subset of production data based on ad hoc or predefined criteria, mask sensitive fields, and install it in a test

environment while preserving referential integrity. The last point is the hard part: Sensitive fields need to be masked in a way that preserves the original linkages between the data. For example, if an account number value needs to be masked and replaced by another unrelated value, every account number reference within the database needs to be masked with the same value.

- Data transformation and masking capability that satisfy audit requirements such as traceability of updates. It may be helpful to include data masking capabilities for popular file formats such as Extended Markup Language (XML) or Comma Separated Values (CSV) because some test data may be generated in those formats. In addition to data masking, some data manipulation features may be useful, for example, the ability to apply nulls to a specific column of data. It may also be useful to have the capability to add custom data masking algorithms to the tool if required. Finally, it should be possible to run an automated comparison between the premasked data and the masked data to ensure that there was no data loss and there are no data integrity issues created by the masking process.
- Data upload capability: a process for uploading the extracted, masked data into a test bed with integrity. This process should include insert, edit, update, and delete functions.
- Data refresh capability: a periodic process of clearing the test data from the test bed and loading another set of fresh data.
- Data extraction and subsetting capability, which is the ability to create smaller copies of production data based on predefined criteria.
- Data aging capability, which is a technique in which data is altered to match necessary conditions by seeding the data and making it flow through specific processes, or simulating periods of time.
- Ability to create or extract test data and interface with testing tools and third-party applications.
- Data set management and library capabilities which enable management of multiple data sets including ability to archive and version.

THE QUALITY ASSURANCE GROUP IN A CONTINUOUS DELIVERY WORLD

Several companies, including Pivotal Labs and Microsoft,[9] have eliminated their formal Quality Assurance groups and moved the testing function back to the developers. These companies believe that moving the testing function back to the developers together with the appropriate automated tools to deploy and test software empowers them and enables them to produce higher quality software. When developers are responsible for testing their software and supporting it in production, they become concerned with how hard their applications are to deploy, test, and run, not just with how quickly they can write software.

However, this approach may be too radical for some companies, and we believe that there is still a role for Quality Assurance groups in a Continuous Delivery world. The key is to ensure that the testing group collaborates closely with development and operations as part of the DevOps process.

According to Bret Pettichord's 2007 Schools of Software Testing talk,[10] testers can be grouped into the following five "schools":

- Analytic school: sees testing as rigorous and technical with many proponents in academia
- Standard school: sees testing as a way to measure progress

CONTINUOUS ARCHITECTURE AND HYBRID CLOUD DEPLOYMENT

Why Use a Cloud Infrastructure for Continuous Delivery?

From a Continuous Architecture perspective, using a cloud infrastructure (see definition in the Glossary) provides several key benefits. The most

with emphasis on cost and repeatable standards
- Quality school: emphasizes process, policing developers, and acting as the gatekeeper
- Context-driven school: emphasizes people, seeking bugs that stakeholders care about (Pettichord aligns himself with this school)
- Agile school: uses testing to prove that development is complete; emphasizes automated testing

Testing groups aligned with the Agile or the context-driven schools are likely to be the most supportive of the Continuous Delivery process; testing groups aligned with the three other schools may have a challenge adapting to that process. When testers act as gatekeepers as emphasized in the "quality school," they negatively impact the collaboration among development, operations, and testing, which is at the core of the "DevOps" process.

Please refer to Pettichord's 2002 article[11] for a discussion of how positioning the testing group in the "process police" role may generate confrontation and could degrade relationships with development and operations.

important of these benefits is the ability to support the development, deployment, scaling, and updating of applications without having to deal with the underlying cost and complexity of hardware, software, and middleware. This capability is provided by a specific type of cloud computing service known as "PaaS." (Please refer to Chapter 10 for an overview of the "As a Service Family.") This cloud platform is defined as follows:

> *Platform as a service (PaaS) is a category of cloud computing services that provides a platform allowing customers to develop, run and manage Web applications without the complexity of building and maintaining the infrastructure typically associated with developing and launching an application.*[12,13,14,15]

Infrastructure autoscaling is an especially important feature offered by PaaS cloud platforms to applications running on those platforms.

A PaaS cloud service can be delivered in three ways:

1. As a **public** PaaS cloud service from a provider, in which the consumer controls the application software layer, and the provider provides the networks, servers, storage, and other services to host the consumer's application
2. As a **private** PaaS cloud service, in which the software is installed in private data centers and managed by internal IT departments
3. As a **hybrid** PaaS cloud service, which is a combination of the previous two models

The third model (hybrid model) is the most flexible and the most effective for supporting Continuous Delivery because it enables nonproduction workloads to instantly provision if necessary additional infrastructure that may not be available on the premises. Most production workloads, especially in the financial services industry, are expected to reside on private cloud infrastructures for the foreseeable future. However, targeted production workloads could be run on public cloud infrastructure, assuming that intellectual property and data security concerns can be properly addressed.

Guidelines for Cloud Readiness

From an architecture viewpoint, it is very important to architect and design applications for cloud readiness. The guiding principle in architecting these applications is to loosely couple the application and its infrastructure. Any organization that has gone through an operating system conversion such as converting from Microsoft XP to Microsoft Windows 7 knows how expensive it is to remediate applications that are tightly coupled to the infrastructure and how these applications can turn a simple, straightforward project into a massive endeavor.

The following guidelines were established as a result of a number of large-scale computing projects, and they directly apply to cloud computing. Please note that their objective is to decouple the application layer from the infrastructure and that by doing so, they significantly reduce the "technical debt" (see Glossary) of the IT organization.

1. Externalize and standardize application configuration: The application configuration should not be part of the application code and should be standardized (i.e., the configuration technique should not be application specific).
2. Scale horizontally not vertically: Applications should scale by using more servers, not bigger servers.
3. Eliminate operating system use: Applications should not be "hard wired" to the operating system. They should make no assumptions about which operating system or operating system version they are running on.
4. Do not hard code to infrastructure: Applications should not be tightly coupled with the infrastructure. Applications should have no knowledge of server, storage, or network names (either physical or logical).
5. Architect for failure: Applications and their services should anticipate failures (including those caused by unreliable infrastructure) and be able to recover from them.
6. Tune applications for minimal resource usage: Applications and services should not waste infrastructure resources by implementing inefficient logic.
7. Rely less on proprietary technology: There is a cost in using proprietary technology. For example, using the proprietary features of a vendor database makes conversion to another database much more difficult. Similarly, using vendor-specific extensions to the Java Messaging Service (JMS) standard creates tight coupling of the application with the vendor software. Avoid using proprietary technology if at all possible.
8. Do not make assumptions on runtime geography: An application running in a public cloud may end up running in a totally different time zone from the one used by the IT organization that built it. Being aware of this will avoid unexpected results when an

ARCHITECTING FOR FAILURE: SHOULD RESILIENCY BE BUILT IN THE INFRASTRUCTURE VERSUS IN THE APPLICATION?

Traditionally, architects rely on the infrastructure to provide most of the resiliency needed for the applications that they are designing. For example, database vendors such as Oracle offer strong resiliency capabilities in their offerings. However, these capabilities come at a cost in terms of proprietary software and proprietary hardware (e.g., Oracle's Exadata systems). In addition, relying on these capabilities increases the coupling of applications with the infrastructure. To make applications "cloud ready," architects need to start thinking about building resiliency in the application instead of relying on proprietary vendor offerings to achieve this. Fortunately, a lot of cloud offerings (e.g., Pivotal Cloud Foundry) offer some resiliency capabilities, but it is always best to architect for running an application on the "least common denominator" infrastructure, which means architecting applications and services to anticipate failures and to recover from them.

application is moved from a private cloud to a public one or from a primary data center to a disaster recovery data center that happens to be located in a different part of the world. This also implies that there should be no assumptions on timezones in the application code. Using Coordinated Universal Time (UTC) would enable this.

9. Use stateless and asynchronous application architectures: Stateless and asynchronous architectures scale much better than stateful and synchronous architectures. Using them when possible will eliminate issues when the load applied to the application suddenly surges because of an unexpected event (e.g., a weather-related catastrophe impacting the claim processing systems of an insurance company).
10. Partition sensitive and confidential data: Sensitive and confidential data need to be carefully protected and most likely should not be stored in a public cloud in an unencrypted format. Segregating it from regular data makes the process of handling the data much easier.

We offer these guidelines as a point of departure. Additional guidelines may be found at "The Twelve-Factor App" web site (12factor.net). Each company may want to build on these guidelines to create its own cloud readiness checklist. However, we have found these basic guidelines to be very effective at improving the quality, robustness, performance, and flexibility of most applications, whether they are to be hosted in a cloud infrastructure or not.

SUMMARY

In this chapter, we described how the Continuous Architecture discipline can be leveraged to implement an effective and efficient Continuous Delivery process and enable an IT organization to adapt and respond quickly to business needs. The goal of Continuous Architecture in the Continuous Delivery project life cycle is to speed up the software development and delivery process by systematically applying an architecture perspective and discipline to each element of the process. We described how to bring an architecture perspective on the following six key components of the process in this chapter:

- The "DevOps" process
- Continuous feedback and monitoring
- Continuous Integration
- Continuous release and deployment
- Continuous testing
- Hybrid cloud deployment

This was done by leveraging the Continuous Architecture principles, specifically *Principle 3: Delay design decisions until they are absolutely necessary; Principle 4: Architect for change—leverage "the power of small"; Principle 5: Architect for build, test, and deploy;* and *Principle 6: Model the organization after the design of the system.*

The next chapter in this book describes different techniques and approaches for validating the architecture and verifying that it fulfills its requirements before the bulk of the system is built.

ENDNOTES

1. Adapted from Wikipedia. DevOps, <https://en.wikipedia.org/wiki/DevOps/>.
2. Loukides M. What is DevOps? O'Reilly Media; June 7, 2012.
3. Floris D, Amrit C, Daneva M. A mapping study on cooperation between information system development and operations. December 10, 2014. <http://eprints.eemcs.utwente.nl/25415/01/A_Mapping_Study_on_DevOps-Erich-Amrit-Daneva-PROFES2014.pdf>.
4. Sharma S, Coyle D. DevOps for dummies. 2nd IBM limited edition, John Wiley & Sons; 2015. <http://www-01.ibm.com/software/rational/dummiesbooks/devops/>.
5. Humble J. There's no such thing as a "DevOps team." Continuous Delivery, October 19, 2012. <http://continuousdelivery.com/2012/10/theres-no-such-thing-as-a-devops-team/>.
6. Service Virtualization. <https://en.wikipedia.org/wiki/Service_virtualization>.
7. Allen J. Service virtualization as an alternative to mocking. eBizQ, April 22, 2013.
8. Lawton G. Service virtualization arises to meet services testing obstacles. SearchSOA, May 15, 2012.
9. Bass D. Microsoft CEO Satya Nadella looks to a future beyond Windows. Bloomberg Businessweek, February 19, 2015. <http://www.bloomberg.com/news/articles/2015-02-19/microsoft-ceo-nadella-looks-to-future-beyond-windows/>.
10. Pettichord B. Schools of Software Testing, March 2007. https://www.prismnet.com/~wazmo/papers/four_schools.pdf.
11. Pettichord B. Don't become the quality police. Stickyminds, June 26, 2002. <http://www.stickyminds.com/article/dont-become-quality-police/>.
12. Platform as a Service. <https://en.wikipedia.org/wiki/Platform_as_a_service>.
13. Butler B. PaaS primer: what is platform as a service and why does it matter? Network World, February 11, 2013.
14. Understanding the cloud computing stack: SaaS, PaaS, IaaS. Rackspace support, October 22, 2013. <http://www.rackspace.com/knowledge_center/whitepaper/understanding-the-cloud-computing-stack-saas-paas-iaas>.
15. Chang WY, Abu-Amara H, Sanford JF. Transforming enterprise cloud services. London: Springer; 2010, pp. 55–56.

Chapter 6

Validating the Architecture

Nothing is as empowering as real-world validation, even if it's for failure.

—Steven Pressfield, *The War of Art: Break Through the Blocks & Win Your Inner Creative Battles*

This chapter discusses various approaches for validating the architecture of a software application within the Continuous Architecture approach. There are four primary reasons for validating architectures:

1. Architectures are the foundation of software systems. Inadequate, poorly designed or carelessly assembled architectures will cause a software system to fail, either during development or, in the worst possible case, after the system has been deployed into production.
2. Validating the architecture early in a Software Development Life Cycle (SDLC) makes a lot of economic sense. Fixing defects early in the Software Development Life Cycle is much less painful and costly than fixing them later or even fixing them after the system has been deployed in production.
3. Architecture validations also encourage communication among the project stakeholders. According to Continuous Architecture, the communication and collaboration aspects of architecture are just as important as developing it. Architecture evaluations help significantly with the collaboration of the architecture.
4. Conway's law (see discussion of Principle 6 in Chapter 2) implies that the structure of a project or an organization determines its architecture to a large extent, and this in turn means that a poorly organized project team will result in a poorly designed architecture. Validating the architecture tells us whether we have the right team structure.

We believe that the architecture should be validated continuously throughout the Software Development Life Cycle. Assessing it at the beginning of a project is simply not enough, and waiting for unpleasant surprises to do damage control is an ineffective strategy.

The techniques used to validate architectures are often grouped into two broad categories:

- **Qualitative approaches**, which include meeting-based architecture validations that can be conducted by either external or internal resources. Both internal and external approaches use the same review techniques, such as questionnaire-driven reviews, scenario-based reviews, and decision-based reviews. (We will briefly discuss these techniques later in this chapter.) We think internal validation of the architecture is better than validations conducted by external resources. We also strongly favor peer reviews over reviews run by a central organization such an Enterprise Architecture group.
- **Quantitative approaches**, which attempt to predict the application system's behavior before it is fully built (or modeled) and try to answer questions about Quality Attribute Requirements (QARs) such as performance or scalability. Quantitative approaches assume that some part of the system has been already built in order to calculate metrics, and therefore are well suited to Continuous Delivery. Quantitative approaches produce a set of metrics used to evaluate a software system. For example, complexity metrics suggest areas where modifiability is poor or errors are likely to occur. Performance metrics help identify the presence of bottlenecks. In addition to running tests against the application code delivered so far, automated architecture validation tools (e.g., the CAST Application Intelligence Platform [AIP]) can be used to calculate a set of standard metrics by scanning code. Other tools validate architecture and design models against the code delivered by the development team. For example, Linaro has developed an automated open source testing system called LAVA (Linaro Automated Validation Architecture).[1]

The most effective way is to combine qualitative and quantitative approaches. We recommend using quantitative techniques such as automated tests run against the software components delivered so far to supplement qualitative approaches, for example, to answer questions such as: "How do we really know that the performance of the system will be acceptable?"

This chapter describes how to validate architectures using our Continuous Architecture "toolbox." We will introduce architecture validation concepts in the following manner:

- Define what we mean by architecture validation.
- Focus on when we need to conduct architecture validation (we will introduce a case study).
- Discuss the roles required in an architecture validation.

- Detail how we can conduct architecture validations by including some industry-recognized techniques such as questionnaire-driven approaches, scenario-based approaches, and decision-based approaches.

WHAT DO WE MEAN BY "ARCHITECTURE VALIDATION"?

An "**Architecture Validation**" is a structured process conducted by a team of architects, designers, and other qualified IT specialists. Architecture validation sessions can range in complexity from a narrow, focused evaluation conducted by a small technical team with specific governance roles to a broad and deep evaluation conducted by a collective of technical experts drawn from across the organization. They all share a requirement for a well-defined approach, review etiquette, and ground rules. All participants must be aware of the purpose of the process and how that purpose will be achieved.

Architecture validation sessions differ from code reviews in their objectives:

> *The code review is designed to answer, "Does this code successfully implement its specification?" The architecture validation is designed to answer, "Will the computer system to be built from this architecture satisfy its business goals?"*[2]

Code reviews are concerned mainly with the conformance of source code against a set of specifications and are designed to answer clearly defined questions. Architecture validation sessions, on the other hand, are concerned about the conformance of a system to a set of business goals that are frequently not well defined, at least initially. As a result, architecture validation sessions nearly always have to gain a better understanding of the business goals and quality attribute requirements of the software architecture being examined.

Architecture and design decisions are constantly being executed when an application system is being delivered, which results in trade-offs being continuously made. As a result, the validation of the architecture has to be conducted in a continuous manner. An initial architecture validation is performed after some initial architecture decisions have been made as part of an "architectural runway"[3] phase if an Agile methodology is used. After the first session, the architecture validation sessions continue throughout the delivery life cycle by running a series of "mini peer validations" or architecture heath checks to catch any emerging architecture issue as soon as it manifests itself and deal with it quickly. We will discuss later in this chapter how to conduct these architecture health checks quickly and inexpensively by combining qualitative and quantitative techniques. This approach will prevent objections that would stand in the way of conducting reviews as often as they are needed.

Architecture Validation Objectives

The overall objectives of an architecture validation session are to ensure that the architecture of the application system will support the achievement of the system's business and technical objectives. It must also exist in a form that is easy to understand by the diverse stakeholders of the system. This often means that it conforms to the architectural principles and standards established by the organization and that it deals reasonably and appropriately with foreseeable business and technical risks. In practical terms, this means that quality attribute requirements such as performance, usability, scalability, resiliency, and cost effectiveness have been adequately addressed and that the key architecture and design decisions are compatible with both the functional and the quality attribute requirements.

Architecture Validation Benefits

The architecture validation process identifies previously unseen risks and evolves the maturity of the application, informed by defined standards, reference architectures, and technical strategies. The collaborative approach used in the validation sessions improves the overall quality of the system and can result in faster delivery by catching design errors earlier in the life cycle.

Architecture validation also promotes knowledge sharing across the enterprise. Architecture validation sessions disseminate good software delivery practices within the enterprise because the review teams document these practices for all projects being reviewed.

Finally, architecture validation sessions enable cross-organizational transparency within the enterprise and better management of software suppliers across the enterprise and can identify areas in which IT teams need more training, such as information security and performance.

> *Since 1988, we've conducted more than 700 project reviews. Starting with AT&T, architecture reviews have grown across all our companies. We estimate that projects of 100,000 non-commentary source lines of code have saved an average of US$1 million each by identifying and resolving problems early.*[4]

Architecture Peer Validation Versus External Architecture Validation

As mentioned earlier in this chapter, architecture validations can be conducted by either internal or external resources. However, we believe that more benefits can be achieved by internal architecture validations conducted by peers of the project team members (we will call this type of reviews "architecture peer validations" in this book) than by external validations or by validations conducted by a central organization.

If the IT organization is unfamiliar with this approach or lacks trained resources, it may make sense to obtain external expertise to perform an initial architecture validation. This validation session should be viewed as a training session, with a prime objective of training the internal team on conducting subsequent sessions. In addition to and ideally before that initial training session, internal IT resources should be formally trained on architecture validation techniques so that they will be able to handle subsequent architecture validation sessions without external help.

Architecture peer validations can be thought of as an extension of the "pair programming" technique, at a larger scale. Leveraging pair programming ensures that the application code being produced is of better quality than using traditional approaches because two sets of eyes constantly validate the software being produced. Similarly, architecture peer validations ensure that the architecture of a system being developed is of better quality than a similar architecture developed without the benefit of a validation process.

WHEN DO WE NEED TO VALIDATE?

How can we "continuously" evaluate architectures in Continuous Architecture, and what is the best approach for each stage of the delivery of a project? Let's return to the case study introduced in Chapter 2 to provide an answer to this question with an example.

As you will remember from Chapter 2, an IT group in a large U.S. financial services corporation has decided to leverage the Continuous Architecture process to deliver its new "WebShop" system, a web-based system to allow prospective customers to compare their offerings with the competitions' offerings. As we saw in Chapter 3, the team has started capturing both their functional and quality attribute requirements. However, their decisions to leverage open source products such as the "MEAN" stack (see Chapter 3 for a discussion of the MEAN stack), to use JavaScript as their development language for both the User Interface and the server components, and to leverage a cloud infrastructure for development and for most of their testing have started worrying some of the IT leadership. As a result, the enterprise chief architect is asked to conduct an architecture evaluation of the system to ensure that the project is not in jeopardy.

Fortunately, the enterprise chief architect is familiar with Continuous Architecture and with the evaluation techniques we presented earlier in this chapter. She sets up a small review team with experienced architects, a trained facilitator, and a scribe. The review team is created as a peer review team by involving active architects from other project areas.

Initial Evaluation

The review team meets with the WebShop project team, and given that the project is still in the early stages, decides to focus on reviewing architecture and design decisions made so far. The WebShop team members (especially their solution architect) are skeptical of the value of this exercise and initially participate reluctantly. However, they agree to provide the review team with some documentation, including their decision log and an early draft of their Quality Attribute utility tree. They also provide a conceptual view of their proposed architecture and agree to participate in the review session together with one of their business stakeholders.

Based on the business drivers, the review team decides to focus on a small subset of Quality Attributes, including cost effectiveness, performance, and security. Using the project's architecture and design decision log, they group the decisions by Quality Attribute and update the preliminary utility tree; see Figure 6.1 for an example. They prioritize the

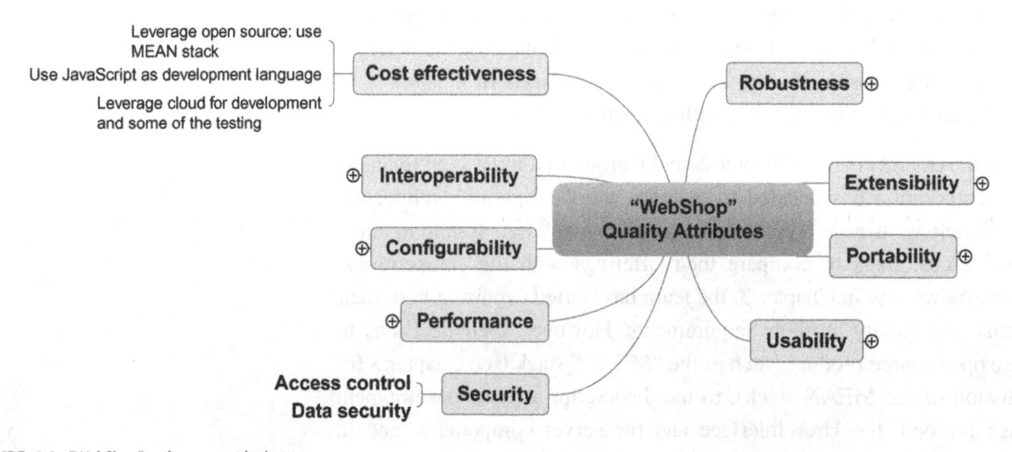

■ FIGURE 6.1 "WebShop" utility tree with decisions.

Quality Attributes using the business drivers, which then enables them to further create a list of prioritized decisions.

Using these prioritized decisions, the review team runs a short 3-hour architecture evaluation session and is able to confirm that the decisions are appropriate and do not conflict with the existing IT standards and practices. As new insights into the system emerge during the review, the solution architect and the "WebShop" project team get more comfortable with the evaluation process and realize that this is not a "finger-pointing" exercise. On the contrary, they understand that this review improves the architecture and the system that they are in the process of delivering.

For example, the review identified a potential issue with the lack of configurability of the solution, which may not meet the system's quality attribute requirements. Because the review occurred early in the Software Development Life Cycle, the project team was able to react quickly and find an appropriate solution to the problem, by externalizing some key configuration parameters in a database table. By the end of the review, the "WebShop" team members (including the solution architect) are enthusiastically participating in the process.

Continuous Evaluation

A few weeks later, the team believes that they now have a solid architecture, and they start delivering well-tested code. Their architecture and design decision log has been growing rapidly since the initial review, and they seem to have reached a point where they are not frequently adding decisions to the log. Based on their positive experience with the initial review session, the team decides that it is time for another review and meets with the enterprise chief architect and the architecture peer review team.

Given that the architecture is now fairly stable and that Quality Attributes, associated refinements, and associated scenarios have now been captured in a well-documented utility tree, the enterprise chief architect suggests running a full-day evaluation session based on a few scenarios designed to stress the architecture. The project team agrees, and they proceed with the evaluation process. As part of this evaluation, the validation team creates several tests based on the scenarios and tests the code produced so far against those scenarios.

Two key risks are discovered during the evaluation session: performance and security. As part of the analysis and tests of the scenarios associated with the Quality Attributes, the evaluation team discovers that the

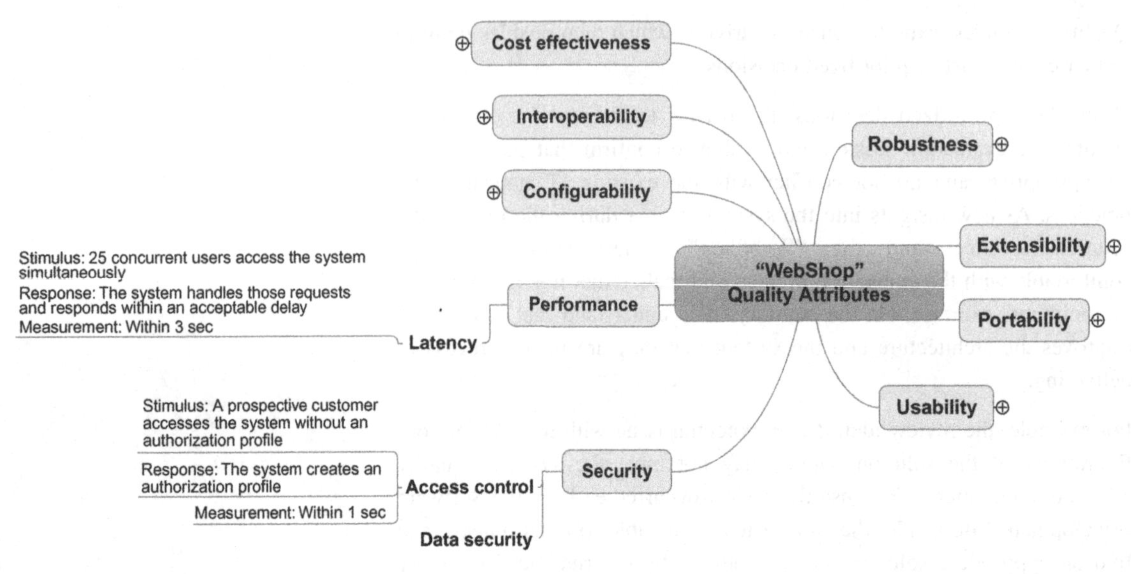
Cost effectiveness
Interoperability
Configurability
Robustness
Extensibility
"WebShop" Quality Attributes
Portability
Usability
Performance
Latency
Stimulus: 25 concurrent users access the system simultaneously
Response: The system handles those requests and responds within an acceptable delay
Measurement: Within 3 sec
Security
Access control
Data security
Stimulus: A prospective customer accesses the system without an authorization profile
Response: The system creates an authorization profile
Measurement: Within 1 sec

■ **FIGURE 6.2** "WebShop" utility tree with scenarios.

"WebShop" system may not be able to provide the expected response time with the anticipated load (Figure 6.2 shows the utility tree with the performance and latency scenario). Further discussion with the project team reveals that the architecture "sensitivity point" associated with this risk is the set of back-end services that the "mobile shopping" system is planning to use (Figure 6.3). In addition, the architecture peer review team has an extra concern: If the business stakeholders decide to add a mobile interface to the system, the usage frequency may significantly increase and exceed the scenario stimulus of 25 concurrent users accessing the system simultaneously. This in turn would cause additional stress on the back-end services, possibly causing performance issues in other systems that use the same services.

Similarly, the validation team analyzes and tests the scenarios associated with security and discovers that the security services may not be able to handle the access control requirements associated with the system. Those services were designed to control access from existing customers who have already established a security profile. However, the "mobile shopping" system is expected to be used by prospective customers without a preestablished security profile (Figure 6.2). Access control is noted as a risk, with security services as the associated sensitivity point (see Figure 6.3).

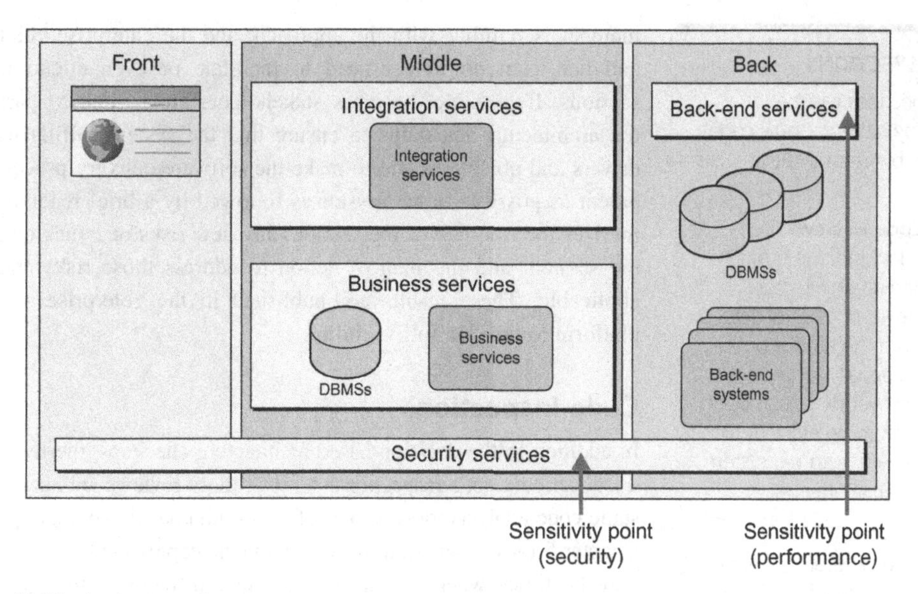

■ **FIGURE 6.3** "WebShop" architecture with sensitivity points.

Based on the feedback from the architecture validation session, the team addresses the two risks flagged by the review. They meet with the team responsible for maintaining the back-end services and jointly design some improvements that greatly increase the performance and scalability of those services. Likewise, they meet with the team responsible for maintaining the security services and negotiate the inclusion of their requirements in a future release to be delivered in time to support their delivery schedule.

Periodic Architecture Checkups

Based on the recommendation of the enterprise chief architect, the team decides to schedule periodic architecture checkups, triggered by significant additions to the architecture decision and design log.

The team monitors the decision log on at least a weekly basis and organizes a review when the team believes that one or several decisions have significantly impacted the architecture or the design of the WebShop system. These reviews can be suggested by any member of the team who thinks that the architecture or the design has significantly changed at any time. As a result, the team meets and decides whether an architecture checkup is warranted.

These architecture checkups follow a decision-based approach and include tests run against the code produced so far. By now, every team member is familiar with the approach, and the enterprise chief architect and her team no longer need to facilitate or even attend the review sessions. If possible, business stakeholders are invited to participate in the architecture checkups to ensure that the system fulfills its business drivers and objectives and to make the software delivery process as transparent as possible. Each session is followed by a brief readout that summarizes the findings of the session, any new risks or issues discovered in the session, and the plan of action to address those risks and issues if applicable. These results are published in the enterprise social media platform to provide full visibility.

CODE INSPECTIONS

Code inspections can be achieved by either manual code reviews or by using static analysis tools.

Manual Code Reviews
A code review process is much simpler than an architecture review. A team of experts gets together with the author of the code and manually inspects that code to discover defects. It is, of course, much more efficient to discover defects before a system is deployed than after deployment.

Depending on the programming language being used, a typical code inspection review would look at 200 to 400 lines of code, so a decision needs to be made before the meeting on which component needs to be manually inspected.

Static Code Analysis
Static program analysis is the analysis of computer software that is performed without actually executing programs (analysis performed on executing programs is known as dynamic analysis). In most cases the analysis is performed on some version of the source code, and in the other cases, some form of the object code. The term is usually applied to the analysis performed by an automated tool, with human analysis being called program understanding, program comprehension, or code review.[5,6]

A number of static code analysis tools are available to save time on most code reviews. Their advantage is that they are able to inspect 100% of the code, but they may not be able to find

Code Inspections

In addition to the decision-based architecture checkups, the team also conducts periodic code inspections. Most of those reviews are automated using static code analysis tools as part of the continuous deployment process (see Chapter 5 for a discussion of the continuous deployment process), but there may be times when a manual evaluation is required to supplement the static code analysis tools, for example, when a component is unusually complex or exhibits some issues when performance testing the system. These reviews are simple checklist-based validations that essentially ensure that the architecture decisions have been properly implemented in the code and that the code is well written and easy to understand.

WHO SHOULD VALIDATE?

Let's assume that an IT group similar to the one we introduced in Chapter 2 would like to continuously validate the architecture of one of their projects. Let's also assume that this IT group includes a number of architects, designers, and developers familiar with the Continuous Architecture approach. Who should participate in the architecture validation process, and which skills should they have to effectively contribute to the process?

One option is to have a central authoritative group such as an enterprise architecture group do the validation, but a better option in our opinion is to perform peer validations. We know of a financial services company where all the senior architects and developers were pulled from their normal assignments for a period of 3 weeks to peer review the top 100 projects. This was an intense effort and worthwhile because of the value the organization got out of this exercise. For example, they were able to identify and to remedy several areas where enterprise services could be effectively leveraged.

The Validation Team

It is important to have the correct team structure and balance to ensure a successful validation exercise. A sample validation team consists of four architects experienced in this process, a facilitator, and a scribe (Figure 6.4). All of the participants are peers of the project team members. They are able to secure a trained facilitator with experience running similar sessions, as well as a dedicated scribe who will document the validation sessions and help produce a brief report summarizing all the findings.

every defect that an expert would, assuming the expert had time to inspect 100% of the code. Static code analysis tools can be either open source or proprietary. Please see Wikipedia[7] for a list of tools available for each commonly used programming language.

An experienced facilitator keeps validation sessions on track, avoids "rat holes," and ensures that as much value as possible is obtained from the evaluation session. A dedicated scribe documents important aspects of the session and provides invaluable input into the validation readout session.

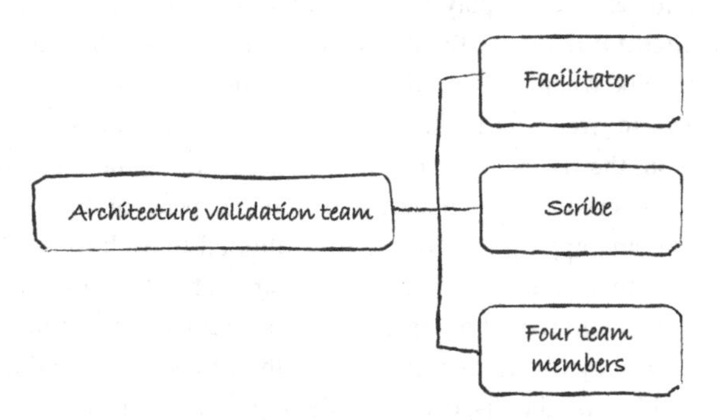

■ **FIGURE 6.4** Sample architecture validation team structure.

After it is formed, the validation team meets with a subset of the project team and agrees with them on the scope of the architecture validation effort, the number of validation sessions necessary, and the schedule of these validation sessions. Because one of the key objectives of the validation process is to verify the alignment of the architecture with the business goals, the team ensures that key business stakeholders will be in attendance for the validation sessions.

The team also understands the importance of selling the participants on the value of the validation effort. Some participants are unhappy with the fact that their system is being validated and believe that this activity is a waste of their time. Demonstrating that a system supported by an architecture that has been continuously validated is more likely to achieve its business objectives will go a long way toward convincing the participants to adopt a positive attitude. In Continuous Architecture, frequent architecture, design, and code validation steps are part of the software delivery process, and ensuring that validation steps are part of the culture is as important as conducting them.

The validation team carefully explains to all the participants the goals and the process that will be followed during the session. This is an important part of the validation process. The team members are, of course, familiar with the process, but the other participants are not. Ensuring that everyone is familiar with the process builds trusts and eliminates unpleasant surprises, for example, when a participant disrupts the process by suddenly asking, "Why are we doing this?" The team also sets expectations with the participants; for example, because session duration is limited, there usually is not sufficient time to perform detailed technical analysis.

Specific Roles

The facilitator and scribe play very important roles in the validation process. The **facilitator** guides the discussion and ensures that everyone gets a chance to talk when they need to and that the discussion does not get bogged down in irrelevant topics. To maximize the usefulness of the validation session, the facilitator makes sure that she keeps the meeting under control, that everyone participates, and that the pace of the meeting is under control and appropriate for the time allotted to each topic. She also ensures that either agreement is reached after each discussion or that the participants agree to record an open issue if agreement cannot be reached. In either case, they obtain consensus from the project team and the business stakeholders on the disposition of the topic under discussion.

Deciding whether a discussion should be allowed to continue or not is almost an art: Some discussions can reveal important risks and issues, but others may end up in a "rat hole" if allowed to continue much longer. The facilitator for this session is able to quickly distinguish between the two situations and direct the meeting accordingly. She is able to get feedback and consensus from the participants at that time. Her experience is invaluable in handling these situations.

Interruptions are kept to a minimum, and breaks are scheduled often enough for the participants to relax and have offline conversations. At times, the facilitator and scribe roles are switched to give the main facilitator a mental break.

The **scribe** records the results of each discussion, the potential risks and issues uncovered, recommendations, and potential follow-ups. The scribe also maintains a "parking lot" of items that need to be discussed and resolved at a later time. She is able to assist the main facilitator by taking over the facilitation of the meeting at times to give her a chance to relax, especially after intense discussions.

The **team members** are peers of the project team creating the application being validated. They are experienced architects and designers but are also able to design and build automated tests to supplement qualitative validations with quantitative techniques and demonstrate whether the architecture is likely to meet its quality attribute requirements.

HOW SHOULD WE VALIDATE?

There are several software architecture validation techniques available to Continuous Architecture practitioners, including the following three common industry techniques:

- **Checklist-driven architecture validation:** This technique leverages a set of questions prepared in advance by the review team.
- **Scenario-based architecture validation:** Scenarios describe specific interactions between the user of an application system and the system itself. Using this approach, the validation team tests the architecture against those scenarios that are associated with the quality attribute requirements for the system.
- **Decision-centric architecture validation:** Using this technique, the review team systematically reviews, analyzes, and records the rationale behind the architecture and design decisions made so far by the project team. These decisions are evaluated against the quality attribute requirements for the architecture of the application. Please note that in Chapter 4, we state the importance of architecture and design decisions, and therefore this approach is a good fit with the Continuous Architecture approach.

We recommend that all of the above techniques are supplemented by automated tests that exercise key aspects of the application system being validated, such as performance. Even at early stages, the "sparse" executable components built can be tested against existing criteria or scenarios.

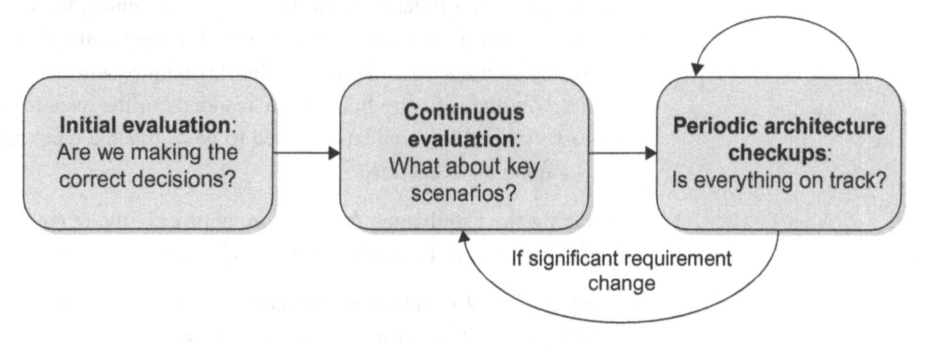

■ **FIGURE 6.5** Combining architecture validation techniques.

These techniques can be combined for and adapted to a given project, as we described in the case study and illustrate in Figure 6.5. In the case study, the validation team first used a decision-based technique for the initial validation session and then used a scenario-based technique for the second session. The team reverted to the decision-based technique for the periodic architecture checkups and used the checklist-based approach for the code reviews as well as to ensure that the system was ready for production. If requirements (either functional requirements or Quality Attributes) significantly change in the future, conducting another scenario-based validation session may become necessary in addition to the periodic architecture checkups.

We will discuss the three techniques in detail in the following sections.

The Checklist-Driven Validation

The checklist-driven approach is the simplest and the most straightforward of the three evaluation techniques[8] discussed in this chapter, and it may be the most in use today because of its simplicity. It leverages familiar concepts such as checklists and requires less training than other approaches.

The checklist contains questions that will guide the architects during the validation session and lead to additional exploration into the architecture being validated. Please note that we are using the word "checklist" loosely here because it generally implies simple yes/no responses. However, some of the questions in the architect's "checklist" need to be open ended to initiate relatively broad discussions rather than eliciting yes/no responses.

The checklist evolves over time to focus on the most important issues uncovered by the validation sessions. In our experience, these issues tend to cluster around performance and security for most commercial systems. It is very important to complement this technique with actual tests that measure how the software built so far responds to the questions from the checklist. Architecture validations need to be as much a quantitative exercise as a qualitative exercise.

Leveraging the Continuous Architecture approach, the team can organize its checklist around the two following main review categories:

1. Application of Continuous Architecture principles, especially *Principle 3: Delay design decisions until they are absolutely*

necessary; *Principle 4: Architect for Change—leverage "the power of small*; *Principle 5: Architect for build, test and deploy;* and *Principle 6: Model the organization after the design of the system*

2. Quality attribute requirements, leveraging *Principle 2: Focus on Quality Attributes, not on functional requirements.* A useful tool for organizing those requirements is the utility tree (see Chapter 3 for a discussion of the utility tree). As we saw earlier in this book, the utility tree is organized as follows:
   a. Highest level: Quality attribute requirement (performance, security, configurability, cost effectiveness, and so on)
      – Next level: Quality Attribute refinements. For example, "latency" is one of the refinements of "performance"; "access control" is one of the refinements of security.
   b. Lowest level: architecture scenarios (at least one architecture scenario per Quality Attribute refinement)

The team can use the first two levels of the utility tree to organize its checklist and ignore the lowest level (architecture scenarios) in the questionnaire-based technique. This third level will be used in scenario-based validations, discussed later in this chapter.

Figure 6.6 shows a sample utility tree with its first two levels.

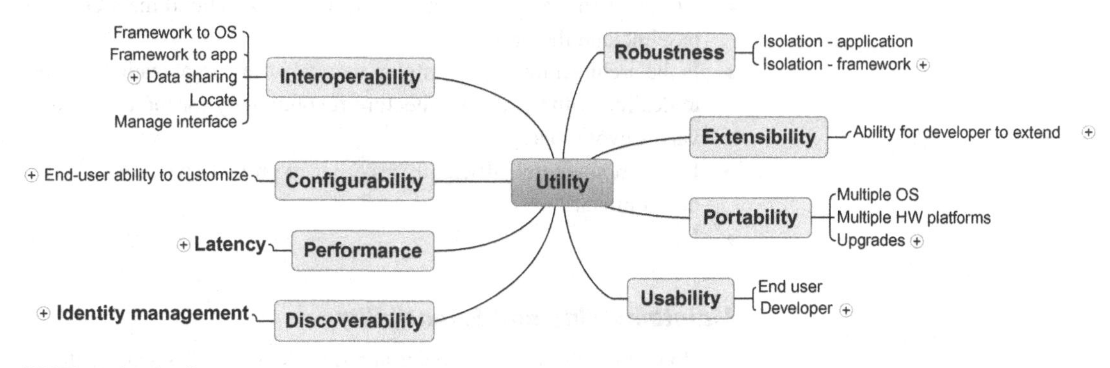

■ **FIGURE 6.6** Sample utility tree.

Over time, checklists morph into a list of important points to remember when designing an architecture and act as a practical guide to the architects. The next section shows an excerpt from a representative architecture validation checklist.

Essential Architecture Validation Checklist

Strategic and Principle Alignment

- Does the solution embody the Continuous Architecture principles?
- Is the application (or the capabilities it delivers) explicitly identified as strategic or enabling on the roadmap?
  - If not, what is the business driver for developing this application, and is this effort adequately funded?
  - Is the application or application architecture enabling from a technical perspective?
  - Does the application provide competitive market capabilities?
  - Are there any plans to replace this technology with more strategic technology in the near term?
- Will the application portfolio be easier to manage after this solution is implemented?
- Will this implementation retire a significant number of portfolio assets?
- Does the solution address all the defined business requirements?
- [...]

Cost Effectiveness

- Are there enough time, money, and resources to build the architecture baseline and the project?
- Is the architecture more complex than what the organization is used to dealing with? Is the architecture revolutionary for the organization versus evolutionary?
- Is the architecture sufficiently modular to promote parallel development?
- [...]

Maintainability and Extensibility

- How often will a change be required to the system? What are the scenarios?
- What new functionality do you anticipate adding in future versions of the system?
- How will you handle new releases of the execution platform?
- Do any components have access to the implementation details of global variables?
- Do you use decoupling mechanisms such as publish and subscribe?
- How do you handle changes in message formats?
- Were design compromises made to enhance performance?

- How many interfaces must change as a result of a change in a piece of functionality?
- [...]

Performance

- What is the expected response time for each use case, based on typical load and based on exceptional load?
- What are the average, maximum, and minimum expected response times?
- What infrastructure resources are being used (e.g., CPU, LAN, private cloud, public cloud)?
- What is the resource consumption (e.g., CPU, memory, other resources)?
- What is the expected number of concurrent sessions given a typical transaction mix?
- Are there any particularly long computations that occur when a certain state is true? Can these be run in the background?
- Are server processes single or multithreaded? If single threaded, is it a requirement for the application to function satisfactorily?
- [...]

Advantages and Challenges of the Checklist-Driven Technique

Architects do not need much training (typically 1 day or less) on how to work with checklists, and the checklists themselves are not hard to build, especially after the team has gained experience conducting validations. The validation team may be able to build on existing checklists, either obtained from consultants or available from several websites such as the Open Group's TOGAF website.[9]

Checklists work well for IT organizations that deliver similar software architectures over time such as systems with low to moderate performance requirements. They become challenging when IT groups start venturing into designing new software architectures such as systems with high performance requirements and a large number of concurrent users. In addition, checklist-centric validation sessions tend to take a significant amount of time because the review team may systematically go through each question (and run associated tests) in their checklist, regardless of the likelihood of uncovering a risk, an issue, or a recommendation.

Another challenge with this approach is associated with the psychology and sociology of architecture validations. Most project teams dislike the "evaluation" aspect of an architecture validation, and unfortunately, checklists reinforce that aspect. The objective of an architecture validation session should be for both teams (validation team and project team) to work collaboratively and jointly examine a software architecture to enhance it. The checklist-based technique may go against that objective by giving the project team the feeling that they are being graded on their work unless the review team is very careful and flexible when using their checklist.

In addition, the validation team needs to anticipate the architecture topics that they need to review when building their checklist. Starting from the Continuous Architecture principles and the utility tree narrows the possibilities, but there still is a danger of taking the review down the wrong path by using a checklist that does not fully address the challenges that the system is facing. For example, under "Performance," the checklist may contain questions related to the response time of an application's website, but the actual architecture issue may be the excessive execution time of batch processes running in the background that prevent them from returning information in a timely manner.

Scenario-Based Validation

Given some of the challenges of the checklist-based technique, several researchers and practitioners have proposed an alternative approach: using scenario-based techniques to perform architecture evaluations. The concept is fairly simple: The review team comes up with a series of scenarios that describe specific interactions between the proposed system and its stakeholders. The project team describes how the proposed system would respond to each scenario, and the review team records associated risks and issues based on their analysis of that response. In addition, the response of the system to each scenario may be quantified by running tests against the software components delivered so far.

The Software Engineering Institute (SEI) at Carnegie Mellon University has developed two scenario-based methodologies: first the Software Architecture Analysis Method (SAAM) and more recently the Architecture Tradeoff Analysis Method (ATAM).[10] We will focus on the Architecture Tradeoff Analysis Method in this section because it is the best known scenario-based evaluation approach.

A Brief Overview of the Architecture Tradeoff Analysis Method

The objective of the ATAM is to evaluate how architecture decisions impact a software system's ability to fulfill its business goals and satisfy its quality attribute requirements. Architecture Tradeoff Analysis Method uses scenarios grouped by Quality Attributes to uncover potential risks and issues with the proposed software architecture decisions. In addition, Architecture Tradeoff Analysis Method explicitly brings together the following three groups during the review:

1. The review team
2. The project team
3. Representatives of the system's stakeholders

The team conducts two validation sessions: an initial evaluation with a small group of technically oriented project stakeholders and a second, more complete validation with a larger group of stakeholders. The Architecture Tradeoff Analysis Method technique recommends that each session lasts 2 days.

In session 1, the team identifies the architecture decisions and the reasons for each of them. The team then lists the Quality Attributes that are important to the system. The Quality Attributes are derived from the business goals and drivers, and they are prioritized using the business drivers. The team breaks down each Quality Attribute into Quality Attribute refinements (see later discussion).

Finally, for each Quality Attribute refinement, the team documents at least one scenario that illustrates how the quality attribute requirement is being met. The results of this exercise are documented in a utility tree (see Chapter 3 for a detailed discussion of the Quality Attribute utility tree) using the structure that we are now familiar with:

- **Highest level:** Quality attribute requirement (e.g., performance, security, configurability, cost effectiveness)
    - **Next level:** Quality Attribute refinements. For example, "latency" is one of the refinements of "performance"; "access control" is one of the refinements of security.
- **Lowest level:** architecture scenarios (at least one architecture scenario per Quality Attribute refinement). Scenarios are documented using the following attributes:
    - **Stimulus:** describes what a user of the system would do to initiate the architecture scenario
    - **Response:** how the system would be expected to respond to the stimulus
    - **Measurement:** quantifies the response to the stimulus

Figure 6.7 repeats the sample utility tree used in Figure 6.2 in our case study. It provides an example of two documented scenarios.

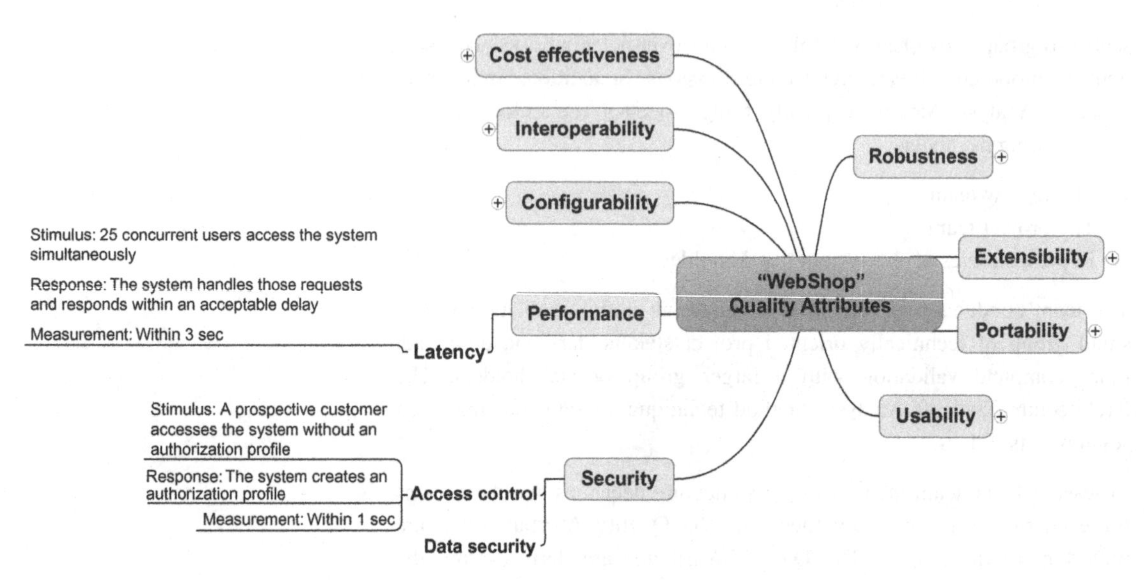
Cost effectiveness
Interoperability
Configurability
Robustness
Extensibility
"WebShop" Quality Attributes
Portability
Usability
Performance
Security
Stimulus: 25 concurrent users access the system simultaneously
Response: The system handles those requests and responds within an acceptable delay
Measurement: Within 3 sec
Latency
Stimulus: A prospective customer accesses the system without an authorization profile
Response: The system creates an authorization profile
Measurement: Within 1 sec
Access control
Data security

FIGURE 6.7 Sample utility tree with scenarios.

The validation team identifies which **architecture decisions** are important to the support of the scenario. This enables the review team to identify the **risks** (potentially problematic architecture decisions), the **nonrisks** (good architecture decisions that may either be explicit or implicit), the **sensitivity points** (architecture features that affect the response to a quality attribute requirement), and the **trade-off points** (architecture decisions that are compromises between conflicting responses to quality attribute requirements). This qualitative analysis may be supplemented by running one or several tests associated with each scenario against the software components delivered so far.

After session 1 is completed, the review team schedules a second session with a larger group of stakeholders. The goals of this session are to verify the results of the first session and to elicit more diverse points of views from the stakeholders.

In session 2, the review team works with the larger group of stakeholders to create a list of prioritized scenarios that are important to them and merges them into the utility tree created as part of session 1. It then analyzes new scenarios and updates the results of session 1.

Advantages and Challenges of the Architecture Tradeoff Analysis Method–Based Approach

An Architecture Tradeoff Analysis Method-based technique is the most rigorous of the three approaches discussed in this book and as such may yield the best results, providing that the review is conducted by closely following the Architecture Tradeoff Analysis Method process and the review team has gone through the formal Architecture Tradeoff Analysis Method evaluator training. The Architecture Tradeoff Analysis Method is excellent at uncovering significant architecture-related risks. It enables a review of the proposed system from both a business and a technical perspective and shows how the two perspectives are related. It provides a very important point of view of risks, nonrisks, sensitivity points, and trade-offs associated with the proposed architecture approach.

> *In summary, the ATAM drives to the essential quality attribute requirements by using business drivers as a key prioritization criterion. The ATAM drives to the essential architectural decisions by exploiting the quality attribute expertise of the architecture evaluation team and the architect. The ATAM offers and understanding of the business ramifications of important architectural decisions.*[10]

There are some challenges with an Architecture Tradeoff Analysis Method-based approach: To conduct a successful Architecture Tradeoff Analysis Method-based review, the team members need to be fully trained on the methodology, and having experience in participating in Architecture Tradeoff Analysis Method-based reviews with other more experienced evaluators helps a lot. In addition, performing an Architecture Tradeoff Analysis Method-based review can be time consuming; each of the two sessions lasts 2 days, which is a significant amount of time for an architecture evaluation. In our experience, the Architecture Tradeoff Analysis Method-based approach is appropriate for conducting an in-depth architecture review at a critical phase of a project, but its requirements in terms of time and resources may prevent it from being used repetitively as part of the Continuous Architecture approach for sizeable systems.

Decision-Centric Validation

A third approach to conducting architecture validations has recently emerged as an alternative to checklist-driven and to scenario-based approaches: the Decision Centric Architecture Review (DCAR) approach.[11]

The goal of Decision Centric Architecture Review is to allow more organizations to perform architecture validations by lowering the barriers of entry in terms of time, resources, and training. Using this approach, the review team analyzes the rationale behind each architecture decision. Decision

Centric Architecture Review significantly differs from the other two approaches discussed in this chapter. Whereas the checklist-driven approach attempts to challenge every key aspect of the proposed architecture, a scenario-based approach tests the proposed architecture against scenarios that are linked to prioritized quality attribute requirements. (Business drivers are used to prioritize the quality attribute requirements.)

In terms of resource utilization, Decision Centric Architecture Review practitioners report that "an average session takes a half-day, requiring the presence of three to five members of the project team, including the chief architect,"[11] which is significantly lower than the time and resources required for a similar review using either a checklist-centric approach or Architecture Tradeoff Analysis Method. Decision Centric Architecture Review is also a good technique for reviewing an updated architecture after some additional architecture decisions have been made rather than verifying that the entire system satisfies its quality attribute requirements.

A key concept in Decision Centric Architecture Review is the analysis of a set of decisions in the context of relevant project- and company-specific "**decision forces**." A decision force is defined as "any non-trivial influence on an architect seeking a solution to an architectural problem."[11] A force could have a positive or a negative impact on a decision. For example, whereas improving response time and the familiarity of an organization with a caching tool are positive forces for a decision to use a caching tool, increased architecture complexity is a negative force.

Because decisions are interrelated and the forces impacting a decision may also have an impact on a related decision, one of the objectives of the Decision Centric Architecture Review decision analysis is to clarify the relationships between decisions.

During the validation session, the validation team reviews the business drivers as well as the proposed architecture and records any potential impact on architecture decisions. This information is used to validate and complete their preliminary list of decision forces.

The team then clarifies the architecture decisions by drawing a simple relationship diagram; see Figure 6.8 for an example. This diagram shows all the decisions identified so far and uses two types of relationships between decisions: "caused by" and "depends on." Figure 6.8 shows how a small set of decisions are interrelated:

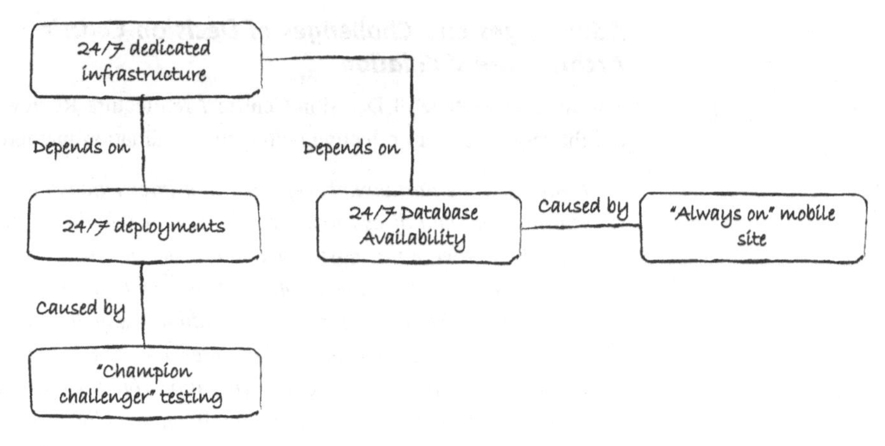

■ **FIGURE 6.8** Sample decision relationship diagram.

- A decision to enable "champion challenger testing" in a mobile website creates the need for 24/7 code deployments so that "challenger" versions of the application can be immediately moved to production to measure whether they have a positive impact.
- A decision to have an "always on" mobile website creates the need for 24/7 database availability because the system cannot be available if its database is not.
- The "24/7 deployments" and "24/7 database availability" decisions depend on a decision to use a dedicated infrastructure to meet a 24/7 availability requirement.

Decisions need to be prioritized because realistically, no more than 10 decisions can be effectively analyzed in a half-day session. In Decision Centric Architecture Review, this is done by having the participants vote on the decisions. Instead, we recommend to associate decisions with quality attribute requirements using a utility tree. They prioritize decisions based on quality attribute requirement priorities, which are themselves based on business drivers. You can leverage the Quality Function Deployment (QFD) technique to do this (see Chapter 4 for a discussion of Quality Function Deployment).

For each decision, the team reviews the forces impacting the decision (both positive and negative) as well as its relationships with other decisions. Each decision is discussed by the participants, and risks and issues associated with the decision are recorded. Based on the team's review of the decision, the team agrees whether the decision is appropriate or needs to be reconsidered. This qualitative analysis may be supplemented by running one or several tests associated with quality attribute requirement against the software components delivered to far.

Advantages and Challenges of Decision-Centric Architecture Validation

The main advantage of Decision Centric Architecture Review is that it is a lightweight yet very effective architecture validation method.

> *Generally, the participants reported that interactions between the stakeholders and discussions with the review team as external contributors were the most valuable advantages of the evaluation session. The chief architect noted that the evaluation report, produced by the review team, was a valuable supplement to the existing system documentation. The interviewees estimated that the decisions elicited during the evaluation roughly covered the most important 75 percent of all significant architecture decisions; this was regarded as an excellent result given the short amount of time invested in the evaluation.*[11]

Some of the challenges associated with Decision Centric Architecture Review include the lack of available training on the methodology and the lack of familiarity of some project teams with documenting decisions and decision forces that impact decisions. Decision Centric Architecture Review is a relatively new technique, and limited assistance is available from consulting companies, unlike what is available for checklist-based techniques and for Architecture Tradeoff Analysis Method. Some additional Decision Centric Architecture Review information and materials are available on the DCAR website.[12]

Despite these challenges, Decision Centric Architecture Review is an innovative and effective approach to architecture validations. It especially works well at the beginning of a project, when most information is not available yet. It also works well to perform periodic architecture check-ups after important architecture decisions have been made.

Recommendations

As described in the case study earlier in this chapter, we are recommending blending the three techniques as follows. Please note that the time-frames are for illustration purposes only and depend on the delivery cycle of the project being validated. Projects with short delivery cycles such as weekly will need more frequent but shorter validation sessions than projects with longer delivery cycles such as monthly.

- Use a **decision-centric** validation technique (Decision Centric Architecture Review or some variant of it) in the early stages of the project (perhaps even as soon as during the first week for projects on

very short delivery cycles) as soon as some key requirements have been captured and some decisions have been made.
- Use a **scenario-based** validation technique (Architecture Tradeoff Analysis Method or some variant of it) a couple of iterations later after a few software releases have been delivered. Alternatively, a **checklist-driven** validation technique could be used at this time if the team is unfamiliar with scenario-based validation techniques.
- Use a **decision-centric** validation technique (Decision Centric Architecture Review or some variant of it) for periodic (perhaps weekly or every other week) architecture checkups as more architecture and design decisions are being made and more software releases have been delivered.
- Use a **checklist-driven** validation technique for code reviews in addition to using the static code analysis tools when the team believes that the quality of the code is deteriorating and it may be time to refactor parts of it.

VALIDATION PROCESS

All of the techniques recommended follow a similar validation process consisting of four simple steps illustrated in Figure 6.9.

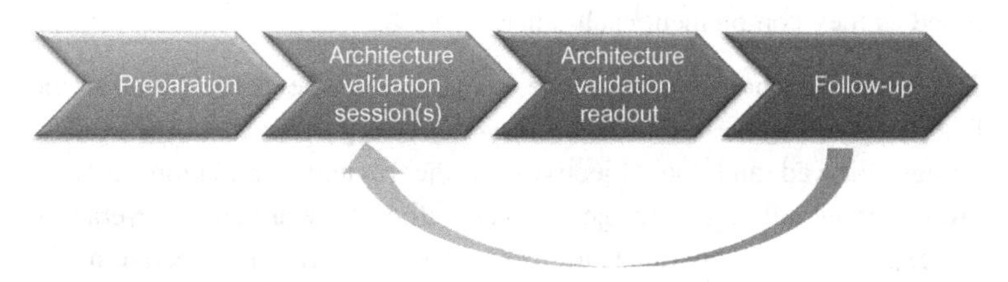

■ **FIGURE 6.9** Validation process.

Step 1: Preparation

Because architecture validations are unlike any other activity handled by an IT group, good preparation is essential to their success. Making sure that the project team, the business stakeholders, and the validation team are prepared ensures that the validation exercise will be effective and interesting.

In this step, the project team assembles the artifacts and delivers them to the validation team before the session. The artifacts may include quality attribute requirements (documented by creating a utility tree; see Chapter 3 for an in-depth discussion of quality attribute requirements and utility trees), functional requirements (refer to the "Leveraging Value Chains to Understand the Functional Scope of a Product" section in Chapter 3 for more information on using value chains and user story themes for defining functional requirements), architecture blueprints and views, architecture and design decision logs (see Chapter 4 for an in-depth discussion of architecture and design decisions), and other relevant artifacts such as a project organization chart. In addition, the project team provides the validation team with access to the software components that they have delivered so far.

Step 2: Architecture Validation Session

The project team starts the session by presenting its business goals and objectives and its proposed architecture. As part of this presentation, the team explains how the architecture addresses the business objectives. The validation team asks questions and identifies risks and issues that may prevent the system from fulfilling its goals. In addition, the evaluation team creates and runs several tests against the software components that have been delivered so far. The joint team reviews the test results and documents any identified risks and issues.

Validation sessions should be conducted openly, and every project team member should be invited to attend and participate. As mentioned earlier in this chapter, qualitative and quantitative techniques should be combined as they complement each other.

The validation process should be explained to the participants at the beginning of the session so that everyone is very clear about the process being followed and the objectives of the review. Validation sessions are not about solving the project issues; rather, they are about leveraging the expertise of the review team to provide a different perspective to the project team and help them uncover new issues. Validation sessions are about asking questions and carefully listening to and analyzing the answers to uncover potential risks and issues with architecture decisions, not about offering solutions.

What is the ideal duration of a validation session? It really depends. It could be as short as a couple of hours for straightforward architectures or as long as a few days, especially if implementing the Architecture Tradeoff Analysis Method technique. If more time is needed, follow-up meetings can be scheduled in the following week to avoid running a multiday marathon session that may exhaust most participants.

The validation session is immediately followed by a brief work session attended by the validation team only to summarize the findings and create a preliminary list of risks, issues, observations, and recommendations identified during the validation session while the discussions are still fresh in the validation team members' minds.

Step 3: Architecture Evaluation Readout

The next step in the process is for the validation team to discuss their findings with the project team.

This session is highly collaborative and may be organized around the following topics: summary of findings and recommendations, risks and issues identified during the review, and detailed observations and recommendations. The readout session may also include the discussion of a brief action plan.

Step 4: Follow-up

In the Continuous Architecture approach, projects need to be validated continuously as mentioned earlier in this chapter under the "Validation Techniques" discussion. The initial validation happens as soon as the first set of architecture requirements—especially quality attribute requirements—are captured; when an initial architecture is drafted; and when a few initial architecture and design decisions are made, such as which platform the system will run on, which database management system it will use, and which existing services it will leverage. This initial validation session is brief because there may not be a lot of content to be reviewed or software to be tested at this time. However, it is important because it validates the architecture in broad terms and initiates a series of architecture health checks that are an integral

A GREAT WAY TO RUN A VALIDATION SESSION: PLAY WITH LEGOS!

The challenge with most architecture reviews is that they can become a tedious exercise, almost like an unwanted school exam. Using scenario-based approaches and strong facilitation can help, but it is easy to fall into a dry exercise. One energizing technique we find useful is to conduct review sessions with LEGO blocks*—but they have to be large ones. The approach is quite simple:

- Get a set of giant LEGO blocks and similar size foam structures. These giant LEGO blocks can be found easily as educational toys for toddlers on the Internet.
- Have the team presenting their architecture depict their system by using the large structures at hand. Having some masking tape is quite useful for drawing boundaries.
- The team then presents their system by doing a physical walk through. Reviewers are free to step into the model and ask scenario-based questions. For example, they can question the fail-over capabilities by kicking over a particular component.

We find that such sessions become a much more entertaining and insightful way of conducting reviews. There are no boundaries, and everyone participates by walking around the "system model." The only ground rules you need are around basic meeting etiquette. Initially, we were tempted to give a certain structure by trying to give certain shapes or colors a meaning (e.g., server, database, container). But we found that letting the teams interpret the shapes resulted in a much more creative and free-flowing exercise.

One challenge with such sessions is capturing the outcome. Taking pictures and quickly drawing a two-dimensional diagram of the LEGO model does help. However, the only people who can understand the diagram are people who attended the session! This is where having a very good scribe helps.

*We would like to thank Martin Yates for introducing this concept and his view that architects should think in a physical dimension.

part of the Continuous Architecture approach. Also, course corrections are very easy at this stage because the architecture is still tentative at best.

Subsequent validation sessions are likely to take longer and get into more details as the proposed architecture is being elaborated. As the project team progresses through the Software Development Life Cycle, architecture checkups are scheduled when necessary. The architecture is reevaluated when an important decision has been made. The architecture and design decision log (see Chapter 4 for more details on architecture and design decision logs) is reviewed often by the project team to decide when a validation session becomes necessary. Over time, the architecture reviews morph into design reviews and eventually code inspections as the architecture and design become more stable. However, we have seen projects in which new information uncovered at a late stage in the process requires a drastic architecture change, so keep on updating and monitoring the decision log for last-minute changes!

SUMMARY

Architecture validations are a key component of the Software Development Life Cycle, and they are essential to the successful implementation of Continuous Architecture. Architecture validations are becoming part of the processes used by IT groups to ensure software quality, and architecture review knowledge, reference materials, and trained resources are becoming increasingly available. In this chapter, we have assumed that reviews would be conducted by a team composed of representatives of various project teams. However, an alternative may be having different teams review each other's architectures. This might even be preferable.

Architecture validations deal with far more than just the technical issues because business drivers are a key force in shaping an architecture. One of the key benefits of architecture validations in Continuous Architecture is that they periodically review the relations between business goals and architecture. As a result, they ensure that the system is designed, built, and delivered in a way that provides the greatest benefit for its stakeholders.

This chapter has described how Continuous Architecture can be leveraged to validate architectures in any type of project, especially in a Continuous Delivery project. First, we defined what we mean by architecture validation. Then we focused on when to conduct architecture validations. We then discussed the roles required in an architecture validation. We finally detailed how we can conduct architecture validations by detailing some industry-recognized techniques such as questionnaire-driven approaches, scenario-based approaches, and decision-based approaches.

We also gave an example of Continuous Architecture evaluation in practice, showing how various approaches can be combined to effectively validate an architecture.

Of course, the continuous customer feedback loop described in Chapter 5 would ideally be the best architecture validation process. Unfortunately, the system would need to be fully delivered to get that valuable feedback, and the cost of adjusting a software architecture after the system has been delivered is usually very high. The objective of the architecture validation techniques described in this chapter is to ensure that the future system meets its business objectives and quality attribute requirements without slowing down the pace of delivery associated with Continuous Delivery.

The next chapter will discuss a Continuous Architecture case study, showing how the various principles, tools, and techniques we introduced in Chapters 2 through 5 can be used in practice.

ENDNOTES

1. Linaro. Test & validation, <http://www.linaro.org/projects/test-validation/>.
2. Kazman R, Bass L. Making architecture reviews work in the real world. IEEE Software, January/February 2002.
3. Scaled Agile Framework. Architectural runway abstract, July 22, 2014. <http://www.scaledagileframework.com/architectural-runway/>.
4. Maranzano JF, Rozsypal SA, Zimmerman GH, et al. Architecture reviews: practice and experience. IEEE Software, March/April 2005.
5. Static program analysis. <https://en.wikipedia.org/wiki/Static_program_analysis>.
6. Wichmann BA, Canning AA, Clutterbuck DL, et al. Industrial perspective on static analysis. Softw Eng J 1995;(March):69–75.7.
7. Wikipedia. List of tools for static code analysis, <http://en.wikipedia.org/wiki/List_of_tools_for_static_code_analysis/>.
8. Maranzano JF, Rozsypal SA, Zimmerman GH, et al. Architecture reviews: practice and experience. IEEE Software, March/April 2005.
9. The Open Group. Architecture review checklist—system engineering/overall architecture, 2001. <http://www.opengroup.org/public/arch/p4/comp/clists/syseng.htm/>.
10. Clements P, Kazman R, Klein M. Evaluating software architectures—methods and case studies. Addison-Wesley; 2002.
11. van Heesch U, Eloranta V-P, Avgeriou P, et al. Decision-centric architecture reviews. IEEE Software, January/February 2014.
12. DCAR—Decision-Centric Architecture Review. Lightweight Architecture Evaluation, October 5, 2012. <http://www.dcar-evaluation.com/>.

Chapter 7

Continuous Architecture in Practice: A Case Study

Be patient toward all that is unresolved in your heart and try to love the questions themselves, like locked rooms and like books that are now written in a very foreign tongue. Do not now seek the answers, which cannot be given you because you would not be able to live them. And the point is, to live everything. Live the questions now. Perhaps you will find them gradually, without noticing it, and live along some distant day into the answer.

—Heinrich Rainer Maria Rilke

Chapter 2 introduced the six principles of Continuous Architecture and then in subsequent chapters we discussed several tools that are applicable to the architecture lifecycle. The Continuous Architecture principles look simple enough, but how does an architect leverage them when faced with working with legacy and monolithic systems, and stringent deadlines? We will use a simple hypothetical case study throughout this chapter to illustrate how a team gets started with Continuous Architecture and how the architecture evolves over time.

Let's go back to the information technology (IT) group in a large U.S. financial services corporation that first mentioned in Chapter 2. They have received a request to build and implement a new mobile application to allow prospective customers to do price comparisons with their competition and place orders to purchase products at the prices they are being quoted. Their first foray into Continuous Architecture (building and implementing the "WebShop system," a web-based online system to allow prospective customers to compare one of their products with the competitions' offerings) was a success. Their business partners really love the flexibility of being able to come up with "testable hypotheses" instead of requirements and having them implemented within 1 week (our IT group is still struggling with releasing application software more often than weekly).

Fresh from their initial success with Continuous Architecture, the IT group decides to leverage the same approach to tackle this new challenge, although it is a larger and more complex project than the "WebShop" system. They form a team that includes a full-time solution architect to work on this project. All the team members are familiar with Continuous Delivery, and the solution architect is a proponent of Continuous Architecture. Let's follow them through their journey, as they architect, design, build, test, and deliver this new system; we will call it the "MobileShopping" system.

HOW TO GET STARTED WITH CONTINUOUS ARCHITECTURE? START SMALL

Refactor Existing Architectures Rather Than Creating from Scratch

The team starts with *Principle 1: Architect products, not just solutions for projects.* They understand that they should not start with creating a new product, at least initially. Instead, their goal is to look at existing products and look for similarities. After similarities among existing products are discovered, the next step is to refactor these products into a common platform. The team applies the following guideline: "If you are struggling to define what a product is, remember that a product is targeted to a certain market segment or client base. Think of how your customers would view the product rather than how IT is organized."

Leveraging this approach, our team discovers that the "MobileShopping" system is very similar to an existing web-based system that allows prospective customers to obtain an online quote for the company's products. They contact the product manager for this system and review her roadmap. They find out that the product manager was planning to implement a mobile User Interface (UI) capability 6 months from now, so it makes sense to consolidate the two initiatives.

After the similarities have been identified, the team's next step is to consolidate requirements (both functional and nonfunctional) among projects and design an architecture that supports both projects. In this case, the midtier (service tier) and back-end tier are the same. The main architectural difference between the two systems is the User Interface (front-end tier) layer (Figure 7.1).

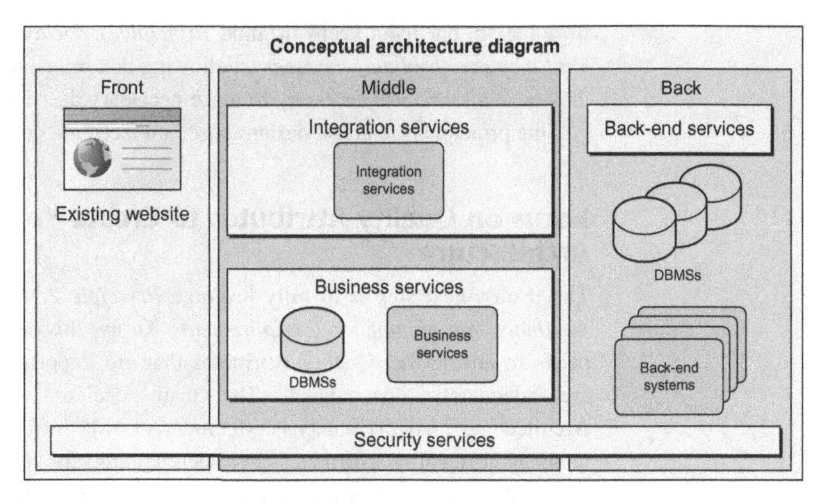

■ **FIGURE 7.1** Conceptual architecture of an existing web-based system.

At this point, the team remembers *Principle 2: Focus on Quality Attributes, not on functional requirements.* One of the nonfunctional requirements of the new system is to be device agnostic. In addition, the team knows that prospective customers are not likely to access the new system frequently, and therefore requiring them to download a "mobile app" to their mobile devices is not a good idea. Based on these requirements, the team decides to opt for a mobile website style of architecture using HTML5 and creates the following candidate architecture shown in Figure 7.2 refactoring the architecture of their existing web-based system.

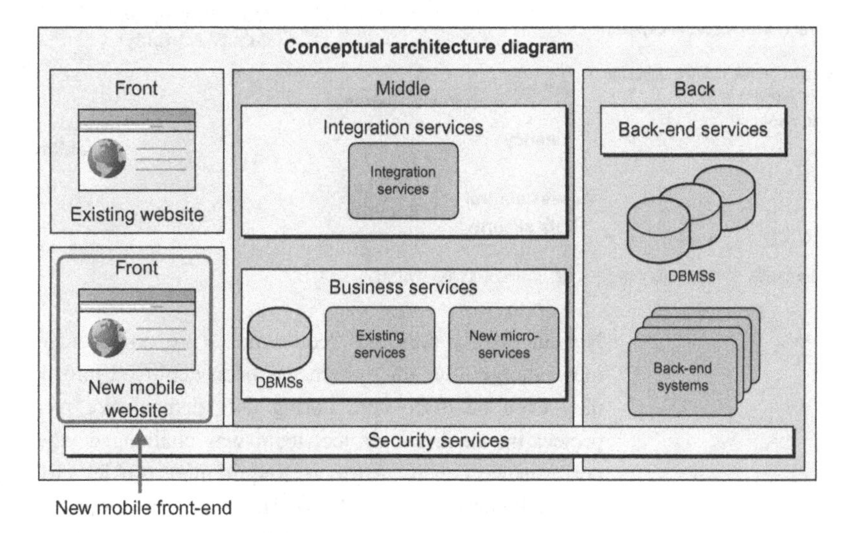

■ **FIGURE 7.2** Proposed conceptual architecture for the "MobileShopping" system.

In doing so, our team keeps in mind *Principle 3: Delay design decisions until they are absolutely necessary.* Following that principle, they wait until they have all the facts necessary to make necessary decisions. Their overall guiding principle is to create designs based on facts, not on guesses.

Focus on Quality Attributes to Create Your Architecture

The team's next step is to fully leverage *Principle 2: Focus on Quality Attributes, not on functional requirements.* To use this principle, the team needs to ensure that Quality Attributes that are important to the system are adequately documented. The team decides to leverage the Architecture Tradeoff Analysis Method (ATAM)[1] utility tree to better understand Quality Attributes by documenting the Quality Attribute refinements (e.g., performance and latency) and the associated scenarios in terms of stimulus, response, and measurement (see Chapter 3 for details about this approach). The team creates the following Architecture Tradeoff Analysis Method utility tree based on the Quality Attributes documented so far (Figure 7.3).

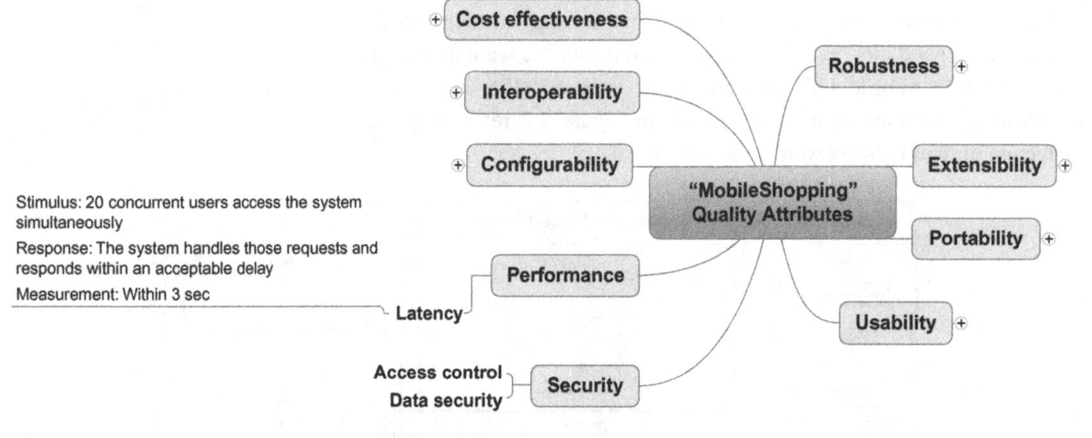

■ **FIGURE 7.3** Preliminary Quality Attribute utility tree for the "MobileShopping" system.

Not all quality attributes requirements are documented up front. Some may emerge after the system has been deployed into production. Others may even be discovered during user demos! We recently reviewed a project in which the project team was challenged when an unexpected performance Quality Attribute Requirement (QAR) surfaced in customer feedback during a user demo. However, the project team was able to quickly design a strategy to adjust the architecture to implement this new requirement without disrupting the main development process. In a short period of time, the team was able to analyze the requirement, architect a solution to the performance issue, implement a solution in a prototype, and get feedback from the business partner at the next demo. After the business partner accepted the prototyped implementation, the team was able to merge the new code into the project baseline for a future release.

At this point, our team is satisfied that the Quality Attributes that have been identified so far and documented in the Architecture Tradeoff Analysis Method utility tree can be accommodated with their candidate architecture. However, performance is an area of concern; although the performance of the existing web-based system is adequate, introducing a new component (a mobile website) in the architecture could potentially create some issues. To address this concern, the team decides to quickly create a prototype of the "MobileShopping" application. The prototype has very limited functionality—a very small subset of the fields is displayed on a single screen, and there is only one field available for user input. However, the team is able to create this prototype in 1 week and perform some preliminary performance tests. The results of those tests are encouraging, and the team decides to proceed with detailed design.

Delay Design Decisions Until They Are Absolutely Necessary to Keep the Architecture Manageable

Now our team turns their attention to *Principle 3: Delay design decisions until they are absolutely necessary*. This is a key principle to ensure that the architect does not design superfluous features into a system. For example, performance is often listed at the top of the Quality Attributes that a system must satisfy. However, it is easy to go overboard when designing for performance. Our team is tempted to introduce some caching capabilities into the design "just in case," but they realize that this would add complexity to the design and make testing and deployment harder. They also feel comfortable with the results of the test they performed using their simple prototype, and they make a decision to delay implementation of caching until it becomes absolutely necessary.

Similarly, the team is tempted to include a configuration engine (in this case, a rules engine) in the design to implement the "configurability" Quality Attribute documented in their Architecture Tradeoff Analysis Method utility tree. They recently read and discussed an article on architecture requirements for new digital systems published by a well-known and well-respected management consulting company. This article advocates the use of configuration rather than coding to automate business processes. After reading that article, the team members wonder if the authors of that article realize that *configuration* is just another name for

FOCUSING ON THE TOP TECHNICAL RISKS WHEN PROTOTYPING THE ARCHITECTURE

Any project has technical risks, and it is important to identify these risks up front to anticipate and mitigate them, if possible, or to respond to them when our mitigation strategies fail to address those risks.

To adequately address technical risks, it is important to create a *prioritized* list of those risks and to review that list periodically to evaluate the effectiveness of our risk mitigation strategies. As a result of this review, the team may need to adjust the project plan to include additional remediation activities—such as prototyping risky aspects of the architecture—in order to better address those risks.

In the context of Continuous Architecture, the team will be using the Architecture Tradeoff Analysis Method utility tree to identify the technical risks and prioritize them. Going back to our case study, the team identifies performance as their top risk and configurability and their second top risk. They are not worried at this time with the risks associated with the other Quality Attributes from the Architecture Tradeoff Analysis Method utility tree.

Do not wait until a technical risk turns into an issue to address it. It is almost always less costly and painful to manage technical risks upfront than to deal with a potentially major issue after it has occurred. Applying *Principle 3: Delay design decisions until they are absolutely necessary* does not mean ignoring technical risks!

Identifying Architecture Scenarios That Address the Top Risks
Each top risk can be mapped to one or several architecture scenarios, depending on the nature of the risk. To mitigate those risks, the team leverages the Architecture Tradeoff Analysis Method utility tree and identifies the architecture scenario (in terms of stimulus, response, and measurement) that best represents the top risk to be mitigated and that can be prototyped in a short period of time and at a reasonable cost. The team then incorporates the implementation of the prototype in the project plan and executes the plan. Using our case study to illustrate this point, the team addresses the performance risk by creating a prototype that they can run performance tests against.

After this risk has been adequately mitigated by creating the appropriate prototype, the team reviews the risk list and decides when the next priority risk needs to be addressed in their project plan; in this case, they address the configurability risk by planning to create a second prototype, incorporate the implementation of the prototype in the project plan, and execute the plan.

This approach can also be leveraged to address technical risks associated with elements of the infrastructure, such as middleware, operating system, hardware, and cloud services. Prototyping architecture and user stories that mitigate the top risks allows us to create a solid architecture

code in a different language. Both approaches still need to go through a full testing cycle, and including a rules engine in the architecture adds several challenges at deployment time. The team knows that their priority should be to keep things as simple as possible. Ideally, they would like to make a small number of design decisions based on the few facts known at the beginning of the project. Leveraging Quality Function Deployment (QFD) to trace architecture and design decisions back to the known quality attribute requirements helps a lot at this stage (see Chapter 4 for details on the Quality Function Deployment technique) and prevents design guesses.

Leverage "The Power of Small" to Architect for Change

The team now faces the usual challenge faced by nearly every IT project since computers were invented: What about the unavoidable changes in requirements? Because they do not want to guess and build "just in case" capabilities in their design, how can they accommodate change? This is where *Principle 4: Architect for change—leverage "the power of small"* comes to their rescue. As explained in our discussion of the Continuous Architecture principles in Chapter 2, the team's objective is to design their architecture based on smaller, loosely coupled components. Loose coupling reduces the intercomponent dependencies and allows our team to quickly substitute one component for another.

For example, not using any of the vendor specific extensions to SQL would allow them to swap one Database Management System (DBMS) for another if they discover at some point in the life cycle of the "MobileShopping" system that they need scalability at a reasonable cost beyond what their initial choice of Database Management System provides. Similarly using small, loosely coupled components (and even microservices if possible; see Glossary for a definition of microservices) allows them to replace a component when necessary instead of attempting to enhance it and perhaps introducing some new defects. Also keep in mind that changing existing code increases the complexity of a service, making it harder to understand, and of course, harder to replace if this is required. Additional advantages of using small, loosely coupled components include:

- Stand-alone components can be individually released.
- They use lightweight, standard industry interfaces such as the Representational State Transfer (REST).
- They can be transparently implemented in different languages.
- They can transparently use their own databases if necessary.
- They are business oriented rather than technology oriented.
- They can be tested separately.

- They can be replicated as required.
- They are scalable in the cloud (either on or off premises).
- They can be released incrementally rather than all at once.

Our team needs to augment the existing service layer (midtier) with new services to implement the new capabilities provided by the "MobileShopping" application rather than designing the new services in the same fashion as the existing ones, the team elects to implement those new services as microservices that can coexist with existing integration and business services. The resulting architecture for the system is depicted in Figure 7.4.

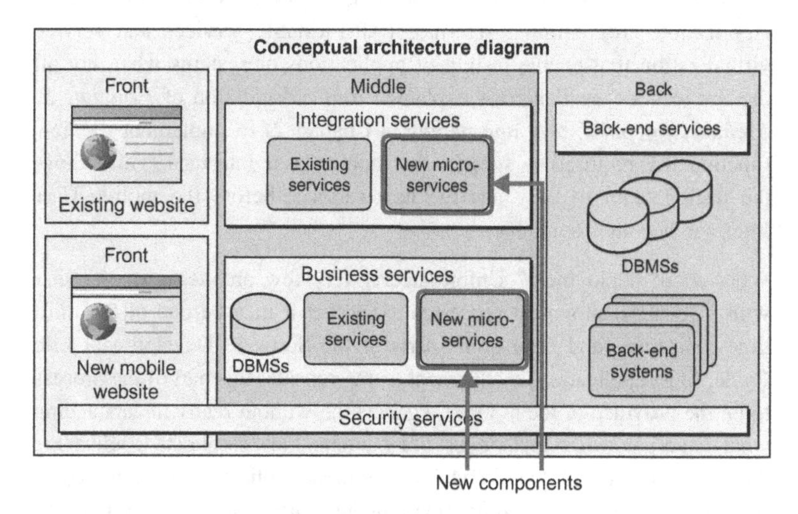

■ **FIGURE 7.4** Conceptual architecture for the "MobileShopping" system with new components.

Architect for Build, Test, and Deploy to Deliver Capabilities Continuously

Principle 5: Architect for build, test, and deploy is a key enabler of Continuous Delivery. By following this principle, the team makes sure that their architect is concerned about and involved in all aspects of the software development process, not just build and design activities but testing and deployment as well. In addition to traditional quality assurance (QA) testing by a central testing group, other forms of testing have started emerging, especially for the systems of engagement. Although quality is still a key requirement in areas such as security, it becomes somewhat less important in our systems of engagement in which users can be part of the testing process using techniques such as "pretotyping"[3] (please refer to callout) and A/B testing (a form of user experience testing where two versions [A and B] are compared, which are identical except for a small number of changes of that might affect a user's behavior).

foundation that is capable of evolving as quality attribute requirements change during the project life cycle.

Risk Management Strategies

There are three main strategies to manage risk[2]:

1. **Risk avoidance:** Reorganize the project so that it cannot be affected by that risk.
2. **Risk transfer:** Reorganize the project so that someone or something else bears the risk (customer, vendor, bank, another element, and so on). This is a specific instance of the risk avoidance strategy.
3. **Risk acceptance:** Decide to live with the risk as a contingency. Monitor the risk symptoms and decide on a contingency plan of what to do if a risk emerges.

Even if the team decides to accept the risk, it is still important to mitigate that risk by taking some immediate action to reduce its impact such as prototyping some aspect of the technical capability that may create the risk.

PRETOTYPING

What is pretotyping (no, it is not a typo!)? According to Alberto Savoia's blog,[4] the formal definition of pretotyping is "Testing the initial appeal and actual usage of a potential new product by simulating its core experience with the smallest possible investment of time and money." A working definition is as follows: "Make sure—as quickly and as cheaply as you can—that you are building the right it before you build it right."

The team realizes that it is critical for their architect to understand how the system is being tested and to design its architecture accordingly. Historically, architects have not usually considered how the application will be tested when designing a system and therefore may create an application that is hard to fully test until all the components are ready, which results in the majority of defects being discovered toward the end of the development process.

In this case, the architect is aware of the challenges associated with a traditional testing approach in which most of the defects are found late in the process. He decides to use techniques such as designing small, Application Programming Interface (API)-testable services and service virtualization that enable testing of applications or systems when not all the services are available (as explained in our discussion of *Principle 5: Architect for build, test, and deploy* in Chapter 2) to implement the new functionality required to support the mobile User Interface. This allows the testing team to fully test the new services before the mobile User Interface becomes available.

What about deployment? Unfortunately, very few architects are familiar with software deployment processes today, yet it may be one of the most time-consuming and error-prone parts of the Software Development Life Cycle. Most application development teams consider this part of the process to be the province of their "Ops" organization without really understanding what that organization really does. For example, most architects would agree that it is a bad idea to "hard code" values in an application, yet few people see an issue with hard coding environment configuration values (e.g., IP addresses) in the deployment scripts. Beyond optimization of scripts, recent advances in virtualization technologies (e.g., software-defined networks) enable some advanced application deployment features, including:

- Ability to run production on the same code and virtual environment that testing was performed on, therefore causing fewer mistakes
- Faster promotion of applications through the development and test environments
- Ability to roll back application changes in an easier and quicker fashion
- Very easy comparison of different application code versions

The solution architect supporting this project is very familiar with infrastructure virtualization techniques and is able to leverage some of these techniques when designing the "MobileShopping" application. Specifically, she elects to use a "virtual container" approach to facilitate deployment of the application. Using that approach, the application and its associated services are packaged and configured once in a "virtual application container." Figure 7.5 depicts the "virtual application container" concept at a high level and how it allows applications and associated components to be seamlessly deployed in multiple environments, including cloud environments, both internal and external to the enterprise.

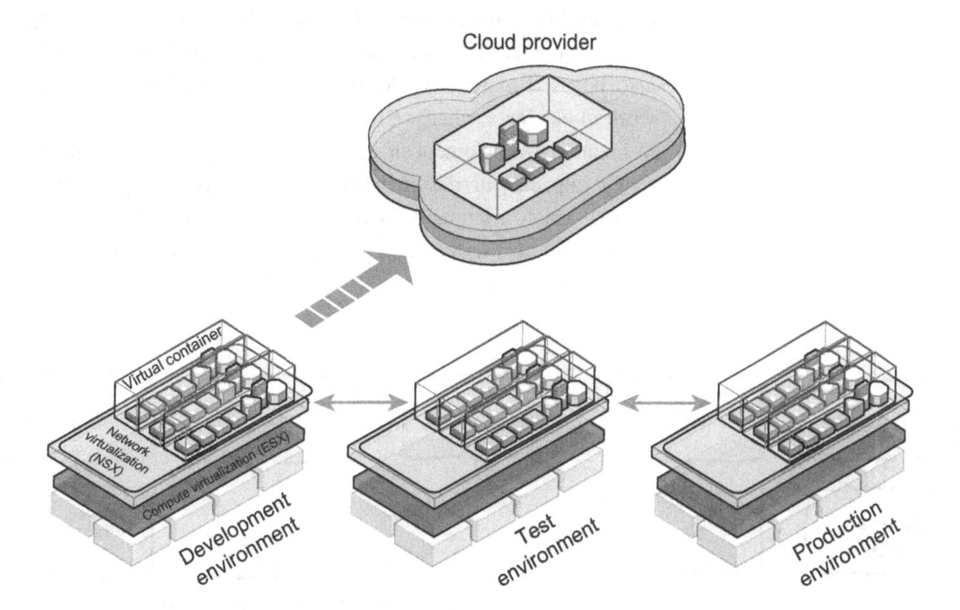

■ **FIGURE 7.5** Virtual application container concept.

After that initial configuration is complete, it is automatically translated by the "virtual container" to every environment that the application needs to be ported to, including on premise off premise clouds.[5] Please note that this diagram illustrates an implementation on the virtual container using 3 VMware products:

- vApp: a collection of preconfigured virtual machines (VMs) that associate applications and their associated services with the operating systems and middleware components that they require
- ESX: compute virtualization
- NSX: network virtualization

A virtual container can be implemented using similar tools from other vendors. Also, using VMware products does not restrict the virtual container to run on VMware-based clouds; it can also be deployed on other clouds such as Amazon's EC2 or Microsoft's Azure by adding a translation step.

Model the Organization After the Design of the System to Promote Interoperability

The final step in getting started with Continuous Architecture is to consider *Principle 6: Model the organization after the design of the system* to promote interoperability, especially the impact of Conway's law. (See Chapter 2 for a description of Conway's law.) The "MobileShopping" project team realizes that architectures affect the organization, but the law can also be used in reverse. As mentioned earlier, Conway's law can either work in our favor when we model our teams after the design we would like to create and implement or against us if a legacy team organization negatively impacts our design because of interoperability issues between the teams, which eventually will result in multiple defects and associated rework. Figure 7.6 illustrates a typical project structure that could have been used for this project.

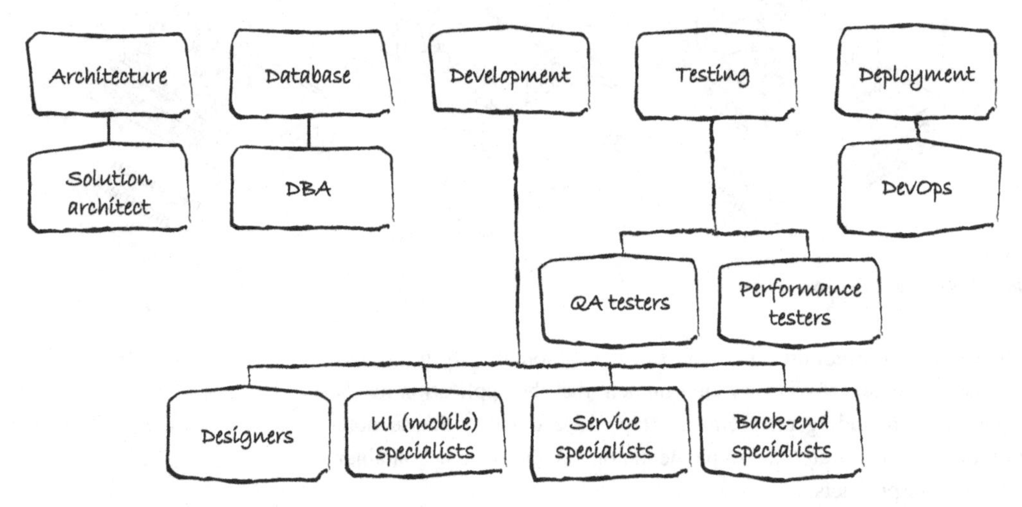

■ **FIGURE 7.6** Traditional project structure.

The team realizes that this project structure would result in a siloed application architecture, with multiple integration and interoperability issues. Instead, they decide to organize themselves around the following capabilities that will be delivered by the new "MobileShopping" application:

- Capability 1: Obtain quotes for a product, including competitors' quotes
- Capability 2: Place an order
- Capability 3: Order fulfillment

This structure is illustrated in Figure 7.7.

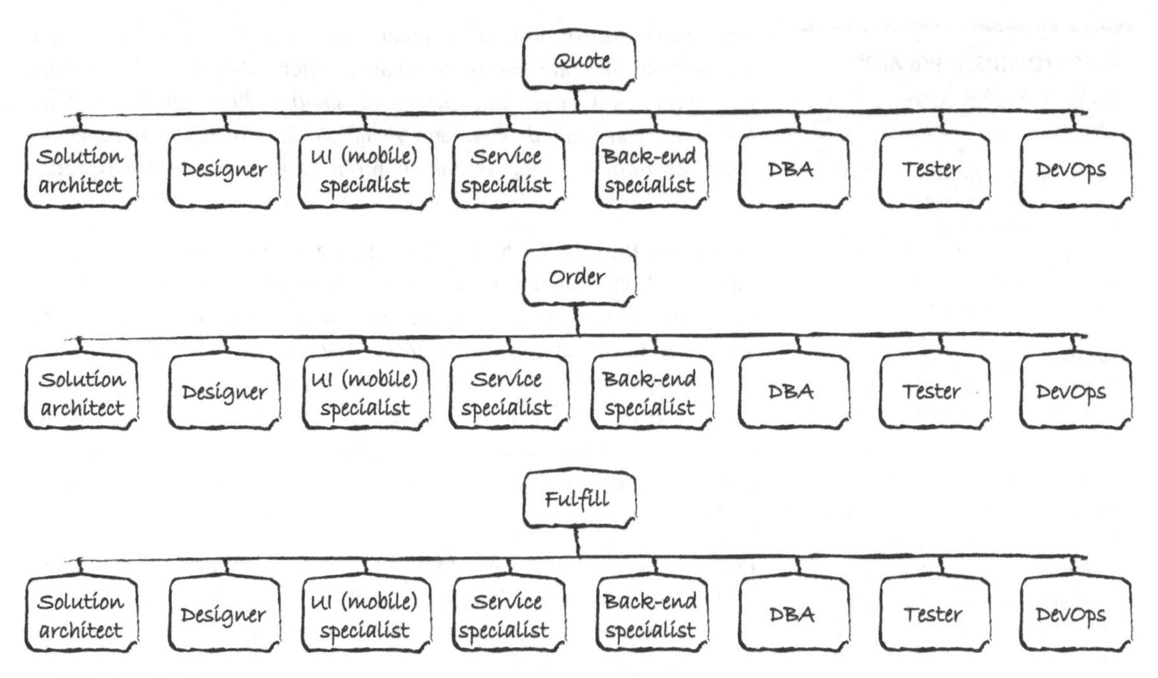

■ **FIGURE 7.7** Updated project organization structure.

Please note that this diagram depicts a role structure and does not depict an organization chart; some of the roles (architect, designer, database administrator) are filled by the same individual across the three teams. Also, because we would like to architect for test and deploy as well as for design and build (*Principle 5: Architect for build, test, and deploy*), it is important to include representatives of the testing and operations organizations in each team; this helps bring the testing and deployment requirements up front and ensure that they are taken into account by the architect at design time.

Leverage Continuous Architecture to Modernize Monolithic Systems Over Time

This approach used by the "MobileShopping" team is a good fit for situations when we are asked to develop a brand new system of engagement, but what if the project involves enhancing an existing, monolithic system? The IT ecosystem of most modern enterprises includes applications developed over decades, when today's needs could not possibly have been anticipated. How can Continuous Architecture principles be applied to evolving those applications?

REFACTORING: A PRIMER[6]

Wikipedia defines code refactoring as

the process of restructuring existing computer code—changing the factoring—without changing its external behavior. Refactoring improves nonfunctional attributes of the software. Advantages include improved code readability and reduced complexity to improve source code maintainability, and create a more expressive internal architecture or object model to improve extensibility.[7]

In practice, code refactoring is driven by the need to simplify a section of code that is difficult to understand, change, expand, and maintain going forward. Code that is easy to ready is also easy to maintain—finding bugs

The answer is to start on a small scale and focus on the areas of the system that are likely to change often. *Principle 4: Architect for change—leverage "the power of small"; Principle 5: Architect for build, test, and deploy;* and *Principle 6: Model the organization after the design of the system* to promote interoperability especially apply.

Of course, this approach, especially following Principle 4, is simple in theory but challenging in practice: Refactoring large, coarse-grained applications into smaller components divides a monolithic system into small services that are much more manageable and eventually will increase speed of delivery. However, refactoring and componentization of large code bases can be a daunting task, especially in the absence of accurate system documentation that defines what the system is expected to deliver. Fortunately, a few patterns deal effectively with this problem.

Let's return to our case study to illustrate this point. The IT team working on building the "MobileShopping" application has determined that they need to change the quoting system (one of their back-end systems) as part of this project (Figure 7.8).

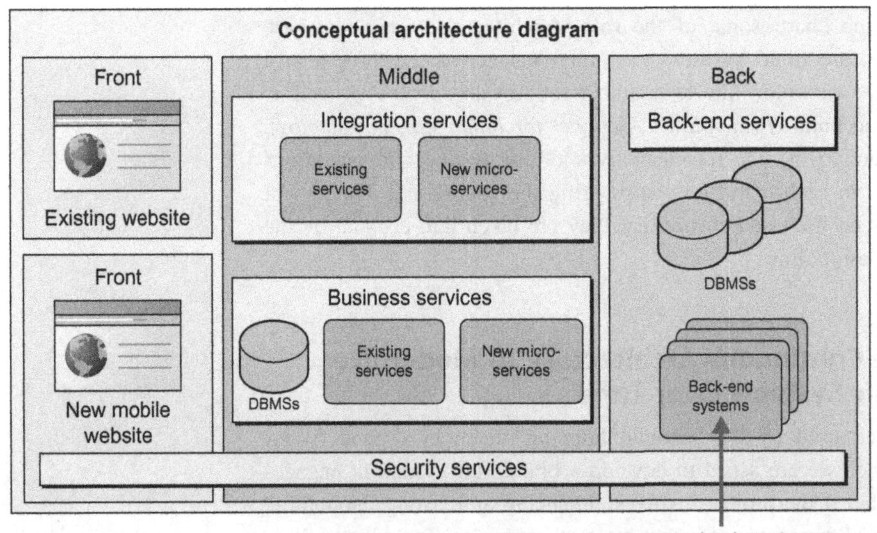

■ **FIGURE 7.8** "MobileShopping" conceptual architecture with impact of change on back-end systems.

The quoting system is an older, mainframe-based application that was designed and built a few decades ago. It includes three subsystems as depicted by Figure 7.9.

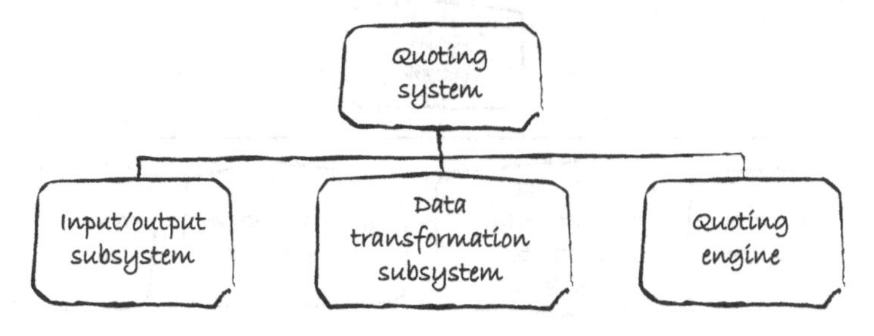

■ **FIGURE 7.9** Conceptual structure diagram for the quoting system.

1. The input/output subsystem, which is responsible for reading and updating data from permanent storage (a DB2 database)
2. The data transformation subsystem, which is responsible for formatting and transforming data from its input format into a format compatible with the quoting engine
3. The quoting engine subsystem, which is responsible for interfacing with a third-party quoting engine

The quoting system was originally well designed for its time and written in COBOL. Unfortunately, over the years, its data transformation subsystem was modified by dozens of programmers; adding an input variable to a screen often meant creating a new transformation. To achieve this, it was often expedient to find a section of code that did a similar transformation to the one being implemented, copy the code, and modify it to achieve the desired behavior. Over time, this approach polluted the design to a point where it has become very hard to understand, and the code base has become very large (more than a million lines of COBOL). The system has also become very unstable because new data transformation modules added to the code may create issues in other parts of the code, a direct result of tight coupling between the various modules within the subsystem.

The team needs to implement a new transformation for a new input variable and does not want to follow the current practice of "copying and pasting" code in the data transformation subsystem. They decide to tackle this problem by leveraging the "strangler" pattern (see "Examples of refactoring" callout).

They create a new microservice written in Java because they have the ability to run Java on the mainframe. They also modify the existing application code to invoke the new transformation microservice instead of the old data

becomes easier when the code is readable and the original design becomes apparent!

Because the goal of code refactoring is not to change the functional behavior of the component being refactored, it is important to have a comprehensive set of automated unit tests that will demonstrate that the behavior of the component has not changed after the refactoring took place.

The following pages in this chapter give an example of how a large, unwieldy body of code can be refactored over time using the "strangler" pattern.

EXAMPLES OF REFACTORING AND COMPONENTIZATION PATTERNS FOR LEGACY MONOLITHS

"Strangler" — see http://paulhammant.com/2013/07/14/legacy-application-strangulation-case-studies/

"Feature Toggles" — see http://martinfowler.com/bliki/FeatureToggle.html

"Branch by Abstraction" — see http://continuousdelivery.com/wp-content/uploads/2011/05/branch_by_abstraction.png

"Wrapping" and "strangling" legacy applications increase modularity by working outside in; branching by abstraction works inside out to eliminate application dependencies.

transformation subsystem when the new transformation is required. The updated structure for the quoting system is illustrated in Figure 7.10.

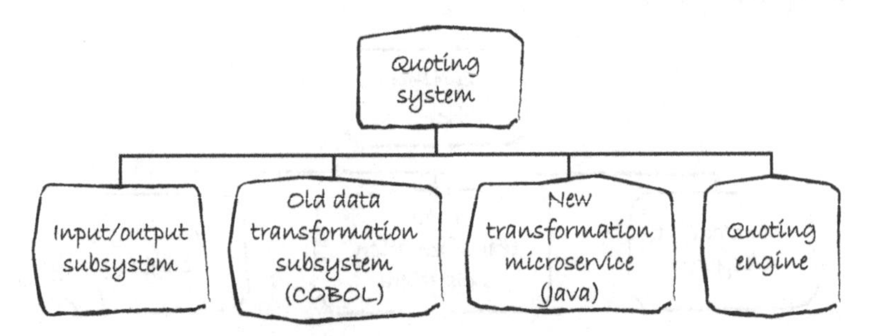

■ **FIGURE 7.10** Updated conceptual structure diagram for the quoting system.

They also obtain the agreement from the quoting system application owner to "freeze" the old data transformation subsystem; from now on, any new transformation or change to an existing transformation will be implemented by either creating a new transformation microservice or replacing an existing one. As result, the number of lines of code in the old data transformation subsystem starts decreasing, and the code becomes more stable.

As noted earlier, this approach requires creating a set of comprehensive regression tests, which must be automated. The tests must demonstrate that the behavior of the system was correct before the refactoring took place. If one of the tests fails, then the team needs to fix the code (assuming that the test case is correct) before the refactoring takes place, or it would be very difficult to distinguish between defects introduced by refactoring and existing defects.

The team carefully tests the new transformation with as many automated test cases as possible. They also run the regression tests to demonstrate that they did not alter the behavior of the existing transformations. Their goal is not to prove the old transformation subsystem is defect free. Instead, their objective is to demonstrate that the new transformation service has as few defects as possible and that their refactoring was safe enough and did not introduce new defects in the existing code base.

The good news about this approach is that refactoring and componentization both get easier with practice. Also, focusing on *Principle 5: Architect for build, test, and deploy* and *Principle 6: Model the organization after the design of the system* first is likely to yield some early successes by streamlining interteam communication (which may result in fewer defects) as well as simplifying the testing and deployment processes. After the team has had some early successes, they may find it less intimidating to tackle the "hard stuff"—refactoring and componentization of legacy monoliths.

HOW TO EVOLVE CONTINUOUS ARCHITECTURE OVER TIME?

Think "Minimum Viable Architecture"

Let's return to our case study. The team has successfully implemented the "MobileShopping" application by following the six Continuous Architecture principles. Now we will turn our attention to their next challenge—how does the team evolve the architecture to cope with the unavoidable requirement changes that are already piling up on them? This is where they need to leverage a "Minimum Viable Architecture" strategy.

Let's first explain what we mean by "Minimum Viable Architecture." This concept is often associated with the concept of "minimum viable product" (MVP), so we will start by giving a brief overview of this concept.

What Exactly Is a "Minimum Viable Product"?

An minimum viable product can be defined as follows:

> *In product development, the minimum viable product (MVP) is the product with the highest return on investment versus risk....*
> *A minimum viable product has just those core features that allow the product to be deployed, and no more. The product is typically deployed to a subset of possible customers, such as early adopters that are thought to be more forgiving, more likely to give feedback, and able to grasp a product vision from an early prototype or marketing information. It is a strategy targeted at avoiding building products that customers do not want, that seeks to maximize the information learned about the customer per dollar spent.*[8,9,10,11,12,13,14]

The concept of minimum viable product has been actively promoted by proponents of Lean and Agile approaches, and it certainly has worked very well at several startups. The concept sounds attractive at first—being able to quickly and inexpensively create a product to gauge the market before investing time and resources into something that may not be successful is a great idea.

However, in a highly regulated industry such as insurance or banking, the concept of minimum viable product has limitations—some product capabilities such as regulatory reporting, security, and auditability are not optional and cannot be taken out of scope. Also, software vendors routinely launch their products as "alpha" or "beta" versions, but very few financial services companies would consider launching anything but a production-ready version, especially to external audiences.

Of course, some other features such as some inquiry screens or activity reports may be omitted from the initial release, but these features are usually easy and inexpensive to build, so taking them out of scope for the initial release may not save much time or money.

In addition, implementing new products may involve leveraging existing capabilities implemented in older back-end systems (e.g., rate quoting in insurance), and interfacing with those systems is likely to represent a significant portion of the effort required to create a new product unless those interfaces have already been encapsulated by developing reusable services as part of a previous effort. Unfortunately, this is not often the case, and teams attempting to implement a minimum viable architecture in financial services companies often struggle with defining a product that has enough capabilities to be moved to production yet that is also small enough to be created quickly and with a minimal investment of time and money.

Let's illustrate this point by returning to our case study. As mentioned earlier, the team was able to create the "MobileShopping" system by reusing the architecture of the existing "WebShop" system, adding a new mobile front-end and some microservices (Figure 7.11).

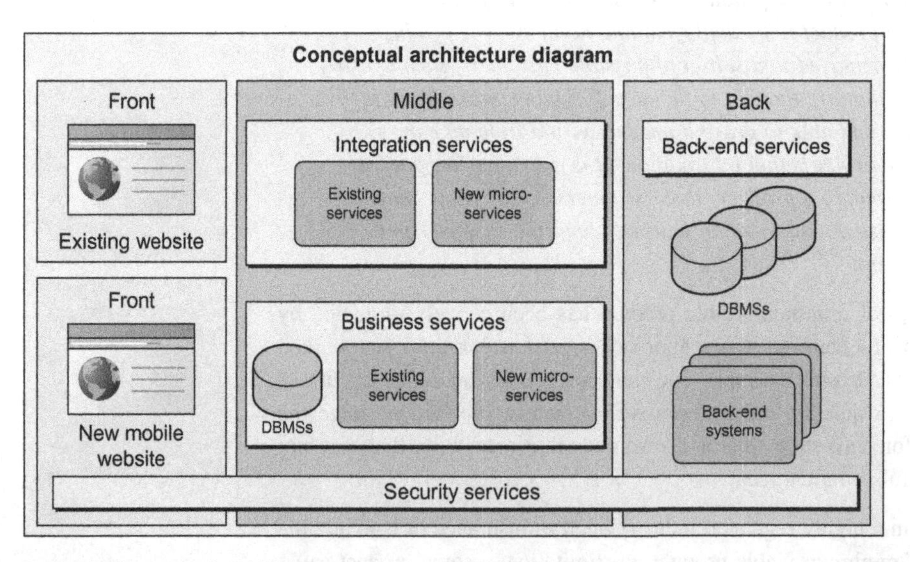

■ FIGURE 7.11 Conceptual architecture for the "MobileShopping" system.

In product management terms, what they did was to extend the "WebShop" product to include a new feature—a mobile front end. As mentioned earlier in this chapter, the "WebShop" system is expected to provide the following capabilities:

- Capability 1: Obtain quotes for a product, including competitors' quotes
- Capability 2: Place an order
- Capability 3: Order fulfillment

Because their competition already has a product with similar capabilities on the market, the minimum viable product has to be at least feature competitive with alternative offerings.

What About Minimum Viable Architecture?

On the other hand, using a Minimum Viable Architecture strategy is an effective way to bring a product to market faster with lower cost. Let's return to the Quality Attributes utility tree for the "WebShopping" system to clarify this point (see Figure 7.12).

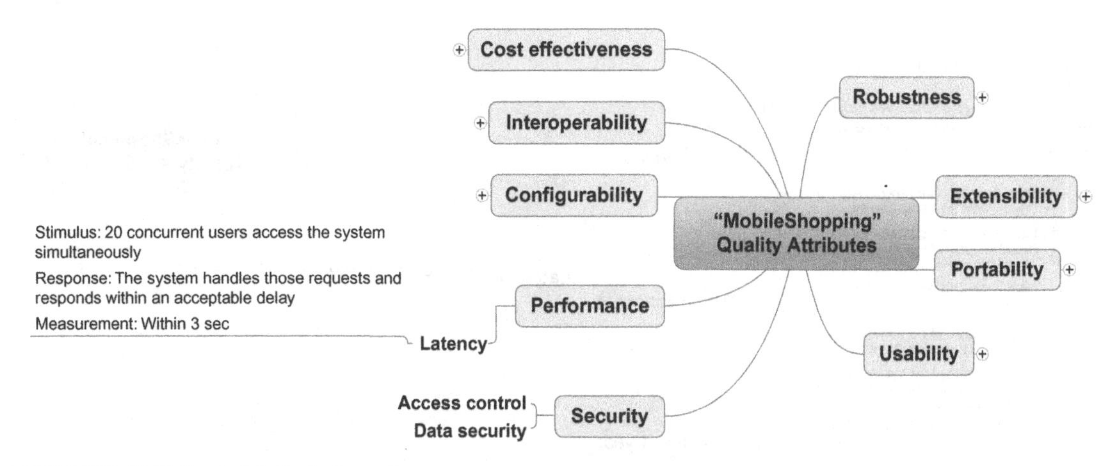

■ **FIGURE 7.12** "MobileShopping" Quality Attributes utility tree.

As we discussed earlier in this chapter, under each of those Quality Attributes are specific Quality Attribute refinements; for example, "latency" further refines "performance." In addition, a Quality Attribute refinement is illustrated by an architecture scenario (see the Glossary for a definition of architecture scenarios) in terms of stimulus, response, and measurement. The architecture scenarios themselves are a very effective way to express quality attribute requirements because they are concrete and measurable and should be easy to implement in a prototype.

There is also a time/release dimension to Quality Attributes analysis that answers the following questions:

- How many concurrent users will be on the system at initial launch?
- How many concurrent users will be on the system within the first 6 months?
- How many concurrent users will be on the system within the first year?
- How many transactions per second is the system expected to handle at initial launch?
- How many transactions per second is the system expected to handle within the first 6 months?
- How many transactions per second is the system expected to handle within a year?

This time dimension can be represented in the Quality Attributes utility tree as shown in Figure 7.13.

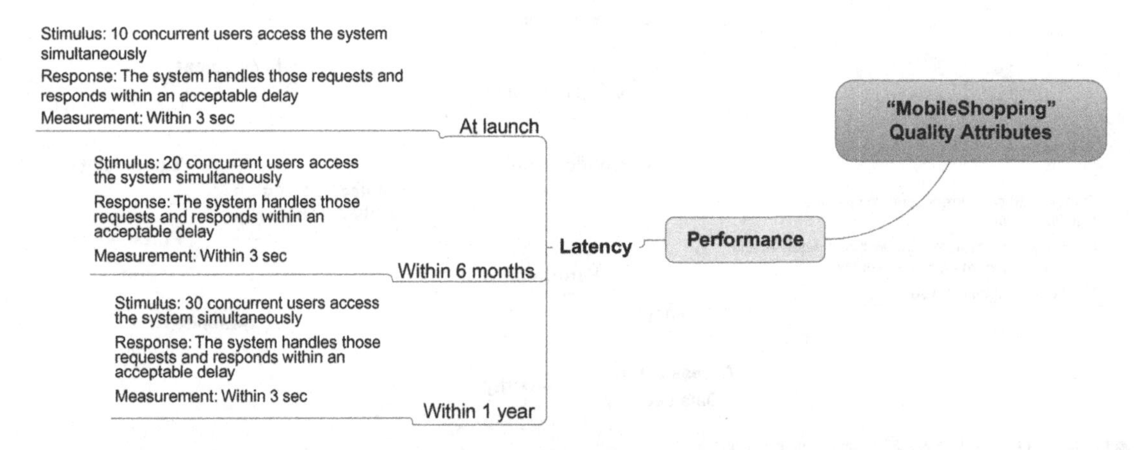
Stimulus: 10 concurrent users access the system simultaneously
Response: The system handles those requests and responds within an acceptable delay
Measurement: Within 3 sec
At launch
Stimulus: 20 concurrent users access the system simultaneously
Response: The system handles those requests and responds within an acceptable delay
Measurement: Within 3 sec
Within 6 months
Stimulus: 30 concurrent users access the system simultaneously
Response: The system handles those requests and responds within an acceptable delay
Measurement: Within 3 sec
Within 1 year
Latency
Performance
"MobileShopping" Quality Attributes

■ **FIGURE 7.13** "MobileShopping" Quality Attributes utility tree with time dimension.

Many architects consider the worst-case scenario when designing a system; in this case, they would ask their business partners for the "maximum number of concurrent users the system should be able to support" without mentioning a time frame and would add a "safety margin" on top of that number just to be on the safe side. Unfortunately, they do not realize that the number of concurrent users provided by the business is likely to be an optimistic guess (business partners would like to believe that every new system is going to be a big success!) unless the system that they are architecting replaces an existing system, and usage volumes are precisely known.

As a result, they end up architecting the new system to handle an unrealistic number of concurrent users, which may not be reached for a few years, and sometimes add unnecessary complexity (e.g., caching components) to their design. We are recommending instead to adopt a "**Minimum Viable Architecture**" approach based on realistic estimates at launch time and **evolve** that architecture **based on actual usage data**. Also keep in mind that technology becomes more efficient over time, and keep in mind *Principle 3: Delay design decisions until they are absolutely necessary*. Design the architecture based on facts, not guesses!

As mentioned earlier in this book, a useful strategy is to limit the budget spent on architecting. This forces the team to think in terms of a minimum viable architecture that starts small and is only expanded when absolutely necessary.

Delay Design Decisions Until They Are Absolutely Necessary to Cope with New Requirements

Returning one more time to our case study, let's assume that the team has just received a request to add the following capability to the "MobileShopping" application:

- Allow the user of the "MobileShopping" application to take a series of pictures to quickly capture information about the products they are interested in buying in order to customize it up front and obtain an accurate quote in a minimum of steps, as opposed to doing this iteratively.

This new capability is going to be used heavily by prospective customers, and response time is critical. In addition, implementing this new capability involves modifying some existing services in the mid-tier. The impact of change created by this new capability is illustrated in Figure 7.14.

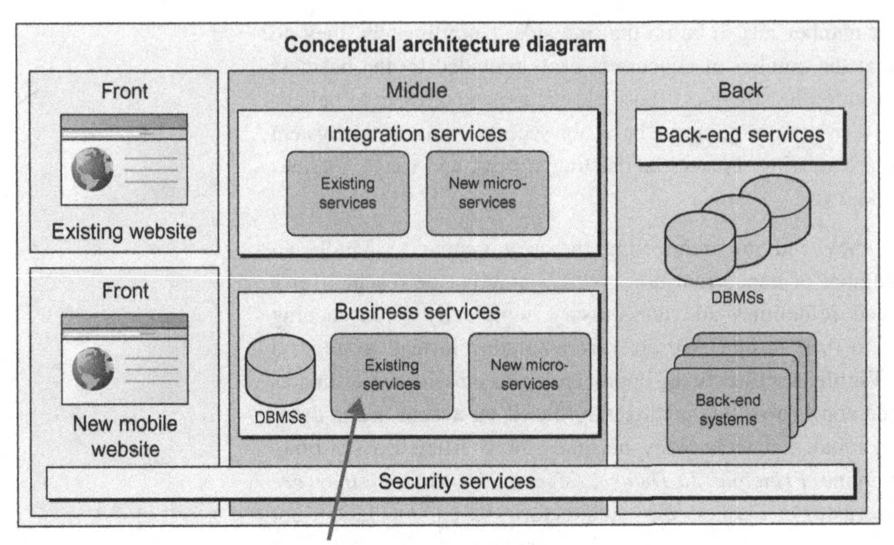

■ **FIGURE 7.14** Conceptual architecture for "MobileShopping" with change impact.

The team's first ally is *Principle 3: Delay design decisions until they are absolutely necessary.* They want to ensure that they make or change design decisions only when additional facts are known, and not a moment before. Because the new capability requires taking pictures with a mobile device, the team considers switching the User Interface design from a mobile website model to a mobile app (or perhaps a hybrid) model to better leverage the device capabilities. However, they conclude that they only require one mobile device function (taking a photo), so there is no need to incur the added cost and complexity of creating a mobile app for each device that their prospective customers might be using. This capability can be provided by leveraging HTML5. Performance may be a concern, so they create a quick prototype and demonstrate that performance remains acceptable.

The team may still have to do some limited refactoring but because they followed *Principle 4: Architect for change—leverage the "power of small"* when initially designing the architecture, the amount of refactoring required to accommodate new requirements should be minimal. A note of caution here: Beware of refactoring—it could be expensive and time consuming! One of the advantages of using microservices is that refactoring is limited to replacing services, not modifying them. In this instance, the team needs to decide whether they should modify or refactor the existing services impacted by the new capability, and they need to evaluate this on a case-by-case basis. They do this by applying the following rules:

- If the amount of change to a service is minimal, then refactoring is unnecessary and should not be done. The change should be implemented by modifying the service without refactoring it.
- If the amount of change is material (e.g., more than 50% of the existing code would be affected by the change) and this service is not expected to significantly change in the future, then refactoring is still unnecessary. The service should be modified without refactoring it rather than replaced.
- If the amount of change is material (e.g., more than 50% of the existing code would be affected by the change) and additional requirements may impact this service in the future, then they should refactor (i.e., replace) the service as one or several microservices.

Based on their analysis of the impact of the change on their 20 existing services, the team determines that they should do the following:

- Replace three of their existing services with new microservices.
- Modify seven of the existing services.
- Leave the remaining 10 services unchanged.

Leverage "What If" Analyses to Test the Architecture

A useful way to ascertain whether the architecture is truly resilient to change and if the team used *Principle 4: Architect for change—leverage "the power of small"* effectively is to perform a few "what if" analyses using architecture scenarios. What if they no longer want to use an Oracle DB and switch to SQL Server for cost reasons? What if they no longer want to use a relational database and switch to a NoSQL DB, also for cost or performance reasons? Was it a good idea to put business logic in stored procedures to save some development time? A more formal approach to this technique is to leverage the Architecture Tradeoff Analysis Method,[1] which looks for risks that the architecture will not satisfy Quality Attributes. As discussed in Chapter 2, Architecture Tradeoff Analysis Method uses a tool called the "utility tree" (see Chapter 3 for more details) to better understand Quality Attributes and their impact on the architecture.

Let's assume that the team determines that an adjustment to the architecture is necessary as a result of performing a "what if" analysis. They expect the new functionality they just delivered to be heavily used, and unfortunately, performance will suffer. As a result, they decide to include a caching tool in the architecture. How can they do this without introducing major changes to the architecture and potentially delaying the delivery of the product? See Figure 7.15.

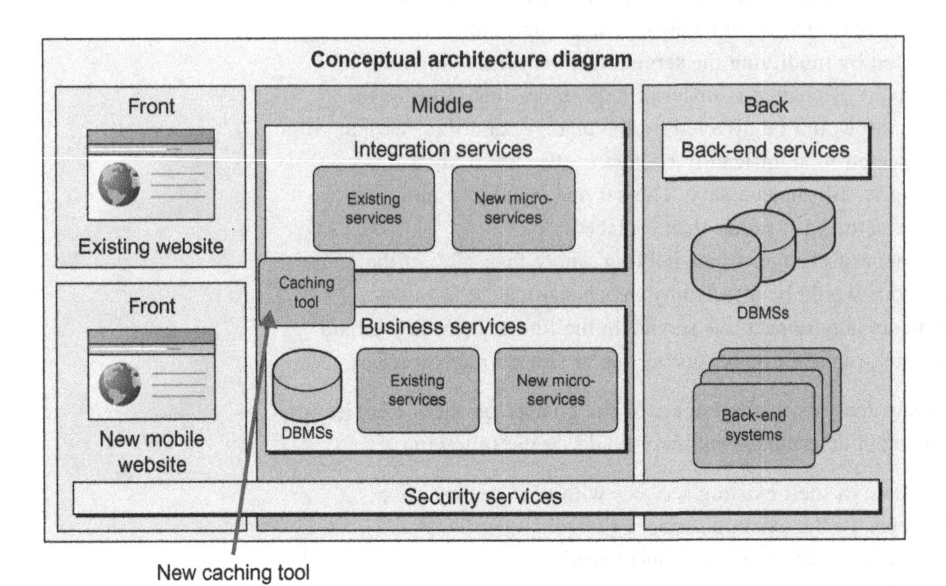

■ **FIGURE 7.15** Conceptual architecture for "MobileShopping" with new caching tool.

They address this challenge by leveraging *Principle 4: Architect for change—leverage "the power of small"* and keeping "the power of small" in mind. Their goal is to replace (not modify) architecture components while keeping coupling between components to a minimum. This strategy enables them to minimize the impact of change caused by the addition of the caching tool to the architecture. They also need to keep *Principle 5: Architect for build, test, and deploy* in mind at all times and keep on architecting for all phases of the Software Development Life Cycle, including testing and deployment. Their objective is to preserve the **Minimum Viable Architecture** they created as part of building the "MobileShopping" application. Architectures unavoidably acquire unnecessary capabilities and to eliminate them use the removal test, another example of "what if" analysis. What if this capability was not part of the architecture? Would the system still meet its requirements?

Continuous Architecture Is Driven by Feedback

A key advantage of Continuous Architecture is that it is driven by feedback; in fact, the team actively solicits feedback from the development teams, the testing teams, the DevOps teams, and their business partners. They use this feedback to continuously test the architecture and govern the evolution of the architecture based on data. This data is collected through a number of channels, for example, "pretotyping" (see earlier discussion), A/B testing, feedback loops from continuous testing, manual reviews, and automated code inspection or any number of approaches that provide substantive feedback on architectural qualities.

The Continuous Architecture evolution process is summarized in Figure 7.16.

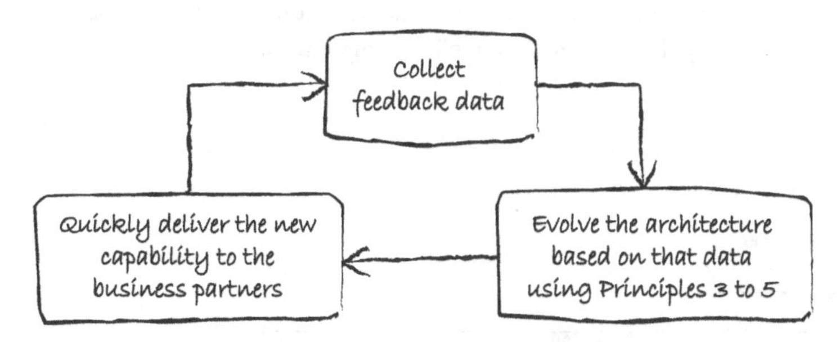

■ **FIGURE 7.16** Continuous Architecture evolution process.

Continuous Feedback Can Be Used to Govern the Evolution of Legacy Monoliths

Now it is time to turn our attention back to the legacy monoliths. The same process as discussed can be used to govern the evolution of the architecture of those systems. The goal is to *continuously collect data* and use that data to *drive the architecture*.

As discussed earlier in this chapter, refactoring and componentization of large code bases can be a daunting task, and the task does not get much easier as the architecture evolves. Eventually, using the patterns that deal effectively with this problem (such as the ones listed under "Leverage Continuous Architecture to Modernize Monolithic Systems Over Time") will break the monolith down into manageable pieces, but this process takes time, and the transition from a monolithic architecture to a flexible, component-based structure can be long and challenging. Of course, the architect needs to keep in mind that all change has to be driven by business demand and not for the sake of it.

SUMMARY

In summary, this chapter has depicted how a team gets started with Continuous Architecture and how the architecture evolves over time, using a case study to illustrate the principles, the techniques, and the tools described in the previous chapters.

When applying the Continuous Architecture principles, it may be helpful to keep Figure 7.17 in mind. This figure depicts the Continuous Architecture principles from the perspective of two dimensions:

1. The topics that they are most closely aligned with: people, process, or technology
2. If they are more relevant when initiating a new project or in the day-to-day decision making while in implementation mode.

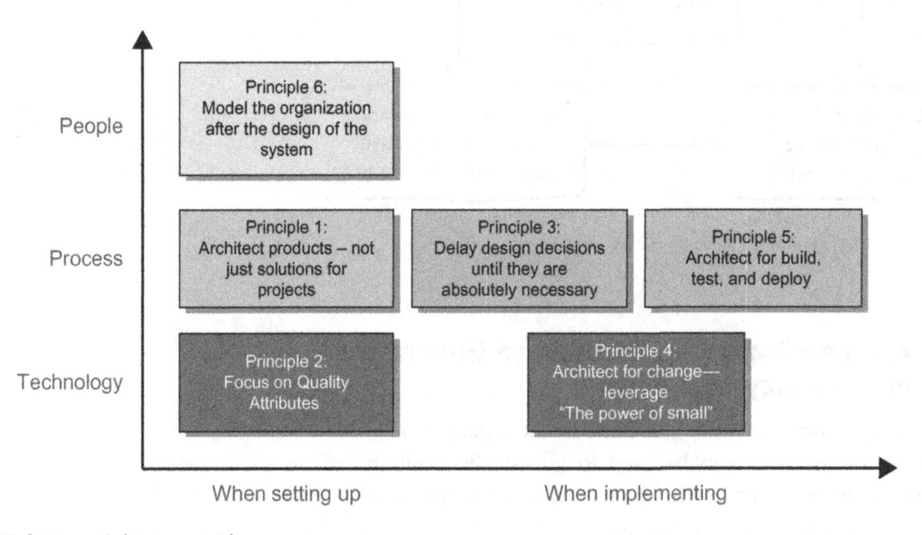

■ **FIGURE 7.17** Continuous Architecture principles.

The next few chapters describe how Continuous Architecture impacts the role of the architect, as well as its applicability in the enterprise.

ENDNOTES

1. Clements P, Kazman R, Klein M. Evaluating software architectures—methods and case studies. Addison-Wesley; 2002.
2. Boehm BW. Software risk management: principles and practices. IEEE Softw January 1991:32–41.
3. Preotyping.org. <http://www.pretotyping.org/>.

4. Preotyping. What is preotyping? <http://pretotyping.blogspot.com/p/what-is-pretotyping.html/>.
5. Intigua. The value of virtual containers. <http://www.intigua.com/intigua-blog/the-value-of-virtual-containers/>.
6. Fowler M, Beck K, Brant J, Opdyke W. Refactoring: Improving the Design of Existing Code, Addison-Wesley Professional, July 8, 1999.
7. Code refactoring. <https://en.wikipedia.org/wiki/Code_refactoring>.
8. Minimum viable product. <https://en.wikipedia.org/wiki/Minimum_viable_product>.
9. Junk WS. The dynamic balance between cost, schedule, features, and quality in software development projects. Computer Science Department, University of Idaho, SEPM-001, April 2000.
10. Ries E. Venture hacks interview: what is the minimum viable product? Lessons Learned. March 23, 2009. <http://www.startuplessonslearned.com/2009/03/minimum-viable-product.html>.
11. Perfection by subtraction—the minimum feature set. <http://www.startupshk.com/perfection-by-subtraction-the-minimum-feature-set>.
12. SyncDev. MVP: Minimum viable product, 2015. <http://www.syncdev.com/index.php/minimum-viable-product/>.
13. Holiday R. The single worst marketing decision you can make. The Next Web, April 1, 2015.
14. Ries E. Minimum viable product: a guide, August 3, 2009. <http://www.startuplessonslearned.com/2009/08/minimum-viable-product-guide.html>.

Chapter 8

Role of the Architect

All the world's a stage,
And all the men and women merely players;
They have their exits and their entrances,
And one man in his time plays many parts,
His acts being seven ages.

—William Shakespeare, *As You Like It*

In the case study provided in Chapter 7, we looked at how a team can apply Continuous Architecture principles and the techniques and the tools described in the book. One of the most important roles in a team is of the architect, which is the focus of this chapter. Although the topic of architecture is widely discussed in the software industry, there are varying views on who an architect is and the meaning of being an architect.

This is also our first chapter in the final section of the book that focuses on applying Continuous Architecture at the enterprise scale. From this perspective, we will not only look at the role of the architect within a particular team but also at different levels from product to division to the entire enterprise.

We will address the topic of the role of the architect initially in a generic manner and then specifically in the context of Continuous Architecture. The sections of this chapter are constructed as follows. We will first discuss the architecture role in general by focusing on what an architect does. Then we will have a look into personality types of people who become architects by referring to well-recognized techniques in this area. Finally, we will define the role of the architect within Continuous Architecture.

WHAT DOES AN ARCHITECT DO?

The role of the architect is widely accepted in the world of technology. However, what is meant by it is not that clearly defined.

In most organizations, architects are the technologists who have experience—the proverbial gray hair and battle scars of dealing with technology solutions throughout their careers. It is definitely a requirement that an architect has to have sufficient experience to be able to resolve significant architectural decisions. In some ways, being an architect is something you pick up while working rather than being formally trained on.

There are two extremes to the experienced technologist becoming a senior architect: We will call them the "Oracle of Delphi" and the "Retired Gunslinger."

At one extreme is an individual who is well recognized in the organization for his or her expertise. This person's opinions are well regarded by senior management and developers alike. The person is normally quite active and participates in multiple projects in formal and informal manners. We call such an individual the "Oracle of Delphi." This person's opinions are considered a final say in hot debates. If the "Oracle of Delphi" says a particular solution does not need such a technical component such as caching, that is the end of the discussion.

At the other extreme, we have the case of the role of the architect becoming a semi-retirement spot for revered individuals. These people have contributed their years to the organization, and the role

In general, the term exemplifies anyone who makes key decisions about the structure and behavior of a system, whether it is software or other technology areas. Although *software architect* is the most commonly used term, there are also application architects, network architects, storage architects, information architects, security architects, and even cloud architects. In some manner, you can say that any technology subject area has people who identify themselves as architects.

Forrester Research describes six foundational architecture roles in the organization report of their Enterprise Architecture playbook: business, information, application, infrastructure, solution, and enterprise.[1] Architects who take on those roles focus on one of the basic architecture domains (business, information, application, or infrastructure), as do the solution architects who apply the domain knowledge to projects and the enterprise architects who ensure coordination and coherence across domains.[1] Similar to Forrester Research's classification, The Open Group Architecture Framework (TOGAF)® also identifies four key architecture domains: business, data, application, and technology. We can identify the following common traits among all these types of architects:

- The term *architect* implies a level of deep knowledge in the domain of interest.
- Architects generally do not directly implement (some architects can create executable prototypes during architecture sprints or runways). Instead, they deal with higher levels of abstraction by defining the structure of a system in the domain of interest.
- Architects are explicitly or implicitly the authority of making decisions in the domain of interest.

Let us look at the responsibilities of an architect. In his book *Mythical Man-Month* Frederick Brooks[2] talks about the conceptual integrity of a software product. This is a good place to start in defining the role of the architect; basically, they are accountable for the "conceptual integrity" of the entity that is being architected or designed.

It is true that architects deal with a higher level of abstraction than implementers, developers, or engineers do. They are concerned about the main components of the system and how they interface. They consider Quality Attributes and continuously validate the architecture against different scenarios. They have to have the ability to traverse different levels of abstraction between concepts, models, and implementation details.

From a Continuous Architecture perspective, we believe the key responsibility of an architect is to drive architectural decisions to a conclusion.

In Chapter 4, we already stated that the unit of work of architecture should be considered the architectural decision. We purposely used the term *drive to a conclusion* rather than *make*. Although we do support the need for the conceptual integrity of a system, we do not think that it can be derived from the views of a single individual who makes all the decisions or from the views of the "Oracle of Delphi" as mentioned earlier. The term *drive to a conclusion* implies that the architect engages with stakeholders and works through the options to arrive at a decision. The term *drive to a conclusion* does not mean that an architect can abdicate responsibility for making sure that architectural decisions are made. An architect has to make sure that decisions are made in a timely manner.

Peter Eeles defines the following characteristics of an architect[4]:

1. Technical leader
2. Understands the software development process
3. Knowledge of the business domain
4. Has technology knowledge
5. Has design skills
6. Has programming skills
7. **Is a good communicator**
8. **Makes decisions**
9. **Is aware of organizational politics**
10. **Is a negotiator**

We think these points exemplify all the good capabilities an architect should embody. In particular, we think the last four highlighted capabilities are critical for a successful architect.

We will next look into different personality traits and how they relate to such capabilities. But before that, let us expand on how Continuous Architecture defines the role of an architect: *Continuous Architecture states that an architect is responsible for enabling the implementation of a software product by driving architectural decisions in a manner that protects the conceptual integrity of the software product.*

WHO IS AN ARCHITECT? TYPES OF PERSONALITIES

We have already provided an example of a typical path to becoming an architect and two extreme stereotypes, the "Oracle of Delphi" and the "Retired Gunslinger." But what personalities do software architects have in general? Do architects have the required capabilities to meet the demands of their role?

becomes a nice way to ride into the sunset like a cowboy who has solved the problems of the town, hence the name the "Retired Gunslinger." The value the organization gets from such an architect can be questioned, but as a social contract, it might not be such a bad result.

Most architects are somewhere between these two caricatured types. They also do not need to be old men. Quite a lot of good architects are young. Unfortunately, there are very few women architects in an industry that already has a low representation of women. We encourage more women to step into these roles and believe that better solutions will evolve with input from a more diverse background, not only in terms of gender.

It is quite interesting to note that the role of software architect is #1 in CNNMoney/PayScale's 2015 top 100 careers with big growth, great pay, and satisfying work. CNNMoney defines the software architect as follows:

In the same way an architect designs a house, software architects lay out a design plan for new programs. That usually means leading a team of developers and engineers, and making sure all the pieces come together to make fully-functioning software.[3]

The key benefits quoted by CNNMoney are that the role is in high demand and diverse in the sense that each new day architects can relate to addressing a new challenge. It also is cited as paying relatively well. The second listed career is a video game designer. To find another role related to the software industry, you then have to go to #8, which is a database developer. Information technology (IT) program managers come in only at #17.

Architects can be seen as uber technologists and just by this are boxed into a vision of a geek or a nerd. They are stereotyped into people who are not that good at social skills in the same manner as the main characters of the U.S. sitcom *The Big Bang Theory*. Is this a fair representation?

To help answer these questions, let us look at some research that has been done in the area of personality types of people in the software industry. For this, we will look at a few different techniques used in corporations to analyze personality types.

Myers-Briggs Type Indicator

The most well known personality type technique is the Myers-Briggs Type Indicator (MBTI). (The exclusive publisher of MBTI is CPP. More information on MBTI can be found on its website.[5]) It is a psychometric evaluation of how people view and engage with the world. It has been around since the 1940s and is based on famous psychologist Carl Jung's theory of psychological types. It groups people along four dimensions or indexes:

- **Extraversion (E) and Introversion (I):** This is fairly self-explanatory and defines an individual's preference in engaging with people. Whereas extraverts prefer engaging with group or social activities, introverts prefer inner reflections and solitude. This dimension is also described as where people get their energy from. Extraverts get energy through interacting with people or doing things. Introverts get energy through reflecting on information, ideas, or concepts.
- **Sensing (S) and iNtuition (N):** This focuses on an individual's preferred manner in how he or she perceives the world. If you prefer sensing, you notice and trust facts, details, and present realities. If you prefer intuition, you attend to and trust interrelationships, theories, and future possibilities.
- **Thinking (T) and Feeling (F):** This focuses on how individuals make decisions. If you prefer thinking, you make decisions using logical, objective analysis. If you prefer feeling, you make decisions to create harmony by applying person-centered values.
- **Judging (J) and Perceiving (P):** This focuses on how individuals interact with the outer world. If you prefer judging, you tend to be organized and orderly and to make decisions quickly. If you prefer perceiving, you tend to be flexible and adaptable and to keep your options open as long as possible (Figure 8.1).

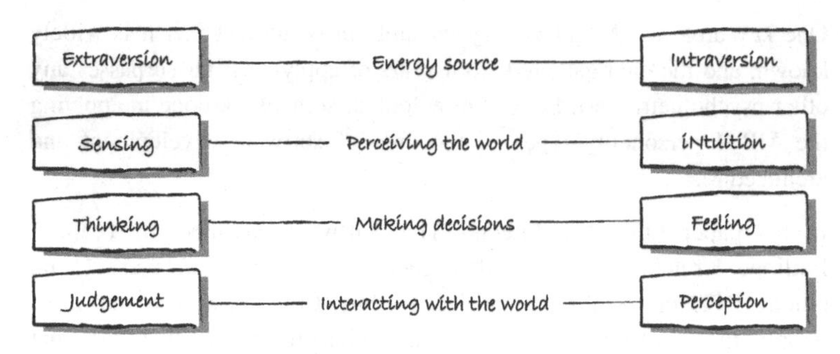

■ **FIGURE 8.1** Myers-Briggs Type Indicator indexes.

The MBTI analysis is conducted by individuals filling in questionnaires and then being categorized into a personality type along each of the dimensions. This results in each individual being given a four-letter personality type such as ENTP, ISTJ, and so on. If you work in a corporation, it is highly likely that you have been through such an assessment and can quote your four letter type in a water cooler conversation.

In recent years, MBTI has been criticized for not being a valid assessment. (Good overviews of the criticism are provided by Stromberg[6] and Michael.[7]) The argument put forward by the critiques has two key elements. First is that it is not a repeatable process; that is, the same person might end up a different personality type each time she or he takes the test. It is claimed that as many as 50% of people come up with a different result when they take the test a second time. The second criticism is that Jung's theory is based on his interpretation of clients and not on controlled experiments or data.

We are not psychologists and do not have a particular view on the exact scientific validity of MBTI. Similar to any such tool, what determines its value is how it is used. If done superficially like a magazine quiz, we agree that its value is limited. If done professionally with a balanced view (and a pinch of salt), it can provide interesting insights to individuals. A detailed MBTI analysis not only gives you your four-letter type but also details your clarity of preferences (i.e., how dominant your preference in a particular dimension is). You can also conduct further analysis by breaking down each dimension into five further facets. This gives you a more detailed view on the dominance of a certain trait. For example, you can prefer extraversion but still have characteristics of introversion in one facet (e.g., be more reflective than active while still being expressive, enthusiastic, and so on).

One key area that MBTI is very valuable in is the fact that it is widely known, and the data gathered from years of applying it far surpasses any other psychometric test. Let us know look at some work done in applying the MBTI personality types to the area of software development and architecture.

In his paper titled "Architects—The Software Architecture Team,"[8] Philippe Krutchen proposed that good software architects are found among INTJ or INTP personalities. He based this on a view that most people in scientific or technological fields are introverted and that the NT combination is the "Promothean temperament: the 12% of the population who loves intelligence, power of nature, competence, skills and their work."

A few studies have focused on applying MBTI to software teams.[9] These papers also state that a suitable personality type indicator for a software architect is NT. This seems logical because N emphasizes trusting interrelationships and theory rather than pure fact. Being able to be abstract is a key feature of an architect. T emphasizes focusing on using objective analysis while making decisions instead of emotions. Where you lie on the extraversion–introversion and judging–perceiving dimensions is less relevant for an architect. An interesting point made is that a suitable personality type for a developer is IST. The main difference with an architect is the S versus N dimension. This basically says that a developer needs to have attention to detail, but an architect can sacrifice that to be able to think in theories and abstract terms. What does this say for the notion that architects tend to be recruited from senior developers? Does a person's personality trait change with experience? Of course, if you are a critic of MBTI, then this is further evidence pointing to MBTI being an inappropriate tool.

The Center for Application of Psychological Type (CAPT) has published its data on the distribution of personality types in the U.S. population.[10] According to this, if we take a view that architects are either INTJ or INTP types, then we can say that 5% to 9% of the population fits these criteria. If we ignore the introversion dimension and just focus on NT, then 9% to 19% of the population fits the criteria. If we say that developers should be IST, then that gives us 15% to 20% of the population. So, we have a slightly higher percentage of the population who are more suitable for development than architecture tasks.

Big Five Personality Traits

As stated earlier, MBTI has attracted criticism in recent years. The proposed alternative by most critics is the big five personality traits.

The five-factor model (FFM), which the big five personality traits is based on, was developed by several researchers throughout the past decades, including Norman (1967), Smith (1967), Goldberg (1981), and McCrae and Costa (1987).[11] The key strength claimed by the FFM model is that it is based on empirical research that shows consistency across time, culture, and age groups. It is also considered more structured because the five traits do not overlap. At a high level, the traits are (Figure 8.2):

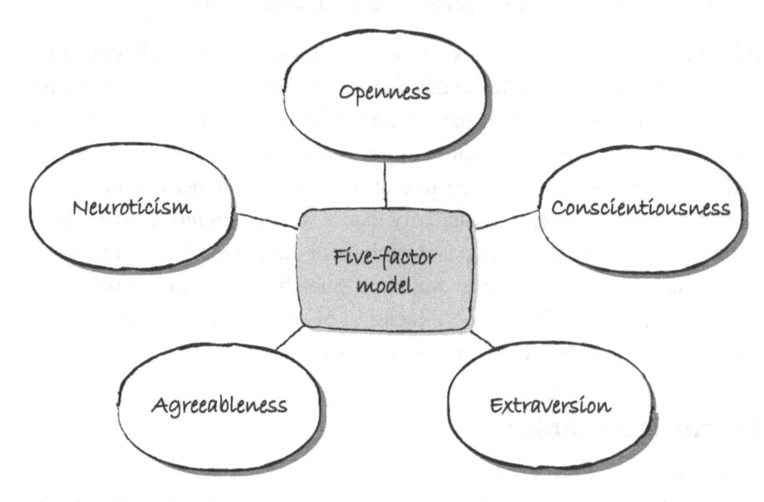

FIGURE 8.2 Five-factor model.

- **Openness to experience:** People with a strong tendency in this trait are considered to be imaginative and creative. They are willing to try new things and are open to ideas.
- **Conscientiousness:** People with a strong tendency in this trait are considered to be goal focused and organized and have self-discipline. They follow rules and plan their actions.
- **Extraversion:** People with a strong tendency in this trait are considered to be outgoing and energetic. They obtain their energy from the company of other people and are defined as being assertive and enthusiastic.
- **Agreeableness:** People with a strong tendency in this trait are considered to be compassionate, kind, and trustworthy. They value getting along with other people and are tolerant.
- **Neuroticism:** People with a strong tendency in this trait are considered to be anxious, self-conscious, impulsive, and pessimistic. They experience negative emotions relatively easily.

There also have been studies that investigate applying the FFM to software engineering teams.[12,13] These studies focus on multiple roles within a software team and not particularly on software architects. However, they do look at key traits for software designers. Based on their analysis, the key trait that has to be strong for software architects is agreeableness. This result supports the Continuous Architecture view that at least 50% of the role of an architect is to focus on communication. (We discuss this in detail in Chapter 9.) The other traits that we think are important for architects are openness to experience and conscientiousness.

It is interesting to note that most of these studies do not explicitly define the role of an architect but refer to the role of a software designer. We are not particularly concerned about the difference between what we would call a solution architect and a software designer. The main differences are in the scale they are operating in. The role of a software designer can be said to happen at a lower level of granularity than a solution architect. Regardless, both are involved in making architecture or design decisions related to a software product. Because we have already stated that Continuous Architecture also applies to the dimension of scale, then both roles should reflect similar capabilities and responsibilities.

Belbin Team Roles

Both MBTI and FFM are based on a view that as human beings, we have common personality traits that define the way we engage with the world, make decisions, and resolve conflicts. It is also recognized that architects operate as part of teams that need to work as a cohesive unit. Although the studies based on personality traits do recognize that different roles require certain personality traits, there is another approach based primarily on identifying different team roles. This is the Belbin team roles based on the work of Meredith Belbin[14] while studying numerous teams at Henley Management College. A high-level overview of the team roles is provided in Table 8.1.

Table 8.1 Belbin Role Types

Plant	Resource Investigator	Coordinator	Shaper	Monitor Evaluator	Team Worker	Implementer	Completer Finisher	Specialist
Solves difficult problems	Explores opportunities, develops contacts	Clarifies goals, promotes decision making	Drives to overcome obstacles	Sees all options, judges accurately	Listens, builds, averts friction	Turns ideas into practical actions	Delivers on time	Provides knowledge and skills in rare supply

If we look at the role of the architect, we can say that four of the Belbin types are more applicable: Plant, Resource Investigator, Monitor Evaluator and Specialist. For each type we will provide the definition we sourced from Wikipedia and provide comments related to Continuous Architecture.

- **Plant:** "Plants are creative, unorthodox generators of ideas. If an innovative solution to a problem is needed, a plant is a good person to ask. A good plant will be bright and free thinking. Plants can tend to ignore incidentals and refrain from getting bogged down in detail. A plant bears a strong resemblance to the popular caricature of the absent-minded professor or inventor and often has a hard time communicating ideas to others."[15]

  At the end of the day, we want architects to solve difficult problems and make key architectural decisions, so the Belbin role of the plant seems to be quite aligned with that view.

  However, this definition can also be viewed as being very close to the commonly perceived vision of the ivory tower architect. They have in-depth knowledge and experience in solving complex problems but find it difficult to communicate with people.
- **Resource Investigator:** "The resource investigator gives a team a rush of enthusiasm at the start of the project by vigorously pursuing contacts and opportunities. He or she is focused outside the team and has a finger firmly on the pulse of the outside world. Where a plant creates new ideas, a resource investigator will quite happily appropriate them from other companies or people."[16]

  At first glance, this seems to be quite the opposite of the plant, but this role type has some key advantages that an architect requires. First of all, we should challenge the perception of the architect who knows everything and can make all decisions. In most cases, solutions to similar problems have been solved elsewhere, and a good architect is one who can find them. We believe that a collaborative architect who gets different perspectives before coming to a conclusion is more suitable in the Continuous Architecture world.
- **Monitor Evaluator:** "Monitor evaluators are fair and logical observers and judges of what is going on in the team. Because they are good at detaching themselves from bias, they are often the ones to see all available options with the greatest clarity and impartiality. They take a broad view when problem solving, and by moving slowly and analytically, they almost always come to the right decision."[17]

  We have said that the primary role of an architect is to make decisions, so a monitor evaluator seems initially like a good fit.

However, there are a few drawbacks. One known weakness of monitor evaluators is that they lack drive and ability to inspire others. Given that a key part of an architect's job is to communicate with stakeholders and at times convince them of the key decisions, this seems like a major drawback. The other challenge with this role is the fact that they take their time to make decisions; however, most times architects need to make decisions quickly without the luxury to analyze all aspects.

- **Specialist:** "Specialists are passionate about learning in their own particular field. As a result, they are likely to be a fountain of knowledge and enjoy imparting this knowledge to others. They also strive to improve and build on their expertise. If there is anything they do not know the answer to, they will happily go and find out. Specialists bring a high level of concentration, ability, and skill in their discipline to the team but can only contribute on that specialism and will tend to be uninterested in anything that lies outside its narrow confines."[18]

  At first glance, this definition seems to be aligned with what an architect should be like. However, we believe that in a Continuous Architecture world, the architect is not a specialist. We would actually argue the contrary, that an architect is a generalist, a technologist with a wide range of expertise. What makes a person a good architect is not specialist knowledge but the ability to apply the required tools of the trade at the appropriate time. In the current software world, we believe that except for in a few unique areas, such as security and embedded systems, the role of a specialized architect is no longer relevant. A model that works quite well is a T-shaped approach in which the architect has the generalist capabilities we mentioned but also has depth in one or two areas. This also enables the architect to keep technical skills in a particular area up to date.

Additional Methods

Psychometrics is defined as *the measurement of mental traits, abilities, and processes.*[19] So far we have covered two major methods, the MBTI and the big five personality traits, or the FFM. But there are several more methods that attempt to uncover the personality traits of individuals. Corporations are increasingly interested in applying psychometric tests. This can be viewed in both a positive and negative manner. On the positive side, corporations want to make sure that their employees understand their strengths and weaknesses. When you know who you are and how you react to common work scenarios, you can develop yourself by emphasizing your strengths and avoiding your weaknesses. This will make you a happier and more successful employee. On the negative side, you could say that corporations want to box people into categories and manage them accordingly. Regardless of what view you take, we can say that psychometric testing is here to stay.

Another interesting method is the Herrmann Brain Dominance Instrument Survey,[20] which was developed by Ned Herrmann while working at General Electric's Crotonville facility. His initial research was published in 1981, and he bases his approach on identifying four key thinking preferences:

- **A- analytical thinking:** This preference focuses on logical and fact-based thinking.
- **B- sequential thinking:** This preference focuses on procedural and methodical thinking.
- **C- interpersonal thinking:** This preference focuses on emotional and sociable thinking.
- **D- imaginative thinking:** This preference focuses on innovative and lateral thinking.

The Herrmann Brain Dominance Instrument Survey ranks an individual's thinking preferences in order of priority. It then looks at how dominant the person's favored thinking preferences are. For example, one of the most commonly found types includes people who are dominant in both analytical and sequential thinking but are not dominant in imaginative and interpersonal thinking (Figure 8.3).

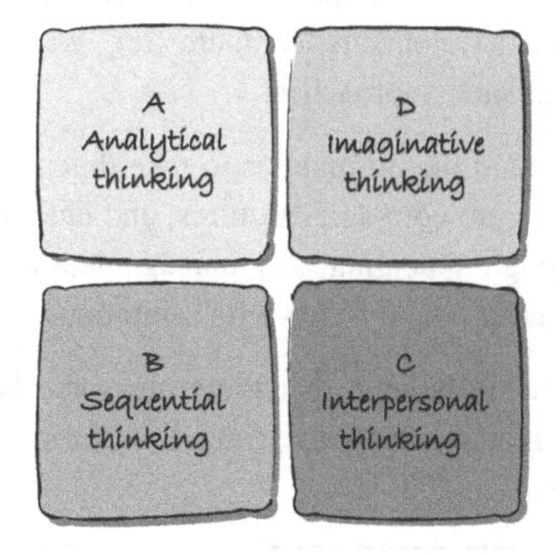

FIGURE 8.3 Herrmann Brain Dominance Instrument survey preferences.

For a Continuous Architecture practitioner, we would like to have someone who has the ability to see the big picture and think outside the box (imaginative thinker) while working effectively with his or her colleagues in driving through decisions (interpersonal thinker). We would also like the person to base his or her decisions on logical thinking (analytical thinker). Applying procedures or methods (sequential thinker) is less relevant. According to Herrmann Brain Dominance Instrument Survey, this would be a triple-dominant individual strong in A, D, and B. Based on the Herrmann's database, this is approximately 5% of the population.

Another method is the Strength Deployment Inventory (SDI®)*. SDI® is based on identifying the motivational values of an individual. SDI® identifies three major motivational value systems. They are assertive, nurturing, and analytic. Obviously, all individuals carry a blend of these values. What is most interesting about the SDI® is that it looks at how the motivational values are exhibited in two circumstances: when things are going well and when in conflict. For example, a person can be a nurturing person when things are going well but switch to being analytical in conflict. SDI® also looks at how a person changes her or his behavior as the conflict escalates. It is difficult to apply the SDI® directly to architectural roles because each of the motivational value systems can provide value in dealing with decision making and managing conflict. Having said that, we believe that a balance of nurturing and analytical value systems is preferable to being assertive while dealing with stakeholders. However, a level of assertiveness is also required to make sure difficult choices are made.

Summarizing Personality Types

This section provided an overview of multiple approaches to identifying personality traits and gave examples of how they apply to a role of an architect. Although it is intellectually interesting, we can also take away practical advice from such approaches.

The first point we would like to make is to take this analysis with a pinch of salt. Human beings are complex creatures, and enterprises are complex organizations. Although appealing, any management approach on boxing people into categories is bound to have its limitations.

Having said that, we do believe that there are some key points we can take away from analyzing personality traits both from a management and individual perspective.

*The SDI®, Strength Deployment Inventory Tool®, was developed in the USA by Dr. Elias H. Porter.

From a management perspective, it is important to recognize that success is based on building well-performing teams. Having a diverse and balanced set of individuals is a foundational requirement to construct a high-performing team. As a manager, using a set of the techniques introduced in this section can give you a structured tool to enable this. If you are focused on building a team of architects, then the personality traits can provide you a good framework to evaluate individuals and look at the role of the architect in a more balanced manner.

From an individual perspective, continuous improvement of skills and capabilities is a lifelong activity. Using such techniques is a good way to evaluate yourself and identify improvement areas. Any of these techniques will provide a mirror in which you can evaluate yourself. As an architect, you can also see how you align with our views of the traits required for Continuous Architecture.

THE ROLE OF THE ARCHITECT IN CONTINUOUS ARCHITECTURE

We have covered general views on the role of a software architect and investigated some of the research done based on different personality types. But what happens to the role of the architect in a Continuous Architecture project? What exactly—if anything—changes? Does she or he need to learn new skills?

We will try to offer some thoughts and advice on these questions. We will look at what capabilities are emphasized by Continuous Architecture. Then we will look at general architecture responsibilities that underpin Continuous Architecture.

But first let us try to bring some of these concepts to life in "A Day in the Life of a Continuous Architect." Here we are using the term *continuous architect* as an architect who applies Continuous Architecture principles and tools. We do not propose to create yet another type of architect; there are sufficient subcategories of architects (solution, software, information, security, and so on) already. We believe that any of these architects can take a Continuous Architecture approach.

A Day in the Life of a Continuous Architect

Let's call our architect Sophia, after Sophia Hayden Bennett, the first graduate of the 4-year architecture program at MIT in 1890.

Sophia is the architect of the MobileShopping platform we discussed in the previous chapter. She starts her day by participating in the daily stand-up. At this stage of the project, the team is in a regular delivery cadence and is releasing code into deployment in cycles of 2 weeks.

Sophia participates actively in the meeting and is particularly interested in some of the deployment challenges the team is dealing with; she takes a note to follow up on this topic. She also provides updates on her "story" that is part of this sprint. This is part of her architectural backlog and deals with the performance and latency challenge uncovered in an architecture validation session. She provides an overview on the work she is doing with the back-end service providers to test a proposed new configuration of the back-end services.

After the session, she sits down with the product manager, Rajeev, and the delivery manager, Doug. They discuss updates to the roadmap that Rajeev is going to publish the following week. There is a big demand from the marketing team to add additional analytic capabilities to the platform. At the same, time Doug is feeling extremely pressured to deliver on the current roadmap features that have already overfilled his backlog. Sophia acts as the voice of reason in this conversation and states that although she understands the extreme demand for the feature, it is a significant architectural enhancement. She takes an action to research different architectural options through her network of architects in the organization. Rajeev is happy that the feature is being considered, and Doug is relieved that the request is being handled in a structured manner. Sophia adds this to her architectural backlog as a new decision to be made.

She also has a short conversation with Doug after the meeting. She has noticed that some of the developers have started tightly coupling their components to meet strict timelines. Although this is understandable and the concern can always be refactored later, she wants to make sure that Doug gets the message that she is watching out for the architectural integrity of the product. She also adds this to her technical debt registry that she keeps on the side.

She then spends the rest of the morning running some executable test scripts she has written to try out the new configuration prototyped jointly with the back-end services architect and team. She is in a good mood because so far, the results are promising. The major performance test will be run in a few days, but so far, it looks like the solution is holding up.

She has lunch with the some of the team members and goes back to the deployment challenge that she noted in the morning stand-up. She realizes that the team is struggling with some of the container capabilities and puts them in touch with an expert that she knows in another team. Although not strictly an architectural decision, she is happy that she has helped the team overcome another roadblock.

The afternoon starts off with a joint session of all the key architects of other products in her business unit. This is facilitated by the Enterprise Architecture team. The session is quite useful in that she gets to hear about what other architects are doing and is able to present her challenge around the analytical capabilities. She schedules a few follow-up sessions to discuss this topic in more detail. She also takes a note that the entitlements enterprise service they use is introducing new features that the MobileShopping product can take advantage of.

She then attends a session with Rajeev, in which he is meeting with a few business users of the platform. It is a fairly informal meeting, but it gives her a chance to get direct input from the users as well as highlight some of the key architectural features of the MobileShopping product.

Her final task of the day is to document the different options for a key architectural decision the team needs to make. The topic of including a configuration engine has been on the agenda for several weeks. There have been different views within the team, as well as the members of the architecture peer review team she has consulted. They are at risk of delaying implementation timelines of the next sprint, so she decides to take a firm stand and strongly recommends not including the configuration engine. She will make sure that her recommendation is ratified in the next enterprise governance meeting they have on this topic.

Sophia has had a productive day, and before leaving work, she spends 30 minutes on the social media platform of the organization. She reads a few posts and responds to some. This is a key activity that keeps her network live, but she does have a hard rule not to spend more than 30 minutes a day on such activities. Otherwise, she might be a popular individual but probably would not deliver much for her team.

In this fictional account of the day in the life of Sophia, she has demonstrated several traits that we deem as critical for applying the Continuous Architecture approach. She is part of a team and is working collectively with them to remove roadblocks. She is fully integrated with the development activities and contributes to the sprints with elements from her architectural backlog. She is involved with architecting how the application is deployed and tested. She is an effective communicator and engages with business users and other architects as well as her development team.

Let us now consider these capabilities in a more structured manner.

Continuous Architecture Responsibilities

The following diagram provides an overview of the key responsibilities and capabilities from the perspective of Continuous Architecture. We have separated the responsibilities into two categories:

- **Emphasized by Continuous Architecture:** These are the responsibilities that are particularly emphasized by the Continuous Architecture approach.
- **Underpin Continuous Architecture:** These are the more generic responsibilities that Continuous Architecture considers an architect should adhere to (Figure 8.4).

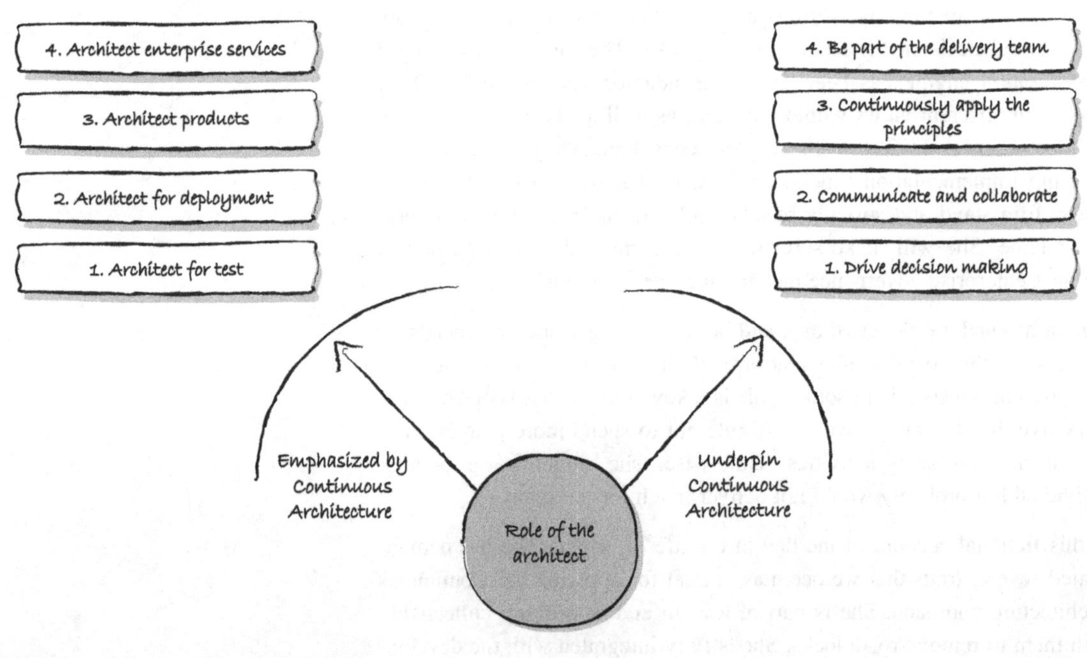

■ **FIGURE 8.4** Continuous Architecture responsibilities.

Responsibilities Emphasized by Continuous Architecture

The most obvious aspect to differentiate in Continuous Architecture is the scope of the architect's responsibility. An architect applying Continuous Architecture should:

- Architect and design the system so that it can be incrementally tested (including system, Quality Assurance [QA], and performance tests). This requires the architect to fully understand the testing processes.
- Architect and design the system so that it can be easily and quickly deployed to the various environments (development, test, and production), potentially on internal and external clouds. This requires the architect to have a very good grasp of the deployment processes.

1. Architect for test (please refer to Figure 8.4).

   Traditionally, architects focus on the design and development portion of the Software Development Life Cycle (SDLC). If it is a more enlightened organization, you will also engage architects in requirements capture and client engagement activities. However, the testing and deployment phases are considered to be the responsibility of the testing or user acceptance testing (UAT) and operations teams, respectively. Those teams follow preset, standard processes that are usually not tailored for the system being tested and deployed. These processes also tend to be monolithic—every component of the system needs to be delivered (and presumably unit and integration tested) for the system, QA, and user acceptance tests to take place. Similarly, all the components of the system are simultaneously deployed from environment to environment, and application usually needs to be reconfigured for each environment (e.g., development, test, and production) (Figure 8.5).

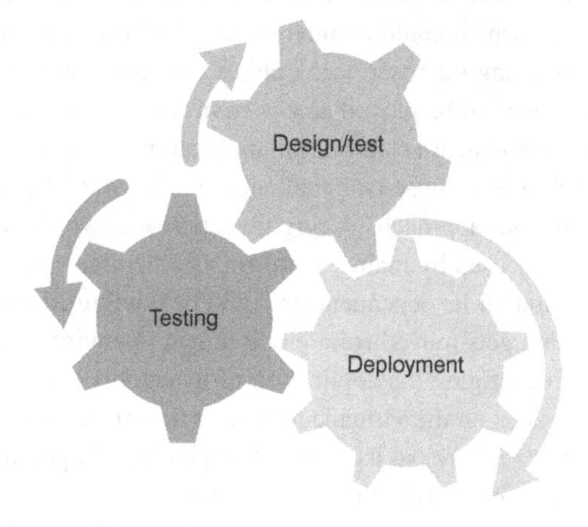

■ **FIGURE 8.5** Continuous Delivery cycles.

So what is changing for the architect? Specifically, adopting a Continuous Architecture approach requires the architect to fully understand how the application software is being tested and how it is being deployed. To be sure, making unit testing an integral part of software development has been one of the key Agile practices since its inception, and Agile approaches have a deliberate focus on "testability" in the software development process. However, implementing Continuous Delivery requires the architect to go beyond Agile practices and to think about how the application software could be tested (including user and performance tested) in an incremental and automated fashion before all the components are built. Manual testing should be avoided as much as possible. Back-end components should not require a front end to be built to fully test them, and similarly, front-end components should be fully testable regardless of the degree of completeness on the front-end components. This may require designing a set of "testing APIs" as part of the architecture. This may also require working with the testing teams to understand their processes and design strategies to automate them.

2. Architect for deployment (refer to Figure 8.4).

   In the same fashion, architects need to understand how the operations group deploys application software in the various environments (dev, test, and prod) and how the overall process can be optimized to save time while keeping quality as high as possible. This is getting even more important as companies are increasing their usage of clouds (both internal and external) and microservices start appearing in architectures. The trend toward using clouds implies that applications should be quickly and seamlessly deployed across environments, which could be internal or external to a company. The trend toward using microservices implies that many more application components need to be moved across environments and configured in the target environment as part of an application deployment. One potential solution to those two challenges could be to implement a "virtual container approach." Using this approach (which is similar to the one already used by many "Platform as a Service" providers), the application and all its dependencies could be configured in a "virtual container" that gets moved from environment to environment without needing to reconfigure the application or its components. This technology relies on the virtualization of infrastructure components, especially the network, so its adoption is predicated upon the adoption and general use of these technologies.

The architect should also be involved in the architecture and design of the environments required for the testing and deployment of the product. This should not only be from the perspective of ease of testing and deployment but also focus on topics such as determining where different levels of validation occur during the test cycles and an approach for validating Quality Attributes.

If we move up the scale and start operating at the department or enterprise level, an architect applying Continuous Architecture should:

a. Architect products, not just solutions for projects. As described in our discussion of Principle 1 in Chapter 2, as IT organizations evolve from today's project-centric focus to a product-centric focus, it is critical for software architecture to lead the way by focusing on products.

b. Architect enterprise services by leveraging the Continuous Architecture principles, especially *Principle 4: Architect for change–leverage "the power of small"* (see Chapter 2).

3. Architect products (refer to Figure 8.4).

The role of the architect in a product-centric world is twofold. First, at the enterprise level, the architect must focus on defining the correct set of products and managing any overlaps and dependencies between or among them. In addition, as part of a product team, the architect has to drive the architectural decisions for the product.

At the enterprise level, the architect needs to understand both the product roadmaps of each product as well as the underlying components and technology used for building them. The product roadmaps enable the architect to understand the capabilities being offered and planned by each product. She or he can then determine if there are any overlaps or key dependencies that have to be managed. This should be aligned with investment governance so that the organization is investing efficiently and not building similar capabilities in different products. The architect also needs to have a view on the internal components and technologies used for each product. This ensures that there is a consistent technology infrastructure and that products can leverage each other's components where appropriate. We can summarize these two aspects by saying that the architect is responsible for ensuring the external and internal consistency and efficiency of the products within the enterprise.

The role of the architect in Agile development is a point of debate in the industry. A dominant view is that there is no need for an overall architecture because the software evolves through the implementation of stories and refactoring. We believe that such a view can be applied only to fairly self-contained projects. If you are architecting a product or trying to operate at a large scale, you do need to think of the architecture; however, this does not mean that you need a separate architect. However, the role of the architect is still crucial to success.

According to Dean Leffingwell,[21] the architect's responsibilities and accountabilities in the Agile world can be summarized as:

- Continuously evolve architecture strategy that supports the needs of the business stakeholders
- Take the full systems view
- Facilitate the flow of architectural initiatives in support of the enterprise value streams
- Understand and communicate Nonfunctional requirements
- Provide architectural governance and guidance, support the teams through routine planning and execution activities
- Empower teams, foster Emergent Design, educate team members in Agile design techniques
- Collaborate with teams on building the Architectural

Runway — near term enablement for business features and capabilities

- Foster innovation by involving team members into exploration activities early and often

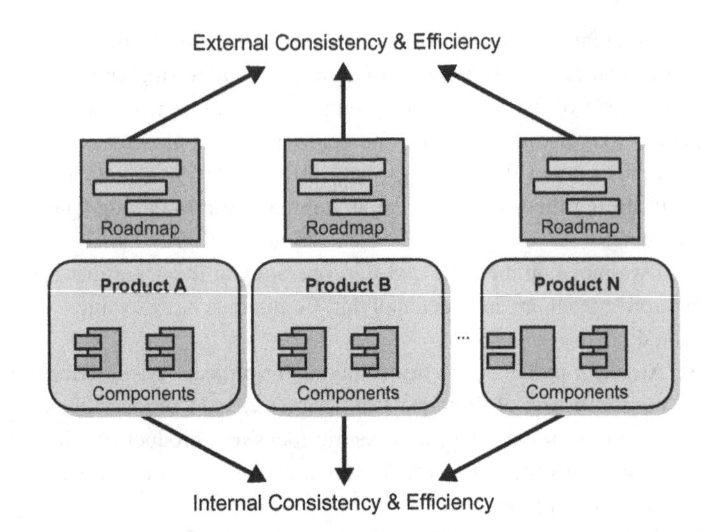

■ **FIGURE 8.6** Product consistency and efficiency.

However, this responsibility should be handled in a flexible manner and not stifle the agility of the product development teams. From an external perspective, products need to meet their customer demand. Trying to be too strict to align products can result in unnecessary delays, which defeats the purpose of Continuous Architecture. The same view applies to being too strict on the internal components and technologies. You could also state that having a level of redundancy and competition among products is a good thing. This enables the organization to try different approaches and technologies to determine which one is most successful. We would only advocate such an approach for more mature technology organizations. As long as these choices are governed effectively and decisions are made transparently, having a more "free market" view of products can be valuable (Figure 8.6).

From the perspective of a single product, the architect plays a key role in the product team. The main responsibility is to balance the demand from the client as represented by the product manager, with the delivery focus provided by the product delivery manager. The architect has to make sure that the architecture of the product is coherent and sustainable. Especially at the beginning of a product, there is often a "negotiation" between product management and the art of the possible. Managing this conversation is a key responsibility of the architect. To do these activities effectively, the key principles to keep in mind are:

a. *Principle 3: Delay design decisions until they are absolutely necessary*: Even though the product needs to have a sustainable architecture, this does not mean to load it up with extra complexity, such as the rules engine example given in Chapter 2.

b. *Principle 2: Focus on Quality Attributes, not on functional requirements*: The best way to make an architecture sustainable is to focus on Quality Attributes. This enables you to create a solid foundation which can be extended, in particular if you combine this with *Principle 4: Architect for change—leverage "the power of small."*

It is also important to point out that in Continuous Architecture, the architect operates as part of a team—in this case, the product team. This implies that the communication and collaboration skills become highly relevant. We believe that "Oracle of Delphi" architects who know all the answers are mythological beasts like unicorns (Figure 8.7).

In Continuous Architecture, architects facilitate, not dictate.

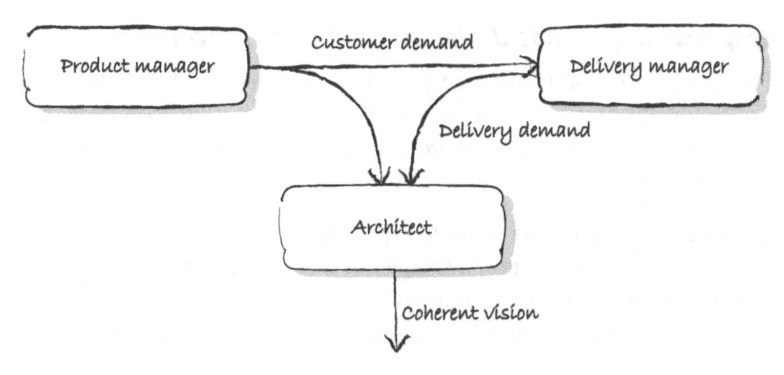

■ **FIGURE 8.7** Architect's balancing role for a product.

4. Architect enterprise services (refer to Figure 8.4).

As with all levels of software at the enterprise level, it is very important to create loosely coupled services based on the "microservices" design philosophy. This approach ensures that enterprise services are reusable across the enterprise and evolve as requirements change. Whether enterprise services are developed by an enterprise-level group, by a business unit group, or even by various development groups using an "internal open source" model, the role of the architect is to ensure that these services are properly designed and (more important) that the application development groups are

In his short work "On Exactitude in Science" ("*Del rigor en la ciencia*" in the original Spanish), Jorge Luis Borges describes a mysterious guild of cartographers who build a map of the empire at a ratio of 1:1. (The idea was formerly presented in Lewis Carroll's *Sylvie and Bruno Concluded*.) As a result, the map is an exact representation of the empire's territory. In the story, the descendants of the guild find the map useless and leave it to nature's elements.

By stating that architects should deal with the realized architecture, are we recommending that architects try to replicate the 1:1 map? Definitely not! A key role of the architect is to be able to abstract to make the necessary definitions. To do this, they are required to build models, diagrams, and documents to describe the architecture. What we should not do is fall into the fallacy that the artifacts we create are the realized architecture.

There are several technologies that claim to enable technologists to engage with and abstract the realized architecture. Modeling tools have been reverse engineering models from code since the 1990s. Several Enterprise Architecture tools generate lists of assets from configuration management databases and business activity monitoring tools provide a view of real-time data and transactions flowing through the infrastructure. However,

aware of their existence so they can use them. In addition, the architect is responsible for managing (i.e., build, define, standardize, and reuse) the APIs associated with these services. At some level, the responsibility of the architect is similar to what was described for the external consistency and efficiency of products. However, there is one significant difference. For enterprise services, the architect is a key customer. In other words, the view of architects is a primary input in determining which enterprise services should be invested in within the organization.

A final aspect of an architect's responsibility is to continuously incorporate feedback into new versions of the architecture. We discussed the topic of continuous feedback loops in Chapter 5. We believe that the days of architecture only represented as a set of documents are over. "Every system has an architecture."[22,23] This architecture is represented by the code that is running on the physical infrastructure. We will call this the "realized architecture."

In Continuous Architecture, the role of the architect is to understand, influence, improve, and communicate the realized architecture.

Responsibilities That Underpin Continuous Architecture

The previous section focused on providing an overview of key responsibilities for architects who are applying Continuous Architecture. Now we will provide an overview of more generic responsibilities that underpin Continuous Architecture.

1. Drive decision making (refer to Figure 8.4).

   As explained in detail in Chapter 4, driving the right architecture decisions is a key responsibility of an architect.

   If architects do nothing else, they need to drive architectural decisions.

   Principle 3 of Continuous Architecture recommends that all design decisions should be delayed until they are absolutely necessary. This means that architects need to start thinking in terms of a Minimum Viable Architecture that starts small and is only expanded when absolutely necessary.

   This does not mean that architects should avoid making decisions until they have all the facts and have analyzed all options. Going into an analysis-paralysis mode is directly opposite of what Continuous Architecture recommends. When a decision has to be made, the architect needs to move quickly and facilitate the decision-making process. The main reason organizations respect good architects is their ability to make the correct decisions in an ambiguous context.

Some of this comes from experience (hence the fact that most architects are senior technologists with significant experience), and some of it is based on applying the relevant tools (e.g., Quality Function Deployment for prioritization) at the appropriate time.

2. Communicate and collaborate (refer to Figure 8.4).

   Communication and collaboration is another key responsibility of an architect. As we will see in more detail in Chapter 9, Continuous Architecture emphasizes the importance of communication and collaboration, with the motto "We cannot overcommunicate."

   No matter if you are a solution architect focused on one product line or an enterprise architect, we believe that more than 50% of your time needs to focus on effective communication and collaboration.

   Specialized architects (business, information, application, infrastructure, solution, and enterprise) tend to work in silos, hence the "ivory tower" label often used to describe architecture groups. The role of an architect is to share knowledge rather than keep it within the group. In addition, getting outside-in views (including views from other industries) is very important. Each architect needs to be encouraged to look outside his or her respective competency domain, look for new ideas, and leverage those ideas on the various programs and projects within the enterprise.

3. Continuously apply Continuous Architecture principles (refer to Figure 8.4).

   It goes without saying that we would expect an architect working with Continuous Architecture to apply the core principles. We have already touched upon quite a few of the principles, implicitly or explicitly, in this chapter. Let us complete the picture by referring to two principles that we have not discussed yet.

   All architects need to respond to the functional and nonfunctional requirements while driving decisions. As stated by *Principle 2: Focus on Quality Attributes, not on functional requirements*, Continuous Architecture states that quality attribute requirements have the most impact on the architecture. As a result, the architect's role is to put special emphasis on Quality Attributes. This should be done in a balanced manner with *Principle 3: Delay design decisions until they are absolutely necessary*. It is very tempting to architect for extreme nonfunctional requirements. Taking this approach will lead to overengineered solutions that are not cost effective and can be difficult to manage. All Quality Attributes should be defined in a manner that dictates their immediate need.

   What helps an architect balance these two principles is *Principle 4: Architect for change—leverage "the power of small"*. By

all of these solutions provide a part of the puzzle and most often with disappointing results. As architects, we have to understand that we are constrained by the limitations of our representations and be comfortable in the ambiguity that this brings.

In his fascinating book *The Hour Between Dog and Wolf*,[24] John Coates delves into the details of how biochemistry and the way the brain functions impact the decision making of bankers. Even if you are not a banker, the book provides insights into how the brain operates in conjunction or in partnership with our body to act and make decisions.

An intriguing topic covered is gut feelings. Apparently, there is a scientific basis for calling an initial hunch we have about a decision a gut feeling. The body and brain are in constant communication, most of it outside our conscious mind. As stated by Coates: "A great deal of our sensation, thinking and automatic reactions take place rapidly and preconsciously."[24] In essence, we have two types of thinking, preconscious and conscious thought. (This is what Nobel Prize winner Daniel Kahneman calls "fast and slow thinking" in his 2011 bestselling book *Thinking, Fast and Slow*.[25]) Our intuition or gut feeling is basically the automatic reactions we make.

The interesting aspect about this is that people specializing in a certain topic (e.g., firefighters and paramedics) have specialized intuitions that can be trusted in their area of expertise. Basically, our bodies and brains are experts in recognizing patterns and being able to react to them without the need for the high energy-consuming act of conscious thought.

Aren't architectural decisions all about abstracting, recognizing patterns, and choosing the correct option? In these cases, should architects who have experience in solving problems trust their gut instincts? This is more cost effective than conducting time- and resource-consuming analysis activities. More times than not, the results of our analysis just validate what we thought in the first place. Interesting food for thought.

leveraging "the power of small," architects should design solutions based on small (e.g., microservices), loosely coupled components.

The most difficult part of applying the Continuous Architecture principles is doing it continuously. For example, we mentioned the importance of the architectural decision log in Chapter 4. All architects at one point in time create such a list, but what usually happens is that the list quickly gets out of date and is not referred to. Similarly, clearly documenting architectural decisions is also usually ignored in the heat of the battle. As a result, anyone looking back a year later will find it difficult to understand why certain decisions were made.

Being able to apply the principles continuously takes discipline and hard work. The level of effort to do this should not be underestimated. If we refer back to the different psychometric evaluations described in this chapter, we can come to the conclusion that following of detailed process and procedures is not usually a capability that we associate with or would prefer to have in architects. As architects, we should acknowledge where our shortcomings are and learn to balance them with being part of a team that has individuals with the required process and procedure skills. For example, an architect can partner with people who are Belbin role types of implementer and completer finisher to make sure that the principles are applied continuously.

This leads us into the final key responsibility of an architect—being part of a team.

4. Be part of the delivery team.

In Continuous Architecture, we do not believe in the architect as an isolated individual or team, the stereotypical ivory tower architect. If you apply *Principle 6: Model the organization after the design of the system*, you will naturally end up with a team structure that has the architect embedded as part of the delivery team.

If you are operating in a Continuous Delivery project, the overall goal of the architect is to clear roadblocks and support the delivery teams with the resources they need to get things done, for example, creating an "architecture runway." (See Glossary for a definition of architecture runway.) This includes proving that new technologies will actually work by creating prototypes as part of the architecture runway.

In a Continuous Architecture model, the role of the architect is likely to evolve from a specialist in one of the traditional architecture domains to being more of a generalist—not unlike the role that a solution architect plays on a project. The main difference is that the architect applying Continuous Architecture works along three dimensions: design/build, testing, and deployment.

What about the traditional enterprise architect role? We assert that Continuous Architecture principles apply in both the time and scale dimensions. If we take this view, then an enterprise architect is an architect who operates at an enterprise scale. There is definitely a need for roles operating at this scale. However, the focus should not be an ivory tower view that creates strategy and architecture artifacts that do not have an immediate relevance on the "realized architecture." Enterprise architects need to alter their views to focus more on a product-centric architecture that leverages enterprise services. They should also look at ways they can engage more effectively with actual delivery teams as we will expand in Chapter 10. We also believe that traditional architects tend to produce lots of e-paper. We recommend that architects applying Continuous Architecture focus on producing implementable code—and avoid the BARF (big architecture up front) syndrome.

A final point we would like to make in terms of integrating with delivery teams is the idea of architects cycling through different delivery teams. We have stated that architects need to be integral to delivery teams and that the more experience an architect has, the more value she or he provides in facilitating architectural decisions. A key way of enabling architects to gain experience is to expose them to different problem and technology domains. A deliberate initiative of architects cycling through different development teams is of tremendous value to the individuals and the enterprise. When we say cycling, we would also encourage architects to minimize multitasking across different projects at the same time. This we believe will be counterproductive because it will make it difficult for the architects to become part of a delivery team.

SUMMARY

In this chapter, we focused on the role of the architect in the world of Continuous Architecture. We started by looking at how the term *architect* is interpreted in general terms. We then defined the role of the architect as follows:

> *Continuous Architecture states that an architect is responsible for enabling the implementation of a software product by driving architectural decisions in a manner that protects the conceptual integrity of the software product.*

We then looked at what types of personality traits are normally perceived as belonging to architects. For this, we looked at multiple psychometric evaluation tools used within the industry. While doing this we attempted to call out common traits that are more suitable for architects. Research is not widespread in applying such techniques to the particular role of an architect. Regardless, we can draw some conclusions on key traits that would make an architect successful.

We expect architects to be analytical thinkers and have the ability to abstract. This would be realized as NT in MBTI, openness to experience in FFM, analytical, and imaginative thinking in the Herrmann Brain Dominance Instrument Survey. Because collaboration and communication are key for an architect, traits that focus on these areas are also key for success. This would be realized as extraversion in MBTI, agreeableness in FFM, and interpersonal thinking in the Herrmann Brain Dominance Instrument Survey. Please note that we do not see these psychometrics tests as a mechanism to evaluate if a particular individual can be a good architect. We believe career choices are up to each individual. However, using these methods is important for architects to become more self-aware and work on areas they need to improve.

We also noted the importance of an architect being part of a team. For this, we looked at the Belbin role types and observed that the most suitable role type for an architect is plant, and to a lesser extent monitor evaluator. However, we also realized that, in particular, Continuous Architecture emphasizes the role type of the resource investigator.

We then described the role of an architect within the context of Continuous Architecture. After providing a fictitious day in the life of an architect, we highlighted responsibilities that Continuous Architecture emphasizes:

1. Architect for deployment.
2. Architect for test.
3. Architect products.
4. Architect enterprise services.

We also discussed more generic responsibilities that underpin Continuous Architecture:

1. Facilitate decision making.
2. Communicate and Collaborate.
3. Continuously apply principles.
4. Be part of the development team.

We believe that the role of the architect is more relevant than ever in the technology world that is moving toward Continuous Delivery. However, to be successful, architects have to expand their responsibilities beyond their traditional comfort zones. While doing this they also have to work collaboratively as part of the delivery teams and engage effectively with a wide group of stakeholders.

ENDNOTES

1. Peyret H. The foundational architecture roles and how they are changing. Forrester Research, July 10, 2014.
2. Brooks F. The mythical man-month: essays on software engineering. Addison-Wesley, 1975, 1995.
3. CNNMoney. Best jobs in America, 2015. <http://money.cnn.com/gallery/pf/2015/01/27/best-jobs-2015/index.html/>.
4. Eeles P. Characteristics of a software architect, IBMDeveloper Works, 2006. <https://www.ibm.com/developerworks/rational/library/mar06/eeles/>.
5. The Myers & Briggs Foundation. <http://www.myersbriggs.org/>.
6. Stromberg S. Vox. <http://www.vox.com/2014/7/15/5881947/myers-briggs-personality-test-meaningless>.
7. Michael J. Using the Myers-Briggs Type Indicator as a tool for leadership development? Apply with caution. J Leadersh Organ Stud 2003;10(1):68–81.
8. Krutchen P. Architects—the software architecture team. Proceedings of the first working IFIP conference on software architecture. San Antonio; 1999.
9. Parteek J. Role of different personality types in software engineering team, September 2011. <http://recipe4developer.files.wordpress.com/>.
10. Center for Applications of Psychological Type. Estimated frequencies of the types in the United States population, 2015. <http://www.capt.org/mbti-assessment/estimated-frequencies.htm/>.
11. Cherry K. The big five personality dimensions. About Education. <http://psychology.about.com/od/personalitydevelopment/a/bigfive.htm/>.
12. Rahman M, Mahmood AK, Salleh R, Amin A. Mapping job requirements of software engineers to big five personality traits. International Conference on Computer & Information Science, 2012.
13. Sodiya AS, Longe HOD, Onashoga SA, et al. An improved assessment of personality traits in software engineering. Interdiscip J Inf, Knowl Manag 2007;2.
14. Belbin. Belbin team roles, <http://www.belbin.com/>.
15. Wikipedia. Team role inventories: plant, <http://en.wikipedia.org/wiki/Team_Role_Inventories#Plant/>.
16. Wikipedia. Team role inventories: resource investigator, <http://en.wikipedia.org/wiki/Team_Role_Inventories#Resource_Investigator/>.
17. Wikipedia. Team role inventories: monitor evaluator, <http://en.wikipedia.org/wiki/Team_Role_Inventories#Monitor_Evaluator/>.
18. Wikipedia. Team role inventories: specialist, <http://en.wikipedia.org/wiki/Team_Role_Inventories#Specialist/>.
19. Dictionary.com. Psychometrics, <http://www.dictionary.com/>.
20. Herrmann International. <http://www.herrmannsolutions.com/>.
21. Leffingwell D. Agile software requirements.
22. IEEE 1471 Conceptual Framework.
23. Bass L, Clements P, Kazman R. Software architecture in practice, third edition. Addison-Wesley, Upper Saddle River, NJ; 2013.
24. Coates J. The hour between dog and wolf: risk-taking, gut feelings and the biology of boom and bust. Penguin Random House Canada; 2012.
25. Kahneman D. Thinking, fast and slow. Macmillan; 2011.

Chapter 9

Continuous Architecture in the Enterprise

Translation is the art of failure.

—Umberto Eco

Chapter 8 discussed the role of the architect in today's world. This chapter already had a more "enterprise" feel to it. We want to expand on this with views on how to implement Continuous Architecture (or in fact any form of architecture) successfully in an enterprise. When we talk about operating at the enterprise scale, we are not focusing on what is traditionally called Enterprise Architecture. Our focus is more on building out solutions at a significantly large scale.

Remember that Continuous Architecture can be considered in two dimensions, time and scale. In the time dimension, we focus on continuously applying the principles and tools outlined in this book rather than following a staged or Waterfall process. In the scale dimension, we can implement the principles and tools to a single team or application to a product suite and finally to the enterprise. However, operating at a larger scale brings its own challenges and more complexity. A majority of the challenges and complexity are social rather than technical and are usually not a focus point of most Continuous Delivery and Agile approaches (Scaled Agile Framework [SAFe] being the most significant exception).[1]

We will start this chapter off by creating the context of operating at an enterprise scale by presenting a set of known enterprise antipatterns. These help provide examples of the types of challenges faced at large scale.

We will then focus on the topic of communication and collaboration. As we increase the scale we are operating, the communications and "soft skills" side of architecture become more relevant.

A key enabler for communicating is to have a common language, which will be our next area of focus. We will look at some industry examples and then provide a set of recommendations on how to create a common language.

We will then revisit the topic of decisions but from the perspective of making them in the enterprise. This will lead us into the topic of architecture governance within the context of wider governance that exists in the enterprise.

We will finally provide some views on the topic of having an architecture process at the enterprise scale.

CONTEXT FOR THE ENTERPRISE AND ANTIPATTERNS

Most architects (including the authors of this book) operate within the context of a large organization—what we call the enterprise. On the one hand, we are lucky enough to operate in an environment that requires solving complex problems and recognizes the need for a level of design and planning. On the other hand, we deal with complexities and conflicting dynamics of any organization. In this section, we will first look at some of the dynamics related to working in such an environment and the constraints that all architects have to deal with.

Communication and Autonomy

The organization's impact on the architecture is so dominant is that we recognize this in *Principle 6: Model the organization after the design of the system.* This is based on Conway's law, which we can repeat as follows:

> *Organizations which design systems ... are constrained to produce designs which are copies of the communication structures of these organizations.*[2]

It is interesting to note that the article Conway's law originated from is called "How do committees invent?" In this article, Conway gives quite a few software examples, such as:

> *A contract research organization had eight people who were to produce a COBOL and an ALGOL compiler. After some initial estimates of difficulty and time, five people were assigned to the COBOL job and three to the ALGOL job. The resulting COBOL compiler ran in five phases, the ALGOL compiler ran in three.*[2]

Rather than software systems, his focus was more on design in the context of large organizations. In the same article, he also points out that there is a certain point at which large system design efforts disintegrate because of the organizational structure they create and the subsequent complexity in team organization and communication. You can say that without *Principle 4: Architect for change—leverage "the power of small,"* design is doomed to fail because of organizational complexity.

Another classic for computer engineers is the *Mythical Man-Month* by Frederic Brooks.[3] Frederic Brooks wrote his essays based on the experience of managing the development of the IBM OS/360 operating system. The insights he provided from the experience several decades ago still ring true today. He is most famous for indicating that adding more people to a late project would delay it even further; hence the title *Mythical Man-Month*.

Similar to Conway, Brooks had good insights on the dynamics of the organization. For example, he spoke about the risk of keeping too many implementers busy while the architecture is not fully defined. As he clearly points out, people like to be productive. So if you have a lot of people without any structured guidance, they will still produce output, but it will most likely result in disappointing results.

Another entertaining analogy Frederic Brooks provides relates to the communication challenge with the Tower of Babel. He does a parody of a postmortem of the Tower of Babel project, or in his own words:

> *Management Audit of the Babel Project. They had all the criteria: clear mission, manpower, materials, time, technology yes—but they were not able to communicate.*[3]

Finally, Brooks discusses the point of organizing enterprises for creativity and a term not used that much in IT literature: *enjoyment of workers*. He refers to a term defined by E.F. Schumacher: the principle of subsidiary function. Again, in Brook's words:

> *E.F. Schumacher, in his classic,* Small is Beautiful: Economics as if People Mattered,[4] *proposes a theory of organizing enterprises to maximize the creativity and joy of workers. Schumacher goes on to interpret:*
>
> *The Principle of Subsidiary Function teaches us that the centre will gain authority and effectiveness if the freedom and responsibility of the lower formations are carefully preserved, with the result that the organization as a whole will be 'happier and more prosperous.'*
>
> *How can such a structure be achieved? . . . The large organization will consist of many semi-autonomous units, which*

The mid 1990s was an era when object-oriented development was taking the industry by storm. All information technology (IT) departments had started key initiatives with this technology. At a major U.S. firm, the chief information officer (CIO) had decided that SmallTalk was the future. As a result, it was decided that all the billing and accounting systems would all be rewritten in SmallTalk. The effort was seen as a huge task, and first priority was given to hiring and training up to 100 developers. Unfortunately, the team was very successful in hiring and training the developers. As a result, the organization ended up with a huge number of developers without the architecture or even the project plan being defined. No developer likes to stay idle, so in the absence of any structure to guide them, the teams started writing code. After several months, they had developed a mass spaghetti of code and a series of unnecessary and contradictory components. At the end, the company had to throw away everything and restart with a smaller team and a more architecture-driven focus.

> *we may call quasifirms. Each of them will have a large amount of freedom, to give the greatest possible change to creativity and entrepreneurship.... Each quasi-firm must have both a profit and loss account, and a balance sheet.*[3]

We can interpret Schumacher's principle of subsidiary function as applying *Principle 4: Architect for change—leverage "the power of small"* to organizational design.

Enterprise Antipatterns

Now that we have touched upon the importance and challenges of communication in the enterprise, let us provide a brief view on antipatterns. Antipatterns refer to common approaches to problems that result in an undesirable outcome. Several of them have been articulated for software development, design, and architecture. A good example of an antipattern that can be applied to an enterprise is design by committee. In *AntiPatterns: Refactoring Software, Architectures, and Projects in Crisis*,[5] the authors define this antipattern as

> *A complex software design is the product of a committee process. It has so many features and variations that it is infeasible for any group of developers to realize the specifications in a reasonable time frame. Even if the designs were possible, it would not be possible to the test the full design due to excessive complexity, ambiguities, overconstraint, and other specification defects. The design would lack conceptual clarity because so many people contributed to it and extended it during its creation.*

The book continues to provide an interesting story of how the Structured Query Language (SQL) became an international standard in 1989. At that time, the specification was 115 pages. In 1992, SQL92 was documented in 580 pages, and the next version, SQL 3, runs to thousands of pages. As a result, no database vendor implements the standard in a similar manner. The consequence of this has been the need for standards: ODBC (Open Database Connectivity) and JDBC (Java Database Connectivity). These standards define the client interface and as a result hide the complexities of vendor-specific extensions.

One antipattern we would like to coin is the "default decision." This is when in the absence of clear decisions, organizational momentum results in a default, normally suboptimal, decision. These are the architectural decisions that happen anyway and most of the time contribute to the entropy of the organization's IT system landscape. We can also interpret this antipattern as not applying *Principle 3: Delay design decisions until they are absolutely necessary* effectively. In this antipattern, decisions happen implicitly rather than explicitly. The problem is not that the design decisions are done too quickly or too late; it is more that design decisions are not recognized or understood. As a result, the organizational dynamics result in certain design choices becoming a reality. It should come as no surprise that this results in Conway's law being realized in a negative manner.

One example of this antipattern is when several applications exist in the enterprise that provide similar functionality. For example, in absence of a focus on enterprise services (as will be articulated in Chapter 10), it is quite common to find competing platforms that provide entitlements (here we are using a fairly broad definition of the term: a service that manages access of roles to particular capabilities) functionality. Because entitlements capabilities are common across applications, teams normally tend to try to reuse these capabilities between a set of applications that are managed by the same team. Over time, these applications increase in number, and as the organization is restructured, some are deprecated, and others join the long list of orphaned applications that exist in the enterprise.

Another example of this antipattern is with lack of a view on how applications should integrate, the organization ends up with multiple point to point application interfaces. These interfaces also use a wide variety of technologies from file transfer to database links.

These examples might seem to conflict with *Principle 3: Delay design decisions until they are absolutely necessary*. If we delay design decisions, then don't we fall into the "default decision" design pattern? This view ignores the second part of the principle, "*until they are absolutely necessary.*" If you explicitly list and prioritize all your design decisions (as recommended in Chapter 4), you actually reduce your risk of falling into this antipattern.

The "default decision" antipattern basically follows from simple human behavior: Without structure, all application teams will take the path of least resistance. This normally ends up in increasing the technical debt of the organization.

Now that we have provided some examples of enterprise antipatterns, let us look at some recommendations on how we can address these challenges. The first step is on collaboration and communication.

COLLABORATION AND COMMUNICATION

"Ivory tower" is a label quite often applied to architects, especially to enterprise architects. They can be seen as people who draw pretty

Trying to demonstrate the value of architects can result in quite interesting scenarios. At one point, an enterprise decided that all architects needed to be formally part of a central organization. This was to ensure that all architects were trained and applied a consistent approach, but was really more like a "power play" by a senior manager.

About six months after this change, the senior manager realized he had a group of a couple of hundred people and was getting challenged by his management about the value his architects provided. To make sure that he could justify the group, he decreed that all architects had to charge their time to actual projects.

This resulted in a scenario in which anyone in IT who launched a project suddenly found a queue of five or six architects knocking on their door, from the data architect to the network architect. Obviously, this did not feature so well in increasing the trust of the architecture function.

WHAT DO REAL ARCHITECTS DO?

The recent decades have seen an increase in the concept of the "celebrity" architect. (By "real architects," we mean the ones who deal with physical buildings.) They are successful because of their ability to sell an expensive vision and fund it, but they also have the ability to execute.

If you look at the opening page of Gehry Partners'

diagrams and add no value. In the extreme, these architects can be viewed as people who create insane standards and try to govern accordingly.

The overall objective has to be to make architects be a part of the overall IT organization and not perceived as a separate entity.

Most architects focus their effort in "building" the architecture. This is natural because normally, fairly technical people who enjoy building systems become architects. However, "socializing" the architecture is equally (if not more) important. In summary, *improving the perception of the architecture function requires soft skills.*

Again, there is no easy cookbook on how to improve communication around the architecture function. However, focusing on a set of communication levers would be a good starting point. We will present these from the perspective of a separate architecture function. This is mainly because this is where the challenges are most explicitly observed within the context of the enterprise. However, we believe that the levers presented here can be applied by architects at all levels. The communication levers we recommend can be articulated as:

1. **Vision and storyboard:** This is stating the obvious—you have to know what your product is before you can try to market it. It is important for an architecture function to clearly identify how it is adding value to the enterprise. This is usually done at the senior management level via a set of PowerPoint presentations. Although we do agree that a vision and mission statement for architecture is required, after it is articulated, the value of the architecture should be self-evident.
2. **Communication channels:** The architecture function in an enterprise has to communicate with all sets of stakeholders. This goes from the Executive Officer (CxO) level, which has to be convinced of the value of the architecture, to the database administrator (DBA), who is trying to figure out if he or she should use stored procedures. Creating channels for open and bidirectional communication with the different stakeholders is required to reach out to such a wide variety of groups. Although we talk about different communication channels, we should not underestimate the value of face-to-face meetings. We are human beings, and the impact of in-person engagement is invaluable. We recommend that when possible, all engagement should be conducted in person.
3. **Artifacts and tools:** One way we like to define an approach to architecture is "a bag of tools and the wisdom to know when to use them."

Crystallizing and packaging architecture artifacts and tools so that they can be easily digested and used by different stakeholders is another key success factor. The most important principle here is self-service. In other words, the artifacts and tools should not require the reader to have a PhD to understand them. In addition, different stakeholder groups will need to be communicated in separate "languages" (e.g., Unified Modeling Language [UML] or presentations).

4. **Process:** At the end of the day, the architecture activities live within existing processes within the enterprise. It is important to understand how architecture aligns with multiple IT processes ranging from the development process to production support activities.
5. **Financials:** Architecture should not be seen as an abstract ivory tower exercise. It is important to have the ability to articulate value in financial terms.

As can be seen from these points, focusing on the collaboration and communication aspects of architecture is not an effort that is left as an after-hours exercise. It should be taken seriously, and any architecture function in a large enterprise should have dedicated roles focusing on these

■ **FIGURE 9.1** Dancing House by Frank Gehry and Vlado Milunic in Prague. *Photo by Dino Quinzani is licensed under CC BY 2.0.*

website,[6] you see the following quote:

Gehry Partners employs a large number of senior architects who have extensive experience in the technical development of building systems and construction documents, and who are highly qualified in the management of complex projects.

It is interesting to note the emphasis given to management of complex projects, which most projects at the enterprise scale are. In IT, architects are very rarely known as the people who you would trust with complex projects; you would give them the complex technical problems instead. In contrast, in the world of real architecture, you will give the difficult technical problems to engineers. In a newspaper article on February 25, 2015,[7] a leading British architect, Ken Shuttleworth, criticized architects for taking all the credit. As quoted by the *Independent* newspaper in a speech addressed to engineers, he said:

Architects take all the credit for all [engineers'] hard work . . . you [engineers] need to tell the architects, when they try and call the shots, to sod off.

However, sometimes form does take over function. For example, the Dancing House by Frank Gehry and Vlado Milunic in Prague is situated next to a very busy road and depends on forced-air circulation (Figure 9.1). It is claimed that this makes the interior somewhat less pleasant for its occupants. If this claim is true, we could interpret this challenge as the architect not implementing *Principle 2: Focus on Quality Attributes , not on functional requirements.* In essence, the Quality Attribute focused on the comfort of the occupants was not fully realized.

aspects. Let us now focus a little more on how architects should engage with different stakeholder groups.

Table 9.1 provides an overview of how the communication levers defined earlier can be applied to each stakeholder group. It is color coded, where white represents most relevant, light grey somewhat relevant, and dark grey not relevant at all.

Table 9.1 Communication levers for Stakeholders

Stakeholder	Vision and Storyboard	Communication Channels	Artifacts and Tools	Process	Financials
Development teams	Not very relevant; they just want to know that architects add value	User forums and social platforms	Self-service tools and advice	They require clarification on when to engage architects	Not relevant
Operations	Somewhat relevant; make sure the vision incorporates operational stability	Participation in operations forums (incident or problem management, deployment)	Focus on tools to support operations	Align operations processes with architecture	Ability to demonstrate Total Cost of Ownership is important
Testers	Somewhat relevant, particularly around approach to testing	User forums and social platforms	Focus on tools to support testing	Align testing processes with architecture	Not relevant
Technology executives	Without a clear sell to executives, architecture is a no-starter	Senior management meetings, one-on-one sessions with key stakeholders	Provide data-driven insight	Interested in impact of KPIs	Need to demonstrate positive financial impact of architecture
Business	Need to clearly articulate the value of architecture in business terms	Senior management meetings, one-on-one sessions with key stakeholders	Data driven insight	Not relevant	Relevant within the wider context of financials of the IT organization

As can be seen, different levers are required to address different stakeholder groups. One point of interest is that one lever that is highly relevant for all stakeholder groups is the establishment of the correct communication channels. Let us look in a little more detail at how the architect should communicate with these different stakeholder groups. For each stakeholder group, we will first focus on how they view architects and then demonstrate how some of the communication levers can be used. For this, we will walk through a story of a fictional architecture function within the enterprise. Although radically simplified, we think that presenting the levers within such a context highlights some of the key points.

Architects and Development Teams

It is quite common for application development teams to just want to get on with their sprints; any notion of an architect is usually seen as a necessary evil to deal with. They normally want to avoid any direct challenge and questioning from the architects. It is quite common for development teams to try to hide their architectural decisions from outside scrutiny. This should not be seen as bad behavior; it is just human nature.

On the flip side, without any influence over the development teams, architects can gain no traction. In such cases, they risk being banished to the land of PowerPoint and pointless meetings.

Implementing *Principle 6: Model the organization after the design of the system* greatly reduces the above friction. In this case, the architects are already a part of the team. The only external architects should be focused on setting standards for particular domains (e.g., security, databases).

As can be seen from Table 9.1 on communication levers for stakeholders, the place to start with development teams is communication channels and artifacts and tools. Let us illustrate with an example.

In a large organization, there is a central architecture team that consists of a small group of high-caliber technologists and a similar sized governance team. The technologists in the architecture team spend a lot of their time investigating upcoming technologies. As a result, they have built good relationships with vendors and open source providers. Meanwhile, the governance team has spent significant effort in customizing an industry standard architecture approach with the help of an external consulting organization. They have developed a series of processes and templates. They are currently rolling out a three-step governance process across the organization.

Meanwhile, the development teams are all operating in an Agile manner and striving for Continuous Delivery. The technologist architects are seen as a traditional ivory tower group. Development teams just ignore them. The governance team is in worse shape in its relationship with the development teams; they are actually disliked and seem like a force of evil. Development teams view the governance team as a group that asks them to create unnecessary documents and attend pointless review meetings. Why waste time, when you have a sprint to deal with? Most development teams assign one team member to worry about the documentation and try to get by the governance reviews by exposing minimal information.

Let's see how some of the Continuous Architecture principles and tools can help our central architecture team. The head of the architecture team notices the challenge his group faces. So he starts by making sure that the technologists are adding value to the organization. He asks them to stop all external interaction and research. Instead, they are given two tasks to complete in a month's time. Each of them has to

1. **Actively participate** in the development blogs that are popular in the organization. This will enable them to understand the hot topics that the developers are dealing with. By being active participants, they will become known within the organization. The more engaging architects start showing up at development team social gatherings and even daily stand-up meetings.
2. **Create a set of artifacts** that solve a challenge they have identified while "socializing" with the development teams. There is no restriction on what such an artifact can be. Suddenly, by producing artifacts that help development teams, our architects are not just friendly technologists but people who provide value. For example, one architect understands that many development teams face challenges in correctly tuning their caching solutions. He ends up documenting a set of best practices for tuning caching for different application types. He also actively helps the teams to configure their caching solutions.

In a short period of about a month the entire perception of our architecture team has changed. More important, our team suddenly feels valued and is excited about solving real challenges.

To create this success, all that was required was a shift in emphasis. Our architecture team focused on two levers: First they used existing **communication channels** within the organization that were recognized by developers. Then they created a set of **artifacts and tools** that were useful to the development teams.

At this point, our manager of the architecture team has solved one big problem: He made his technology-focused team relevant within the eyes of the development community. But he is still left with the governance side of his organization. Although they are creating a lot of presentations and dashboards about the number of documents they have reviewed, he is doubtful they are really having an impact. Maybe he should focus them not on the development team but operations, which will be our next topic.

Architects and Operations

Operation teams are critical to the success of the IT estate of any large organization. They are responsible for the day-to-day running of the applications and data centers. They are also the first line of defense for incidents and engaging with users during these stressful moments. *Principle 5: Architect for build, test, and deploy* recognizes the importance of operations within Continuous Architecture.

It is important to separate operations versus DevOps. As articulated in Chapter 5, DevOps is a process to better integrate the development and IT operations teams to enable Continuous Delivery. Even when the DevOps process is implemented in an effective manner, at the enterprise scale, there is still an IT operations group that focuses on "running" the IT platforms.

The nature of operations is very different to development in that it is very process driven. IT operations have had considerable success in standardizing their processes. For example, the IT Infrastructure Library (ITIL) defines a set of common practices and processes. IT Infrastructure Library has been adopted widely. (The IT Infrastructure Library was initially developed by the U.K. Government's Central Computer and Telecommunications Agency in the 1980s.) Most help and service desks in the world implement IT Infrastructure Library, and the approach to processes such as incident, problem, and capacity management are quite common among different organizations.

Contrary to operations, the software development world has been less successful in being process driven. Efforts to develop common processes have not lived up to expectations. In some aspects, software development is still not an industrialized process and operates more in a craftsmanship model. There is also a culture of creativity among software developers, which naturally rejects restrictions imposed by formal processes. The huge uptake in Agile development should not only be attributed to the ability to deliver business benefits quickly. It has also been successful because it taps into the zeitgeist of the software developer mind-set.

Obviously, the best place to start engaging with the operations group is to use the process lever. Let us go back to the architecture group we introduced in the previous section. After being able to engage effectively with the developers, the head of the architecture function decides to focus on operations by asking his governance team to engage with them. They start by understanding the standard processes used by the operations team. The governance team has learned from the success of the technologists and decides to apply a similar approach and start participating in key meetings of the operations team, focusing on problem management and capacity planning. They also look into applying some of the Continuous Architecture tools relevant to the DevOps process, in particular the concept of a continuous feedback loop.

As a result of these activities, they identify two pain points:

1. The operations team believes that they are involved too late in the development process and have no input into some key features of systems. In particular, they highlight monitoring, capacity management, and disaster recovery as areas where they struggle.
2. The runbooks they use are very manual and result in a high risk of human error. (A runbook is a set of procedures required to run a system in a daily manner.) This is seen as one of the top root causes of production incidents.

To address these challenges, the architecture team conducts the following activities:

- Update the problem management processes to have an architecture focus and provide a feedback loop to the architecture governance process.
- Develop a common monitoring architecture and solution by reaching out to some of the technologists within the architecture team.
- Develop a set of tools that help with capacity management. These are basic excel templates that define a set of key questions for applications that can be used to size appropriate storage and CPU metrics.

As a result of these recommendations, the operations team starts to see the architecture team as an ally. They believe that jointly, they can improve working practices within IT and in particular influence the development teams.

In this effort, the architecture team focused on three levers. They started with **process**, which created a common language and understanding with operations. Then they participated in **communication channels** relevant to the operations team. Finally, they created a set of **artifacts and tools** that were useful to operations.

The head of the architecture function is now starting to feel better about the impact of his group. The technologist side has a good relationship with the developers, and the governance team is seen as a positive contributor by operations. The next step is to bring these two worlds together. Maybe testing could be a good area to do this, which will be our next focus area.

Architects and Testers

Testing is an area with which most enterprises struggle. Although the current trend in the software community is toward test-driven development and automated testing, large enterprises usually encumber themselves by building separate testing teams. (See Chapter 5 for a more detailed discussion on continuous testing.) One claim behind this approach is that testing is a unique expertise and having a third party test the software enables more defects to be uncovered.

If you look at it at a high level, we have three types of testing:

- **System focused:** This type of testing is usually conducted by the development team. It ranges from unit testing to integration testing, but the focus is the application being developed.
- **Quality Attribute focused:** This is when the system being developed is tested against multiple Quality Attributes. The most common one is performance and scalability. But testing for high availability, disaster recovery, and security can also be conducted.
- **User focused:** This is the infamous user acceptance testing (UAT), in which the end user actually gets to test the system in anger using it in a as close-to-real-live-business scenario as possible.

From a Continuous Architecture perspective, we strongly believe in test-driven development, and that there should not be a separate group that focuses on testing. The only exception could be around Quality Attribute focused testing. Quality Attribute focused testing usually requires expertise on how to create test harnesses for different volumes and stress conditions. It also can require significant infrastructure to be provisioned to conduct the tests, as well as specialized tools.

Let us now look at "testers" as a community and what communication levers are most appropriate to engage with them. We called operations teams process driven, similarly, we would like to call testers procedure driven. This is a subtle difference. What we are trying to say is that testers strive in a structured environment where they can execute well-defined procedures. The fact that these procedures might be aligned to a

One challenge with the approach of having a central team focus only on testing is that this could end up creating a fragmented tooling environment, particularly if not aligned with other areas creating tooling (e.g., requirements, integration). A much better approach is to have a central team that is responsible for defining the tooling strategy and architecture across practice areas.

larger process is not that relevant. Testers are also very data driven and focus on developing metrics that demonstrate their progress.

Let us go back to our fictional organization. System testing and UAT testing are done by the development teams. A separate team focuses on performance testing. Test specialists have been embedded in application teams, but they still operate within a wider community of practice. This testing community is managed by a central testing team that defines the standards, tools, and procedures throughout the enterprise.

The head of architecture has had success in his two separate teams engaging with both the development teams and operations. He now wants to pull this together. He decides to drive this through the testing community. He does this by creating a combined team that has a representative from his two areas. He chooses the architect that focused on driving caching solutions and pairs him with a member of the governance team. They are asked to work with the testing community to create a test harness for caching solutions. They also update the testing procedures and align them with operational checkpoints. As a result of this, test and release of applications that have a caching component performance improves significantly. In parallel, the architecture team works with the performance testing team to help architect the technology stack and integrate it with the Continuous Delivery toolset used within the organization.

In this effort, the architecture team focused on two levers. They started with **artifacts and tools** by creating the test harness and defining the integration architecture with performance test environment. Then they focused on **process** by aligning the test procedures with release and operations processes.

Architects and Technology Executives

Senior IT management is conceptually supportive of architecture, most likely without truly understanding what it means. They are also very busy people who have limited time to focus and really understand what is meant by architecture. It is also common that the senior architects in an enterprise are probably the most senior people in the IT organization who still have a solid understanding of technology. As a result, they do not speak a common language with their peers. It should be recognized that senior management spends a majority of their time focusing on budget and people (human resources) issues. So when communicating with them, we have to recognize:

1. They have limited bandwidth to engage and understand the details.
2. Presenting hard-core data, particularly around financials and resource efficiency, is what they will listen to.

Let us see how our head of architecture engages with his senior IT colleagues. As illustrated in the former sections, he put in great effort to work and communicate with development teams, operations, and testers. The architecture team is seen as a valuable partner by a large portion of the IT organization. This is a huge benefit but on its own is not sufficient for success with IT leadership.

He decides to form an Insight team and tasks them with gathering information related to the software development process and IT estate in general. The team produces very interesting statistics on topics such as:

- Number of project managers versus developers and their geographic distribution
- Vendor spend with key software and services providers
- Percentage of open source code used in production systems
- Correlation between production incidents and average release cycle of applications

Specific focus is spent on two aspects while presenting the insight. First, special techniques are used to make sure the data is presented in a consumable manner. (We particularly recommend reading the books by Edward Tufte[8] on how to represent information.) Second, the data is correlated wherever possible to the financial impact on the organization.

At each senior management briefing on architecture, the head of architecture consistently covers two agenda points:

1. Present a success story of the architecture team's engagement with the wider IT organization
2. Provide a set of insights from the data his team has gathered

As a result, instead of providing a dull update on some technology focused topics, our head of architecture is able to actively engage with senior IT leadership and provide them with valuable insight on how to improve the organization. The insight results in projects being launched to address the pain points. The head of architecture insists that a majority of these projects are owned and run by areas such as application development or operations. In this manner, he is seen as working collaboratively with his colleagues. We should point out that there is one danger in this approach of focusing on insights. It could be perceived as a threat by some senior IT leaders if they are protective of their areas. To avoid this risk, the head of architecture spends a significant amount of his time sharing his results in one-on-one sessions before any large group briefing. As a result, no one is surprised and do not feel that they have to defend themselves in a stressful meeting.

While dealing with technology executives, our head of architecture has successfully used three levers. He has presented a **vision and storyboard** to senior management but more critically, backs this up with **artifacts and tools** that provided a data-driven analysis. He has also been able to tie this analysis to **financial impact**.

ARCHITECTURE HYPE CYCLE

Ask any business or IT executive, and it is highly likely that they would be supportive of having a business and IT architecture. They would argue that without a strong architectural foundation, it is difficult to build a sustainable business or IT function. However, the tenure of "chief architects" and architecture functions in the industry seems to go against this belief. Chief architects and central architecture functions seem to follow a trend similar to the Gartner hype cycle (Figure 9.2). (The hype cycle is a branded graphical presentation developed and used by IT research and advisory firm Gartner for representing the maturity, adoption, and social application of specific technologies.)

The main difference is that very few of these individuals or groups manage to get out of the "trough of disillusionment." This results in a vicious cycle of change in the leadership and structure of the architecture function.

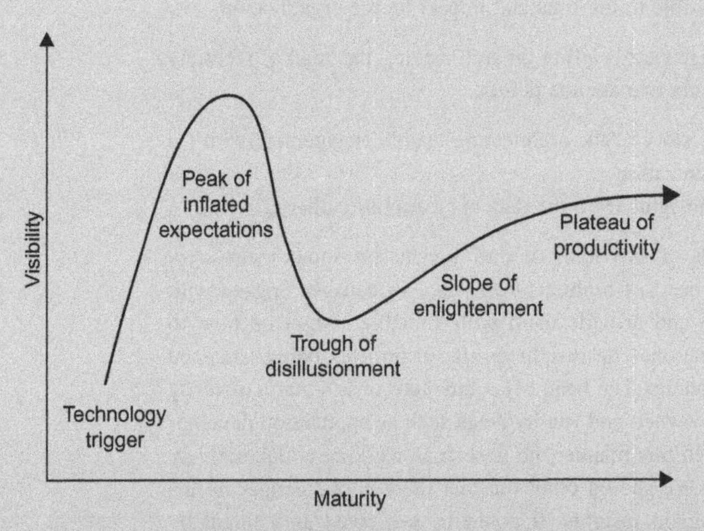

■ **FIGURE 9.2** Gartner technology hype cycle. *Reproduced with permission from Gartner. Gartner hype cycle. http://www.gartner.com/technology/research/methodologies/hype-cycle.jsp.*

Because of this constant churn, which normally is around 18 months from trigger to trough of disillusionment, development teams tend to ignore any output coming from an architecture function. A typical architecture hype cycle can look like:

1. A new head of architecture is appointed. He decides to start from scratch and stops all initiatives started by his predecessor. Sometimes he even creates a whole new team.
2. The head of architecture spends his first 3 months meeting senior business and IT stakeholders to formulate the "new strategy" and finally do architecture in a business-driven and effective manner. At the same time, there is a long queue of technology vendors waiting to pitch the architect their products.
3. The new architecture strategy is presented to senior management. This strategy is normally a long PowerPoint presentation prepared by a consulting firm that the head of architecture has hired. Senior management like what they see; a whole new vision and way of operating has been presented to them with colorful graphics and case studies.
4. We are now 4 or 5 months into the tenure of the head of architecture. This is the "peak of inflated expectations." The head of architecture is finally ready to make an impact. He does two things: First he hires the consulting firm that helped him with his senior pitch to implement the vision. Second, he picks one of the technology vendors that has been courting him to introduce a highly visible technology that is claimed to give dramatic business benefits.
5. The next phase usually lasts between 6 and 9 months. In this period, there is a flurry of activity where the consulting firm creates a lot of artifacts and conducts reviews; PowerPoint is the normal mode of communication. The chosen technology vendor is busy creating proof of concepts and signing an enterprise license agreement. The challenge is that during these activities, two communities have been ignored: the development teams and the actual business. They are being spoken to but not being listened to. The disillusionment and frustration of these two communities eventually start coming out, and the infamous comment of: "He's been here so many months, what has he delivered?" starts being circulated in different forums and water cooler conversations.
6. We are now quickly approaching the "trough of disillusionment." The same business and IT senior management who were so enamored by the initial pitch suddenly wake up and realize that they are not getting any value out of the new head architect. They abolish the function and roll the architecture capabilities into another IT lead, for example, the head of infrastructure or application development.
7. A few months later, it becomes obvious that the IT lead who has been asked to look over architecture does not have sufficient bandwidth to focus on this topic. Senior leadership starts saying, "How can we not have an architectural foundation and vision? It is like steering a ship without a navigation plan." The search for the new head of architecture commences.

Architects and Business

At the end of the day, IT exists to support a business. Understanding the business context is relevant to any individual in the IT organization, and this applies to architects as well. Businesses can view IT on two extremes of the value scale. At one extreme, IT can be seen as an inefficient cost center causing nothing but headaches. On the other end, IT can be seen as a partner that enables the business to rapidly evolve and grow. The larger an enterprise is, the more likely that IT will be seen from a negative perspective. This is mainly because large organizations, by their sheer size and history, have accumulated a lot of technical debt and have a relatively inflexible IT landscape that is difficult to change and expensive to maintain.

How should the architecture function engage with the business? Should architecture be internally focused within the IT organization? Our view is that architecture needs to be visible to the business to be successful. In Chapter 3, we introduced tools such as value chains and user story themes to understand the business context. However, understanding the business is not sufficient; the business has to understand what architecture does.

What levers can we use to communicate with the business? There are lot of similarities in the techniques used for communication with IT executives and with the business. The business is interested in understanding the architecture **vision and storyboard** and the **financial impact**. The business will also be engaged when presented with **artifacts and tools** that provide a data-driven analysis. The main difference is the scope of information that they would be interested in. Whereas for IT executives, we have to focus on internal workings of IT, for the business, we have to focus on an external view, that is, the impact of IT.

Our head of architecture applies a similar approach to dealing with business counterparts as he did with senior IT executives. He spends a lot of time meeting with different business representatives to understand their drivers and frustrations. He feeds this information to his insight team that produces views relevant to the business, for example, linking sales data to investment in platforms that support different products. They quickly realize that they have been underinvesting in IT for some key growth areas. This results in additional funding being released for those areas, to the delight of the CIO.

But the relationship with the business is not only driven by the head of architecture. He makes sure that his team engages with relevant business partners at all levels. This ranges from defining stories jointly with the business, architects, and developers for Agile sprints to the architects investigating how new technologies can help address key business challenges. Business representatives are also invited to join architectural validation sessions.

As a result of these activities, the business no longer sees the architecture group as a vague entity that hopefully provides value to IT. Instead, they have a very clear understanding of how they can engage with the architects and understand the value they provide.

Applying the Levers and Principles

In this section, we have presented a set of levers that we believe help architects communicate and engage with different stakeholders. We tried to bring these levers to life through a fictional architecture function. We are aware that the example we provided is overly simplified and that the complexities of an enterprise and individual personalities can create very different dynamics. However, this should not take away from the fact that communication is critical to the success of an architect. As a result, architects should explicitly focus on developing a communication plan and improving how they engage with stakeholders.

Let us also look at some of our key principles and how they support collaboration and communication. The most obvious one is *Principle 6: Model the organization after the design of the system.* In this model, the architect role is part of the core development team. The level of friction between the architect and the developers is minimized. In most organizations, there is still a central architecture function. But they focus on defining the high-level "rules". (see Chapter 4 for a more detailed discussion around rules and architectural decisions). They can effectively engage with the architects via building a community of interest.

Consulting organizations and IT vendors spend a lot of effort on building relationships at all levels within an organization. This is the only way that they can be successful. Most opportunities come from existing relationships and return business. One technique they use quite often is to build a relationship map of the organization. On this map, they group stakeholders in three categories:

- Sponsors who are supportive of the vendor.
- Neutrals who have either no opinion or are indifferent to the vendor.
- Antagonists who are explicitly against the vendor, either because of a bad experience or because they are supportive of a competitor.

A sample relationship map might look like the one shown in Figure 9.3.

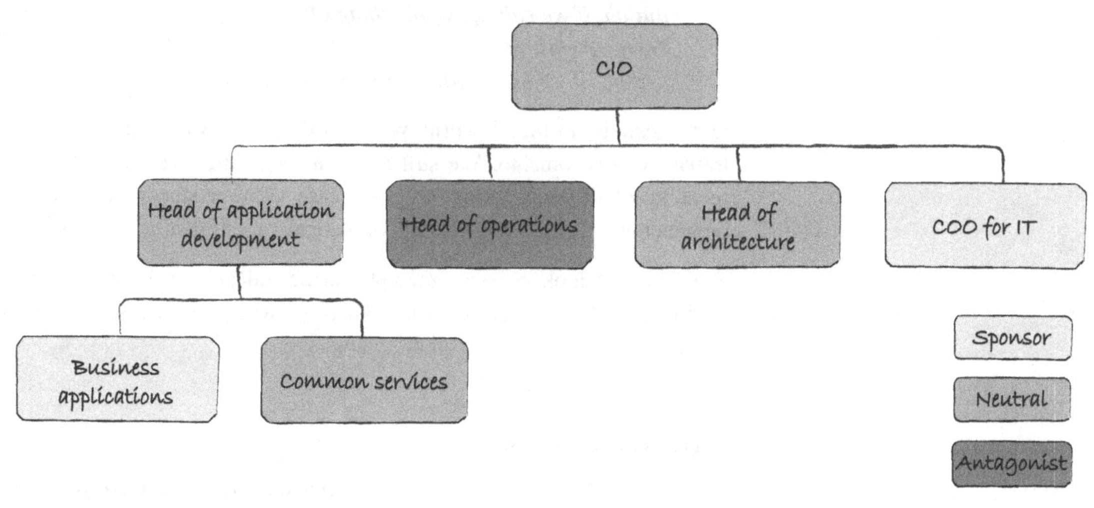

■ **FIGURE 9.3** Illustrative relationship map.

You will notice that to be able to understand a complex organization, vendors are constantly trying to obtain the latest organization charts.

We do not recommend that architects go to such extremes, but we might be able to learn a thing or two on how to understand our stakeholders and their views.

Applying *Principle 1: Architect products, not just solutions for projects* also improves collaboration and communication. The discipline of product management is inherently focused on understanding consumer demand and engaging with stakeholders. As a result, introducing the role of product managers into the organization on its own should lead to improved collaboration and communication.

Principle 5: Architect for build, test, and deploy changes the focus of the architect. To apply this principle, the architect has to understand how release management, testing, and operations work within the organization. This on its own increases the stakeholder base with which the architect has to engage.

COMMON LANGUAGE

As articulated in the previous section, communication is key to the success of architecture within the enterprise. A common language is the foundation of successful communication. This is best articulated by the song written by George Gershwin and Ira Gershwin for the 1937 film *Shall We Dance?*:

> *You like potato and I like potahto*
> *You like tomato and I like tomahto*
> *Potato, potahto,*
> *Tomato, tomahto.*
> *Let's call the whole thing off*
> *But oh, if we call the whole thing off*
> *Then we must part*
> *and oh, if we ever part, then that might break my heart*

Unfortunately, in the IT world, we are still a long way from agreeing on tomato versus tomahto. We still spend a long time discussing the exact meaning of different terms (e.g., use case vs. user story), notation, and architectural artifacts (conceptual vs. logical vs. physical architectures).

We will first look at some attempts in the industry to drive a common language in the software industry. Then we will provide a set of recommendations for creating a common language.

Industry Examples

We believe there are two key developments in the past 20 years that greatly contributed to the creation of a common IT language: the Unified

Modeling Language (UML) and design patterns. Let us take a look at these in a little more detail.

Unified Modeling Language

If you were doing object-oriented development in the early 1990s, your team would have had to initially decide on which design notation to use. Should it be the Booch clouds versus Rumbaugh's more box-like notation or the domain object circles of Jacobson? What about use cases? Should they even be considered as part of an object-oriented approach?

Then suddenly, one company, Rational Software, ended up employing three of the big names in this field—Grady Booch, James Rumbaugh, and Ivar Jacobson. They became known as the three amigos, and UML was born. It was then adopted by the Object Management Group (OMG) as a standard in 1997.

Today a majority of developers and designers use UML notation when visually communicating design options and decisions.

Interestingly, agreeing on a common process was not that successful. The Rational Unified Process (RUP) originated at the same time from the same company but did not gain as much universal acceptance as UML. This is somewhat understandable because a common language makes peoples' lives easier, but a common process can be considered stifling to creative software developers.

> The value of a common process can be exemplified by the experience of one of the authors while acting as a consultant while using a precursor to Rational Unified Process. A consultant using the same process had been working for 1 year helping with the design of a major system for a U.S. entertainment organization. When it was decided that a new consultant would take over the role, the two consultants agreed to have a week's handover with the viewpoint that transferring all the inherent knowledge on the project would take some time. To both of the consultants' surprise, knowledge transfer was completed in half a day. All that they needed to communicate was the artifacts and the state they were in; the rest was self-explanatory. The new consultant was effective on his second day.

Design Patterns

In 1994, the gang of four, Erich Gamma, Richard Helm, Ralph Johnson, and John Vlissides, published their seminal book *Design Patterns—Elements of Reusable Object-Oriented Software.*[9] In this book, they identified 23 patterns that addressed well-known challenges in object-oriented software development. Almost as important as the solutions they provided is the fact that they introduced the concept of the design pattern and defined a manner to explain the patterns consistently.

Several publications after this book have expanded the pattern concept to different areas from analysis to enterprise applications. More importantly, software designers were able to communicate with each other by referring to design patterns.

Architecture Frameworks

There also have been several architectural approaches that provide a starting point for a common language. The Zachman framework has been around since 1987.[10] As illustrated in Figure 9.4, this framework is basically an ontology of how to categorize different aspect of an enterprise.

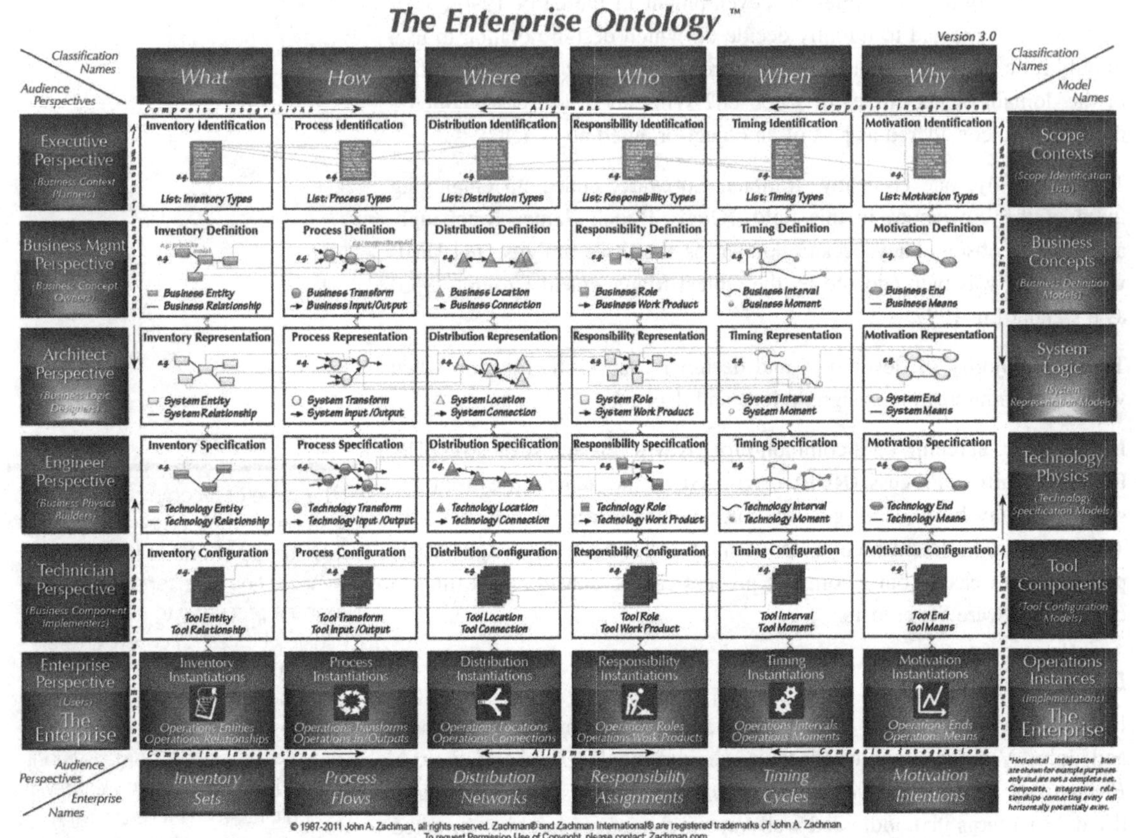

■ **FIGURE 9.4** The Zachman framework.[23] *Published with the permission of John A. Zachman and Zachman International®, Inc. (www.zachman.com).*

Although it is not used that widely anymore and can be critiqued as being too much of a static view of the world, it is still a valid model for defining different architecture categories.

Another more recent architectural framework is The Open Group Architecture Framework (TOGAF).[11] It is advertised as an Enterprise Architecture methodology and framework. Contrary to the Zachman framework, TOGAF puts more emphasis on methodology and process.

This core is defined by the Architecture Development Method (ADM). In terms of defining a common language, two elements of TOGAF are important. The Architecture Content Framework defines the set of key artifacts produced to support an architecture, and the Technical Reference Model (TRM) provides a model and taxonomy of generic platform services. TOGAF has gained a lot of traction in the industry, and most enterprise architects seek to acquire its accreditation. However, our view is that it has not been that successful in creating a common language among architects, and the wider IT community.

In summary, we would consider the design-focused efforts of UML and design patterns more successful than architecture-focused efforts such as the Zachman framework and TOGAF.

Creating a Common Language

Are we doomed to stay in our Tower of Babel and continuously struggle with the challenge posed by lack of a common language? In some aspects, yes:

> *A successful architect is comfortable operating in ambiguity.*

Most of us have a drive for precision and perfection in our thoughts and designs. However, we have to accept that the world around is composed of humans and natural behavior. As a result, we will never have the level of precision in language and notation we strive for.

But what level of precision do we require in an architecture? One definition of architectural practice that we like is:

> *Architecture is the ability to abstract at the right level to make the required decisions.*

This is very much aligned with our *Principle 3: Delay design decisions until they are absolutely necessary*. We believe that trying to get to a level of precision not required for the decision you need to make is a waste of energy and results in fractured architectures.

This does not mean we should not strive to create a common language. We are all human beings and prefer to be understood and communicate with our peers. We will provide a few key recommendations we believe will enable converging on a common language within the enterprise. But first let us look at how some of our Continuous Architecture principles can enable a common language.

One good example of unnecessary attention to level of precision is the obsession we find with key performance indicators (KPIs) in most enterprises. It is quite frequently quoted by senior IT management that you cannot make any progress if you are not able to measure your current state and where you are going. This results in a series of KPIs being defined and an industry formed around the generation of the KPIs. But what normally happens is that the decisions driven from the KPIs are fairly high level (e.g., stopping a certain program or increasing or decreasing the size of a particular team). In hindsight, management would have been able to make the same decisions with much fewer data points. A good way to look at this is the following saying:

Measure with a microscope, mark with a chalk, and cut with an axe.

In other words, if our instrument is as blunt as an axe, why do we need to measure with a microscope?

Let us start with *Principle 6: Model the organization after the design of the system*. This results in cross-disciplinary teams focusing on solving the same problem. As a result, regardless of what notation or process is used, the team members start creating their own terminology in understanding and communicating the problem and solution domain it is dealing with. Consider the following two scenarios:

1. A DBA is part of a large enterprise resource pool and gets assigned to projects based on where the key demand is. This is mostly prioritized to focus on areas that are having performance or delivery requirements. The DBA spends her time multitasking between the core general ledger system and the mobile shopping systems.
2. A DBA is assigned to two product teams, both a "system of engagement" type system. She spends her time in meetings that not only focus on database tasks but the overall system design and deployment architecture.

It is obvious that in the second scenario, our DBA will have a much better understanding of the business problems being addressed and start using a common language with the developers and testers.

Then apply *Principle 1: Architect products, not just solutions for projects*. One key benefit of thinking of your IT landscape in terms of products is that you will always have to take a client-based perspective. This inherently creates two outcomes. First you naturally focus on communicating to generate client-focused product material, being product definitions or roadmaps. This on its own is a huge step in simplifying the language. Second, if the product management discipline is mature, all products are presented and communicated in a similar manner. So, when you view a product roadmap, it is represented consistently across the organization.

Finally, focus on the recommendations made in Chapter 4, particularly on creating architectural decision backlogs and explicitly communicating these within the organization. Again, if you reach a certain level of maturity in this area, all architectural decisions will be represented in a common manner. More important, teams will start understanding the design decisions in other areas and determine any applicability in their area. Done successfully, such an approach will emulate the success of design patterns that has happened in the industry.

The examples provided illustrate that applying a Continuous Architecture approach will already start creating a common language. However, more is required to address this challenge. Here are some additional recommendations:

1. **Create a common business-focused language.** The first thing that any IT architect will do is to understand the business requirements and context. So why not start the creation of a common language from the business first? This does not have to be an extremely complex mechanism. A great technique to use for this is the value chain and user story themes (or use cases) as illustrated in Chapter 3. Another tool that we highly recommend is to create a data glossary and use industry reference models (when applicable) as a starting point. Just having a set of basic terms defined and documented can be a very powerful tool. However, we should urge a level of caution in this exercise. Defining a detailed data model with agreement on every term can be an exhaustive and counterproductive effort. We recommend capturing just a sufficient set of key terms to enable a common understanding of the business. We also found that training architects on the business and financial side of the business helps create a common language.
2. **Define a common architecture language.** Now that we have a common business language, we can focus on defining a common IT language. The best mechanism for this is to standardize on a set of key artifacts that are used throughout the organization. It does not matter what Software Delivery Life Cycle approach or architecture methodology you want to use; the idea is that there should be a handful of key artifacts that are required for each product area and IT project. Key examples include product roadmap, conceptual and logical component models, architectural decisions, and Quality Attribute definitions. Again, the challenge here is to keep the common set minimal and provide best practice recommendations from real project examples. Enterprise groups can get carried away by enforcing a series of architectural artifacts on IT teams that are counterproductive. These are normally treated as a box-ticking exercise by teams. The emphasis should be on creating these artifacts as part of the regular rhythm of a project and not as an afterthought.

   Several large organizations outsource a significant portion of their IT development, either on a short- or long-term basis. Getting vendors on board to use the common language is key as well. An interesting approach would be for the supplier to present their common language, which you can use as an input into defining your own language.
3. **Agree on a common notation and tools.** "A picture says a thousand words," they say. The challenge becomes when there is not a common understanding of what the picture represents. We do not

want our architectural depictions to be similar to some forms of modern art—the only way you can interpret is to rush to the museum wall and read the explanation. We already touched on the huge benefit delivered by UML in the software industry. Unlike our recommendation to not drive a huge level of precision in a data glossary, on the topic of notation, we strongly encourage a level of rigor. This can be further enforced by using a common tool. The freedom to create random sets of figures and lines in PowerPoint and Visio normally leads to more confusion.

4. **Emphasize communication.** We already mentioned the importance of communication in this chapter. We would like to reemphasize this point and state that:

   We cannot overcommunicate.

   The communication levers already discussed in this chapter can be used, for achieving a common language. However, a common language has its own nuances, and we recommend creating a set of training material that enables people to come together and communicate. This definitely should not be in a traditional classroom style setting. Instead we would recommend that groups come together (face to face is preferred) to solve a problem and use the common language in context.

Achieving a common language is not a milestone you can put in a project plan. It comes naturally by communicating and interpreting the problems domains in a common manner. Just like in our callout of two consultants, you will know you have achieved success in a common language when a handover is easy to accomplish or a workshop suddenly ends early when everyone agrees on a common outcome.

DECISION MAKING IN THE ENTERPRISE

In Chapter 4, we discussed the importance of architectural decisions in Continuous Architecture. We even stated that the key role of an architect is to drive architectural decisions. So if an architect does nothing else, she or he should focus on making sure that the architectural decisions are resolved in a timely manner and with sufficient transparency to the organization.

Let us now look at decision making at the enterprise scale, which leads us to the topic of governance. A good definition of governance we found is:

> *The structure, oversight and management processes which ensure the delivery of the expected benefits of IT in a controlled way to help enhance the long term sustainable success of the enterprise.*[12]

In most organizations, explicitly or implicitly, there are three types of governance:

1. **Investment governance** focuses on the IT budget and makes sure that it is allocated effectively based on the business drivers. Success is achieved if the IT budget focuses on key business drivers while not sacrificing stability and performance of the overall IT estate.
2. **Program governance** focuses on delivery of programs and resolving challenges. (If your organization is product driven, then this can be replaced with product governance.) Success is achieved if all programs deliver on time and in budget.
3. **Architecture governance** focuses on driving architectural decisions and enforcing standards. Achieving success is, to be honest, not that clearly understood. Normally, just being able to establish architecture governance is considered a success in its own right. Another common form of success is the ability to enforce standards. We define the success of architectural governance as follows:

   Success of architectural governance is that all architectural decisions are made to enable effective and timely delivery of IT products while not introducing additional technical debt.

There is a natural tension in architectural governance: time to deliver versus deliver for the enterprise. Another way of looking at this is centralized governance versus decentralized application development.

Development team view
Enterprise view
Decisions need to be made quickly in order to make the deadlines
Time
Decisions need to be made with proper consideration of impacts on the wider IT landscape
Technology most appropriate for the current effort is required
Standards
Technology most appropriate for long-term sustainability is required

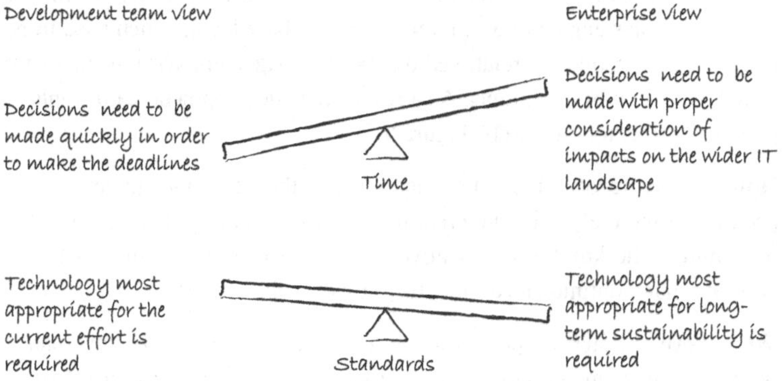

■ **FIGURE 9.5** Balancing development versus enterprise views.

In many cases, project teams need to move quickly to meet their timelines. However, this can result in suboptimal solutions from an enterprise perspective. The entitlements area is a good example that illustrates this tension.

There is an industry standard, COBIT 5 (Control Objectives for Information and Related Technology), that defines a framework for IT management and governance. It focuses on defining key processes and controls for implementing governance. We believe that the challenges addressed by Continuous Architecture are orthogonal to implementing such structured approaches as COBIT 5. As a result, we will not refer to them in the book.

Regardless if they use COBIT 5 or not, many organizations use an overarching governance and management process (e.g., PRINCE2). These normally apply defined gates or stages at which certain artifacts have to be created to pass to the next phase. This does create a conflict with an Agile and Continuous Delivery approach. What can we say about the role of Continuous Architecture within such an environment?

The first point is to accept the overarching process as a constraint. Just as architecture is about making decisions within known constraints, we have to work with constraints while applying the Continuous Architecture principles.

The second point is to influence the overarching process. This can be done by aligning the architecture artifacts required by the overarching process with the Continuous Architecture approach. For example, in terms of architecture artifacts, making sure that architectural decision backlogs are considered or that the architectural validation follows the approaches recommended in Chapter 6. In this way, project teams do not need to do any additional work to comply with the architectural aspects of gates or stages, as defined by the overarching process.

In an interesting article, Alex Yates[13] proposes a term called *technical debt singularity*.

The term *technical debt* has gained significant traction in recent years and is a metaphor that addresses the challenge with several short-term decisions resulting in long-term complexity. (Refer to Chapter 10 for more detail on technical debt.)

The term *technology singularity* is defined as the point at which computer (or artificial) intelligence will exceed the capacity of humans. After this point, all events will be unpredictable. The term was first attributed to John von Neumann:[14]

... ever accelerating progress of technology and changes in the mode of human life, which gives the appearance of approaching some essential singularity in the history of the race beyond which human affairs, as we know them, could not continue.

Although the technical debt singularity does not have such dire consequences for humankind, it is still quite

Every application needs to manage the security of its users and provide different levels of access to the data based on roles. The quickest way for most application teams is to handcraft this functionality themselves. They are under extreme time pressure to deliver business functionality, and trying to normalize or externalizing their entitlements capability is not considered a high priority. If we have 20 new applications delivered to the enterprise within 1 year, we are at risk of having 20 approaches for solving the same problem. In addition, the ongoing day-to-day management of users and entitlements becomes a very complex process. To do the right thing for the enterprise, an effective architectural governance process would ensure that there is alignment among these approaches, and potentially, as illustrated in Chapter 10, a common service is used. The tension is that aligning 20 projects to agree and use a common approach takes time and effort, which is in direct conflict with the delivery timelines. The concept of technical debt can be reintroduced here. At times, you might need to respond tactically and accrue technical debt. The important thing is to make this decision explicitly and record your technical debt so that it can be addressed in the future.

Another tension in architectural governance is how technology standards are enforced. It is common and preferred for central architecture teams to set a set of standards. Why should an organization have to deal with the overhead of maintaining and paying for several different technologies that provide the same functionality? These days you would find few software development teams that care about which network switches or operating systems are used. But the higher you go up in the technology stack, the more challenging standards become. There can be religious debates over which workflow solution or rules engine to use. Even at the database level, which used to be dominated by traditional relational database management systems, there are now several non-SQL entrants. As a result, each development team wants to pick the correct tool for itself (Figure 9.5).

How can we resolve these tensions so that the development teams can progress effectively without creating an unsustainable IT landscape for the future? The key tension is governance versus agility, which is at the core of what Continuous Architecture tries to address.

We believe the starting point for this is aligning architectural governance with investment and program governance. Too often all of these governance models operate independently. Not only does this lead to inefficiency at the enterprise level, but it also creates an environment where the development team is constantly asked similar questions by different governance bodies.

What we are recommending is a unified governance model that combines the three aspects of governance: investment, program, and architecture (Figure 9.6).

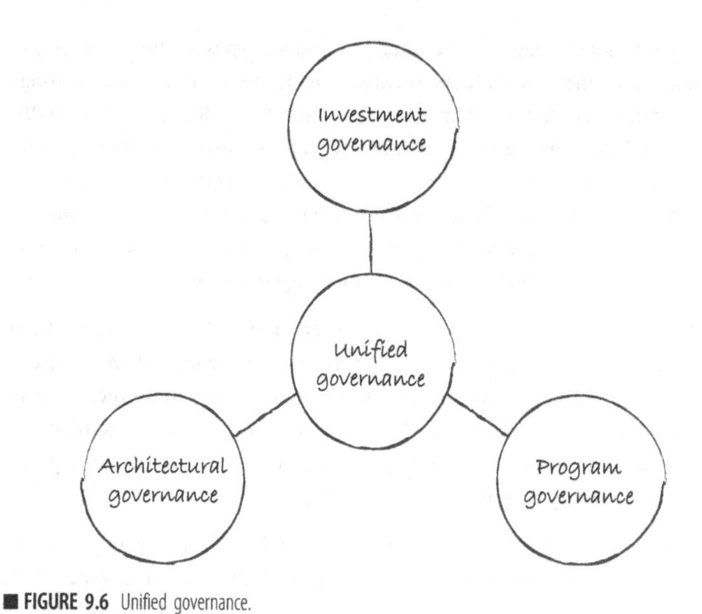

■ **FIGURE 9.6** Unified governance.

significant for the impacted teams. Yates defined the technical debt singularity as:

So what happens if the interest we owe on our technical debt starts to exceed the number of man-hours in a working day? Well, I call that the technical debt singularity. This is the point at which software development grinds to a halt. If you spend practically all your time firefighting and you can't release often (or ever?) with confidence, I'm afraid I'm talking about you. You've pretty much reached a dead-end with little hope of making significant progress.[13]

We can expand this to the wider enterprise and say that:

An enterprise has reached an architectural debt singularity when it cannot balance delivery of business demand and ongoing stability of the IT landscape in a cost efficient manner.

Let us remind ourselves of the purpose, success definition, and participants of the three types of governance (Table 9.2).

Table 9.2 Aspects of Governance Types

Type	Purpose	Success Definition	Participants	Frequency
Investment	IT budget is allocated effectively based on the business drivers	IT budget delivers on key business drivers while not sacrificing stability and performance of the overall IT estate	• Business signs off on overall IT budget • IT management signs off on the allocation of the budget	Annually
Program	Effective delivery of programs and resolution of key challenges	Programs are delivered on time and in budget	• Business stakeholders • IT senior management • Program team	Program dependent; varies from weekly to monthly
Architecture	Drive architectural decisions and enforce standards	Architectural decisions are made so that IT solutions can be delivered in an effective and timely manner while not introducing additional technical debt to the organization	• IT architects • Program team representatives	From monthly to quarterly

The key differences between the three governance types are the frequency of execution and the stakeholders involved. In terms of frequency, a rough approximation is that investment governance tends to operate annually, architectural governance operates quarterly, and program governance operates monthly or even more frequently. While all this activity is going on, the development teams are striving for Continuous Delivery. As a result, there is a natural mismatch between the decisions the program teams need to make and the governance structures the enterprise imposes on them.

Similarly, there is a mismatch between the different stakeholders involved. The development team deals directly with business users. Normally, the management of these business users is represented in program governance, but only senior business management is involved in investment governance. Meanwhile, on architecture governance aspects, there is seldom any business representation.

The mismatch in frequency of execution and stakeholder engagement involvement is a natural result of operating within a large enterprise. As a starting point, we have to acknowledge this as a fact but change some of the dynamics involved. Let us look again at our analysis of how architectural decisions are made in Chapter 4 (Figure 9.7).

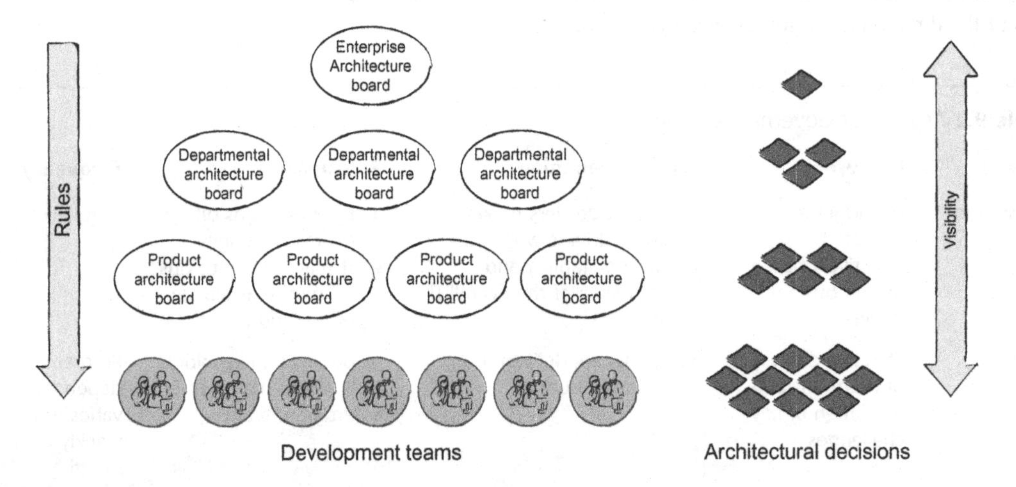

■ FIGURE 9.7 Levels of architecture decisions.

As can be seen from the diagram, a majority of architectural decisions are made at the development team level. There is nothing wrong with this; this is where "the rubber hits the road" and implementation occurs. If we want Continuous Delivery, we have to let the development teams progress with all their decisions. What the wider enterprise context has to provide are the basic rules of the road that the development teams need to adhere to.

From a Continuous Architecture perspective, our recommendations for governance can be defined as:

- **Define the constraints (i.e., the "rules of the road"):** Use senior enterprise governance structures to define the boundaries of that the development teams need to operate within. This can vary from available budget for a particular area to technology standards.
- **Empower development teams:** After the "rules of the road" are defined, empower the development teams. This means that each development team should not believe that they need senior approval for allocating budget spend or every technology choice. For example, a development team should be able to decide to use its budget to increase its team size or allocate additional infrastructure capacity. As long as they are within the overall budget allocated, there is no reason for them to require additional sign-offs. Similarly, they should be free to make any technology choice as long as they are aware of the technology standards that the enterprise imposes.
- **Provide transparency:** Empowering teams does not mean that they operate in a black hole. There has to be exact transparency on all the decisions that a development team makes, architectural or otherwise. There is a reason senior management exists. This is not to sign off on all decisions made and be a bottleneck. However, they need sufficient transparency on all the decisions being made by multiple development teams. This enables them to have confidence that all delivery is going in the right direction but also to take action when they see multiple development teams making conflicting decisions on a wider scale.
- **Use governance for ratification:** After we have been able to define the "rules of the road," empowered the development teams, and enabled transparency, the purpose of governance forums change. They are not meant to be bodies where long debates take place and where the side with the better argument wins—or more likely, where the most senior person makes a judgment call. Instead, they are bodies that ratify decisions made by the development teams within a well-structured context. There can be cases when the governance body disagrees with the presented decision. In this case, there has to be a level of rework done by the team that presented the decision. However, we believe that if done correctly, the few cases when this occurs highly outweigh the efficiency and expediency gained by operating in the recommended manner.

IMPACT OF OPEN SOURCE

Setting technology standards is one of the more common activities that Enterprise Architecture groups fulfill. Setting standards is challenging enough when considering commercially available products. The past 15 years has seen the emergence of open source software that has increased the challenges in this space. According to the Open Source Initiative,[15] the term is defined as:

Open source software is software that can be freely used, changed, and shared (in modified or unmodified form) by anyone. Open source software is made by many people, and distributed under licenses that comply with the Open Source Definition.[16]

(This is further detailed by the Open Source Initiative[16] and refers to the key topics such as free redistribution, source code, derived works, integrity of the author's source code, and so on.)

Commercially, open source has been quite successful and has acted as a true disruptive source within the software industry. At its best, open source can be considered to embody all the good things about the Internet age. It demonstrates the ability of individuals to collaborate to achieve a common goal, the common wisdom being that multiple people addressing the same problem solve it more elegantly with fewer defects. The open source movement has also taught us quite a lot about how communities can collaborate effectively across different geographies and time zones. Although seemingly very democratic, it is interesting to note the concept of a "benevolent dictator" (also known as the "committer") being key to quite a few of the successful open source initiatives. Briefly, the benevolent dictator can be considered the architect, or the person responsible for the conceptual integrity of the solution.

The impact of open source can be seen from the market-leading solutions it has given rise to, from Linux to the multiple projects under the Apache Foundation (TomCat, Camel, and Hadoop, to name a few well-known ones). From a commercial perspective, open source has also created new business models in which companies provide versions of open source software that are supported in a more traditional software model. These have been instrumental in making large organizations feel comfortable using the open source technology. You could say that at some point in the future, we may get to a point where there are only two types of software left: open source and software as a service (i.e., software delivered via the cloud).

Does open source have any significance from an architectural approach perspective? From one perspective, open source code has been a huge asset for software reuse. Effectively used open source components can significantly reduce the time to market of a software development team. On the other hand, open source technology creates significant challenges in terms of introducing unknowns into the software code base. This can happen from multiple angles:

- Commercially, the teams might not be aware of what open source licensing they are operating under. This could cause significant headaches if it is found that the organization is not fully adhering to the license conditions, for example, legal headaches when signing a new contract for open source support (e.g., indemnification!).
- The development teams might not be downloading the most recent version of the open source component, or more likely, they will not be keeping their version of the component up to date with newer versions. This can result in nonperforming or defective code existing in the code base.
- In addition, if a development team wants to fix an issue found in the source code, this must be made available to the open source community. Several large companies do not permit this activity.
- A special challenge is around security risks. There is no guarantee that all security flaws will be fixed rapidly in the code base, and the alerting mechanisms for known security breaches can be suboptimal.
- Finally, there is always the possibility of the community losing interest in the open source initiative, resulting in a portion of the code base being orphaned with no one really supporting it or understanding it fully. From our perspective, this is no different than the legacy COBOL code base existing in organizations.

From a Continuous Architecture perspective, we are very supportive of the ethos of open source initiatives. We believe that the code itself and the community models it espouses are tremendously valuable. We encourage organizations to embrace open source and apply some of the open source development approaches internally as well, commonly known as internal open source models. An area where this approach can be used is for orphaned enterprise services that the enterprise no longer wants to maintain because there is not enough demand for them. If a few groups still want to use those services, they can continue to maintain them using our internal open source model.

While implementing open source within a commercial enterprise, a controlled approach in terms of tracking open source usage and addressing the challenges highlighted is required. We believe that following the Continuous Architecture principles such as *Principle 4: Architect for change—leverage "the power of small"* and *Principle 1: Architect products, not just solutions for projects* will help in addressing the challenges. Both of these principles enable you to manage the scope and context of your code base so that you can keep track of the areas where you use open source more effectively. In addition, open source software tends to be more cloud friendly than proprietary software, and this helps with applying *Principle 5: Architect for build, test, and deploy.*

Let us now go back to our three types of governance and see how they operate from a Continuous Architecture viewpoint. Investment and architecture governance are mostly focused on defining the "rules of the road." They basically create the context in which program-level governance operates. Program governance focuses on unblocking challenges that occur during implementation. Most key decisions are made at the development team level. We recommend a decentralized manner in which decisions can be made closest to the implementation rather than by some abstract groups that do not have sufficient context. The key aspects of this model are:

- Architecture and investment governance focus on setting context for the rest of the organization. They also should operate with a feedback loop. Investment governance requires input from the wider architecture drivers while allocating budget. At the same time, architecture standards cannot be set without an understanding of the business and overall budgetary context. There is also a feedback loop from the rest of the organization to these enterprise governance bodies. The feedback can be a challenge to a rule or a recommendation to set up a rule in a new area.
- The majority of the decisions are made by the development teams. They are closest to the problem and have a better understanding of the context. They have to provide transparency to the higher level governing bodies about the decisions that they are making.
- Program Governance is there to support the development teams and not as a major decision maker. Its main inputs are the decisions being made by the development teams and the challenges they face. Program governance focuses on resolving the challenges and making sure that the decisions are aligned with the enterprise rules. It can also provide a set of recommendations to the development teams when it sees decisions drifting away from the rules or the overall direction of the program (Figure 9.8).

The Continuous Architecture approach we are recommending can be interpreted as applying Schumacher's principle of subsidiary that we referred to earlier in this chapter. To quote him again:

> *The large organization will consist of many semi-autonomous units, which we may call quasifirms. Each of them will have a large amount of freedom, to give the greatest possible change to creativity and entrepreneurship.... Each quasi-firm must have both a profit and loss account, and a balance sheet.*[4]

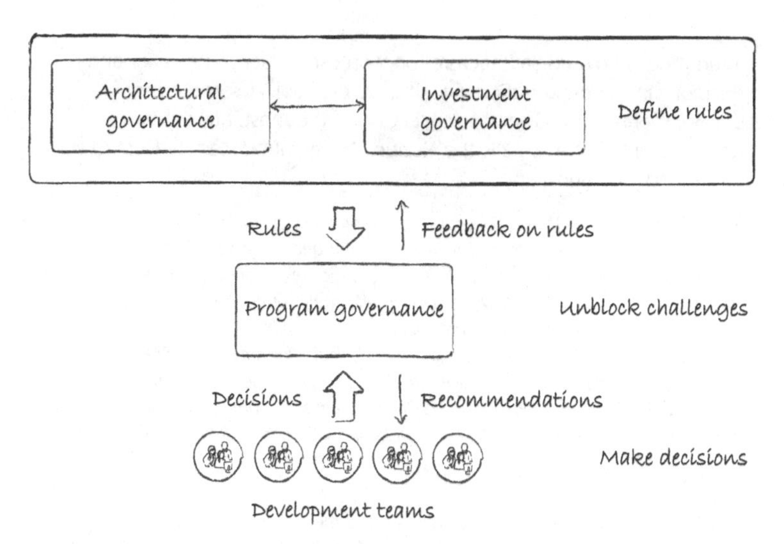

■ **FIGURE 9.8** Decisions aligned with governance.

It is clear that the model we are presenting is fairly simplified, and the ability to implement such a model depends on the overall culture of the enterprise. Regardless, we still believe that governance in a Continuous Architecture world can only be effective by applying Schumacher's principle of subsidiary. The key question then becomes at what level do we set up our quasifirms? Are they major departments in our IT group, should they be individual development teams, or should they be some combination of them?

This is when we apply *Principle 1: Architect products, not just solutions for projects*. The quasifirm that Schumacher refers to should be the products we have defined. This is the right level of granularity to make the correct financial and architectural decisions. We will be fully in a Continuous Architecture world, when we are thinking of terms of products. In essence, we should be replacing the role of program governance with product governance. The additional benefit of product governance is by its nature it is extremely focused on delivering value to its end consumers.

NUDGE THEORY FOR ARCHITECTURE?

Influencing decisions is a strong social skill required for architects. At a personal level, this depends a lot on individual traits of the architect and the groups he or she is trying to influence. We have discussed some of these capabilities in the role of the architect (see Chapter 8). What is also interesting is how an architecture function can influence behavior and decisions in the organization. For this, we can look at some recent developments in behavioral science. One of the most interesting developments in this area is the Nudge Theory introduced by Richard Thaler and Cass Sunstein.[17]

Nudge Theory (or Nudge) is a concept in behavioral science, political theory and economics which argues that positive reinforcement and indirect suggestions to try to achieve non-forced compliance can influence the motives, incentives and decision making of groups and individuals, at least as effectively—if not more effectively—than direct instruction, legislation, or enforcement.

Nudge Theory's most celebrated influences include the formation of a British Behavioural Insights Team, often called the 'Nudge Unit', in the British Cabinet Office, headed up by Dr David Halpern and US President Barack Obama's appointment of Cass R. Sunstein as administrator of the Office of Information and Regulatory Affairs.[18]

As stated by Thaler and Sunstein:

A nudge, as we will use the term, is any aspect of the choice architecture that alters people's behavior in a predictable way without forbidding any options or significantly changing their economic incentives. To count as a mere nudge, the intervention must be easy and cheap to avoid. Nudges are not mandates. Putting fruit at eye level counts as a nudge. Banning junk food does not.[17]

Some examples of how nudge theory was applied by the nudge unit are[19]:

- Automatically enrolling individuals on to pension schemes has increased saving rates for those employed by large firms in the United Kingdom from 61% to 83%.
- Informing people who failed to pay their taxes that most other people had already paid increased payment rates by more than 5 percentage points.
- Encouraging jobseekers to actively commit to undertaking job search activities increased their chance of finding a new job.
- Prompting people to join the Organ Donor Register using reciprocity messages ("If you needed an organ, would you take one?") adds 100,000 people to the register in 1 year.

We personally have not applied Nudge Theory to the architecture process in the enterprise but think it would be an interesting avenue to pursue.

ARCHITECTURE PROCESS AT THE ENTERPRISE SCALE

Is there a need for a methodology or process for architecting enterprise solutions? As already discussed, although the software industry has made good progress in developing a common language, it has struggled in formalizing a common software development approach or process. Numerous software development professionals have espoused that software development needs move from being a craft to becoming an industry. Most of these attempts at a common process have resulted in books sitting on a shelf.

The Rational Unified Process was one of the more widespread attempts in this area. The same organization that created UML was behind Rational Unified Process. Although encompassing a set of valuable tools such as iterative development, use cases, and sequence diagrams, Rational Unified Process ended up being another process that was interpreted as being too cumbersome. One major challenge was that Rational Unified Process was not seen as a framework to be tailored but an out-of-the-box process to be used as is. This resulted in overly rich processes that were difficult for an organization to absorb. Another challenge with Rational Unified Process was that it was turned into a product. (Rational Unified Process was initially developed by Rational Software Corporation, which was acquired by IBM in 2003.) Similar to any product, it had to be further developed, but how do you further develop a process? You can always improve and provide additional tools and supporting software, but you cannot avoid the need for detailing the process and creating more artifacts. Over time, the process becomes too heavyweight and complicated to understand and implement.

Since the publication of *Extreme Programming Explained* in 1999,[20] the software discipline has been moving toward a practice-driven approach. Rational Unified Process and SAFe have also been broken down into a set of practices. The increased adoption of Agile software practices in today's development community demonstrates that successful tools and techniques are more valuable than highly structured methodologies. The

ENTERPRISE ARCHITECTURE METHODOLOGIES

The term *Enterprise Architecture* has been used in the industry since the 1980s. It focuses on architecture applying architecture concepts consistently across a large enterprise.

A series of Enterprise Architecture methodologies and processes have been developed in the past 30 years. We have already touched on the Zachman framework and The Open Group Architecture Framework.

The Zachman framework can be considered the father of Enterprise Architecture. It is the first approach that covers the different perspectives that have to be addressed at the enterprise level.

In particular, in the United States, the government has driven a few comprehensive Enterprise Architecture approaches; the Department of Defense's framework (DODAF)[21] and the Federal Enterprise Architecture (FEA)[22] framework are the most well-known ones.

There are also more commercially driven approaches developed by consulting companies, of which the Gartner Enterprise Architecture

Framework is the most widely known. Rather than a formal process, this can be considered a set of practices.

TOGAF is probably the most widely adopted Enterprise Architecture approach in the recent years. It has been relatively successful in driving through an accreditation program. Several practitioners see TOGAF certification as a badge of honor.

Finally, although not particularly an Enterprise Architecture approach, there is SAFe,[1] which focuses on applying Agile practices at an enterprise scale.

Although Continuous Architecture is not an Enterprise Architecture approach, it does focus on some of the same challenges. We do not have a particular viewpoint on the merits or drawbacks of Enterprise Architecture methodologies. We also do not believe that you have to adopt an Enterprise Architecture methodology to apply architectural thinking at the enterprise level.

organizations that pick and choose the tools that work for them are more successful than organizations that try to create a highly structured and prescriptive process. This even applies to adopting Agile practices. Just forcing every team to create a backlog and have daily standup meetings will not create a successful software delivery team.

From a Continuous Architecture perspective, we believe the same applies to architecture. There is no need to create a detailed architecture methodology and process. Success boils down to two key building blocks:

1. A common language
2. A toolbox

As long as we can understand each other and use a similar set of tools and techniques, then we can say that we are successfully implementing a consistent architecture approach. This is one of the key tenets of this book. We are not claiming that Continuous Architecture is a new architecture process, nor do we have answers to all challenges. What we do believe is that there is a set of trusted tools that have been used successfully in the industry. Our recommendation is to adopt the appropriate tools for your organization aligned with the Continuous Architecture principles.

One lever we have not covered while focusing on collaboration and communication is training and mentoring. If the objective is to provide a consistent enterprise approach to architecture, then there is a need to launch an effort that enables individuals to learn, understand, and internalize the recommended approach. This education, training, or mentoring effort should focus on communicating the common language and tools effectively to the organization. We recommend that formal training should only be organized for key processes and tools. For example, if architecture validations are going to follow a common approach (as discussed in Chapter 6), then it would make sense to have a formal training program.

SUMMARY

In this chapter, we provided an overview of how Continuous Architecture can help address the challenges faced by architects at an enterprise scale. This is a very wide topic, and the unique aspects of each organization as well as the level (solution vs. enterprise) architecture you are dealing with vastly impact how you focus. Regardless, we believe that there are some common themes and applicable tools and techniques that can be used.

We started off by providing an overview of the enterprise context and sample antipatterns by referring to cornerstone literature on this topic.

We then focused on collaboration and communication, which is key to being a successful architect. Most architects who come from a technical background struggle in this area. Our recommendation is to make an explicit effort in communicating with different types of stakeholders. We introduced a set of levers that we believe can be helpful in this area.

We then discussed the importance of having a common language and provided a set of examples where we believe the industry has been successful, particularly UML and design patterns. We introduced an approach to creating a common language.

We then looked at the topic of decision making in the enterprise and presented an approach to governance. The key premise is empowerment of development teams while providing them a support structure in which to make their decisions.

Finally, we addressed the topic of an architecture process at the enterprise scale. Our view is that having a common language and common set of tools across the enterprise is sufficient to enable success. We believe that focusing too much on an architectural process usually provides little benefit relative to the investment made.

In Chapter 10, we will focus on the concept of enterprise services, which we believe is a logical step of applying Continuous Architecture at the enterprise scale.

ENDNOTES

1. Scaled Agile Framework. <http://www.scaledagileframework.com/>.
2. Conway ME. How do committees invent? Datamation 1968;14(5):28–31.
3. Brooks F. The mythical man-month: essays on software engineering, Addison-Wesley; 1975, 1995.
4. Schumacher EF. Small is beautiful: economics as if people mattered. New York: Harper and Row; 1973. p. 244.
5. Brown W, Malveau R, McCormick S, Mowbray T. AntiPatterns: refactoring software, architectures, and projects in crisis. John Wiley & Sons, NY; 1998.
6. Gehry Partners, LLP. <http://www.foga.com/>.
7. The Independent. <http://www.independent.co.uk/arts-entertainment/architecture/architects-are-branded-arrogant-and-egotistical–by-one-of-their-own-10068030.html>.
8. Tufte, ER. The Visual Display of Quantitative Information (2nd ed.), Graphics Press, Cheshire, CT; 2001 [1983]. <http://wiki/International_Standard_Book_Number/>; <http://wiki/Special:BookSources/0-9613921-4-2/>.
9. Gamma E, Helm R, Johnson R, Vlissides J. Design patterns—elements of reusable object-oriented software. Addison-Wesley; 1994.
10. Zachman J. A framework for information systems architecture. IBM Systems Journal 1987;26(3):276–292.
11. The Open Group. Architecture forum. <http://www.opengroup.org/togaf/>.
12. The Free On-line Dictionary of Computing. Governance, 2010. <http://foldoc.org/>.
13. Working with Devs. The technical debt singularity, January 1, 2015. <http://workingwithdevs.com/technical-debt-singularity/>.
14. Ulam S. Tribute to John von Neumann. Bull Am Math Soc 1958;64(3, part 2):5.
15. The Open Source Initiative. <http://www.opensource.org/>.
16. The Open Source Initiative. The open source definition, <http://opensource.org/definition/>.
17. Thaler RH, Sunstein CR. Nudge: improving decisions about health, wealth and happiness. New Haven, CT: Yale University Press, 2008.
18. Wikipedia. Nudge theory. <http://en.wikipedia.org/wiki/Nudge_theory/>.
19. The Behavioural Insights Team. Who we are. <http://www.behaviouralinsights.co.uk/about-us/>.
20. Beck K. Extreme programming explained: embrace change. Addison-Wesley; 1999.
21. Wikipedia. Department of Defense Architecture Framework. <http://en.wikipedia.org/wiki/Department_of_Defense_Architecture_Framework/>.
22. Wikipedia. Federal enterprise architecture. <http://en.wikipedia.org/wiki/Federal_enterprise_architecture/>.
23. Zachman International Enterprise Architecture. About the Zachman Framework, 2008. <https://www.zachman.com/about-the-zachman-framework/>.

Chapter 10

What About Enterprise Services?

Knowledge speaks, but wisdom listens.

—Jimi Hendrix

The term *enterprise service* is used quite a lot within the industry without a clear definition. In this final chapter of the book, we look at the topic of enterprise services. This is a natural step of applying Continuous Architecture at an enterprise scale.

The most known usage is in relation to the enterprise service bus, which is aligned to the service-oriented architecture (SOA) vision. In this context, an enterprise service is a component that represents a set of functionality that can be exposed to the enterprise via a common interface. One example is a credit check service that can be exposed to multiple business processes that require such functionality.

Part of the SOA vision is focused on software reuse. The software industry has been trying to encourage software reuse for decades. For example, this was one of the key selling points of object-oriented technologies that evolved in the 1990s. The key benefit of reusable assets is that they contribute to:

- Faster = Improved productivity because the asset is already built
- Cheaper = Reduced cost because less effort is focused on building
- Better = Improved quality because the asset has already been used and is therefore proven

The second context in which the enterprise service term is used is more infrastructure driven. In the past decade, virtualization technology and cloud-based offerings have enabled a much more elastic vision of provisioning infrastructure. You no longer need to purchase your own server and install an operating system or database. You can just request the amount of information technology (IT) capacity you need in terms of basic elements such as CPU and memory. In this context, enterprise services represent the types of elastic infrastructure you can use. An example of such an enterprise service would be the ability to provision databases on a shared infrastructure.

Both an service-oriented architecture (SOA) and an infrastructure focus are valid starting points for enterprise services. We believe that enterprise services are a key building block of creating successful architectures at scale.

In this chapter, we discuss how Continuous Architecture approaches the topic of enterprise services. We start off by focusing on the role and definition of enterprise service. Then we drill down into recommendations on how to successfully build out such capability, with a special emphasis on product management. We also introduce a case study and demonstrate the applicability of the Continuous Architecture principles.

THE ROLE OF ENTERPRISE SERVICES

When we talk about Continuous Architecture, the continuum not only applies to the time dimension but also to scale. So whereas the application architect talks about reuse of objects and interfaces at the code or application level, the enterprise architect talks about using enterprise services at the level of an enterprise.

The reason behind the drive for enterprise services can be distilled down to a few aspects:

1. **Architectural simplicity:** In Continuous Architecture, the ultimate end state of an application is to be composed of a set of loosely coupled services. The enterprise services are simply those that are used by more than one application. In a loosely coupled architecture, vendor risks and open source risks can be mitigated by standardizing on interfaces and making them "source independent" so that the specific implementations can be replaced without affecting the consuming application.
2. **Cost and effort:** It is more cost effective to build a commonly used service once. More importantly, the ongoing cost of maintaining a single service is dramatically lower than the cost of maintaining multiple services. In large enterprises, an inordinate amount of effort is spent on keeping software assets up to date and focusing on continuous improvements, like security. Enterprise services greatly reduce the level of effort for such activities.
3. **Knowledge:** It is logical to try to isolate and reduce the areas where specialized knowledge is required. This also aligns with the fact that the role of the architect is becoming more generalized as discussed in Chapter 8. Enterprise services help consolidate and reduce the areas where difficult technical challenges need to be addressed.

Let's take a basic example. Messaging technologies have been around for decades. They enable applications to send messages to each other via pre-agreed interfaces or Application Programming Interfaces (APIs), IBM's MQ solution being one of the first ones to gain widespread usage in the industry. If you look under the cover, these solutions are applications in themselves that need to be installed on a server and require ongoing maintenance. In addition, sufficient capacity needs to be provisioned to deal with the nonfunctional demand (volumes, latency) required by the calling applications. Initially, if two applications wanted to communicate via IBM MQ, each would install a version of the software on its own servers and manage all capacity and security requirements individually.

Over time, this leads to a difficult environment to manage. It is not clear who is responsible for ensuring that the messaging layer performs. Also, as IBM releases new versions of the product or releases critical security patches, it is not clear who is accountable for ensuring that all applications comply with the vendor releases.

To address these challenges, the correct model is to create an enterprise service that is installed on a central set of servers with applications connecting via the common MQ API (or an enterprise API if it is defined). In this model, a central team is responsible for managing all aspects of the environment, including capacity management, release upgrades, day-to-day monitoring, and so on.

Not only is this model more cost efficient, but it also reduces the number of people who have to be familiar with the details of IBM MQ technology in the organization. The application developers can focus on building applications rather than dealing with the intricacies of a particular messaging technology.

We used a fairly technical example to illustrate the point. It should be recognized that enterprise services can range from such technical services to more business-focused functionality. We will see this as we further define the term and provide examples.

What Is an Enterprise Service?

The simple example above provides a scenario for an enterprise service but leaves lots of open questions:

- Are only managed services (i.e., hosted on their own infrastructure) considered to be enterprise services? What about libraries and code reuse?
- How does this relate to the concepts of Infrastructure as a Service (IaaS), Platform as a Service (PaaS), and Software as a Service (SaaS)?
- What level of granularity should an enterprise service be?

We define an enterprise service as a technical capability offered within an enterprise that has the following characteristics:

1. Provides a cohesive set of technical capabilities and features through a well-defined interface (or contract)
2. Has an accountable team that is responsible for delivering and supporting the service
3. Has a well-defined onboarding process that outlines how to use the service
4. Provides build and runtime support in terms of monitoring, resolving and fixing issues
5. Has well-defined service-level agreements (SLAs) outlining the nonfunctional parameters of the service
6. Has a financial model that defines the economics for using the service

Environments
Key aspect: Enable software life cycle
Examples: Development environments, testing tools
Common Platforms
Key aspect: Application platforms that have business users
Examples: Provisioning, ticketing, document management, and workflow
Common Services
Key aspect: Provide common functionality to other services
Examples: Entitlements, static data
Common Libraries
Key aspect: Specialized code that can be reused
Examples: Validation, data serialization
Integration Services
Key aspect: Enable integration of services
Examples: Data Integration (ETL), messaging, service bus
Infrastructure Services
Key aspect: Virtualized infrastructure platforms
Examples: Database, operating system, compute, storage

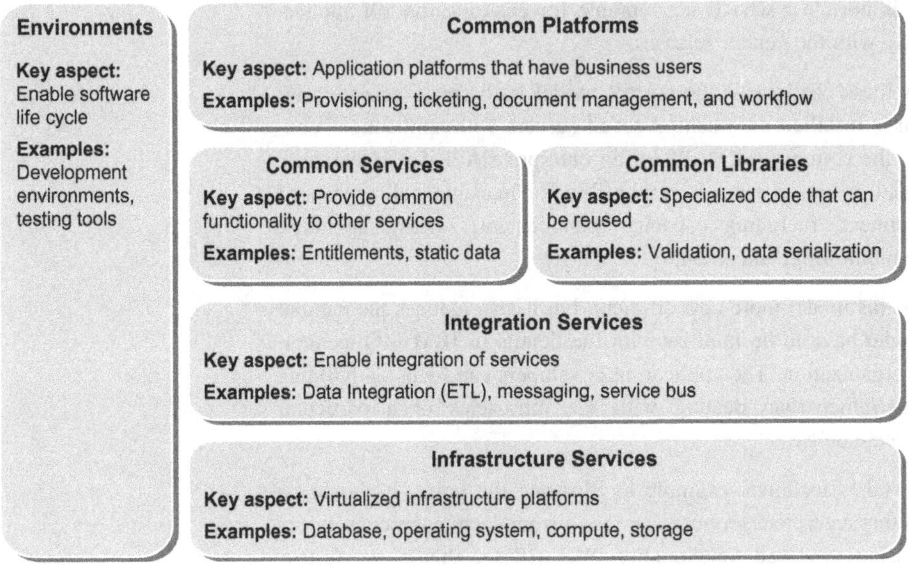

FIGURE 10.1 Enterprise service categories.

Figure 10.1 represents the major categories of enterprise services, which are as follows:

- **Common platforms:** These are more application-like platforms that offer capabilities such as workflow, document management, ticketing, and provisioning.
- **Common services:** These represent callable services from other applications that perform a common functionality. Examples include entitlements and static data sources.

- **Common libraries:** These represent highly specialized code that is written by qualified developers. Examples include data serialization, common validation, and rule implementations.
- **Integration technologies:** These are focused on moving data between applications and range from core messaging (e.g., Java Message Service (JMS), IBM MQ), to managed file transfer, data integration (ETL), and enterprise service bus (Extract, transfer, Load [ETL] software) solutions.
- **Infrastructure:** These represent infrastructure platforms such as virtualized database, compute, and storage platforms.
- **Environments:** These are tools used by application development teams to build applications, such as development, automated testing and deployment tools, and application frameworks.

AS A SERVICE FAMILY

So how do enterprise services relate to the trends toward cloud applications, particularly IaaS, PaaS, and SaaS? (The term Business Process as a Service [BPaaS] is also becoming prevalent in the marketplace.) The short answer is that whereas enterprise services are more of an architectural pattern within an enterprise, the "as a Service family" takes advantage of technology standardization to address a commercial pattern in the marketplace. As a result, the two are related but orthogonal approaches. Because of their nature, enterprise services should be able to leverage what is offered by the "as a Service family."

First let's give a high-level view of the "as a Service family." For years, there has been a vision to make compute resources as pervasive and easily usable as common utilities such as electricity and water. It looks like the industry is starting to make this vision a reality. The "as a Service family" offers clients the ability to take advantage of compute resources, whether they are virtual storage or full-blown applications, without having to actually own any of the physical devices, licenses, or additional infrastructure required. In other words, you can have electricity without having to buy a generator.

All that is different among IaaS, PaaS, and SaaS is the level of granularity of the resource you are paying for. Although the IaaS, PaaS, and SaaS terms have been around for a while, the market is was still evolving. A few years ago, it was all about IaaS. Now the market is maturing, and most vendors have started focusing on PaaS (Figure 10.2).

The development of the "as a Service family" was driven both from an infrastructure focus (bottom up) as well as a software focus (top down). The infrastructure-focused model can be summarized in the story of Amazon Web Services. How did a company that provided an online retailing offering end up with such a massive business in cloud computing? First was the enabling factor, standardization driven from the chief executive officer (CEO)—every architect's dream! In 2002, Jeff Bezos (the CEO of Amazon), insisted that all Amazon services be built in a way that they could easily communicate with each other over a web protocol, and he issued a mandate requiring all teams to expose their data and functionality through service interfaces.[1] This resulted in the company having an ethos focused on building well-defined components that can integrate via standard interfaces. Next came the step taken to apply this to Amazon's computing infrastructure driven by Chris Pinkham and Benjamin Black.[2,3] Because we are mentioning names, it is also important to note that Amazon's chief technology officer, Werner Vogel, was key to the development of Amazon Web Services. The final step was the realization that they could leverage all this investment:

Amazon has spent 11 years and $2 billion building up its network of data centers. Opening up that infrastructure to outside developers is an effort to gain financially from that investment and expertise. "The basic idea is that there are certain pieces of heavy-lifting infrastructure where we can take all that fixed cost and resell it to people by the drink as a variable cost," Bezos said in 2006.[4]

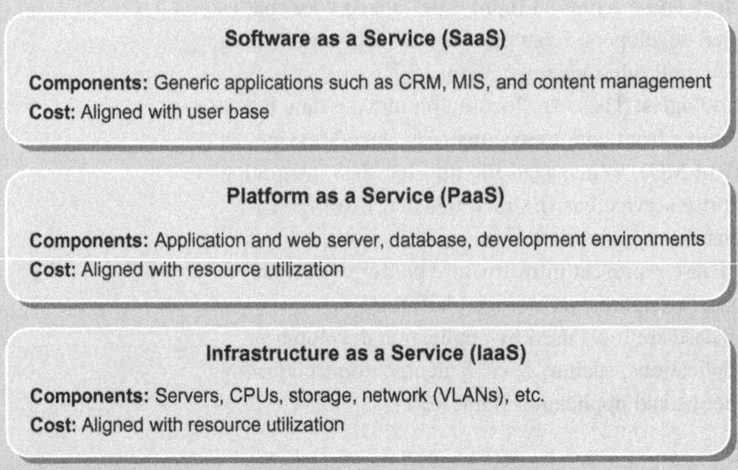

Software as a Service (SaaS)

Components: Generic applications such as CRM, MIS, and content management
Cost: Aligned with user base

Platform as a Service (PaaS)

Components: Application and web server, database, development environments
Cost: Aligned with resource utilization

Infrastructure as a Service (IaaS)

Components: Servers, CPUs, storage, network (VLANs), etc.
Cost: Aligned with resource utilization

■ **FIGURE 10.2** View of "As A Service family."

If we look at the software-focused story, then a good example is Salesforce.com, which started as a provider of customer relationship software in 1999. The visionary aspect was to follow the SaaS model, better known as an Application Service Provider (ASP) at that time. However, similar to Amazon, there is a notion of simplicity and focusing on the developer in this success story. What made Salesforce.com successful was not only the effective manner in which it delivered its business application, but also the development platform that it used. As advertised on Salesforce.com: *Force.com is a set of tools and services that make it faster and easier to create employee-facing applications that are instantly social and mobile.* So, you could say that Salesforce.com started as a SaaS provider and ended up as a PaaS provider (Figure 10.3).

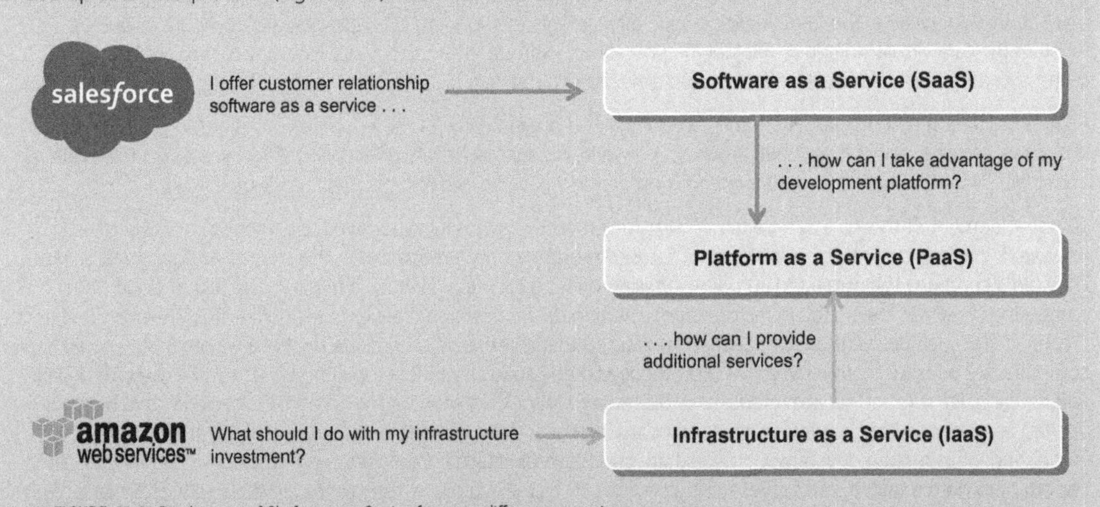

■ **FIGURE 10.3** Development of Platform as a Service from two different perspectives.

In summary, we have two companies that have leveraged their existing investments to create new markets. The purpose of this book is not to provide a market overview of "as a Service family" providers. We picked two of the more well-known companies in this space, Amazon Web Services and Salesforce.com, mainly to illustrate the concepts. This does not imply any view regarding how their offerings compare with competitor products.

Back to our original question on the relationship of the "as a Service family" with enterprise services. We can draw three main conclusions:

1. The cloud trend, like business process outsourcing, is here to stay and will wax and wane in popularity for enterprises.
2. We should learn from the success stories of leading companies in these areas. Their success is driven by three main aspects: standardization, focus on developers, and being commercially driven.
3. Finally, we should note that the successful cloud service providers treat their offerings as products, so by default, they implement *Principle 1: Architect products, not just solutions for projects.*

PRODUCT MANAGEMENT

A common theme running through our view of enterprise services is looking at how commercial technology vendors operate. We should think of enterprise services just like products offered by a commercial software company. This means that for each enterprise service, there has to be a clear understanding of the marketplace and user requirements, which is then reflected in a product definition and roadmap.

A role that is critical to operate in that manner is that of the product manager.

Most large enterprises can be considered to operate as internal commercial markets. Multiple project teams are trying to achieve their individual goals within the budget and time constraints they have. This is the target marketplace for enterprise services. Bringing a product management focus is a key enabler for ensuring that enterprise services are aligned with the demands of this target marketplace.

At the end of the day, the goal of enterprise services is to make delivery and ongoing maintenance of key applications easier, quicker, and more cost effective. So, in an ideal world, the case for enterprise services should be clear-cut, but large enterprises are far from an ideal world.

First let's look at how product management is defined generally and then analyze how it can be implemented for enterprise services.*

The concept of product management has been in the industry for decades and focuses on successfully introducing and maintaining a commercial

*We would like to thank Ian Warford for providing us with his in-depth knowledge of product management.

product for an organization. There is no clear definition, and how it is interpreted varies among industries and individual companies. One of the better definitions we have found is:

> *Product Management is the activity of "product" ownership from Product Conception to Product Withdrawal. It is without any doubt an essential business discipline whereby the Product Manager is analogous to the conductor of an orchestra—without the conductor, uncontrolled pandemonium sets in with each instrument fighting to be heard in continuous cycle of disarray.*[5]

At a high level, there is also a differentiation between inbound and outbound product management:

> *Inbound product management (aka inbound marketing) is the "radar" of the organization and involves absorbing information like customer research, competitive intelligence, industry analysis, trends, economic signals and competitive activity as well as documenting requirements and setting product strategy.*
>
> *In comparison, outbound activities are focused on distributing or pushing messages, training sales people, go to market strategies and communicating messages through channels like advertising, Public Relations (PR) and events.*[6]

Inbound product management is better understood by technologists and architects. It is basically focused on identifying the customer needs and requirements. However, outbound marketing is usually not practiced. This is because technologists tend to underestimate the amount of communication and "marketing" required. (We discuss the topic of communication and collaboration in detail in Chapter 9).

Let us now consider some of the dynamics of the enterprise service marketplace. First of all, the size of the internal market is limited by the organization size. However, there is still a lot of work to understand the "voice of the customer" and requirements. A second difference is that the market can be considered a captive market. In other words, certain choices can be dictated to the market in a different manner than the external software market. This is a double-edged sword—although initially it is tempting to believe that dictating standards will solve all problems, if the offered services do not meet requirements (functional or nonfunctional), the end result can be a huge failure with a lot of money wasted and a political maelstrom. This leads to the third difference; the political and bureaucratic mechanisms of an enterprise can easily lead to an environment where suboptimal services are still kept alive regardless of their capabilities. This easily leads to bloated organizations that provide little value to the enterprise.

We already demonstrated the value of thinking in terms of products rather than projects in Chapter 7. In this example, our team tasked with developing the "MobileShopping" system used *Principle 1: Architect products, not just solutions for projects* and realized that the capability they were asked to build already aligned with the roadmap of the product focused on delivering online quotes. This enabled them to refocus their effort and reuse key elements of an existing product's architecture.

So, how do we create a product management environment that takes advantage of known commercial practices but avoids the pitfalls of traditional enterprise dynamics? There is no easy cookbook for this, but here are three key recommendations that we believe will be helpful.

- Product management as a first class citizen
- Govern properly – Fill or Kill
- Get the financials right

Product Management as a First-Class Citizen

Very few IT organizations value the role of a product manager. The first step is to clearly articulate this role and give it teeth. Regardless of organizational structure a product manager should be responsible for the following activities:

- **Understand the market.** Have a clear view on the scale of the developer community, the different groups, and their priorities and challenges. Although this task might sound easy, for a large organization, it can get quite complex. Because most organizations do not have good data on their current state, even answering basic questions such as "How many of our developers use Java vs. Microsoft?" can be quite challenging.
- **Know the clients.** Treating other application teams within an organization as clients can be quite counterintuitive. But that is exactly the approach required. The product manager has to have a clear understanding of the key clients, in terms of individuals as stakeholders and also in terms of the business line they are supporting. This should not be a one-time exercise, nor should it be confined to one-on-one communications. As software vendors realized years ago, creating customer forums where different clients interact is a very powerful tool.
- **Define the product.** Define what the enterprise service is really offering; this can range from a centrally managed service such as messaging to libraries used for compressing data. The product manager should clearly articulate the service, the functional and

In one organization, a shared platform was built to provide a workflow solution. The initial implementation was quite successful, and about 35 different workflow applications were hosted on the platform. When the team maintaining the platform was asked about the client list, the team produced a list of application names. There was no understanding of the actual client base in terms of business areas supported or senior stakeholders.

nonfunctional capabilities it offers, how users can use or onboard onto the service, and associated service level agreements and financial parameters.

- **Develop a roadmap.** No service will meet all the requirements of its clients, particularly as the world of technology keeps on evolving. It is important that there is a clearly articulated roadmap for the service defining what features and capabilities will be offered in the future.
- **Govern the product life cycle.** All critical decisions regarding the scope and roadmap of a product have to be governed properly. Product decisions should be based on the balanced input of all stakeholders: customers, senior management, and the product delivery team.

Determining where in the organization the product manager sits is as important as determining her or his roles and responsibilities. A model we believe works very well is when the product manager is a peer of the individual accountable for the delivery of the service—the product owner as well as the architect. As a result, there are three roles focused on the service:

- The product manager who is external facing and works with the clients and determines the roadmap
- The product owner who is accountable for the delivery of the service and owns all the resources that are required to build, test, release, and maintain the service
- The product architect who is responsible for the coherent architectural vision and sustainability of the product

In addition, it is common to have a fourth role focused on the day-to-day operations of the service—the operations owner.

This separation between the product manager and product owner is quite important because each requires different skillsets. Too often product managers are subservient to product owners and are not taken very seriously. This results in the dominant and normally very technical product owner making critical decisions, which usually end in overengineered, technically complex products that limited value to clients.

Govern Properly—Fill or Kill

As stated before, enterprises do not operate as efficiently as the commercial software market.

This is mainly because software assets in an enterprise are not treated like products. A tool that we believe greatly helps address this is the fill or kill process. Basically, we are talking about a governance model in which every quarter, all enterprise services are reviewed, and it is determined either to provide them with additional or continued budget (fill) or to stop the investment and wind down (kill).

This process is driven by the product manager, and he or she comes to each review with key data around market penetration, client satisfaction, delivery against roadmap, commercials, and operational statistics (e.g., stability, performance). This data enables the governance body to explicitly make decisions on how to direct funding of enterprise services.

Let us illustrate this for an organization that has 10 enterprise services. They plot their services along two axes:

- **Customer demand**, which represents the amount of demand for a particular service in the enterprise
- **Effectiveness and stability**, which represents a combined score of the service based on how stable it is in production and how well it delivers against its roadmap (Figure 10.4)

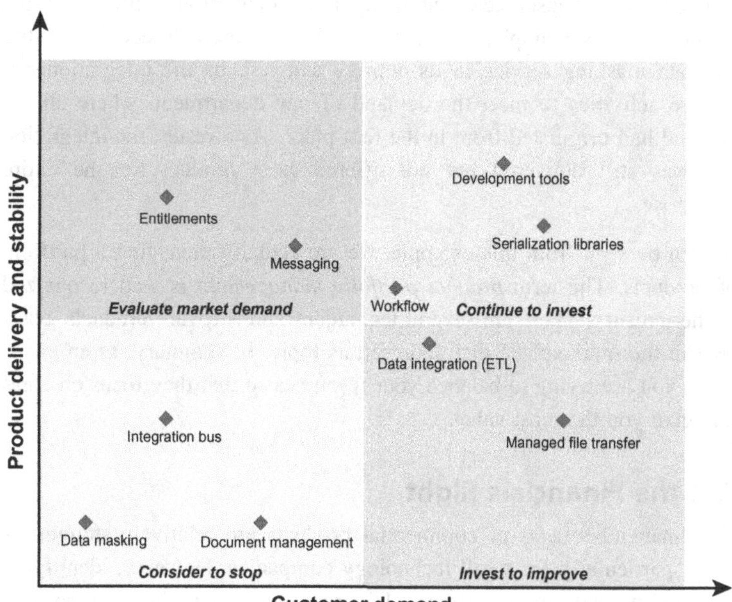

■ **FIGURE 10.4** Customer demand versus product delivery and stability mapping example.

This analysis results in four focus areas:

- **Continue to invest.** These services are both in high demand and achieve an acceptable level of operational and delivery stability. They should be continued to be invested in (fill).

- **Invest to improve.** These services have high customer demand but are struggling to deliver to the client expectations. They should still be invested in but with a focus to improve product delivery and stability (fill).
- **Evaluate market demand.** These services meet client expectations, but the problem is that demand is limited. Market demand should be evaluated, and it should be determined if they can be sustained as enterprise services (if not they become a kill candidate—demote from enterprise).
- **Consider to stop.** These are services that are both struggling from a delivery and stability perspective and also have limited demand. They should be seriously reviewed and considered as activities that should be stopped (kill candidate).

Note that stopping a service can mean two things. The entire activity can be stopped and all resources offboarded, or the activity can still continue but for a limited scope. Alternatively, the service could be "crowd-sourced" or "opensourced" internally if a small group still wants the features. In this example, the governance body eventually decided to stop the data masking service in its entirety and refocus the integration bus service activities to meet the demand of one department, where all the demand had originated from in the first place. As a result, the integration bus was still delivered but not offered as a product for the entire enterprise.

As can be seen from this example, we are actually managing a portfolio of products. The term *product portfolio management* is well recognized in the industry. There are several techniques and software products available in the marketplace that address this topic. In summary, as an enterprise, you are trying to balance your resources so that they focus on areas that give you the most value.

Within the context of financials, justifying Enterprise Architecture teams from a cost perspective is even more difficult; these groups usually get formed and disbanded with a regular rhythm based on the economic cycle. We believe that with the introduction of Agile and Continuous Delivery, the pendulum has swung away from Enterprise Architecture and will not swing back to traditional methods.

Get the Financials Right

The financial aspects of commercial products are relatively straightforward, particularly for small technology companies. However, identifying the commercial metrics for an IT organization can be horrendously difficult. This starts from the fact that the IT organization is a cost to the business rather than a value center, at least for most enterprises. So the commercial aspect for IT is not on producing profit but on the ability to justify its cost basis.

Enterprise services add an extra dimension of complexity to this picture. They are supposed to make IT more efficient and should theoretically result in cost savings. However, it is extremely difficult to create financial models that demonstrate this value. The main challenge is the way data is captured (or not) in large organizations.

Also, we have to recognize that creating a product that can be used by several clients is significantly more costly than tactical solutions that can be implemented. On the other hand, it also has to be understood that multiple short-term tactical fixes accumulate technical debt.

Over the years, people have developed several approaches for funding enterprise services:

- **First come, first pay:** This is the most common approach, in which the initial build out of an enterprise service is funded by a major program. In this model, the enterprise service is in essence riding the wave of a major change effort. The challenge with this approach is catching the train at the right time, that is, the sales pitch for the enterprise service has to be made at the same time that the major change initiative is being launched. This usually leads to an ad hoc collection of enterprise services not aligned to any particular architectural vision.
- **Tax across the enterprise:** In this model, the cost of enterprise services is basically absorbed in the overall IT budget. This results in a tax to all business units regardless of whether they use the service or not. This is a good model if there is sufficient budget and belief in enterprise services. However, it usually ends up in inefficient allocation of budget and no clear alignment of spend versus value.
- **Pooled resources:** In this model, several projects that need the same capability pool their resources to provide a common component. This is a nimble approach and is cost efficient from the perspective of the projects. It has the same drawback of first come, first pay, in the sense that it normally leads to an ad hoc collection of services. It is also difficult to execute because the priorities of the projects diverge over time. As a result, it is not that commonplace.
- **Usage-based pricing:** This is when the cost of an enterprise service is split across consumers based on an agreed usage pattern. This is probably the most sophisticated model and gives the impression of a well-oiled machine. The main challenge with this approach is that it usually takes an inordinate amount of time to develop, agree on, and finally monitor these cost allocations. In addition, the cost is normally allocated to other IT groups, so does it make sense for two cost centers to worry so much about cross-charging?

Another way of looking at this topic is to consider a time-related model. Basically, the costing model is driven to some aspect by when you create

The term *technical debt* has gained a lot of interest in the software industry. It is a metaphor that addresses the challenge with several short-term decisions resulting in long-term challenges. It draws comparison with how financial debt works. It does not mean debt is bad and actually is sometimes preferable (e.g., quick solutions to get a product to market). However, it should be repaid. The concept was first introduced by Ward Cunningham[7] as:

Shipping first time code is like going into debt. A little debt speeds development so long as it is paid back promptly with a rewrite.... The danger occurs when the debt is not repaid. Every minute spent on not-quite-right code counts as interest on that debt. Entire engineering organizations can be brought to a stand-still under the debt load of an unconsolidated implementation, object-oriented or otherwise.

the service. If you are proactive (beforehand), then you will need to consider funding models that are more centrally driven. If you are creating the services just in time (as needed), you will tend to go for models that are more project driven such as pooled resources. If you are creating services after the fact (harvesting), then you can go for a balance of central and demand-driven models.

Covering details of cost allocation mechanisms is beyond the scope of this book. Needless to say, the best financial management approach of an enterprise service will be heavily influenced by organizational specifics. The most important message is not to ignore such a critical aspect of product management when focusing on enterprise services.

A SHORT STORY OF AN ENTERPRISE SERVICE

Now that we have introduced the concept of enterprise services and detailed what we mean by product management, let us take a look at how enterprise services can be constructed using Continuous Architecture.

Let us take an example of the IT organization of a global company. For years, this company has been successful in building applications that support individual business lines, but there is little or no utilization of common components. However, the company does have a common IT infrastructure services group that operates the data centers and networks. In the past 10 years, this infrastructure function has had a level of success in building out shared infrastructure components that are used by development teams.

Their main areas of success have been in storage, compute, and web server hosting. The company started out in the storage and compute areas, where they teamed up with one of the major commercial providers and jointly built out an infrastructure that enabled them to offer different levels of services at a sliding cost scale. Learning from how their commercial partners operated, they created the role of a product manager, who focused on developing a cost model for the services and ensuring there was sufficient capacity to meet the demand.

Seeing the success of these first two services, the company then ventured into the space of building out a web hosting service. This service enabled multitenant web server hosting for one commercial and one open source solution. The service also took care of critical topics such as authentication, load balancing, and caching in an efficient manner. The company had a very skilled engineering team that created a highly scalable environment. The company also put a lot of effort into automating the onboarding process, so that application teams could self-service most standard requests for a web server. As a result, application teams had no reason to install their own web servers. The infrastructure team had another huge success.

While our Infrastructure group was building out the infrastructure components, the Enterprise Architecture group was focused on setting technology standards. They decided to focus on areas where they saw a lot of diversity in the organization and defined standards in the areas of User Interface (UI), Data Integration (ETL), and workflow. Through multiple governance mechanisms, the company tried to enforce these standards, with limited success.

At this point, the infrastructure group was looking for more areas to grow into when they noticed that implementing an enterprise service around workflow made sense. The Enterprise Architecture group was also happy because finally someone was taking their standards seriously. Even happier was the commercial IT vendor that sold an enterprise license to the organization (Figure 10.5).

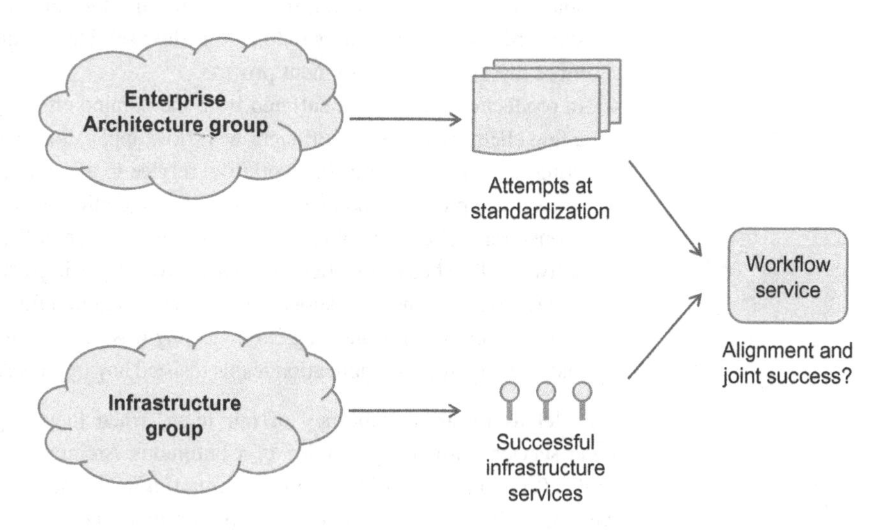

■ **FIGURE 10.5** The story of an enterprise service.

Because this was going to be an enterprise service, it had to be engineered carefully. It was also more complex and had many more moving parts than any of the former enterprise services that the group had worked on. As a result, the group spent eight months carefully engineering a highly scalable multitenant service. With great fanfare, they launched the workflow service. There was an initial set of about ten different application teams using the service.

But after the first year, the service was not as successful as expected. Some of the key challenges outlined by an external consultancy brought in to do a lessons learned exercise were:

- Clients had to use the User Interface of the workflow engine, which was not as flexible and appealing as the custom interfaces they were used to.
- During the implementation, it turned out that there were several workflows that involved management of documents, which were difficult to implement with the limited document management capability provided by the service.
- Moving a workflow through different stages of the development life cycle was deemed as being very complex, resulting in several manual steps and approval chains.
- The testing vendor that the company had outsourced the testing to was not trained on the intricacies of dealing with the workflow solution. The testing vendor unsuccessfully tried to implement their standard testing procedures onto a workflow service, resulting in even more layers in the deployment process.
- In production, the service suffered from the domino effect. In essence, a few clients that wrote inefficient workflow applications were able to bring the performance of the workflow service to a grinding halt.
- The service provided too much run-time configuration flexibility to clients. Each client was allowed to run its own version of the workflow software. This became difficult to manage over time, in particular when security patches and mandatory upgrades were required for the core workflow engine. Because regression testing was such a cumbersome and manual process, application teams resisted any upgrades.

Now let us restart the journey of our team, when they implement the same service with the principles of Continuous Architecture. First they apply *Principle 1: Architect products, not just solutions for projects.* Although they had the concept of a product manager, the role was more focused on developing charge-back mechanisms and ensuring the there was sufficient infrastructure capacity. They therefore decide to bring in a professional product manager from an external company. She turns out to be great at her job and immediately uncovers some key problems. The service had never focused on understanding its marketplace and what clients had wanted from the service. She quickly understands this and pulls together a roadmap that outlines the core capabilities that will meet client demand. She particularly focuses on building a service that can be integrated into the User Interface framework of the organization.

She then initiates the creation of a workflow competency center. Although there is initial pushback from senior management on the workflow competency center, our product manager is able to demonstrate its value by pointing out that a majority of the problems with the service happened because individual application teams were left to implement workflows without any guidance. For example, a competency center would have ensured that application teams knew how to take advantage of the workflow engine's state management capabilities. This would have prevented several daily performance problems. The first two recruits into the competency center are one of the core engineers from the original team and an external hire with years of experience in the vendor product. Their first project is to refactor about 45 workflows for a specific application into a set of six workflow patterns. This results in significant efficiencies in terms of ongoing maintenance and further rollout of these workflows. This project on its own is sufficient to demonstrate the value of the competency center.

Meanwhile, the lead engineer (who in this case also acts as the product architect), who is now called the product owner, is working with his team on using *Principle 3: Delay design decisions until they are absolutely necessary* and *Principle 4: Architect for change—leverage "the power of small."* Note that he is now a peer of the product manager, and they have developed a strong and effective working relationship. He trusts her with understanding the client base and being able to prioritize a roadmap, and she trusts him with making the architectural decisions and never commits to any client deliverable without his input. In actuality, they manage all key client decisions together. This proves to create an extremely effective team because they can bounce ideas off each other and examine alternative approaches.

The first thing the team does is to write down a list of all the design decisions that they need to make. Some of the key decisions identified are:

1. Should the service support integration with external UIs?
2. Should the service support integration with external document management systems?
3. Should a rules engine be made available as part of the service offering?
4. How should entitlements be managed for the service?

5. How should platform upgrades be handled?
6. How should multitenancy work? Should there be a quality of service like offering?

Note that the design decisions at this stage are articulated fairly briefly; there is no need to go into too much more detail until a decision needs to be made. As in line with *Principle 3: Delay design decisions until they are absolutely necessary*, they did not try to address all of them at once but instead focused on decisions 1, 2, and 4, which were critical for developing the roadmap based on customer demand. Focusing on these decisions leads them to leverage *Principle 4: Architect for change—leverage "the power of small."* What they quickly realize is that the service is too much of a monolith and constructed of tightly coupled components. They develop a new roadmap that clearly articulates where the service can be integrated with external UIs and document management systems. They also realize that there is a need for a stronger entitlements solution. But rather than building it just for this service, they bring this up as a new product to the governance board. This will be the genesis of a new entitlements service in the organization. Figure 10.6 illustrates how the service is modified to leverage the "power of small."

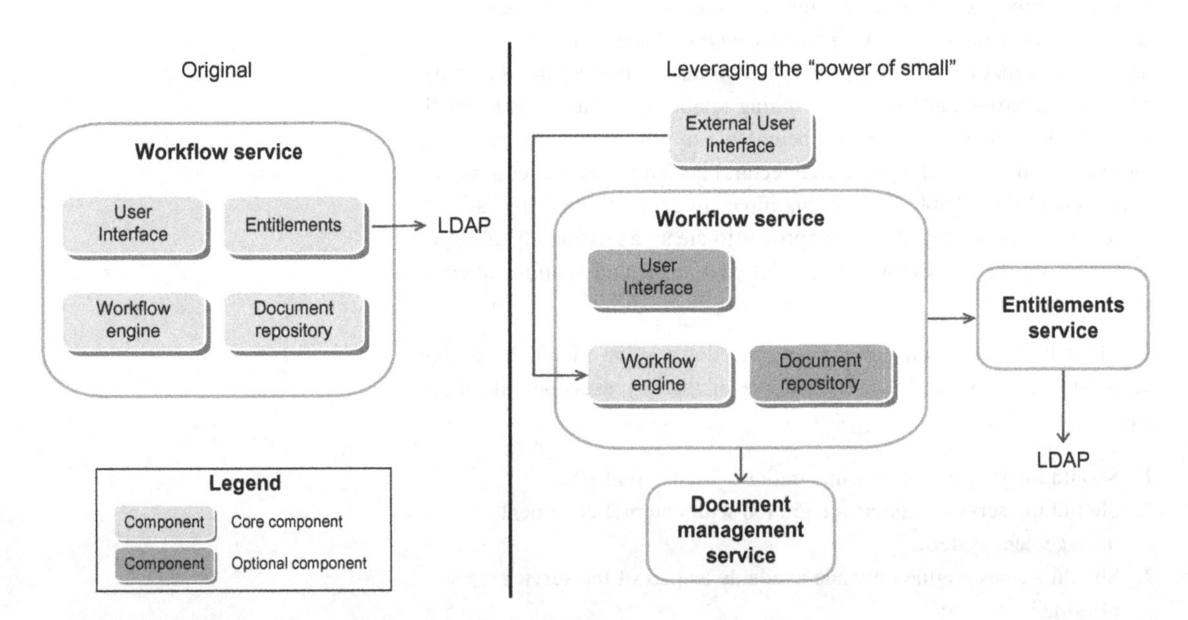

■ **FIGURE 10.6** Before and after view of "workflow service" components.

Note that in this model, the internal User Interface and document repository components still exist within the service. This is to support clients who have simple User Interface or document management requirements. Let us now look at how they leveraged *Principle 2: Focus on Quality Attributes, not on functional requirements*. The team had formerly spent a lot of time focusing on building a scalable multitenant system, so it is unfair to say that they had not focused on nonfunctional qualities. However, before adopting a product management focus, they had not focused on some key Quality Attributes that were important to their clients. That is, they had a very technical instead of a commercial view of the service. In essence, the team had focused on meeting the Quality Attributes for performance and stability while ignoring significant Quality Attributes in the areas of usability, maintainability, and configurability. An example Architecture Tradeoff Analysis Method (ATAM) quality tree contrasting the original focus versus the product-centric focus is provided in Figure 10.7.

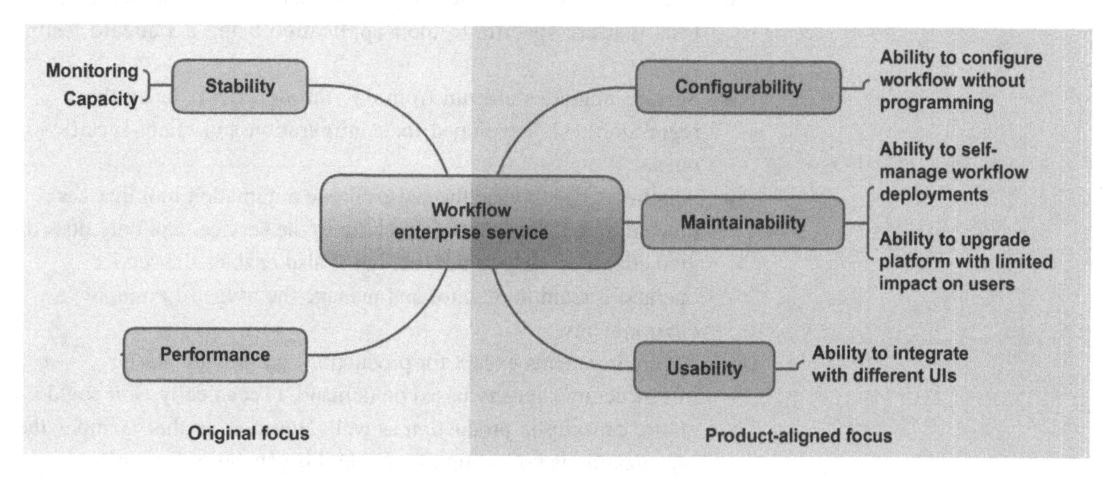

FIGURE 10.7 Workflow service Quality Attributes.

Continuing their focus on decisions important for the roadmap, the team focuses on the fifth design decision (How should platform upgrades be handled?). This leads to leveraging *Principle 5: Architect for build, test, and deploy*. As they observe, challenges with the lengthy deployment process resulted in client dissatisfaction and a complex environment to manage. As with any enterprise service, deployment has three aspects:

- Client onboarding, which is the initial deployment to get a client up and running for using the service

- Client-specific deployments, which result in specific client workflows being delivered into production
- Service deployments related to the underlying platform

First they focus on how to automate the service deployments. Here are some of the key principles they apply:

- Configuration parameters for each client on all environments (dev, user acceptance testing [UAT], preprod, and prod) are kept the same, except for controlled variations because of different capacity constraints. The only difference among the environments is the level of virtualization and underlying infrastructure capacity.
- There are a standard set of regression tests that each client has to run to validate the configuration of the environment. This is the first step that clients conduct after a platform change.
- Each client using the service has to develop a set of regression tests that are specific to their application using a standard testing tool.
- Service upgrades are run from dev through UAT, using the regression tests developed for configuration and client-specific ones.
- All clients have to use the same release automation tool that has preconfigured steps that are specific to the service. Not only does this give clients an easy to use tool but it also enables the service operations team to monitor and manage the usage of multiple environments.
- All environments except for production can provide elastic infrastructure capacity based on demand. (Technically, you could use elastic capacity in production as well. However, in this example, the organization is not set up to provide this capability for business-critical applications.)

The architect and operations team spent significant effort in developing this environment. The most important concept they developed is the **enterprise service ecosystem**. Because the workflow service depends on the document management and entitlements services, to enable rapid development and deployment, all of these services have to be available in all environments. Table 10.1 highlights how the different environments are configured from an enterprise service ecosystem and capacity perspective.

Table 10.1 Enterprise Service Ecosystem

Environment	Purpose	Enterprise Service Ecosystem	Level of Virtualization and Capacity
Dev	Capability for development activities	All dependent enterprise services are available as stubs that can be configured for each client	All client environments share the same virtualized server and database environment
UAT	Conduct acceptance testing with business users	Services are available as callable services with real data samples that are masked from production data	All client environments share the same virtualized server and database environment
Preprod	Conduct performance testing	Services are available as callable services with real data samples that are masked from production data	Reflects the same level of virtualization as production; additional capacity is provisioned on an as-needed basis for the tests
Production	Real-life environment to run business applications	Real services; this is production	Virtualized based on enterprise standards and ability to meet client QARs; capacity is provisioned to meet service QARs

Finally, let us look at *Principle 6: Model the organization after the design of the system.* Our team supporting the workflow service started out as an engineering team focused on building out the service. Then the product manager was introduced as part of the team to create a more client-driven model. She introduced the concept of the competency center. As we can see, a team with disparate roles is starting to take shape. Figure 10.8 shows the main roles that are required to provide an enterprise service.

These just represent roles; the size of the team will dictate how these roles can be distributed among team members. In our workflow services team, the same person is playing the role of the architect and platform owner. Our workflow service also does not have a separate onboarding team; the competency center deals with this aspect of the service as well.

If we apply Principle 6 fully, this results in all of the roles being part of the same service team. However, we recognize that this is not feasible in all organizations. Especially in large organizations, there is a drive to create synergies out of common skills such as project managers and production support teams. Our view on this is that it is possible to create

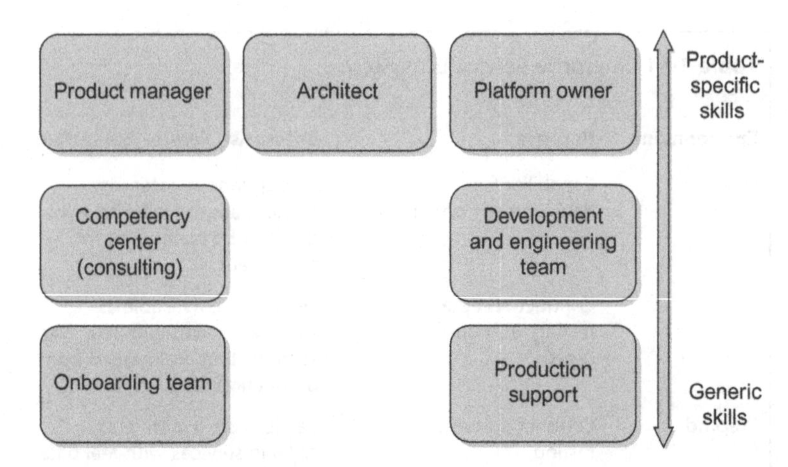

■ **FIGURE 10.8** Enterprise service roles.

these synergies by having the central teams define and develop the skills required for these roles. However, the actual people performing the roles should be part of the delivery team. In other words, the individuals should feel directly accountable to the product team (solid line) while being part of a larger community of practice defined by the central or horizontal teams (dotted line).

DELIVERING ENTERPRISE SERVICES

So far we have defined what we mean by an enterprise service and discussed the topic of product management. We have also gone through a case study of applying Continuous Architecture principles to enterprise services. Now let's look a little more into the elements that are required to deliver an enterprise service. Analyzing a problem from technology, process, and people dimensions is a tried and trusted practice. We think this is a very useful way of looking at key assets that are required for an enterprise service, as illustrated by Figure 10.9.

Let's Start From the Technology Dimension

1. **Interface:** This is the most obvious element, particularly for services that are separate runtime entities. As with any component that is architected successfully with a clear interface, articulating a set of well-understood and unique responsibilities is a must.

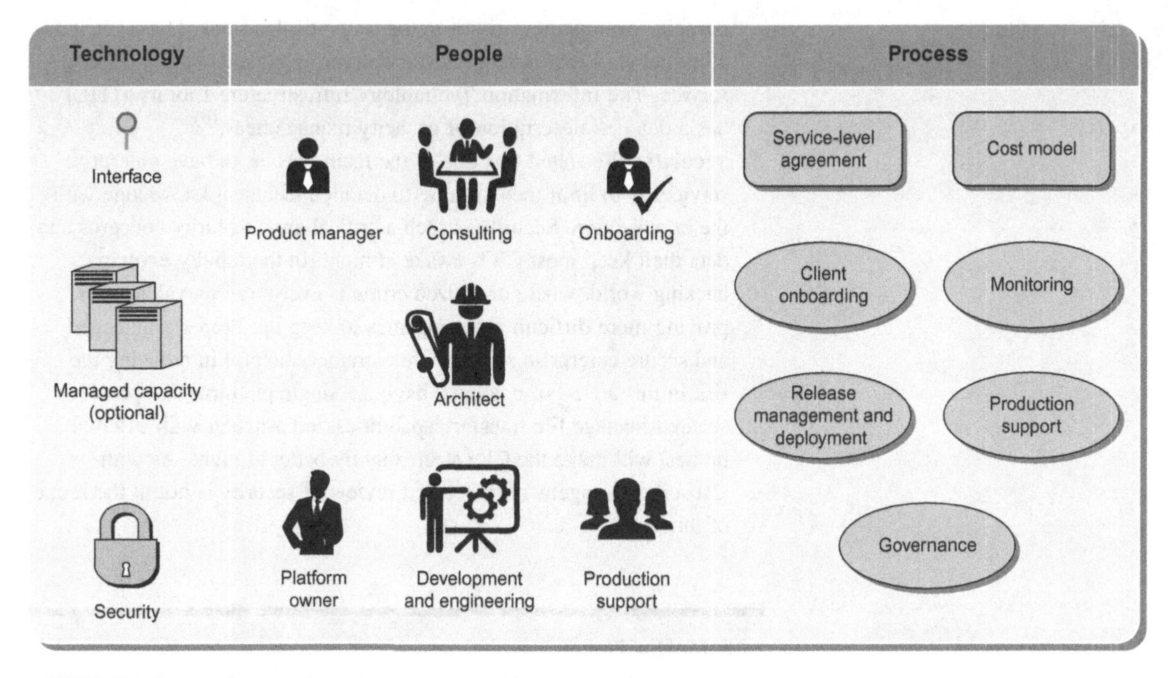

■ **FIGURE 10.9** Elements of an enterprise service.

What about enterprise services such as common libraries and larger components that could be considered applications on their own (e.g., document management systems or development environments)? Both of these types of services still have well-defined interfaces. A library is just a well-written piece of code that you need to insert into your software that has well-documented functions; the difference is that it operates within your runtime environment and namespace. Applications such as document management systems and development environments again have well-defined mechanisms for using them. They have APIs for system access and UIs for human interaction.

2. **Managed capacity:** As stated earlier, the biggest differentiator of the "as a Service" family is the fact that it takes away the pain of managing infrastructure and capacity from the client. Basically, all the client (or user) of the service needs to worry about is the ability to pay for the service you use. Similarly, within the enterprise, being able to emulate the offerings of the cloud vendors by providing capacity that is "elastic" is critical for success. The topic of proper

capacity management is not in the scope of this book. However, it is a critical skill that is required for delivering a successful enterprise service. The Information Technology Infrastructure Library (ITIL) has a detailed description of capacity management.[10]

3. **Security:** We stated that one of the main reasons to have enterprise services is to limit the exposure to detailed technical knowledge with the organization. Security is such a critical area. Security concerns and data theft keep most CIOs awake at night. In the rapidly evolving hacking world, where organized crime is ever more prevalent, it is proving more difficult for companies to keep up. Properly managed and secure enterprise services are extremely helpful in reducing the risk in this area. For example, having a single platform that provides secured manage file transfer capabilities, in particular with external parties, will make the CIO sleep slightly better at night. As with Capacity Management, a detailed review of security is not in the scope of this book.

API MANAGEMENT

The topics of APIs and API management have recently been attracting a lot of attention. We see this interest evolving from two trends, one architectural and the other commercial.

On the architectural side, the concept of RESTful APIs introduced in 2000[8] (first introduced by Roy Fielding at the University of California, Irvine) has seen an increased level of acceptance in the past 5 years. This has resulted in the other dominant standard of SOAP-based interfaces defined via WSDL quickly becoming a legacy mechanism. (SOAP [Simple Object Access Protocol] was introduced in 1998, and WSDL 1.0 [Web Services Definition Language] was developed by IBM, Microsoft, and Ariba in 2000 to describe web services for their SOAP toolkit.[9]) As a result of this trend, even the extremely successful document markup language of XML is being superseded by JSON (Java Script Object Notation).

The beauty of the RESTful API construct is that it is an architectural approach rather than a standard or certain set of technology. The World Wide Web is the best example of how scalable and successful this approach can be. According to Wikipedia:

REST is an architectural style consisting of a coordinated set of architectural constraints applied to components, connectors, and data elements within a distributed hypermedia system. REST ignores the details of component implementation and protocol syntax in order to focus on the roles of components, the constraints upon their interaction with other components, and their interpretation of data elements.[9]

The main difference in the RESTful API approach is to change the focus on interfaces from a verb-centric view to a noun-centric view. In essence, you use a set of very basic methods (e.g., GET, PUT, POST, DELETE) on a noun (normally known as a resource). The downside of the RESTful API approach is that it is a collection of architectural best practices, so as a result, people take different approaches on how to implement these APIs.

On the commercial side, the success of cloud providers as well as social media companies has created a new economy for APIs. In essence, the view is that by exposing their internal resources as APIs to the external world, companies can "monetize" new revenue streams. For example, a financial services institution can externalize its mortgage or loan repayment calculation capabilities. When this is available, the hope is that developers will start using these APIs to develop new applications that will enable the company to expand its reach into the market and potentially obtain income from charging for its API utilization. All major software vendors and consulting companies are now talking about the "API economy."

Suddenly, from being a boring way to access an application, the term API has become trendy, and a new marketplace for API management software has developed. These offerings provide capabilities for companies to manage internal and external APIs, including key features such as mobile enablement, security, monitoring, and scalability.

So what does this trend mean from an architectural perspective, and in particular, what does this say about service-oriented architecture (SOA)?

Our view is that any focus on defining well-defined interfaces is good from an architectural perspective. If this trend enables companies to represent their resources in terms of understandable and consumable APIs, it will be hugely valuable.

Constructing applications from a set of well-defined, loosely coupled components has been best practice in software development for decades. The trend around SOA basically extended this best practice to the enterprise via a set of new technologies such as enterprise service buses. The challenge with most SOA efforts in the enterprise is that they were top-down driven, which led to large investments with limited perceived value.

We see the API management trend in alignment with the overall original objectives of SOA. So hopefully, the output of activities in this area will be supportive of the SOA agenda.

A key difference of API management is the focus on the developer. Basically, the idea is to make the APIs and appropriate tools as usable to the developer as possible.

However, we would like to state a word of caution. As the API management market evolves, we predict that a lot of the capabilities that are provided by

ESB technology vendors will start to be introduced into the API management solutions. So in summary, the API management journey will revisit several of the key topics of SOA but hopefully will take advantage of the lessons learned.

Finally, we would like to call out the risk of developing APIs without an architectural context. Although SOA can be seen as too top-down driven by enterprise architects, API management has the risk of evolving with no architectural oversight. We believe that an enterprise focus aligned with Continuous Architecture will help address this risk.

Next Let Us Move Onto the People Dimension

Toward the end of our case study, we provided a detailed view of the different roles required.

The most important shift in organizing an enterprise services function is to think like a product company. In essence, you need so start creating more roles than the traditional software development, testing, and operations roles. Details of how to organize your overall delivery team should be no different than just following the guidelines of *Principle 6: Model the organization after the design of the system.*

Now let us look into some of the additional roles required for the success of enterprise services. Please note that we are focusing on key differentiated roles for enterprise services and not attempting to create a cookbook by defining all roles. The culture and existing role models within an organization will significantly impact how these roles can materialize.

The most important of these roles is the **product manager**; basically, product managers are responsible for managing the product from vision to retirement. They are the ones who listen to the voice of the customer, develop the roadmap, and market the product. Our case study clearly demonstrates the benefit of having a proper product manager.

Similar to any commercial software product, it is very rare that clients can use the service without any **consulting** support. Clients need to understand the technical details of the product and resolve key architectural decisions that arise during the implementation of the enterprise service. Quite often such activities are provided by groups called centers of excellence or competency centers. Although extremely valuable, such groups can be difficult to justify from a cost perspective. In our case study, the consulting team was able to demonstrate its value quite early on by refactoring existing workflows. Although this might not always be the case, the ability to demonstrate the value of such an organization is key to the success of an enterprise service. The main recommendations we can make regarding this challenge are to keep this team lean, focus on spreading their knowledge over a series of services, and find ways of circulating core engineering talent into this group. Having the core build and engineering team focus on this role usually does not work because the consulting aspect becomes a best effort endeavor. It is better to state that the service does not offer any consulting than to try to do it on a best effort basis.

The fact that such consulting-focused groups are difficult to justify in an enterprise produces an interesting dynamic. Because these groups are perceived as expendable in difficult times, they do not attract top talent within the enterprise. This is almost opposite of the independent software companies, where the consulting side of the organization can have a strong appeal.

The **onboarding** role is a type of consulting particularly focused on the activities involved when clients are starting to use the product for the first time. We have called this role out because it is important from a client satisfaction perspective. The first time anyone uses a service is when they usually have the most difficulty, and any help in making this experience easy is greatly appreciated. This should not take away from the recommendation that most onboarding activities should be automated. Achieving self-service should be a target for all enterprise services.

The **architect**'s responsibility is to ensure that the product has a functionally and technically consistent vision and implementation. This role provides a balancing aspect between the product manager, who represents the voice of the client, and the **platform owner**, who is responsible for the implementation of the enterprise service. We discussed the topic of the relationship between the three roles in detail in Chapter 8.

As discussed in the case study, the **development and engineering team** is responsible for the technical implementation of the enterprise service. The size and exact roles within this group are highly dependent on the type of service. Regardless, they normally have highly technical and specialized skills because of the following reasons:

1. First it is quite common for enterprise services to make commercially available or open source technology usable within the enterprise.
   As a result, the teams operate in a different model than a traditional software development organization. They focus more on implementing available technology on the standards available within the enterprise,

integrating capabilities such as monitoring, capacity management, and self-service onboarding.

2. Second they focus on specializing in detailed technology areas, so that the rest of the enterprise does not have to know the ins and outs. Most people with these skills would call themselves engineers rather than developers. You can find lots of Java developers, but not many of them will be able to effectively configure a messaging solution or develop a high-performance serialization component.

Finally, the role of the **production support team** should not be overlooked. The main reason we are calling out this role and not rolling it into the core build and engineer team, which should have a DevOps focus, is to highlight the different mentality required to support enterprise services. By their nature, support teams are risk averse, which is a good thing. However, when supporting enterprise services, being too risk averse can turn away clients. Who would want to deal with an external cloud vendor that tells you that you have to wait 2 weeks to implement a change or have to go through a huge bureaucratic process to onboard onto the service?

Being client focused is not just about creating a product management role; this culture has to permeate throughout the entire organization.

Finally Let Us Expand Upon the Process Aspect of Enterprise Services

Remember that operating in a "modern" Agile world does not mean ignoring process. Almost all successful companies are built on well-functioning processes. Because delivering enterprise services is very close to operating a commercial company, this aspect is probably the most important but is normally the most overlooked. First let us consider two key artifacts that are a must for any enterprise service:

- **Service Level Agreement (SLA):** Every consumer of a service wants to know under what terms he or she is using the service. In some ways, this can be considered the articulation of *Principle 2: Focus on Quality Attributes, not on functional requirements* within the context of enterprise services. There is a large amount of available material on the topic of SLAs, and determining what aspects should be covered in a SLA goes beyond the scope of this book. Also, the particular culture and standards of the organization influence the

exact structure of the SLA. With this in mind, here are a few key elements that we believe every SLA should have:
  - Quality Attributes should be defined clearly.
  - The procedure for reporting problems and expected turnaround times should be articulated.
  - The impact of the product life cycle, how often upgrades will be provided, and the expectations of the client should be defined.
  - Remember that services will be deprecated, so defining what happens in this scenario should be defined up front. In other words the SLA should recognize that every service has a life cycle.
- **Financial model:** Costing of enterprise services can be a very complex area and is heavily influenced by the culture of the enterprise. The exact cost implications for every enterprise service need to be clearly articulated, as well as an indication on how the model will potentially evolve over time. More details about costing enterprise services are discussed in the product management section of this chapter.

Now let us look at some of the key processes required at a high level:

- **Client onboarding:** In an ideal world, we would want to emulate commercial providers such as Amazon Web Services. (As discussed earlier, Amazon Web Services is one of the most well-recognized cloud providers of IT resources such as compute, storage, database, analytics, application, and deployment services.) Basically, all you need is a credit card, and off you go. Self-service is a mantra that goes hand in hand with being client focused. Obviously, all services are not as simple as Amazon Web Services. Regardless of how complex and potentially manual client onboarding might be, it still has to adhere to a few key principles:
  - It should be easy to understand and well documented.
  - It should be transparent. The steps required for onboarding should be clearly understood. Clients should be able to track their progress easily without having to resort to endless follow-ups with different approval groups.
  - You should have help ready when required. This is potentially an area where we might not want to simulate web companies. How many people have actually managed to speak to a real person when dealing with issues on your "free" email provider?

Doing all of this seems obvious, but the level of effort required for this should not be underestimated.

Monitoring: Figure 10.10 provides an overview of how monitoring can be conducted for an enterprise service ecosystem.

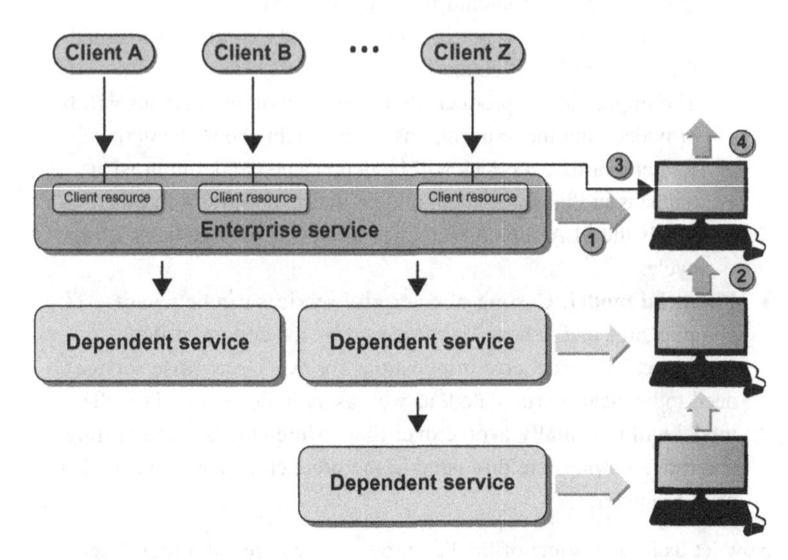

■ **FIGURE 10.10** Overview of enterprise service monitoring.

Monitoring of an enterprise service can be broken down into the following components:

1. **Health of the service itself:** Is the infrastructure of the service functioning and all components in a healthy state? (The health of the service can loosely be defined as a confidence factor that the service is operating within its service-level definitions. This varies by service, but it minimally requires that constituent components of a service are up and running within agreeable capacity limits.)
2. **Health of other services it depends on:** This is an important concept. Nesting services can potentially be very risky. The way to manage this is to have proactive monitoring between the services.
3. **Health of each of the clients SLAs:** The resource pool required for each client needs to be monitored and tracked against the overall health of the enterprise service.
4. **Reporting on utilization and health of the service:** Clients should be able to see regular information regarding the utilization of the service. Although this aspect sounds similar to the first two items, its main focus is providing visibility to clients regarding the health of the service. It normally is a simplified view that depicts key client-

relevant data—ideally, a real-time dashboard; minimally, consistent reporting at regular intervals.

As with client onboarding, the level of effort required for implementing effective monitoring is significant:

Just as with Continuous Delivery, which espouses automation of the build and test process, Continuous Architecture promotes the full automation of the onboarding and monitoring for enterprise services.

Two other areas to highlight are (1) release management and deployment and (2) production support. For both of these, there is nothing unique about enterprise services, but it is expected that they adhere to software development best practices around Continuous Delivery. Please refer to Chapter 5 for more details.

Finally, as discussed in the section about product management, governance is a critical process for enterprise services.

As can be seen from this section, being able to provide enterprise services is more than selecting the right technology and architecting it to meet your needs. You have to have the right processes and teams in place.

CONTINUOUS ARCHITECTURE AND ENTERPRISE SERVICES

There are two ways of looking at how Continuous Architecture and enterprise services align—the micro and macro views. At the micro level, it is obvious that enterprise services should be built using Continuous Architecture principles. On this point, we already went through a detailed case study on building out a workflow service in this chapter. At the macro level, it is interesting to look at how enterprise services can enable Continuous Architecture at the enterprise level.

Let us look at the micro level first. Although the concept of enterprise services has existed for a long time, we believe one reason for their lack of success is due to not applying Continuous Architecture principles effectively. Because enterprise services are technology products, all principles apply, but some are more critical than others. Let's have a quick look at how each of the principles applies to enterprise services:

- **Principle 1: Architect products, not just solutions for projects:** As can be seen from the focus on product management in this section, this principle is a must for any enterprise service.

It is almost impossible to talk about processes around enterprise services without mentioning IT Infrastructure Library. ITIL started out in the 1980s with a focus on capturing a set of recommendations for best practices in managing IT. The key thing to understand about ITIL is that it is technology independent and process driven. As can be inferred from the "infrastructure" in its title, the focus of ITIL traditionally has been on supporting IT infrastructure services, in particular, elements such as service catalogue, SLA, service desk, change management, and configuration management.[11] As a result, the context of implementing ITIL has traditionally been in production management (operations) organizations. However, the definition of ITIL is conceptually much larger and can theoretically be applied to services that support the business.

The ITIL best practices are currently detailed within five core areas:

1. ITIL service strategy
2. ITIL service design
3. ITIL service transition
4. ITIL service operation
5. ITIL continual service improvement

These cover the entire ITIL service life cycle, beginning with the identification of customer needs and drivers of IT requirements through to the design and implementation of the service, and finally to the monitoring and improvement phase of the service.[12]

From a Continuous Architecture perspective, we are supportive of the standardization and best practices that frameworks such as ITIL provide. However, we do not see the implementation of ITIL as critical to being successful in enterprise services.

We should never underestimate the complexity of an enterprise. One interesting factor is the layering of enterprise services, or building dependencies between them. To illustrate this complexity, let us take an example where the enterprise has two enterprise services focused on the infrastructure layer:

1. Compute enterprise service that provides standard X86-based Linux capacity
2. Common database platform that provides a standard commercial relational database platform

They decide to create an enterprise inventory management service based on a commercially available product.

All of the groups implementing the enterprise services are under the same management, and there is a belief that each group should use its own services. As a result, the enterprise inventory management service has to use the common database and compute platforms. However,

- **Principle 2: Focus on Quality Attributes, not on functional requirements:** Given the nature of enterprise services, the nonfunctional requirements become even more important. There can be a tendency to overengineer services to meet future demand. This is normally the case when the enterprise service team is overoptimistic about the demand. Having strong product management is what is required to balance the desire to overengineer.
- **Principle 3: Delay design decisions until they are absolutely necessary:** Following the comments made on Principle 2, there can be a tendency to overengineer for an unknown future state too early on. As a result, complex architectural decisions get made in a vacuum where the "voice of the customer" is not present. Applying Principle 3 in a disciplined manner is what is required to avoid an overengineered product.
- **Principle 4: Architect for change—leverage "the power of small":** The enterprise service itself has to be composed of a set of loosely coupled components. What is critical is to build an enterprise service to avoid the "domino effect." This happens when a rogue client that misuses the services or floods it with requests that end up taking down the whole service for all clients. The power of small by its nature also results in horizontally scalable solutions, which means that you can buy the option to enhance engineering for future requirements. Basically, Principles 2, 3, and 4 go together, each supporting the others.
- **Principle 5: Architect for build, test, and deploy:** Enterprise services do not have the luxury of having all clients upgrade at the same time nor for all clients to wait for a 6-month release cycle. This creates a unique angle on how the build, test, and deploy cycles are managed. Another key consideration required in this area is around versioning and backward compatibility.
- **Principle 6: Model the organization after the design of the system:** The main point is to reiterate the recommendation for having cohesive product teams composed of all roles. We have already discussed the unique roles required for an enterprise service in this chapter.

Now let's take a quick look at how enterprise services enable Continuous Architecture at the enterprise level. Just by introducing enterprise services, you will have already taken a huge step in implementing Continuous Architecture:

Let's start with *Principle 4: Architect for change—leverage "the power of small."* This is basically what each enterprise service should be—a loosely coupled component that has a unique responsibility within the enterprise. Then we move on to *Principle 1: Architect products, not just solutions for projects.* Enterprise services are the best place to introduce the discipline of product management; this can then be extended to other parts of the enterprise. We then focus on *Principle 5: Architect for build, test, and deploy.* What is most critical here is to be able to link your enterprise services into the automated build, test, and deploy environments available for other applications. Without this ability, it would be costly and require manual effort to leverage enterprise services. Enabling this capability is also a huge adoption lever; how can any team say no to working with enterprise services if they can easily link to them as part of their Continuous Delivery cycle? We can now look at *Principle 2: Focus on Quality Attributes, not on functional requirements* and *Principle 3: Delay design decisions until they are absolutely necessary.* Using enterprise services will create "positive constraints" on how you design applications in general. This is because they introduce a level of known Quality Attributes and design constraints. Removing optionality is not always a bad thing, especially if you focus on the enterprise level. Our final principle is *Principle 6: Model the organization after the design of the system.* By creating teams around enterprise services, the implementation of this principle naturally occurs.

SUMMARY

In this chapter, we provided an overview of the concept of enterprise services within Continuous Architecture.

We started by defining the concept of an enterprise service. It is clear that for any large-scale organization, utilization of enterprise services is an important way of providing an architecturally consistent and manageable IT landscape.

However, providing such enterprise services is quite challenging. We recommend approaching this by adopting practices that have been successful in the commercial software market, particularly by introducing the concept of product management. In addition, we believe that utilization of the Continuous Architecture principles supports the creation of successful enterprise services. We clarified this aspect in the case study. We then provided recommendations on implementing enterprise services by looking into technology, people, and process perspectives.

Finally, it is important to reiterate that Continuous Architecture is applicable in two dimensions: time and scale. As explained in this chapter,

there is a slight problem—the compute platform does not provide all the disaster recovery capabilities required, and the database platform is missing some of the key features required by the commercial inventory management product they have selected. This results in the inventory management service not being able to deliver on time, and even when it delivers, it does not meet client expectations. This is not because the team did not clearly understand the requirements of their clients but because they did not manage the dependency to other services and its impact on Quality Attributes. In addition, because there is no consistent capacity management or monitoring across all the services, when incidents occur, it becomes extremely difficult to identify the source of the problem.

At this point, the inventory management service has gone live with only one client. Because other business areas see the problems, they quickly invest in their own inventory management projects. As a result, the organization ends up with three different solutions for a common problem.

How could this have been avoided? There are three main points to consider:

1. Proper product management would have made the missing features of the compute and database platforms more visible, and the product manager for the inventory

management solution would have set client expectations.
2. The "architectural decision" to use the common platforms was based on a management edict rather than proper architectural analysis.
3. When it was obvious that the inventory management service would not attract any new customers, proper governance would have ensured that either the service was discontinued or the service was invested in properly to address the limitations.

Unfortunately, the Inventory Management service limps along and joins a long line of legacy systems being supported in the enterprise.

enterprise services are a natural stepping stone in adopting Continuous Architecture as the scale dimension moves from a project to a department to an enterprise.

ENDNOTES

1. Hernandez JG. Management and leadership notes. Jeff Bezos' mandate: Amazon and Web Services, October 18, 2012. <http://jesusgilhernandez.com/2012/10/18/jeff-bezos-mandate-amazon-and-web-services/>.
2. Wikipedia. Amazon Web Services: history, <http://en.wikipedia.org/wiki/Amazon_Web_Services#History/>.
3. Clark J. How Amazon exposed its guts: the history of AWS's EC2. ZDNet, June 7, 2012. <http://www.zdnet.com/article/how-amazon-exposed-its-guts-the-history-of-awss-ec2/#/>.
4. LaMonica M. Bezos: Amazon Web Services will be "meaningful business." CNET News, November 8, 2006. <http://www.cnet.com/news/bezos-amazon-web-services-will-be-meaningful-business-1/>.
5. Productmanager.co.uk.
6. Inbound and outbound product management, <https://en.wikipedia.org/wiki/Product_management#Inbound_and_Outbound_Product_Management>.
7. Wikipedia. Ward Cunningham. <https://en.wikipedia.org/wiki/Ward_Cunningham/>.
8. Fielding R. Architectural styles and the design of network-based software architectures. University of California, Irvine, Dissertation. <http://www.ics.uci.edu/~fielding/pubs/dissertation/top.htm>.
9. SOAP, <https://en.wikipedia.org/wiki/SOAP>, WSDL, <https://en.wikipedia.org/wiki/Web_Services_Description_Language>.
10. Open Guide. ITIL capacity management, <http://www.itlibrary.org/index.php?page=Capacity_Management/>.
11. Whittleston S. University of Northampton. ITIL is ITIL, Axelos Best Practice 2012. <https://www.axelos.com/best-practice-solutions/itil>.
12. Axelos: What is ITIL? <https://www.axelos.com/best-practice-solutions/itil/what-is-itil/>.

Chapter 11

Conclusion

Designs of purely arbitrary nature cannot be expected to last long.

—Kenzo Tange

WHAT WAS THIS BOOK ABOUT?

In this book, we have described how the Continuous Architecture approach can help architects effectively support software delivery, particularly Continuous Delivery projects. We presented a series of principles, tools, techniques, and ideas that can be thought of as an architect's toolbox.

As we saw earlier in the book, the Continuous Architecture approach is based on the following six simple principles:

1. **Architect products, not just solutions for projects.** Architecting products is more efficient than just designing point solutions for projects and focuses the team on their customers.
2. **Focus on Quality Attributes, not on functional requirements.** Quality Attribute Requirements (QARs) drive the architecture.
3. **Delay design decisions until they are absolutely necessary.** Design architectures based on facts, not on guesses. There is no point in designing and implementing capabilities that may never be used; it is a waste of time and resources.
4. **Architect for change—leverage "the power of small."** Big, monolithic, tightly coupled components are hard to change. Instead, leverage small, loosely coupled services.
5. **Architect for build, test, and deploy.** Most architecture methodologies exclusively focus on software building activities, but we believe that architects should be concerned about testing and deployment activities in order to support Continuous Delivery.
6. **Model the organization after the design of the system.** The way teams are organized drives the architecture and design of the systems they are working on.

These principles are described in detail in Chapter 2 of this book, and they are complemented by a number of well-known tools such as value chains, utility trees, decision logs, and Quality Function Deployment (QFD) matrices. All of these tools are described in detail in this book, and together with the principles, they assist the architect in defining the key components of a software architecture, such as:

- The context of the system
- The key functional requirements that will impact the architecture
- The quality attribute requirements that drive the architecture
- The architecture and design decisions
- The architecture blueprints

As we stated many times throughout this book, the components of a software architecture do not exist in isolation and are interrelated. Creating an architecture is making a series of compromises between the requirements, the decisions, the blueprints, and even the ultimate architecture artifact—the executable code itself. Remember that "architecture is the art of the possible!"

WHY DOES CONTINUOUS ARCHITECTURE WORK?

We strongly believe that leveraging the contents of our "Continuous Architecture" toolbox will help architects address and eliminate the bottlenecks that may be created by traditional architecture methodologies when they attempt to support projects using Agile development. In addition, the Continuous Architecture approach speeds up the software development and delivery processes by systematically applying an architecture perspective and discipline continuously throughout the development process. This supports our goal of delivering software at an ever-increasing speed to create competitive differentiators.

As Kurt Bittner notes in the Preface to this book, Agile development is now "old news," and older Iterative, Incremental, and "Waterfall" ways of developing software have faded from the leading edge of software development. As older applications are replaced, refactored, or retired, these older methodologies are losing their grip on software developers. In the meantime, Agile is evolving thanks to the concepts of DevOps and Continuous Delivery, and software architecture is catching up by changing its old methodologies into modern approaches such as Continuous Architecture. Each of these approaches, processes, and methodologies—Agile, DevOps, Continuous Delivery, and Continuous Architecture—can be thought of as pieces of a software delivery puzzle (Figure 11.1).

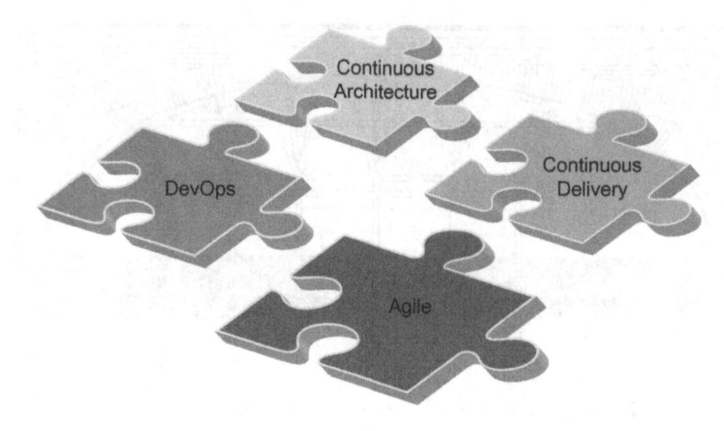

■ **FIGURE 11.1** The software delivery puzzle.

One of the main reasons why the Continuous Architecture approach works is that we do not think of it as a formal methodology. There is no preset order or process to follow for using the Continuous Architecture principles, tools, techniques, and ideas, and you may choose to use only some of them depending on the context of the project you are working on. We have found that using this toolbox is very effective in our projects and that the Continuous Architecture tools are dynamic and adaptable in nature. These tools were built and fine tuned from our experience with real projects and our work with other practitioners. They are practical, not theoretical or academic. They enable the architect to help software development teams create successful software that implements key Quality Attributes such as modularity, maintainability, scalability, security, and adaptability.

Unlike most traditional software architecture approaches that focus on the software design and construction aspects of the Software Delivery Life Cycle, Continuous Architecture brings an architecture perspective to the overall process, as illustrated by *Principle 5: Architect for build, test, and deploy.* It encourages the architect to avoid the Big Architecture up Front (BArF) syndrome when software developers wait and do not produce any software while the architecture team creates complicated and arcane artifacts describing complex technical capabilities and features that may never get used. It helps the architect create flexible, adaptable, and nimble architectures that are quickly implemented into executable code that can be rapidly tested and deployed to production so that the users of the system can provide useful feedback, which is the ultimate validation of an architecture.

> **THE VALUE OF ARCHITECTURE**
>
> What is the real value of architecture? We think of architecture as an enabler for the delivery of valuable software. Software architecture's concerns, quality attribute requirements such as performance, maintainability, scalability, and security, are at the heart of what makes software successful.
>
> A comparison to building architecture may help illustrate this concept. Stone arches are one of the most successful building architecture constructs. Numerous bridges built by the Romans around 2000 years ago using stone arches are still standing, for example, the Pont du Gard, built in the first century AD. How were stone arches being built at that time? A wooden frame known as the "centring" was first constructed in the shape of an arch. The stone work was built up around the frame, and finally a keystone was set in position. The key stone gave the arch strength and rigidity. The wood frame could then be removed and the arch was left in position. The same technique was later used in 1825–28 by Thomas Telford for building the Over Bridge in Cloucester, England (Figure 11.2).
>
> We think of software architecture as the "centring" for building successful software "arches." When Romans built bridges using this technique, we do not believe that anybody worried about the aesthetics or the appearance of

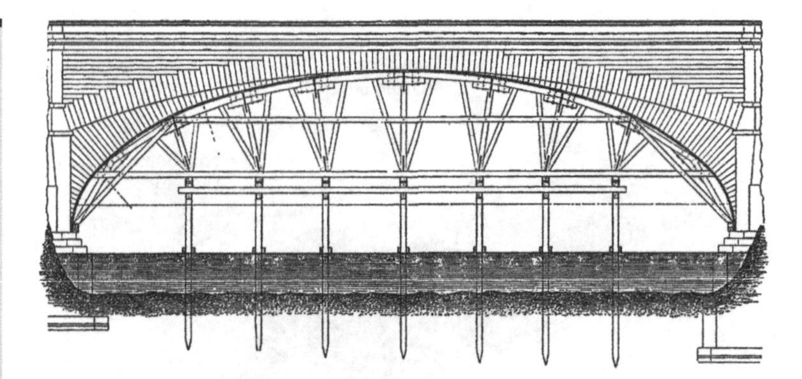

■ **FIGURE 11.2** Centring of Over Bridge, Gloucester, England. *Wikimedia Commons.*

We also realize that some companies may not be ready to adopt Agile software development methodologies. Moreover, even if a company is fully committed to Agile methodologies, there may be situations such as working with a third-party software package when other approaches such as Iterative, Incremental, or even "Waterfall" may be more appropriate.

One of the key benefits of our "toolbox" approach is that its contents can be easily adapted to work with Iterative or Incremental instead of Agile and even to projects following a Waterfall methodology, and therefore even Agile is not a prerequisite to using the Continuous Architecture approach. We still recommend using Agile to deliver software rapidly, but the Continuous Architecture approach will still yield important benefits when used with other software development methodologies.

PUTTING CONTINUOUS ARCHITECTURE IN PRACTICE

If you have read the book cover to cover, you should feel comfortable in putting the Continuous Architecture principles and toolbox in practice. We hope that even if you have looked into sections that you find relevant, you have been able to find useful information and tips. Success in architecture is to be able to influence what we called the "realized architecture," that is, the software product implemented as code on a particular infrastructure. Similarly, success for us would be for practitioners to put Continuous Architecture recommendations into practice.

As mentioned in Chapter 1, we believe that the current trend in the industry is away from traditional architecture methodologies and do not believe that the pendulum will swing back. We strongly believe that is a need for an architectural approach that can encompass modern software delivery approaches, providing them with a broader architectural perspective, and this is exactly what Continuous Architecture is about.

We hope that you have found this book interesting and useful and that you will be inspired by it to adapt the contents of our little "Continuous Architecture" toolbox and extend it with new ideas on how to provide architecture support to projects that want to deliver robust and effective software capabilities rapidly. Good luck and please share your experiences with us!

the "centring." Its purpose was the delivery of a robust, strong, reliable, usable, and long-lasting bridge.

Similarly, we believe that the value of software architecture should be measured by the success of the software it is helping to deliver, not by the quality of its artifacts. Sometimes, architects use the term "value-evident architecture" to describe a set of software architecture documents they created and are really proud of and that development teams should not (ideally) need to be convinced to implement the architecture. However, we are somewhat skeptical about these claims; can you really evaluate a "centring" until the arch is complete, the key stone has been put in place, and the bridge can be used safely?

Glossary

Architecture Epic In the Scaled Agile Framework (SAFe) methodology, architecture epics are "large technology initiatives at the portfolio level. New epics are continuously identified to improve the technology platforms that deliver business functionality."[1,2]

Architecture Feature In the SAFe methodology, an architecture (or architectural) feature is "the technical aspect of a system that is needed to support a business functionality. Over time, architectural features may evolve into Non Functional Requirements (NFRs)."[1,2]

Architecture Scenario "In computing, a scenario is a narrative of foreseeable interactions of user roles (known in the Unified Modeling Language as "actors") and the technical system, which usually includes computer hardware and software. A scenario has a goal, which is usually functional. A scenario describes one way that a system is or is envisaged to be used in the context of activity in a defined time-frame."[3] Architecture scenarios are instantiations of architecturally significant use cases.

Architecture Runway In the SAFe methodology, "with architectural features implemented in a program, the enterprise incrementally builds an architectural runway. Instead of big up-front architecture, Agile teams develop the technology platforms to support business needs during each release."[1,2]

Architecture Tradeoff Analysis Method (ATAM) A risk mitigation process used early in the Software Development Life Cycle. ATAM was developed by the Software Engineering Institute at the Carnegie Mellon University. Its purpose is to help choose a suitable architecture for a software system by discovering trade-offs and sensitivity points.[4]

Architecture Tradeoff Analysis Method Utility Tree In ATAM, utility trees are used to document and organize quality attribute requirements. They are also used to prioritize quality attribute requirements and to evaluate the suitability of an architecture against its quality attribute requirements.

Cloud Infrastructure Cloud computing refers to the practice of transitioning computer services such as computation or data storage to multiple redundant offsite locations available on the Internet, which allows application software to be operated using Internet-enabled devices. Clouds can be classified as public, private, and hybrid.[5,6]

Continuous Delivery A software engineering approach in which teams keep producing valuable software in short cycles and ensure that the software can be reliably released at any time. It is used in software development to automate and improve the process of software delivery. Techniques such as automated testing and continuous integration allow software to be developed to a high standard and easily packaged and deployed to test environments, resulting in the ability to rapidly, reliably, and repeatedly push out enhancements and bug fixes to customers at low risk and with minimal manual overhead.[7,8]

Continuous Integration The practice, in software engineering, of merging all developer working copies with a shared mainline several times a day. It was first named and proposed by Grady Booch in his 1991 method, although practices at that time did not yet support full automation or the performance of integrations more than a few times a day. It was adopted as part of Extreme Programming (XP), which did advocate integrating more than once per day, perhaps as many as 10s of times per day. The main aim of continuous integration is to prevent integration problems.[9,10]

Continuous Testing Practice that uses automated approaches to significantly improve the speed of testing by taking a so-called "shift-left" approach, which integrates the quality assurance and development phases. This approach may include a set of automated testing workflows, which can be combined with analytics and metrics to provide a clear, fact-based picture of the quality of the software being delivered.

DevOps Process An application delivery philosophy that stresses communication, collaboration, and integration between software developers and their information technology (IT) counterparts in operations. DevOps is a response to the interdependence of software development and IT operations. It aims to help an organization rapidly produce software products and services.[11,12,13]

Feature The Institute of Electrical and Electronics Engineers defines the term "feature" in IEEE 829 as "A distinguishing characteristic of a software item (e.g., performance, portability, or functionality)."[14,15]

Microservices In computing, a software architecture style in which complex applications are composed of small, independent processes communicating with each other using language-agnostic Application Programming Interface (API). These services are small and highly decoupled and focus on doing a small task.[16,17,18]

Minimum Viable Product (MVP) In product development, the product with the highest return on investment versus risk. An MVP has just those core features that allow the product to be deployed—and no more. The product is typically deployed to a subset of possible customers, such as early adopters who are thought to be more forgiving, more likely to give feedback, and able to grasp a product vision from an early prototype or marketing information. It is a strategy targeted at avoiding building products that customers do not want, that seeks to maximize the information learned about the customer per dollar spent.[19,20,21,22,23,24,25]

Minimum Viable Architecture (MVA) An architecture that enables the delivery of the core product features to be deployed in a given phase of a project and satisfied known requirements (especially quality attribute requirements)—and no more.

Rational Unified Process methodology An Iterative software development process framework created by the Rational Software Corporation, a division of IBM since 2003. RUP is not a single concrete prescriptive process but rather an adaptable process framework intended to be tailored by the development organizations and software project teams that will select the elements of the process that are appropriate for their needs. RUP is a specific implementation of the unified process.[26,27]

Scaled Agile Framework methodology "The is a freely-revealed, on-line knowledge base of proven success patterns for applying Lean and Agile development at enterprise scale. The SAFe website[28] allows users to browse the "SAFe Big Picture" to understand the roles, teams, activities, and artifacts necessary to scale these practices to the enterprise."[29]

Technical Debt A recent metaphor referring to the eventual consequences of any system design, software architecture, or software development within a codebase. The debt can be thought of as work that needs to be done before a particular job can be considered complete or proper. If the debt is not repaid, then it will keep on accumulating interest, making it hard to implement changes later on. Unaddressed technical debt increases software entropy. Analogous to monetary debt, technical debt is not necessarily a bad thing, and sometimes technical debt is required to move projects forward. Technical debt is also known as design debt or code debt.[30,31]

User Story A tool used in Agile software development to capture a description of a software feature from an end-user perspective. The user story describes the type of user, what he or she wants, and why. A user story helps to create a simplified description of a requirement.[32]

ENDNOTES

1. JL Marechaux: SAFE: Get on the (agile) train. <https://www.ibm.com/developerworks/community/blogs/jlmarechaux/entry/safe_get_on_the_agile_train?lang=en)/>.
2. <http://www.scaledagileframework.com/architectural-epic/>.
3. Scenario (computing). <https://en.wikipedia.org/wiki/Scenario_(computing)>.
4. Architecture Tradeoff Analysis Method. <https://en.wikipedia.org/wiki/Architecture_tradeoff_analysis_method>.
5. Cloud computing, Far Eye Blog. <http://www.fareye.in/cloud-computing-i/>.
6. Qusay H. Demystifying cloud computing. J Def Softw Eng (CrossTalk) 2011(Jan/Feb):16–21.
7. Continuous Delivery. <https://en.wikipedia.org/wiki/Continuous_delivery>.
8. Lianping C. Continuous delivery: huge benefits, but challenges too. IEEE Software 2015;32(2):50.
9. Continuous integration. <https://en.wikipedia.org/wiki/Continuous_integration>.
10. Booch G. Object oriented design with applications. Benjamin-Cummings Publishing Co., Inc. Redwood City, CA, USA ©1991
11. DevOps. <https://en.wikipedia.org/wiki/DevOps>.
12. Loukides M. What is DevOps? <http://radar.oreilly.com/2012/06/what-is-devops.html>.
13. Floris E, Chintan A, Maya D. A mapping study on cooperation between information system development and operations. <http://link.springer.com/chapter/10.1007%2F978-3-319-13835-0_21>.
14. Software feature. <https://en.wikipedia.org/wiki/Software_feature>.
15. IEEE Std. 829-2008 IEEE Standard for Software and System Test Documentation. <https://www.cs.odu.edu/~zeil/cs333/latest/Public/bbtesting/IEEE%20829-2008.pdf.
16. Microservices. <https://en.wikipedia.org/wiki/Microservices>.
17. Fowler M. Microservices. <http://martinfowler.com/articles/microservices.html/>.
18. Newman S. Building Microservices: Designing Fine-Grained Systems, O'Reilly Media, 2015.
19. Minimum Viable Product. <https://en.wikipedia.org/wiki/Minimum_viable_product>.
20. Junk WS. The dynamic balance between cost, schedule, features, and quality in software development projects. Computer Science Department, University of Idaho, April 2000.
21. Ries E. What is the minimum viable product? Lessons learned. Venture Hacks, March 23, 2009.
22. Perfection By Subtraction—The Minimum Feature Set. <http://www.startupshk.com/perfection-by-subtraction-the-minimum-feature-set-steve-blank/>.
23. SyncDev. Minimum viable product, <http://www.syncdev.com/index.php/minimum-viable-product/>.
24. Holiday R. The single worst marketing decision you can make. The Next Web, April 1, 2015.
25. Ries E. Minimum viable product: a guide, August 3, 2009. <http://www.startuplessonslearned.com/2009/08/minimum-viable-product-guide.html>.
26. Rational Unified Process. <https://en.wikipedia.org/wiki/Minimum_viable_product>.
27. Taft DK. IBM acquires Rational. eWeek, December 6, 2012. <http://www.eweek.com/c/a/Desktops-and-Notebooks/IBM-Acquires-Rational/>.
28. <www.scaledagileframework.com/>.
29. Linders B. Lean and agile leadership with the Scaled Agile Framework (SAFe). InfoQ, January 12, 2015. <http://www.infoq.com/news/2015/01/lean-agile-leadership-safe/>.
30. Technical Debt. <https://en.wikipedia.org/wiki/Technical_debt>.
31. Suryanarayana G. Refactoring for software design smells. 1st ed. Morgan Kaufmann, Boston, MA; 2014. p. 258.
32. TechTarget. User story, <http://searchsoftwarequality.techtarget.com/definition/user-story/>.

ENDNOTES

Index

Note: Page numbers followed by "*f*", "*t*" and "*b*" refer to boxes, figures and tables, respectively.

D

E

F

G

H

I

J

K

L

Printed in the United States
By Bookmasters